Also from Academic Foundation :

Spices in Indian Economy
by M.T. Khan

The Author :

S. N. MAHINDRU (b. 1930), a noted consultant, is a product of Delhi University and an elected Fellow of the Institution of Chemists (India).

Mr. Mahindru retired as Chief Chemist, Regional Agmark Laboratory, New Delhi in 1988. He has four decades of experience in the field of analysis, founding of Agmark laboratories, training of new chemists in the theory and analysis of agricultural commodities, 20 years in spices and condiments alone, both for export and domestic markets.

After retirement, his consultancy and advisory services are in great demand (by spices industry in particular) in the specialised area of analysis, product development and Food Legislation.

Mr. Mahindru is : Fellow, Oil Technologists Association of India; Fellow, Essential Oil Association of India; Member, Association of Food Scientists & Technologists; Member, Indian Society of Analytical Scientists; Member, FADC: 9;45;47 of Bureau of Indian Standards as well as a member of the sub-committee of International Standards Organisation dealing with spices and condiments of which India holds the secretariat.

A widely read and appreciated author, his other books are :

1. *Milk Nutrients* (1982) published by National Book Trust of India
2. *Spices in Indian Life : 6500 BC to 1950 AD* (1982)
3. *Handbook of Food Analysis* (1987)
4. *Indian Plant Perfumes* (1992)

Manual of Indian
SPICES

Manual of Indian
SPICES

S.N. Mahindru

ACADEMIC FOUNDATION

24-A, Sriram Road, Civil Lines, Delhi - 110 054, India.
Phone : 233730, 232966, 2911852.

Published in 1994 by
ACADEMIC FOUNDATION
24 - A, Sriram Road, Civil Lines, Delhi - 110 054.
Tel : 232966, 233730, 2911852.

Manual of Indian Spices
S.N. Mahindru
ISBN 81-7188-063-0

Laser-Typeset in Times New Roman by
COMPRINT INDIA, Delhi

The greedy merchants, led by lucre, run,
To the parch'd Indies and the rising sun,
From thence hot pepper and rich drugs they bear,
Bart'ring for spices, their Italian ware.

— *Aulus Persius Floccus*
34 A.D. to 62 A.D.

Contents

Part-I

Part-II

Foreword

INDIA is the largest producer, consumer and exporter of spices in the world. Almost all spices are grown in India. The present production of spices is estimated at 2 Million tonnes per annum. Our exports are roughly 5% of the production sharing 25% of the world trade. A large segment of our population depends upon spices for livelihood.

Spices Research and Development are of recent origin. Technology on production and processing has been developed fairly for pepper, ginger, turmeric, chilli and cardamom. However, there are a number of them belonging to seed spices, herbal spices and tree spices which require more attention.

Unlike other countries spices find varied uses in India. They are essential ingredients not only in cuisine but also in medicinal and beauty and body care preparations. The indigenous system of medicine, Ayurveda uses a variety of spices. Allopathy, Homeopathy and Unani systems also use spices in one form or other.

Commercial grades have been developed in India for spices. They are classified under AGMARK specifications. Being food materials adulteration in spices is punishable under Prevention of Food Adulteration Act of the Govt. of India. Quality of spices is examined not only for intrinsic value but also for freedom from contaminations.

This manual has been prepared by S.N. Mahindru after a careful review of literature on selected subjects of spices. It is difficult to get such an assorted and exhaustive information in a single compilation. I am sure that this manual on Indian spices will become popular soon among those concerned with the spices industry.

Kochi - 18

(C K George)
Executive Director
Spices Board
INDIA

Preface

INDIA, the home of spices and condiments since ancient times, contri-butes in a major way to their production in the world. This is evident from the fact that during 1992-93 India exported 1,23,265 metric tonnes of spices and condiments valued at Rupees 38206.45 lakhs. The share of spices and condiments in total export earnings from agricultural products is now more than 10% which used to be less than 5% in early eighties. This is at the export front. The consumption of spices and condiments within India is much higher. Thus spices and condiments have attained the status of a separate discipline of study in India.

Those involved in the production, processing and market-ing of spices and condiments do not have a Manual/Hand Book on spices and condiments for ready reference and hence arises the need for the present volume. In this Manual an attempt has, therefore, been made to provide information on the historical, social, cultural, agricultural, commercial, tech-nical, and legal aspects beside analytical examination of the issues involved. Up-to-date statistical information has also been given.

This book shall be useful for trading, manufacturing and processing fraternity of spices and condiments, analysts of these commodities, Public Analysts, Advocates handling Food adulteration cases, Oleoresin techno-logists and others inter-ested in spices and condiments.

I am genuinely indebted to Acting Director, analyst friend Shri I. Chakraborty, Central Food Laboratory, Ghaziabad for providing details of pesticide analysis and Shri Subhash Shah, Public Analyst, Baroda Muncipal Laboratory for providing details of estimation of heavy metals like mercury, cadmium and zinc.

I am also grateful to Dr. P.N. Verma, Director, Homeopathic Pharmacopoeia Laboratory, Ghaziabad, for providing details about the testing of tinctures in the Homeopathic System.

Thanking a mentor, the publisher and his establishment has become a formality. Rarely it is an urge. Nevertheless, presently it is an emotional and sincere feeling towards Mr. Raj Kapila, Director, Academic Foundation, Delhi, not only for his academic disposition but for his uncompromising perfectionism in handling this manuscript. I am deeply indebted to him and his associates for bringing out the present work.

I owe a debt of gratitude to Mahashya Dharam Pal, Managing Director, M/s M.D.H. (P) Ltd., New Delhi, also – a doyen in his own right in the field of spices and condiments processing, from whom I learnt a lot about them.

Last but not the least, I owe a debt of gratitude to Dr. C.K. George, Executive Director, Spices Board, India, for not only contributing the Foreword but also for providing very valueable data and suggestions from time to time for making the book more purposeful to its users.

— *S.N. Mahindru*

New Delhi

Part - I

1

Spices, Condiments and Herbs

— An Introduction

Definitions:

SPICES, condiments and herbs are the highly esteemed dried parts of various plants of tropical and subtropical regions cultivated for their aromatic, pungent, or otherwise desirable substances. They consist of rhizomes, bulbs, barks, flower buds, stigmas, fruits, seeds, and leaves. Some spice seeds are the tiny aromatic fruits and oily seeds of herbaceous plants like coriander, fenugreek, anise, caraway, cumin, fennel, poppy, and sesame. Herbs are the fragrant leaves of such plants as marjoram, mint, rosemary, and thyme.

Spices, condiments, and herbs are employed as adjuncts to impart flavour and aroma or piquancy to foods. In the small quantities used to prepare culinary dishes they have little or no nutritive value, but they stimulate the appetite, add zest to food, enhance the taste, and delight the gourmet.

Most of the spices of the tropics had their origin in the orient in a latitude belt lying between 25°N and 10°S of the Equator. While other parts of the world have not provided many spices, the Indian tropics have given the world pepper, cardamom, turmeric, ginger, nutmeg, mace, basil, cassia, mustard, garlic, dry mango, tamarind etc.

The Mediterranean area including North Africa and the Middle-East have supplied most of culinary herbs and seeds such as bay leaves, coriander, cumin, dill, fennel, fenugreek, rosemary and sage. On the other hand, the cold regions of the Northern Europe and Asia have produced very few spices like caraway and horse radish; American tropics contributed vanilla and capsicums only.

The Delhi High Court in its judgement in the case of Hansraj v/s Delhi Administration reported as 1977, Cr.LJ, 92 had decided that condiment is an appetising and usually pungent substance of natural origin (as pepper, vinegar or mustard); any of various complex combinations having similar qualities (as curry or chilli powder, pickle or catsup).

Clinical Dietetics and Nutrition by F.P. Anita, 1986; Oxford University Press, Delhi (pp. 290-294) distinguishes spices and condiments as :

> "Spices are aromatic pungent substances. Condiments are processed spices made into a sauce or relish; spices do not make a significant contribution as they are consumed in small quantities — spices should be used to bring out the best flavour of food and make it more appetising, rather than give to the food a pungency which irritates the mouth and masks the original flavour".

The Bureau of Indian Standards in its Standard IS:1977-1985 defines spices and condiments as : "Such natural vegetable products or mixtures thereof, without any extraneous matter, as are used for flavouring, seasoning and imparting aroma to foods (the term applies to them either in the whole form or in the ground form)."

Nevertheless, condiments are sometimes classified as spices, although they are usually employed in a different manner. Spices are used during the cooking or processing of food, condiments are added to food after it has been served at table. Black pepper may be considered a spice or condiment depending upon its use.

Spices are one of the indispensable factors of the Indian cooking system. There are eighty-seven spices and condiments which have been recognised by the Bureau of Indian Standards and are used in Indian kitchens (Appendix at end of chapt). The three quintessential aspects distinguishing them among themselves are the fragrance, the taste and the colour they impart to the food.

Fragrance in spices and condiments is by virtue of the presence of a class of steam volatile organic compounds termed as volatile oils which belong to groups of chemical compounds like alcohols, aldehydes, esters, ketones, sesquiterpenes, terpenes and sulphides. The taste is accentuated due to the presence of another class of bitter and/or pungent organic compounds called alkaloids like capsaicin in chillies, piperine, piperdine, (piperettine) and chavicine in black pepper. Acidulants like tamarind, *amchur*, *kokam*, and *anardana* impart the sour taste attributed to the presence of aliphatic acids like tartaric, malic, hydroxy citric and oxalic in the aforesaid spices and condiments respectively. Colouring organic compounds like crocin present in saffron, carotene in chillies and curcumin in turmeric provide varying shades of yellow, orange and red.

It is the wide application of spices and condiments in the preparation of foods, imparting different flavours, tastes and colours which is responsible for the distinct characteristics of numerous geographical styles of the culinary art in the world. The primary ingredients used in a dish are not much at variance viz. meat, poultry, pulses, vegetables, rice, wheat and tubers. It is the specific plurality of spices and condiments in a dish which bestows on it its distinct character. Same is the case with preserves, chutneys and pickles etc.

The above mentioned broad classification of spices and condiments can be sub-classified on any of the following basis :

1. *Botanical* - the botanical families to which the spices and condiments belong viz. turmeric, ginger and cardamom all belong to the family of *zingiberaceae* though diametrically different in their spicy character.

2. *Geographical* - the geographical areas like Mediterranean growing umbelliferous fruits.

3. *Useful Part* viz. (i) leaves (ii) roots (iii) fruits (iv) barks (v) flowers (vi) flower umbels (vii) seeds (viii) bulbs etc.

4. *End Uses*

(a) *Preservation* : (i) *Antioxidants* like black pepper, paprika, chilly, nutmeg etc.; (ii) *Germicides* like garlic, clove, cinnamon; (iii) *Cosmetics* by virtue of being dermatologically beneficial plus fragrance like turmeric.

(b) Hedonistic

(c) Medicinal

5. *Commercial value* : Importance as a cash crop and foreign exchange earner through exports like dried ginger and black pepper.

6. *Nomenclature* : Botanical, English and Indian languages arranged alphabetically.

Botanical nomenclature is more authentic in the identification of an individual spice or condiment and is of universal use and hence, a detailed table (Annexure - 1.4) is appended giving their Botanical and corresponding names in English, Assamese, Bengali, Hindi & Urdu, Gujarati, Kannad, Kashmiri, Malayalam, Marathi, Oriya, Punjabi, Sanskrit, Sindhi, Tamil and Telugu.

HISTORY OF THE SPICE TRADE

The role of spices, condiments and herbs in shaping the course of history is significant and it is a long and romantic story. The spice trade is one of the oldest known to man. Overland trade routes across Asia antecede recorded history, and merchandise moved over coastal sea routes in both directions between Arabia and sourthern Cathay (China) in very early times. Cinnamon, cassia, cardamom, ginger, and turmeric were known and employed by the Eastern people thousands of years ago, and these became important items of commerce early in the evolutionary course of trade.

Cinnamon and cassia found their way to the Middle East at least 2,000 years before the Christian Era. There are many references to spices in the Bible, including four to cinnamon and three to cassia. The spice trade in those days was extensive and profitable. Part of the immense yearly income of King Solomon came from "the traffic of the spice merchants".

From time immemorial, southern Arbia (Arabia Felix of antiquity) had been a trading centre for frankincense, myrrh, and other fragrant resins and gums. It is logical to conclude that the Arabian merchants would seek to add to their store of aromatics and no doubt it was the Arabs who first brought the highly esteemed cinnamon and cassia to the Middle East. Shrewd traders as they were, they artfully withheld the true source of these spices. To satisfy the curious, to protect their market, and to discourage likely competitors, they spread abroad fantastic tales to the effect that cassia grew in shallow lakes guarded by winged animals, that cinnamon grew in deep glens infested with poisonous snakes, and that, in consequence, they obtained these spices only at great risk. Pliny the Elder (AD 23-79) ridicules these stories of "fabulous antiquity" and boldly declares that "all these tales, however, have been evidently invented for the purpose of enhancing the price of these commodities." Strabo (c. 64 BC-AD 20) in his *Geography* speaks of the extensive trade in spices carried on by the Arabians, of the wealth of the Arabian spice merchants, and observes that even a camel driver "might attain to some sort of wealth" by trading in spices. Whatever part the overland trade routes across Asia played, it was mainly by sea that the spice trade grew. By rudimentary navigational skill, and aided by the winds called monsoons, the Arabians were making direct sailings before the Christian Era. In the Far East, parallel in time and not less skilled, the Chinese were moving through the waters of the Malay Archipelago and trading in the Spice Islands. Ceylon was the central trading point.

With the advent of the Ptolemies, Egyptian trade with India began and was developed by the Romans who succeeded them. From its early, hesitant start this trade was well developed by the time of Strabo, who said that on a visit to Syene he had found that about 120 ships sailed regularly from the Red Sea port of Myos-Hormos to India.

Under the Ptolemies, Alexandria, founded in 332 BC, had become a great seaport and centre of trade. Its revenues from port dues were already enormous when Ptolemy Alexander bequeathed this ancient city to the Romans in 80 BC. Under the Romans Alexandria became the greatest commercial centre of the world and the emporium for the aromatic and pungent spices of India that found their way to the markets of Greece and the Roman Empire.

Roman trade with India was extensive for over three centuries and then began to decline. It had, no doubt, weakened but not broken the Arabian hold on the spice trade. The Roman trade revived in the 5th century but dwindled in the 6th, whereas the Arabian trade endured into and through the Middle Ages.

By the 6th century Ceylon had become a notable trading centre to which came, according to Cosmas Indicopleustes of Alexandria, the "richest merchandise of the Indies, and all sorts of perfumes and spices."

At about the same time, Venice came into existence. By the 10th century it was beginning to prosper in the trade of the Levant; by the early part of the 13th century it enjoyed monopoly of the trade of the Near East; and by the 15th century it was a formidable power in Europe. Part of Venice's great wealth came from trading in the spices of India, Ceylon, the East Indies, and Cathay, which it obtained in Alexandria and sold to northern and western European buyers-distributors at exorbitant prices.

The Europeans knew very well about the origin of the spices reaching Alexandria and, but unable to break the hold of Venice, determined in the last third of the 15th century to build ships and venture abroad in search of a route to the spice-producing countries. So began the famed voyages of discovery. The Portuguese were first in the race, and the first to bring spices from India to Europe by way of the Cape of Good Hope.

Bartholomeu Dias doubled the Cape of Good Hope in 1488; Vasco da Gama reached Calicut, India, in 1498; and Pedro Alvares Cabral brought spices to Lisbon in 1501.

In 1492, Christopher Columbus sailed under the flag of Spain,

and in 1497, John Cabot sailed for England; but both failed to reach the fabulous spice lands.

Columbus had read, probably, that Eratosthenes of Cyrene (about 250 BC) had calculated the circumference of the world and that Strabo had observed that India might easily be reached from Spain, "still keeping the same parallel were it not for the extent of the Atlantic." Columbus thought, no doubt, that by sailing west he might reach the East before the Portuguese. But the first land he reached was not that of the fabulous Orient but a small island, which he named San Salvador. He thought he had arrived in the Indies "where the spices grow" (hence the name West Indies for the Caribbean islands he discovered). His four voyages resulted in no significant contribution to spices beyond his finding that the natives used capsicums, which they called *aji*, to season their food.

John Cabot fetched up on the barren coast of Cape Breton Island and took possession of the land in the name of Henry VII. He, too, thought he had arrived in the land where the spices grow, but he found none at all.

Ferdinand Magellan took up the quest for Spain in 1519. He discovered the straits that bore his name, and although he was killed in the Philippines en route, he is credited with the first circumnavigation of the world. Of the five vessels that set out from San Lucar under his command only one, "Victoria," returned to Spain, triumphantly, laden as she was with the cloves of Tidore.

In 1577, Sir Francis Drake began his adventurous voyage around the world by way of Magellan's straits and the Spice Islands and brought the "Golden Hind" heavily laden with the cloves of Ternate and other treasures into Plymouth harbour in 1580.

In Holland, a fleet under the command of Cornelis de Houtman sailed for the Spice Islands in 1595; another, commanded by Jacob van Neck, put to sea in 1598; and their ships returned home with rich cargoes of cloves, mace, nutmegs, and pepper.

The market in Europe for spices was considerable; the prices were high and the profits great. The early success of the Dutch gave them a temporary monopoly on pepper, forcing the price of that spice to rise in England from two shillings and eightpence to eight shillings per pound in 1599. The London merchants acted quickly, and after the formation of the East India Company under charter of Queen Elizabeth, on December 31, 1600, Capt. James Lancaster, later Sir James, sailed for the East Indies. His ships returned to England in September, 1603 with 1,000,000 pounds of pepper, which had cost him less than sixpence a pound in Sumatra.

In 1608, a cargo of cloves bought in the Spice Islands for £2,948 realized £36,287 in England.

In 1602, the Dutch East India Company came into existence by authority of the Estates-General of the Netherlands. In 1664, the French East India Company was organized by state authorization under Louis XIV. Other European nations granted charters to East India companies with varying success.

From the time in the latter part of the 15th century when the Portuguese put to sea in search of a southern route to India, European powers vied with one another in the quest for Eastern spices. Numerous vessels set out in search of spice cargoes. There followed struggles and conquests to gain advantage and monopolistic control of the trade. For more than over 100 years Portugal was the dominant power, but later yielded to English and Dutch enterprise and conquest. The 19th century witnessed the British interests firmly rooted in India and Ceylon and the Dutch in control over the greater part of the East Indies.

For mariners it was an age of adventure, risk, hardship, disease, and death; for nations an age of struggle, conquest or defeat; it was an age of acquisition of new, near-primitive lands and of colonizing and gaining dominion over civilized foreign territories. For European commercial interests it was an age of rewarding success, which broke the monopoly of Venice, overcame the Muslim domination of the spice trade that extended from the Red Sea and the Persian Gulf to the China Sea, created a voluminous trade in a great variety of merchandise between Europe and the Far East, and opened up a New World.

The United States entered the spice trade at the close of the 18th century. Capt. Jonathan Carnes is credited with founding the pepper trade with the East Indies. Financed by Salem interests, he put to sea in the brigantine "Rajah," on July 20, 1795, and returned in the following year with a cargo of 1,58, 544 pounds of pepper, which was sold at 37 cents per pound and brought a handsome profit of 700 percent.

This historic voyage began a lucrative pepper trade with Sumatra that flourished for 69 years, bringing pepper to Salem, Boston, and New York. It is recorded that between 1795 and 1845 some 200 merchantmen laden with the pepper of the East Indies entered Salem harbour.

*****

Uses : Ancient and Modern

The most notable uses of spices and herbs in very early times were in medicine, in the making of holy oils and unguents, and as aphrodisiacs. Priests employed them in worship, incantations, magical rites, and rituals.

Ancient herbals, including those of Cathay, Sumer, Assyria, Egypt, Greece, and Rome, testify to the use of spices and herbs in the treatment of disease. Hippocrates, Galen, and Pedanius Dioscorides, among others, employed them. In the first century of the Christian Era, Pliny, the Elder, in his *Natural History*, extols at length the efficacy and healing powers of spices and herbs in the treatment of just about every ailment known in his day. Such virtues, tempered and moderated, filtered down into the Middle Ages and early modern times.

It is not known when man first used spices and herbs in food. Sesame seems to have been known and employed as food, for making wine, and for its oil from time immemorial. Garlic and onions were employed as part of the diet in very early times. Certainly by the time of the ancient Greeks and Romans many spices and herbs had come into use to flavour food and beverages.

Herodotus (c. 484-c. 425 BC) describes the food of people he had met or heard about and relates that fish and pickled meats were staple items of food in many lands centuries after his time, and it requires no effort to imagine the welcome change the gratifying flavour of spices and herbs brought to foods, not only to opulent Greeks and Romans but to the affluent of society everywhere long after them.

Only the wealthy could indulge the use of imported aromatic spices and this was true, apparently, all over the world. Marco Polo observed, in 13th-century Cathay, that the higher class people ate meat that had been preserved in several of their spices, but the poor had to be content with meat steeped in garlic juice.

In Europe, in the course of time, knowledge of the use of spices and herbs to aid in the preservation of food by retarding or preventing rancidity or other deterioration caused by oxidation and to flavour dishes slowly spread. By medieval times large quantities of culinary herbs were in use. Eastern spices were beyond the purse of the greater number of people, but with the ascendency of the western European nations in the Oriental spice trade these conditions gradually changed, and the aromatic and pungent spices finally came into general use by rich and poor alike.

Modern uses of spices, condiments, and herbs are legion. There are few culinary recipes that do not include them, and their judicious use brings a delectable, distinctive aroma and taste to a host of dishes (see Annexure - 1.1).

In the food industry they are employed in the preparation of numerous products including processed meats, fancy sausages, sauces and vinegars, prepared mustard, pickles, chutneys, preserves, mayonnaise, salad dressings, biscuits, cookies, cakes, confections, and beverages.

Their essential oils and oleoresins are the basis of a number of spice flavourings and seasonings employed in food manufacturing, where oil spices are preferred to the whole or ground spices for the preparation of certain products.

Spices and herbs, or their oils where processing temperature permits, go into the preparation of a number of liqueurs including absinthe, anisette, benedictine, creme de menthe, curacao, and kummel.

Their essential oils are the flavouring components of a number of extracts; and they are employed in perfumery, cosmetics, toilet preparations, hair oils, toothpastes, toilet soaps, and tobacco.

In medicine the spices and herbs have not entirely lost their reputation. In India and other Asiatic countries their curative virtues enjoy respect. They still have a place, though limited, in Western medicine. Present-day herbalists extol the efficacies of some of the spices, spice seeds, and herbs in the treatment of certain ailments.

SPICES IN BEAUTY CARE

Beauty is but a flower
Which wrinkles will devour

—Thomas Nashe

In India various spices are used in the raw form for improving the complexion. The beneficial use of spices is being emphasised in today's world of perfumery and cosmetics industry, which uses oils of all the spices like caraway, cinnamon, cassia, cloves, nutmeg, mace, rosemary and cardamom in the blending of volatile and fixed oils to manufacture scores of alluring perfumes far in advance of the crude scents of the ancient time.

Spices and their oils are used abundantly for the manufacture of soaps, tooth pastes, talcum powders, after shave lotions, cologne, vanishing creams, mouth freshners, room freshners, sachets, toilet waters, powders, pomades and hair oils.

The effects of spices on beauty and body care is still not fully understood. Nevertheless, the use of pure spices and their oils is better in many ways when compared to the use of synthetic preparations, as spices can easily assimilate with the human system leading to lasting and superior effect with no side effects usually associated with synthetics.

Mrs. Nita Bhandari of Shahnaz Hussain Beauty Institute, New Delhi, mentions the following effects of various spices in body and beauty care as worked out in her Institute.

1. *Aniseed* coarse powder mixed with curd is good for removing the black as well as white heads. Aniseed prevents dandruff and falling hair.

2. *Bay leaf* water decoction has antiseptic action. Bay leaf prevents pyorrhoea and combined with various herbs is a good mouth freshner. It whitens the teeth and cures spongy gums, checks bleeding in them. Bay leaf is good for blemished skins too.

3. *Black Pepper* cures acne, haggard and sallow skin. It also activates blood circulation, stimulates the follicles, and is an astringent, tightener and toner.

4. *Cinnamon* powder mixed with powders of clove and pepper as well as with curd or milk is a powerful antiseptic pack for acne, headless lump, blisters and/or pimples.

5. *Clove* is antiseptic, antibiotic and hence cures acne and controls the activities of the sebaceous glands.

6. *Cumin seeds* are good for the broken, dilated and split capillaries, have a cooling, therefore, soothing effect. Cumin is good for the complexion too.

7. *Garlic* is good for open pores. It activates or stimulates blood circulation and also reduces obesity. It is a tonic for the hair and is the poor man's musk.

8. *Turmeric* is antiseptic, antitanning healer, good for pigmentation. It makes the skin translucent and glowing thereby maintaining the pH factor. Turmeric has cooling and soothing effect, tightens the breast muscles as well. It protects the skin from water allergy and purifies the blood.

[Source : Nita Bhandari, Spice India, 1990, 9(iii), 13-14]

Modern Trade and Production

In the passage of time, by intentional transplanting and seeding, and by natural dissemination, many of the plants from which we obtain spices, spice seeds, or herbs have become established in lands near to, or far from, their natural habitat. Ginger, native to southeastern Asia, is now cultivated in many countries across the world from East to West; spice capsicum, native to Central America, enjoys almost universal production; pepper, native to and an export spice of southern India, is also cultivated for export in Indonesia, Cambodia, Sri Lanka (Ceylon), Malagasy Republic, Malaysia, Thailand, and Brazil; cardamom and sesame, products of the Old World, now flourish in the New World. Today spices, spice seeds, condiments and herbs come from many parts of the world (see Annexure - 1.2). This has led to increased production, but not overproduction as the consumption of spices and herbs throughout the world has grown, too.

Variations of quality have resulted because of differences in altitude, temperature, soil composition, precipitation, and other environmental factors and because of differences in methods of harvesting, drying, processing, and storing in the various regions.

Spices, spice seeds, condiments and herbs are purchased directly from producers or, more commonly, through brokers specializing in the trade and operating, usually, in major seaports such as New York, London, Hamburg, and Amsterdam.

Organizations or associations exist to promote, facilitate, and regulate trading: the Spices Board, India; Fachverband der Gewurzindustrie C.V., West Germany; and the American Spice Trade Association, United States.

Importation and Sale

Spices and herbs destined for ports overseas are transported in general cargo vessels. On arrival at their destination, these products are subject to examination for adulteration and contamination by port health authorities acting under the imported food laws of their respective countries. For example, spices, spice seeds, condiments and herbs imported into the United States are subjected to sampling and examination by the Food and Drug Administration; spice lots found to be contaminated are reconditioned under their supervision.

Following inspection, spices and condiments imported for or by merchants and manufacturers located in the port of entry are cleared through customs on payment of duty, if any (a procedure usually carried out by customs brokers), and picked up at the pier. Those en route to other areas are shipped in bond to their destination, where they are similarly cleared and then picked up at the bounded warehouse by the merchants concerned.

Spices, spice seeds, condiments and herbs are usually imported whole, some to be sold whole, most to be further processed by grinding. Spice grinding is a specialized business requiring ability to identify the various spices, spice seeds, condiments and herbs; to assess their quality; and to know their structure and principal chemical components.

Bark and root (rhizome) spices must be reduced to a size suitable for introduction into the grinding machine. This is uaually accomplished with the aid of a knife-cutter comminuting machine.

Grinding machines commonly in use in the United States include pulverizers, roller mills, hammer mills, and comminuters.

The ground and sifted spices are mixed to uniformity usually in a ribbon blender or mixer. This machine also prepares spice and herb mixtures.

Excessive heat must be avoided in the grinding process, as it will cause a loss of valuable volatile oil.

Spices, spice seeds, condiments and herbs are sold whole or ground, in small containers for the retail trade, or in bulk quantities. Bulk buyers include meat packers, fancy sausage specialists, pickle manufacturers, producers of condiments, commercial bakers, confectioners, and the catering industry.

The United Nations and the Organization for Economic Cooperation and Development provide statistics of imports and exports reported by several but not all countries. Many countries provide only a partial report; world totals would be greater if all information were included.

Production

Spices in general, after harvesting and collection, are cleansed of extraneous matter, cured if necessary, dried in the sun or by artificial heat or both, sorted, and graded. Spice seeds are obtained by threshing the harvested plants after they have been stacked in the field to mature and dry. Herbs are harvested, suspended, or stacked in the open to dry, and the dried leaves rubbed from the stalks; or following harvesting they are dried by exposure to controlled artificial heat and then processed mechanically to produce herbs of good colour, full flavour, and desired fragment size. Consumer demand at retail differs the world over because cuisine differs.

Blends

Ground mixtures of spices, some long established and some newly introduced, are available.

Meat tenderizers

Meat tenderizers may be seasoned or unseasoned. The seasoned tenderizers contain appropriate ground spices. Both types usually contain salt and dextrose, some contain monosodium glutamate, but the principal tenderizing substance in all of them is papain. Papain is derived from the latex or the unripe fruit of the papaya, or papaw, tree, *Carica papaya*, native to tropical America. Papain is a proteolytic enzyme that acts as a protein digestive.

Peels

Peels such as lemon and orange produced by spice manufacturers consist of the dried and finely comminuted peels blended, respectively, with lemon oil and orange oil.

Condiments

Condiments (Latin *condire*, "preserve") are, loosely, any kind of relish or seasoning added to prepared food dishes. In this sense pepper could be classified as a condiment, but the term usually includes such preparations as chutneys, catsup, tabasco sauce, Worcestershire sauce, barbecue sauce, soya sauce, mayonnaise, salad dressing, prepared mustard, etc. The last mentioned item is more closely allied to spices; the others contain spices among a number of ingredients. The major ingredient of prepared mustard is mustard flour (ground mustard seed), although other spices are present as well as vinegar, salt, and sugar or dextrose. Prepared mustard with horseradish added is also available.

Essential Oils

Essential oils are so called because they contain oils essential to the life of the plant, besides having the aroma and flavour of the plants. They are also called volatile oils because they evaporate when exposed to air.

In addition to the principal flavour component or components of the oils, lesser amounts of other natural organic chemical constituents present in the essential oil contribute to the full flavour of the spice, seed, or herb.

Oleoresins

Oleoresins, as their name implies, are natural combinations of essential oils and resins, more or less liquid in consistency. Resins are complex natural oxidation products of essential oils. Oleoresins occur naturally in capsicums, ginger, laurel (bay) leaves, pepper, star anise, and turmeric.

Commercially, an oleoresin is prepared from a spice or herb by extraction with a selected volatile, organic solvent. This process yields a mixture of the essential oil, soluble resins, and related substances present in the spice or herb depending on the kind of solvent employed. These mixtures contain the flavouring principles present in the original spice or herb.

By combining essential oils and oleoresins in various processes, products are obtained that replace the natural spice or herb and can be used in the manufacture of soluble spice flavourings, stable flavourings for all types of processed meats and fancy sausages.

Soluble spice flavourings are made by distributing the oleoresin product on a dry, soluble edible substance such as salt or dextrose (encapsulation). When other substances such as ground spices are added, the complete mixture is known commercially as a dry soluble seasoning.

Maintenance of quality

Quality control

All bulk spices, whole and ground, are stored in dry, clean, sanitary, rodent-proof, cool premises. Temperature and humidity are controlled to inhibit mold growth and discourage insect infestation in the interest of consumer protection, and to avoid loss to the manufacturer.

Whole spices and herbs intended for grinding should not be stored too long. A slow deterioration of essential oil may occur with the passage of time although the cellular structure is intact. Spices and herbs with oil glands on or near the surface are more vulnerable than those with oil secretion cells deeply seated in the tissues.

Ground spices should not be left exposed to the air but kept in tightly closed containers while awaiting packaging. Grinding fractures and tears apart the tisues and cell walls, and loss of volatile constituents will occur in direct ratio to surrounding air temperature unless the products are properly contained.

All retail packages and containers should afford full protection against this kind of loss.

Laboratory quality-control checks can be made by sampling and routine analysis. For this purpose the spice is ground fine enough to pass through a sieve with circular openings half millimetre in diameter. The sample should be thoroughly representative of the lot.

The procedure usually involves the following determination: (1) moisture, (2) total ash, (3) ash insoluble in hydrochloric acid, (4) volatile oil, (5) nonvolatile ether extract, (6) crude fibre, (7) starch.

Spices and herbs offered for sale to the public are subject to spot sampling and analysis by government agencies responsible under the food laws.

Shelf life

The shelf life of spices depends largely upon the form of the spice and the material used for packaging. The shelf life from the date of manufacture varies as follows: flaked items in tins, 12 months; whole spices in cartons, 18 months; ground spices in tins, 24 months; and spices packed in glass containers, 36 months.

Standards

Standards of identity are promulgated by governments to regulate the industry and protect the public. Minimum and maximum limits for physical and chemical properties insure against inferiority or adulteration. These requirements must be met by foreign exporters and by importers at home.

Not all countries have standards relative to spices, spice seeds, and herbs, but there is universal recognition of the value of such standards to exporters, importers, and manufacturers, and of their necessity in the interests of consumer protection. A trend to the promulgation of standards by more nations is now evident.

Flavourings

Flavouring extracts, essences, and flavours are liquids added to foods to enhance taste and aroma. They are prepared from essential oils, such as cloves and cinnamon; from vanilla; from fresh fruits by expression; from ginger by extraction; from mixtures of essential oils and synthetic organic chemicals; or entirely from synthetic chemicals, with alcohol, glycerol, propylene glycol, alone or in combination, as solvents. Water is added and sometimes certified food colour.

Extracts, essences, and flavours employing only natural flavouring agents are called pure; those employing synthetics (in part or entirely) are called imitation or artificial flavourings.

Essential oils, complex substances derived from plants, consist of a number of organic chemical components including alcohols, aldehydes, ethers, esters, hydrocarbons (terpenes, sesquiterpenes, etc.), ketones, lactones, phenols, and phenol ethers. Nearly all of these organic chemicals have been synthesized, and these are the synthetics that are employed in the manufacture of imitation flavourings.

Essential oil extracts

These extracts are prepared by dissolving an essential oil in alcohol of the proper strength, adding water and, where desirable and permitted by law, a small amount of certified food colour. They include anise, celery, cassia or cinnamon, clove, lemon, nutmeg, rosemary, savory, basil, sweet marjoram, thyme.

Nonalcoholic flavouring extracts

Nonalcoholic flavouring extracts are prepared by employing glycerol or propylene glycol or a combination of these to bring the essential oil into solution, with added water, and sometimes food colour.

True fruit flavours

True fruit flavours are obtained by expression, concentration, or distillation of fresh fruits. The alcoholic content of the finished product is usually between 18 and 22 percent to prevent fermentation.

Imitation, artificial extracts, essences, flavours

Imitation, artificial extracts, essences, and flavours are prepared by bringing into solution with alcohol, glycerol, or propylene glycol various synthetic flavour with the likeness of the flavour of the fruit, spirit, or liqueur for which it is named. These preparations cover a wide range of flavourings including vanilla, lemon, lime, banana, cherry, butterscotch, brandy, and rum.

Some contain few ingredients, others many. Imitation vanilla extract may be prepared with synthetic vanillin, coumarin (this ingredient is now prohibited in the United States and Canada), heliotropin, glycerol, water, and caramel colouring.

Imitation extracts, essences, and flavours must be labelled accordingly.

Quality Control and Analysis

The International Organization of Flavour Industries, IOFI, with headquarters in Brussels, was incorporated under the laws of Belgium. Its main purpose is the continuing evaluation of flavour ingredients for safety, and its aim is directed toward the establishment of a universal code of flavour laws.

ANNEXURES FOLLOW...

ANNEXURE 1.1 Uses of Spices and Herbs With Foods

	bever-ages	*breads, rolls*	*cakes, cookies, biscuits*	*cheese dishes*	*chut-neys*	*des-serts*	*dress-ings*	*egg dishes*	*fish and seafood*	*fruit dishes*	*gravies*	*meat dishes*	*pickles*	*poul-try*	*salads*	*sauces and relishes*	*soups*	*vege-table dishes*
Allspice			+		+	+	+						+			+		
Aniseed	+	+	+										+					
Basil, sweet								+	+			+			+		+	+
Caraway seed		+	+	+								+		+	+			+
Cardamom		+	+			+				+			+					
Cayenne pepper					+			+	+			+				+		
Celery salt								+	+			+					+	
Celery seed							+		+				+		+			+
Chervil							+	+	+			+		+	+	+	+	
Chilli peppers					+								+			+		
Chilli powder								+	+		+	+				+	+	+
Cinnamon	+	+	+			+				+			+					
Cloves			+		+	+	+			+		+	+					

Contd...

...Contd.

	beverages	*breads, rolls*	*cakes, cookies, biscuits*	*cheese dishes*	*chutneys*	*desserts*	*dressings*	*egg dishes*	*fish and seafood*	*fruit dishes*	*gravies*	*meat dishes*	*pickles*	*poultry*	*salads*	*sauces and relishes*	*soups*	*vegetable dishes*
Coriander seed		+	+				+					+	+	+	+			
Cuminseed				+			+	+				+		+			+	
Curry powder								+	+			+		+		+		+
Dillseed							+				+	+	+		+	+	+	+
Fennel seed	+		+			+			+				+					
Fenugreek seed					+													
Garlic powder							+					+						
Garlic salt								+				+						
Ginger		+	+		+	+				+		+	+	+				+
Laurel (bay) leaves									+			+	+			+	+	
Mace			+			+				+						+		
Marjoram, sweet								+	+			+		+	+	+	+	

Contd...

...Contd.

	beverages	*breads, rolls*	*cakes, cookies, biscuits*	*cheese dishes*	*chutneys*	*desserts*	*dressings*	*egg dishes*	*fish and seafood*	*fruit dishes*	*gravies*	*meat dishes*	*pickles*	*poultry*	*salads*	*sauces and relishes*	*soups*	*vegetable dishes*
Mint	+				+				+			+				+	+	+
Mixed pickling spice													+					
Mustard					+		+		+		+	+	+			+		+
Nutmeg			+			+				+						+		+
Onion powder							+					+			+	+	+	
Onion salt												+			+	+	+	
Origanum (oregano)				+			+	+	+		+	+			+	+	+	+
Paprika							+	+	+		+	+						+
Parsley									+			+		+	+	+	+	+
Pepper							+	+	+		+	+	+	+	+	+	+	+
Poppy seed		+	+				+								+			+
Red pepper							+	+	+			+				+		+

Contd...

...*Contd.*

	bever-ages	*breads, rolls*	*cakes, cookies, biscuits*	*cheese dishes*	*chut-neys*	*des-serts*	*dress-ings*	*egg dishes*	*fish and seafood*	*fruit dishes*	*gravies*	*meat dishes*	*pickles*	*poul-try*	*salads*	*sauces and relishes*	*soups*	*vege-table dishes*
Rosemary									+			+		+			+	+
Saffron			+			+												
Sage									+			+		+				
Savory							+	+	+			+		+	+	+		
Sesame seed		+	+															
Tarragon								+				+		+	+	+		+
Thyme							+					+		+		+	+	+
Turmeric				+			+		+				+			+	+	+

ANNEXURE 1.2

Spices and their Regions of Origin

* Major source. + Other sources. ++ Includes dehydrated garlic, onion.

Allspice	Guatemala+ Honduras, British+ Honduras, Republic+ Jamaica* Mexico*
Aniseed	Bulgaria+ Lebanon+ Mexico* The Netherlands* Spain* Syria+ Tanzania+ Turkey+ CIS(USSR)+ Yugoslavia+
Basil, sweet	Belgium+ France* Hungary* Italy+ USA* Yugoslavia*
Caraway seed	Denmark* Ethiopia+ Lebanon* The Netherlands* Poland* CIS(USSR)+
Cardamom	Cambodia+ Costa Rica+ El Salvador+ Guatemala* India* Malaysia+ Sri Lanka (Ceylon)+ Tanzania+ Thailand+
Celery seed	France* India* Indonesia+
Chervil	France+ USA*
Chilli peppers	Chile+ China+ Ethiopia* Fiji+ Greece+ Haiti+ India* Indonesia+ Israel+ Japan* Kenya* Malaysia+ Mexico* Nigeria* Pakistan* Sierra Leone+ Sudan+ Tanzania* Taiwan+ Thailand+ Turkey+ Uganda+ USA*
Cinnamon, Ceylon	Kenya+ Malagasy Republic+ Seychelles+ Sri Lanka (Ceylon)*
Cinnamon, cassia	China* India+ Indonesia* Taiwan+ South Vietnam*
Cassia buds	China*
Cloves	Indonesia* Malagasy Republic Malaysia* Mozambique+ Sri Lanka (Ceylon)+ Tanzania*
Coriander seed	Algeria+ Argentina* Bulgaria+

Contd...

Coriander seed (Contd.)	Cyprus+
	Czechoslovakia+
	Ethiopia+
	India*
	Iran+
	Mexico+
	Morocco*
	Nigeria+
	Pakistan+
	Poland+
	Romania*
	Spain*
	USA+
	CIS(USSR)+
	Yugoslavia*
Cuminseed	Argentina+
	China+
	Cyprus+
	India*
	Indonesia+
	Iran*
	Japan+
	Lebanon*
	Mexico+
	Morocco+
	Syria+
	Turkey+
Dillseed	China+
	India*
	Mexico+
	USA+
Fennel seed	Argentina*
	Brazil+
	Bulgaria*
	China+
	Denmark+
	France+
	Germany, West*
	Greece*
	India*
	Italy+
	Korea, South+
	Lebanon*
	Romania+
	Taiwan+
	Yugoslavia+
Fenugreek seed	Egypt+
	Ethiopia+
	France+
Fenugreek seed (Contd.)	India*
	Iran+
	Lebanon+
	Morocco+
Garlic	Argentina*
	Bulgaria++
	China+
	Egypt++
	Ethiopia+
	Hungary++
	India+
	Iran+
	Italy+
	Mexico++
	Peru+
	Portugal++
	Spain+
	Taiwan++
	USA++
	CIS(USSR)+
Ginger	China+
	Fiji+
	Guatemala+
	Haiti+
	Hong Kong+
	India*
	Jamaica*
	Japan+
	Kenya+
	Nigeria*
	Puerto Rico+
	Sierra Leone*
	Taiwan+
	Thailand+
	Uganda+
Laurel (bay) leaves	Cyprus+
	Greece+
	Mexico+
	Portugal*
	Turkey*
	Yugoslavia+
Marjoram sweet	Chile+
	France+
	Lebanon+
	Mexico+
	Peru+
	Romania+
	USA+

Contd...

Mint	Bulgaria*
	Egypt*
	France*
	Germany, West+
	Greece*
	Morocco*
	Romania*
	South Africa+
	U.K.*
	USA+
	CIS(USSR)*
Mustard seed	Bulgaria+
	Canada*
	Chile+
	Denmark*
	Ethiopia*
	Germany, West+
	Italy+
	The Netherlands+
	U.K.*
	CIS(USSR)+
	USA+
Mace	Grenada*
	India+
	Indonesia*
	Jamaica+
	Leeward Islands+
	Malaysia+
	Sri Lanka (Ceylon)+
	Trinidad and Tobago+
Nutmeg	Grenada*
	India+
	Indonesia*
	Jamaica+
	Malaysia+
	Sri Lanka (Ceylon)+
	Trinidad and Tobago+
Onion	Argentina*
	Bulgaria++
	Egypt++
	Ethiopia+
	France+
	Germany, West+
	Guatemala+
	Hungary++
	Iran+
	Israel++
	Lebanon+
	Peru+
Onion (Contd.)	Portugal+
	Romania*
	Spain+
	Taiwan+
	USA++
	CIS(USSR)+
Origanum (Oregano)	Cyprus+
	Dominican Republic+
	France+
	Germany, West+
	Greece*
	Italy+
	Japan+
	Lebanon+
	Mexico*
	Portugal+
	Spain+
	Turkey+
	USA+
Paprika	Bulgaria*
	Chile+
	Czechoslovakia+
	Egypt+
	Hungary*
	Mexico+
	Morocco*
	Portugal*
	Romania+
	Spain*
	Turkey+
	USA+
	CIS(USSR)+
	Yugoslavia*
Parsley	Belgium+
	Canada+
	France+
	Germany, West+
	Hungary+
	Spain+
	U.K.+
	USA+
Pepper	Brazil*
	Cambodia+
	Ivory Coast+
	India*
	Indonesia*
	Jamaica+
	Malagasy Republic+
	Malaysia*

Contd...

Pepper (Contd.)	Sarawak*
	Sri Lanka (Ceylon)*
	Thailand^{+}
Poppy seed	Bulgaria^{+}
	Denmark^{+}
	Iran^{+}
	The Netherlands*
	Poland*
	Romania*
	Turkey*
	CIS(USSR)*
Rosemary	France^{+}
	Spain^{+}
	USA^{+}
	Yugoslavia^{+}
Saffron	Egypt^{+}
	Greece^{+}
	Spain*
	Turkey^{+}
Sage	Albania*
	Cyprus^{+}
	Czechoslovakia^{+}
	Greece^{+}
	Italy^{+}
	Lebanon^{+}
	Turkey^{+}
	USA^{+}
	CIS(USSR)$^{+}$
	Yugoslavia*
Savory	France*
	Spain*
	USA*
	Yugoslavia*
Sesame seed	Brazil^{+}
	China*
	Colombia^{+}
	Egypt^{+}
	El Salvador*
	Ethiopia*
	Guatemala*
Sesame seed (Contd.)	India*
	Iraq^{+}
	Japan^{+}
	Lebanon^{+}
	Mexico*
	Nicaragua*
	Sudan^{+}
	Syria^{+}
	Thailand^{+}
	USA^{+}
	CIS(USSR)$^{+}$
Star anise	China*
	North Vietnam*
Tarragon	France*
	The Netherlands^{+}
	USA*
Thyme	Cyprus^{+}
	France*
	Greece^{+}
	The Netherlands^{+}
	Spain*
	Turkey^{+}
	USA^{+}
Turmeric	China^{+}
	Haiti^{+}
	Honduras, Republic*
	India*
	Indonesia^{+}
	Jamaica*
	Pakistan^{+}
	Peru^{+}
	Sri Lanka (Ceylon)$^{+}$
	Taiwan^{+}
Vanilla	Indonesia*
	Malagasy Republic*
	Mexico*
	Mozambique^{+}
	Reunion^{+}
	Seychelles^{+}
	Tahiti^{+}
	Uganda^{+}

ANNEXURE 1.3

Names of some Botanists

For reference with Annexure 1.4 on Indian Nomenclature of Spices

Coloumn 2 of Annexure 1.4 contains certain bracketed words which are in fact abbreviated names of the following renowned botanists associated with the discovery of that particular spice

A.Rich.	Richard, Achille
Andrews	Andrews, Henry C.
A.W.Hill	Hill, Arthur W.
Blume	Blume, C.L.
Bullock	Bullock, Arthur Allman
Burk	Burkill, J Iac H.
Cosson	Cosson, E. St-Charles
Czernj.	Czernjaew, V.W.
DC.	Candolle, A.P. de
Dunal	Dunal,MIchel,Felix
Engl.	Engler, H.G.A.
Gaertn.	Gaertner, Joseph
Hoffm.	Hoffman, Georg Franz
Hook. f.	Hooker, J.D.
Houtt.	Houttun, Maarten
J. Moore	Moore, John William
Koch	Koch, W.D.J.
L.	Linnaeus (Linne), C. von
Lf.	Linne, C. von, (filius)
Maton	Maton, William G.
Maxim.	Maximowicz, K.J.
Merr.	Merrill, E.D.
Meyer	Meyer Bernhard
Miller	Miller, Philipp
Nees	Nees von Esenbeck, C.G.D.
Nyman	Nyman, Carl Fredrik
Perry	Perry, Lify May
Pers.	Persoon, C.H.
Pierre	Pierre, J.B.L.
Roscoe	Roscoe, William
Roxb.	Roxyburgh, William
Salisb.	Salisbury, E.A.
Schiede	Schiede, C.J.W.
Scherb.	Scherbius, Johannes
Schumann	Schumann, K.M.
S. Harrison	Harrison, S.G.
Sonn.	Sonnerat, Pierre
Sprague	Sprague, Thomas A.
Sprengel	Sprengel, K.P.J.
Thonn.	Thonning, Peter
Thwaites	Thwaites, G.H.K.
Willd	Willdenow, C.L. von.

ANNEXURE 1.4 INDIAN NOMENCLATURE OF SPICES

S.No.	Botanical	English	Assamese	Bengali	Hindi & Urdu	Gujarati	Kannad	Kashmiri	Malayalam	Marathi	Oriya	Punjabi	Sanskrit	Sindhi	Tamil	Telugu
1	2	3	4	5	6	7	8	9	10	11	12	13	14	15	16	17
1.	Acorus calamus (Linn.)	Sweet flag	Themeprii	Bach	Bach, Garbach, Bacha	Gandhilovaj	Baje, Bajegida	Vabi	Vashampe	Vekhand, Bariboj, Wach		Bacha	Bhadra, Gulami		Vashambu	Vadaja, Vasa
2.	Allium scalonicum (Linn.)	Shallot		Gundhun	Ek-kanda-lasun							Gandana, Gandhan				
3.	Allium cepa (Linn.)	Onion	Piyaz	Palandu	Piyaz	Dunzari	Nirulli		Bawanj	Kanda		Piyaz	Palandu	Dungari	Irruli, Vengayam	Nirulli
4.	Allium fistulosum (Linn.)	Stone leek, Welsh onion		Vilayati lasson					Vellulli	Khorat						
5.	Allium porrum (Linn.)	Leek	–	Paru	–	-	–		–	–						
6.	Allium sativa (Linn.)	Garlic	Nahairu	Rashum	Lasun, Lassan, Lashun	Lassan	Balluli	Ruham	Velluli	Lusoon		Lassan	Lashuna		Ullipundu	Velluri
7.	Allium schoenoparasum (Linn.)	Chive, cive														
8.	Alpina gallanga (Linn.) Willd.	Galanga		Kulanjan	Kulanjan	Kalinjan	Rasmi, Sugandha Vach		Perasatta	Bari Pan kijar, koshi Kulanjan		Kulanjan	Kulanjana	Kathi, Kunjar	Sugandam Tittiram	Pedadum-parashtram kachoramu

...Contd.

1	2	3	4	5	6	7	8	9	10	11	12	13	14	15	16	17
9	Alpinia officinarum (Hance)	Lesser galangal			Kulanjan		Rasna						Rasnab		Chitta-ratlai Sanrashtam	Sannaras-tram
10.	Alpinia speciosa (K.Schum)	Light galangal		Punang champa												
11.	Amomum aromaticium (Roxb.)	Bengal cardamom		Morang elaichi	Moti elaichi Morang elaichi					Veldoda						
12.	Amomum subulatum (Roxb.)	Greater Indian cardamom, Sikkim, Nepal cardamom		Bara elaichi	Bari elaichi	Moto elaichi	Dodda yalakki		Perelam Peri elav, Periya-elattri	Mote veldode moto-eldari		Bari elaichi	Brihadoela Brihat-upa-kunchika Ela		Periya yalam Periya yallakki	Peddayellaki Adavi-Ellakkay
13.	Amomum xanthioides (Wall)	Bastard cardamom		Elach	Illayachi											
14.	Anethum graveolens (Linn)	European dill														
15.	Anethum sowa (Kurz)	Indian dill		Sowa, Soya	Sowa, Soya	Surva	Sabasige	Soi		Surva, Shepu		Sowa, Soya	Satapushpi	Suava	Satha Kau-ppei sompa	sabesige
16.	Angelica archengelica (Linn.) syn. Archengelica officinalis (Hoffmann)	Great angelica American angelica master wort.														

Contd...

...Contd.

1	2	3	4	5	6	7	8	9	10	11	12	13	14	15	16	17
17	Anthriscus cerefolium (Hoffm)	Chervil			Baz-Atrilal											
18	Apium graveolens (Linn.)	Celery seed		Bandhuri, chanu, Randhuni	Shalari, Ajmud	Bodiajmoda				Ajmoda		Karnauli, Bhutghata	Ajamoda, Sigru		Ajmoda	
19.	Apium graveolens var. rapaceum de-Candole	Celeriac			Ajmud											
20.	Armoracia rusticana (Gaertu)	Horse radish														
21.	Artemisia dracanculus (Linn.)	Tarragon, Estragon														
22.	Averrhoa bilimbi (Linn.)	Bilimbing, Tree sorrel, Cucumber tree		Blimbi	Belambu, Tamarang	Blimbu Kalazounsi	Bimblee		Vilimbi	Bilamba					Pilimbi, Pullicha-kai Kachittamar thaki	Bilimbikay, Pulusukayulu Bilibilikayalu
23.	Averrhoa carambola (Linn.)	Carambola, Country gooseberry, Chinese gooseberry	Kardai	Kamranga	Karmal Kamrakh	Kamarakha Kumrak	Darehuli		Tamaratta	Kamrakha, Kumrak			Karmaranga		Tamarattai	Karomonga, Tamaratamu
24.	Brassicanapus (Linn) Syn. B. campestris (Linn.) sub sp. napus (Linn.)	Toria, Indian rape seed, Brown sarson			Kalisarson, Toriya											

Contd...

...Contd.

1	2	3	4	5	6	7	8	9	10	11	12	13	14	15	16	17
25.	Brassica campestris (Linn.) Var. sarson prain or glauca (Linn.)	Yellow sarson			Pili sarson											
26.	Brassica juncea (Linn.) Czernejev & Cosson	Indian mustard		Sarisha Raisarisha	Kalee sarson	Rai	Sasave	Aasur, Sarisa		Mohri, Pivalisiras, Rayan			Asuri, Bimbatta		Kadugo	Avalu
27.	Brassia alba (Boiss) Syn. Sinapus alba (Linn.)	white mustard		Dhop-rai	Safed rai	Safed Rai			Vellakadugu	Mohori-pandri			Swet sarisha Siddhartha		Kadugo	Avalu
28.	Brassica nigra (Linn.) Koch	Black mustard		Banarsi rai, Krishnrai	Banarsi rai Kalo rai, Makra rai	Rai	Sasave Karisasivey	-do-	Kaduka	Mohari, Rai sarson			Sarashpah	Ahur	-do-	-do-
29.	Capparis spinosa (Linn.)	Caper			Kabra		Mullu Kattari			Kabar		Kaur, Brar	Kakadani			Kokila kshamu
30.	Capsicum frutescens (Linn.)	Capsicum, Bird eye chilli		Lanka marich, Jhal	Jhal					Lavangi mirchi				Garho-mirchi	Milagi	Mirappa
31.	Capsicum annum (Linn.)	Chillies, Paprika, Red pepper, Cay-enne pepper		Lal mirchi, Lanka marich Jhal	Lal mirchi	March, Marchu	Kempu menasu	Mirch waungum, Martsu	Upperi paranki, Perangimuluk Kappalmelaka	Mirsinga, Mirchi		Mirch, Mattisa	Marichi-phalam, Katuvira, Bruhi		Molagay, Milagi	Mirapakaya, Galakonda, Mirapasinga
32.	Carum bulbocastanum	Black caraway			Siahjira											

Contd...

...Contd.

1	2	3	4	5	6	7	8	9	10	11	12	13	14	15	16	17
33.	Carum carvi (Linn.) syn. Apium carvi (Linn.) and Crantz Seseli carvi (Linn.) Lamet DC.	Caraway seed Caraway seed		Jira, zira	Shia jira, Siya zira		Shime jeerige	Gunyun	Shima jirakam	Wilayat zirah		Zira siah	Sushavi,	Kalu duru	Shimai shembu	Sima jirakaia
34.	Cinnamomum aromaticum (C.G. Nees)	Cassia, Chinese Cassia		Dalchini, Daruchini		Dalchini, Daruchini	Lovang pattai		Lavangpatta	Dalchini, Daruchini		Kirfa, Dalchini, Daruchini	Guda, tvak Thwak, Varangam		Lovang pattai	Lovang pattai
35.	Cinnamomum tamala (Buch Ham) Nees & Ebermaier	Indian Cassia		Tejpat	Tejpat	Tamalapatra				Darchini,		Tejpat	Tamalaka, Tejpatra		Talishappa-ttiri	Talisapatri
36.	Cinnamomum zeylanicum	Cinnamon		Dalchini	Dalchini, Darchini	Dalchini	Lavangpattai		Lavang-pattai	Dalchini	Dalchini	Dalchini	Darushila		Sanna-lavangpattai	
37.	Coriandrum sativum (Linn.)	Coriander		Dhane, Dhania	Dhania Dhanya	Kothmiri, Libdhana	Kothambri, Kothamiribija	Daaniwal, Kothambalari	Kothum-palaribija	Dhana	Dhania	Dhania	Dhanyaka		Kothamalli	Dhaniyalu
38.	Crocus Sativa (Linn.)	Saffron		Jafran	Kesar, Zafran Jafranekar,	Keshar	Kum Kuma, Kesari	Kong	Kunkum-appu	Keshar, Kesara		Kesar, Zafran	Keshara, Bhavrakta, Saurabh, Mangal		Kungumapu	Kum kuma-puva
39.	Cuminum cyminum (Linn.)	Cumin seed		Safaijira, Zeera	Jira, Zeera, Safaid jeera or Zeera	Jeeru	Jeerige	Zyur	Jeerakam	Jeerigire	Jeera	Safed Jira or Zeera	Jiraka, Jira	Zero	Ziragum, Jeergum	Jidakara, Jikaka

Contd...

...Contd.

1	2	3	4	5	6	7	8	9	10	11	12	13	14	15	16	17
40.	Curcuma amada (Roxb)	Mango ginger	Amada, Pholiya	Amahaldi	Karpura haridra	Arukamlaka, Mamidiallam	Shodgrandika	Ambahalad			Amahaldi, Amba halad					
41.	Curcuma aromatica (Salisb)	Yellow Zedoary, wild turmeric	Ban-halad	Jangli haldi	Vanaharidra	Kasturi manjal	Advipasupa	Kadarasina Kasturi-arishina	Kapur-Kachali	Kattu manjal	Vedi-halad					
42.	Curcuma longa (Linn.)	Turmeric	Halud, Pitras, Haldi	Halud, Haldi	Haldi, Haladi	Haldhar, Haldi	Arishina	Lidar	Manjal	Halad, Haldi	Haldi	Haldi, Haldhar,	Haridra, Harita Rajani, Gauri, Nisha, Varavat Ela		Manjal	Pasupu
43.	Elettaria cardamomum (Linn) Maton. syn. E repans.	Cardamom, Malabar-cardamom Lesser Cardamom		Choti elaichi Garata	Choti elaichi	Elaichi	Yellaki	Aa'l Buduaa'al Elayachi	Elathari	Velchi, Elaichi, Veldode	Alaichi		Ela		Yellakki Elakkai Elem, Elakgai	Elakkayi, yealak-kayulu, Pakkuln
44.	Eugenia caryophyllus (C. Sprengel, Bullock et. Harrison; Syzgium aromaticum (Linn.) Merril et. Perry.	cloves		Lavang	Laung	Lavang	Lavanga		Grambu	Luvang	Labang	Lauang	Lavanga		Kirambu	Lavangalu
45.	Ferula alliacea (Boiss) syn. Ferula rubri caulis (Boiss), F. asafoetida (Linn.) F. foetida (Regel) F. nārthex (Boiss)	Asafoetida, Hing		Hing	Hing	Hing	Hinger	Yang, Sap	Perungayam Kayam	Hing	Hengu	Hing	Badkika, Agudagandhu Bahleeka, Ramatta, Sulanasan, Hingu Bhutnasan,	Vaghayani, Vagharni	Perungayam Kayam	Inguva, Ingumo

Contd...

...Contd.

1	2	3	4	5	6	7	8	9	10	11	12	13	14	15	16	17
46.	Foeniculum vulgare P. Miller syn. F. officinale All., Anethum foeniculum	Fennel, Indian sweet fennel		Pan-Muhiri, Mauri, Methi	Bari saunf, saunf, sonp.	Variari, Warialli	Badi-sopu, sabbasige		Perum jeerakum	Bedi-shep		Saunf	Madhurika, Mettica	Saunf	Shombei, shombu, Sohikire	Sopu, Pedda-jilakara
47.	Garcinia cambogia, (Gaertner), Desrousseaux	Gambodge			Aradal											
48.	Garcinia morella (Desrouseaux)	Indian gambodge		Tamal	Gotaghanba Kokam		Laurel			Kokam					Korakpuli Trevalchi-nippal	Rival-chinipul
49.	Garcinia indica (Choisy) syn. G. purpurea	Kokam Red Mango Kokam butter		Kokam	Kokam	Ratamba, Birandel Kokambel, Kokan	Murginahuli mara, Murgala		Punampulli	Kokam, Amsol, Katambi, Bhirand Ratamba					Murgalmara	
50.	Hyssopus officinalis	Hyssop (Linn.)			Zufah-yabis, Zufah											
51.	Illicium verum (Hook)	Staranise			Anasphal					Badian					Annashupu	Anaspuvu
52.	Juniperus Communis (Linn.)	Juniper		Havasha	Aaraar, Saru Hauber, Abhal			Betar, Petthra, Pama, Chui, Haulber				Betar, Petthri, Chui, Pama Abhal saru	Vapusha			
53.	Laurus nobilis (Linn.)	Bay or laurel leaves			Baz, Hab-el-ghar											

Contd...

...Contd.

1	2	3	4	5	6	7	8	9	10	11	12	13	14	15	16	17
54.	Majorana hortensis (Moench) Syn. Origanum majorana (Linn.)	Sweet marjoram		Murru	Marwa, Marva Khusha Sathra		Maruga		Maru vamu	Murwo, Marwa		Marwa	Maru	Marwo	Maruvu, Marru, Marrau	Maru vamu
55.	Mangifera indica (Linn.)	Mango slices or powder		Kachu kacha aam	Amchur, Keri Kachcha aam	Keri, Ambo	Mavina Kayi		Manga, Mampalam Mavu	Amba	Kanch ambu	Amchur, Kachcha am	Amva, Amra, Chita	Ambi	Mangai	Mamidi kayi
56.	Melissa officinalis (Linn.)	Lemon balm		Bililotan, Baranjiboya												
57.	Mentha arvensis (Linn.)	Japanese peppermint		Pudina	Pudina	Pudina	Chetni-marugu	Pudyanu	Muthina, Putliyana	Pudina		Pudina			Pudina	Pudina
58.	Mentha longifolia (Linn.) Hudson.	Mint			Pudina											
59.	Mentha piperita (Linn.)	Peppermint			Peppermint											
60.	Mentha spicta (Linn.) syn. M. virdis (Linn.)	spearmint			Pahari Pudina											
61	Murraya koenigii (Linn.) C. sprengel syn. Bergera koenigü	Curry leaf	Narsingha, Bisharhari	Barsanga, Kariphulli	Curry patta mitha neem, Gandhela, Barsanga Kathnim.	Goranimb Kadhilimbdo	Karibevu		Kariveppilei Basango	Karhinimb,	Barsan, Basango, Bhursunga	Curry patta	Surabhinimba, krishna nimba		Karivempu, Karuveppilei	Karepaku

Contd...

...Contd.

1	2	3	4	5	6	7	8	9	10	11	12	13	14	15	16	17
62	Myristica fragrans (Hautluyn)	Mace	Japatri	Jotri, Jamtri	Jamtri, Paydpatri, Jayepatri	Javitri Jaepatri	Japatri Jaepatri	Jaabvatiur Jouwatri	Jathipatri	Jaepatri	Jaitre	Jaipatri Jamtari	Jatipatri		Jaddipattiri	Japatri, Jaddipattiri
63.	- do -	Nutmeg	Jaiphal	Jaiphal	Jaiphal	Jaiphal	Jaijikai	Zaaphal	Jathikka		Jaiphala		-do-		Jathikai Jadikkay	Jajikai
64.	Nigella sativa (Linn.)	Black cumin		Kalijira Mugrela	Kalonji, Mangrela	Kadu jeeroo	Karijirigay	Tukhmic-gandna	Karinchirkam, Karun-shiragam	Krishanajira, Kalanjire		Kalonji, Kala jira	upkunchika, Aranyajeerka, Krishan jiraka		Karunshirgam Karunjiragam	Nulanji lakra
65.	Ocimum basilicum (Linn.)	Sweet basil		Babui tulsi	Gulal or Kali tulsi, marva	Damaro, Nasabo, Sabza	Kama Kasturi, Sajjagida	Niazbo, Hazbo	Tirunitnu, Tirunitri, Ram Tulsi	Marva, Sabza	Dhala tulsi, Kapur Kanti,	Furrunj-mushk Niazbo, Baburi	Munjariki Surasa, Varvara, Bisva tulsi	Sabajhi	Tirnirupachai Karpura tulsi Karandai, Tirnut patchi	Bhutulsi, Rudrajada, Vepudu pacha Kukka tulsi, Vebudi patri
66.	Origanum vulgare (Linn.) syn. O. Majorana (Linn.)	Marjoram wild		Murru	Sathra, Marwa					Marwa			Marwa		Marvu, Marau	Maru vamu
67.	Origanum hortensis (Moench)	Marjoram		Murru	Marwa, Marva khusha		Maruga		Maruvamu			Marwa	Maru	Murwo	Maruvu, Marru	
68.	Papaver somniferum (Linn.)	Poppy seed		Kaskash	Khus-khus, Khishkhash	Khus-khush,	Khasksi		Kashakasha	Khus khus		Khush khush, Khas khas	Khasa, khakasa kasa bijam		Gashagasha kasakasa	Kasa Kasa, Gasagarla Gasalu, Nalamanthu

Contd...

...Contd.

1	2	3	4	5	6	7	8	9	10	11	12	13	14	15	16	17
69.	Petroselinum crispum syn. P. sativum (P. Miller) Hyman ex A.W. Hill	Parsley			Ajmood		Achu mooda		Katham belari							
70.	Pimenta dioica (Linn.) Merrill	Pimento, all-spice					Ganda menasu		Kappalamu-laku						Kattukkaruva	
71.	Pimpinella anisum (Linn.) syn. Anisum vulgare (Gaer) A. officinalis (Moench)	Aniseed, Anise, Sweet fennel		Muhuri, Mitha jira.	Saunf, Badian Rumi, Aawonf	Anisi	Sompu		Shombu	Somp, Badishep	Sop	Valaiti Saunf	shatapushapa Madhurimisi Karavee, Shatava, shetpushpa		Shombu	Kuppi, sopu
72.	Piper longum (Linn.)	Long pepper, Dried Catkins	Piplu, Pipal	Pipla more, Pipli, Pepul	Pipli, Piplamul Pipul, Pimpli	Pipli, Pipara	Hippali, Kuva, Hippalibali, yippali		Tippali, Pippali	Pimpli Mothi, Pipli	Pippoli	Maghan, Darfilfil	Pippali, Trikama, Maghadhi, Granthikan	Pippli, fil	Thippli	Tippili, Pippalu, Pippalte Kaue
73.	Piper nigrum (Linn.)	Black or white pepper		Kalamorich Golmirch Vellajung	Kali or safed mirch, Siah mirch	Kalamari, Kalomirch	Kare menasu Volloy menasu	Marutis Martz	Kurumaluku, Nallamulaku Kuru-milagu	Mire, Kali mirch	Gol Moricha	Kalimircha	Maricha Ushana Hapusha Valliyam Krishnam		Milagu	Miriyalu, Miryalatige
74.	Punica granatum (Linn.)	Pome-granate seed	Dalim	Dalimb	Anardana	Dadam, Dalamb	Dalimbri, Dalimbay	Daan, Dhiun	Mathalam pazham	Dalimb	Dalimba	Anardana	Dadima Darimba	Anardakum	Mathalam pazham, Madalai, Madalangkai	Dannima pandu, Dadima, Dalimba
75.	Rosmarimes officinalis (Linn.)	Rosemary			Rusmari, Rajmari											

Contd...

...Contd.

1	2	3	4	5	6	7	8	9	10	11	12	13	14	15	16	17
76.	Salvia officinalis	Sage			Seya kuss, Salbia Selakuss											
77.	Satureia or Satureja hortensis (Linn.)	Summer savory														
78.	Satureia or Satureja montana (Linn.)	Winter savory														
79.	Sinapis alba (Linn.) Boissier	White mustard or yellow mustard		Dhoprai	Sufed rai	Sufed rai			Vella Kadugu	Mohori-pandu					Kadugu	Avalu
80.	Tamarindus Indica	Tamarind	Ttali	Ambli, Tentul Tintil	Imli	Ambli, Amli	Amli, Huli Hunase hannu	Tamar-i-Hind	Puli	Chinch,	Teetuli, Koina, Konya	Imli	Abdika, Amli Tintiri, Tintrani Amlika, Tintik	yippali	Puli, Puliyan	Amlika, Chinth-appandu, Chinta, Asek
81.	Thymus serpyllum (Linn.)	Wild thyme			Banjwain, Ipar, Hasha							Marizha, Masho, Rangsbur				
82.	T. Vulgaris (Linn.)	Thyme														
83.	Trachyspermum ammi (Linn.) Sprague ex. Turril. syn. Carum copticum (Heirn)	Bishop's weed, Ajowan		Jowan, joan	Ajowan, Ajowain	Yavan	Oma	Jawind	Omum	Onva	Jnuani	Ajowani	Ajamoda, yavnika		Omum	Vamu

Contd...

...Contd.

1	2	3	4	5	6	7	8	9	10	11	12	13	14	15	16	17
84.	Trigonella foenumgraecum (Linn.)	Fenugreek		Methi	Methi	Methi	Menthya		Ventayam uluva	Methi	Methi	Methi	Medhika	Methi	Vendayam Venthiyam	Menthula, Mentulu
85.	Vanilla fragrans (Salisbury) Ames, syn. V. planifolia (Andrews)	Vanilla			Vanilla		Vanilla		Vanilla			Vanilla			Vanilla	
86.	Zingiber officinale Roscoe	Ginger		Ada	Sonth, Adrak Adhrak	Adu	Shunti, Adraka	Sho'nt	Inji, Chukka	Ale	Ada	Adrak	Sangavera Ardraka, Varam Sringaberam		Inji, shukhu Chukhu	Allam, Sonti

ANNEXURE 1.5 NAMES OF SPICES AND CONDIMENTS IN FOREIGN LANGUAGES

Botanical name	*English*	*Spanish*	*French*	*German*	*Russian*	*Japanese*	*Chinese*	*Arabic*	*Italian*	*Portugese*
1	**2**	**3**	**4**	**5**	**6**	**7**	**8**	**9**	**10**	**11**
Piper nigrum	Pepper	Pimienta	Poivre	Pfeffer	Pyerets	Kosha	Hu Chiao	Filfil Aswad	Pepe	Pimenta
Elettaria cardamomum	Cardamom (small)	Cardamomo	Cardamome	Kardamom	Kardamom	Karudamon	Pai-tou-kon	Hal	Cardamomo	Cardamomo
Capsicum annuum Capsicum frutescens	chilli	Pimenton	Poaiverede Guinee	Poprika	Struchkovy pyeret	Togarashi	Hsivng-Yale Chiao	Filfil Ahmar	Peperone	Pimento
Zingiber officinale	Ginger	Jengibre	Gingembre	Ingwer	Imbir	Shoga	Chiang	Zanjabil	Zenzero	Gengibre
Curcuma longa	Turmeric	Curcuma	Curcuma	Kurkuma Gelb wurzel	Zholty Imbir	Ukon	Yu-chin	Kurkum	Curcuma	Acafrao-da-India
Coriandrum sativum	Coriander	Culantro	Corriandre	Koriander	Koriander	Koendoro	Hu-sui	Kuzhbare	Coriandolo	Co-entro
Cuminum cyminum	Cumin	Comino	Cumin	Romischer Kummel	Kmin		Ma-chin	Kammun	Comino	Cominho
Foeniculum vulgare	Fennel	Hinojo	Fenonil	Fenchel	Fyenkhel	Vikyo	Hui-Hsiang	Shamar	Finiocchio	Funcho

Contd...

...Contd

1	2	3	4	5	6	7	8	9	10	11
Apium graveolens	celery seed	Apio	Celeri	Sellerie	Syel derey	Seronii	Chin	Karafs	Sedano	Aipo
Anethum graveolens	Dill	Eneldo	Anelt	Dill	Ukrop		Shin-do	Shibith	Aneto	Endro
Papaver somniferum	Poppy	Adermidera	Pavot	Mohn	Mak	Keshi	Ying-shu	Khashkhash	Papavero	Dormideira
Allium sativum	Garlic	Ajo	Ail	Knoblanch	Chesnok	Ninniku	Suan	Thum	Agilio	Alho
Sinapis alba	Mustard	Mastaza	Moutarde	Senfsaat	Gorchitsa	Shiro korashi	chiet	Khardal	Senape	Mastarda
Cinnamomum zeylanicum	Cinnamon	Canela	Cannelle	Zimt	Koritsa	Seiron-Nikkei	Jou-kwei	Qurfa	Cannella	Canela
Cinnamomum aromaticum	Cassia	Canela dela china	Canele de cochin chine	Z Limtkassie		Bokei	Kuei/Kwei	Darasini	Cassia	
Myristica fragrans	Nutmeg and Mace	Nuez Moscada	Muscade	Musketnuss	Oryekh Muskatny	Nikuzuku	Jou-Tou-Kou	Basbasa	Noce Moscata	Noz-Moscada
Syzygium aromaticum	Clove	Clavo	Girofle	Gewarz nelken	Gvozdika	Choji	Ting-Hsiang	Qaranful	Garofano	Cracvo
Pimpinella anisum	Aniseed	Anis	Anis	Anis	Anis		Hnei-Hsiang	Yanisun	Anice	Erva-doce

Contd...

...Contd

1	2	3	4	5	6	7	8	9	10	11
Crocus sativus	Saffron	Azafran	Safran	Safran	Shafran	Safuran	Fanj-Hung-Hua	Zafaran	Zafferano	Acofrao
Vanilla fragrans	Vanilla	Vainilla	Vanille	Vanille	Vanil	Banira	H-siang-Tsao	Wanila	Vaniglia	Daunilha
Pimenta dioica	Pimento	Pimienta-gorda	Piment	Piment	Yamayski Pyerets			Bahar	Pepe si Giamaica	Pimenta-Da-Jamaica
Laurus nobilis	Bay leaf	Laurel	Laurier	Lorbeer	Lavr	Gekkeiju	Yueh-kuei	Ghar	Alloro	Loureiro
Ocimum basilicum	Basil	Alba Laca	Basilic	Besilienkrant	Bazilik	Meboki	Lo-le	Raihan	Basilico	Manjericao
Ferula asafoetida	Asafoetida		Ferule asafoetida	Stinkendes Stecken kraut				Tyib, Haltheeth		
Petroselinum crispum	Parsley	Perejil	Persil	Petersilie	Pyetrushka	Paseri	Yang-Hu-Sui	Bagdunis	Prezzemolo	Salsa
Rosmarinus afficinalis	Rosemary	Romero	Romarin	Rosamarin	Rozamarin	Mannenro	Mi-Tiech-Hsiang	Iklil Al-Jabal	Romerino	Alecrim
Thymus vulgaris	Thyme	Tomillo	Thym	Thymian	Timyan	Jakosa	Pai-Li-Hsiang	Satar	Timo	Tomilko
Carum carvi	Caraway seed	Alcaravea	Carvi	Kummel	Tmin		Yuan-Sui	Karauya	Carvi	Alcaravia

Contd...

...*Contd*

1	2	3	4	5	6	7	8	9	10	11
Origanum vulgare	Oregano	Oregano	Origan	Dost	Dushitsa			Anrar	Regamo	Ouregao
Satureja hortensis	Savory	Ajedrea	Sarriette	Bohnen krabit	Chabyor		Hsiang Potho	Nadgh	Santoreggia	Segurelha
Salvia officinalis	Sage	Salvia	Sauge	Salbei	Shalfey	Sage	Ching-Chieh	Mariyamiya	Salvia	Salva
Armoracia rusticana	Horseradish	Raband Picante	Meerrettich	Meerrettich	Khren	Wasabi	Lagen	Fujl Har	Rafano	Rabana Picante
Artemisia dracunculus	Tarragon	Estragon	Estragon	Estragon	Estragon		Ai-Hao	Tarkhun	Targone	Estragao
Marjorana hortensis	Marjoram	Amaraco	Marjolaine	Majovan	Mayoran	Mayorana	Ma-Yueh-Lan-Hua	Marzanjush	Maggiorana	Manjerona

ANNEXURE 1.6

International Classification of Goods and Services

for the Purpose of the Registration of Marks

World Intellectual Property Organization

Geneva - 1987

Class 30	List of Goods in Class Order (Spices)
Serial No.	Indication of Goods
AO205	All spice
AO301	Aniseed
CO263	Celery salt
CO484	Cinnamon (spice)
CO564	Cloves (spice)
CO996	Curry (spice)
GO114	Ginger (spice)
MO440	Mustard
NO124	Nutmegs
PO209	Pepper
PO217	Peppers (seasonings)
SOO27	Saffron (seasoning)
SO679	Spices
SO781	Star aniseed
TO512	Turmeric for food
VOO28	Vanilla (flovouring)
WO166	Weeds (condiment) Bishop's

(NICE classification --- 5th Edn. Part II).

ANNEXURE 1.7

Spices Growing States in India

(States contributing to more than 80 per cent of the total production)

AJOVAN :	Bihar, Jammu & Kashmir
ANISEED :	Punjab, Uttar Pradesh, Assam
CARDAMOM (Small) :	Kerala, Karnataka, Tamil Nadu
CARDAMOM (Large) :	Sikkim, West Bengal
CELERY :	Punjab, Uttar Pradesh
CHILLIES :	Andhra Pradesh, Gujarat, Karnataka, Maharashtra, Orissa, Rajasthan, Tamil Nadu, Uttar Pradesh, West Bengal, Madhya Pradesh
CINNAMON & CASSIA :	Kerala, Tamil Nadu
CLOVE :	Kerala, Tamil Nadu, Karnataka
CORIANDER :	Rajasthan, Uttar Pradesh
CUMIN :	Rajasthan, Gujarat, Uttar Pradesh
DILL SEED :	Gujarat, Rajasthan
FENNEL :	Gujarat, Rajasthan, Uttar Pradesh
FENUGREEK :	Rajasthan, Uttar Pradesh, Gujarat
GARLIC :	Haryana, Madhya Pradesh, Maharashtra, Orissa, Uttar Pradesh, Bihar, Gujarat, Karnataka, Rajasthan
GINGER :	Andhra Pradesh, Karnataka, Kerala, Madhya Pradesh, Meghalaya, Orissa, Arunachal Pradesh, West Bengal, Mizoram, Sikkim, Himachal Pradesh, Tamil Nadu

HERBAL & EXOTIC SPICES :	Ootty (Tamil Nadu)
KOKAM :	Karnataka
MUSTARD :	Uttar Pradesh
NUTMEG & MACE :	Kerala, Tamil Nadu, Karnataka
PEPPER :	Kerala, Karnataka, Tamil Nadu
POMEGRANATE SEED :	Maharashtra
SAFFRON :	Jammu & Kashmir
TEJPAT :	Arunachal Pradesh, Sikkim
TURMERIC :	Andhra Pradesh, Karnataka, Orissa, Tamil Nadu, West Bengal, Maharashtra, Kerala, Assam, Bihar, Meghalaya, Tripura, Uttar Pradesh, Arunachal Pradesh
VANILLA :	Kerala, Karnataka, Tamil Nadu

ANNEXURE 1.8

List of Spices & Spice–Products Coming Under the Purview of the Spices Board

1.	All-Spice	आलस्पाइस, (पिमेन्टो)
2.	Aniseed	सौंफ
3.	Asafoetida	हींग
4.	Basil	तुलसी
5.	Bayleaf	बे-पत्ता (जयपत्र)
6.	Bishop's weed	आजवाइन (ओवा)
7.	Cambodge	केम्बोज
8.	Caper	केपर (कबरा)
9.	Caraway	काला जीरा
10.	Cardamom (Small & Large)	इलायची छोटी एवं बड़ी
11.	Cassia	अमलतास, तेजपत्ता
12.	Celery	सेलरी, अजमोद, अजमोदा, आजवाइन
13.	Chilli	मिर्च
14.	Cinnamon	दालचीनी
15.	Clove	लौंग
16.	Coriander	धनिया
17.	Cumin	सफेद जीरा
18.	Curryleaf	कढ़ी पत्ता
19.	Dill	सोआ तेल
20.	Fennel	कलौंजी
21.	Fenugreek	मेथी
22.	Garlic	लहसुन
23.	Ginger	अदरक
24.	Greater Galingale	महागेलेंजा (सफेद पनकी झाड़) (बरकुलंजन)

25.	Horse Raddish	हौर्स-रैडिश (शोभाजन)
26.	Hyssop	हिसप, जूफा
27.	Juniperberry	जूनिपर बेरी (आरार)
28.	Kokum	कूकम
29.	Lovage	लवेज
30.	Mace	जावित्री
31.	Marjoram	मुखाक, मरुआ, कुठरा
32.	Mint	पुदीना
33.	Mustard	सरसों
34.	Nutmeg	जायफल
35.	Oregano	ओरगेनो
36.	Parsely	अजमोद
37.	Pepper	काली मिर्च
38.	Pepper Long	पीपला
39.	Pomegranate seed	अनारदाना
40.	Poppy seed	खसखस
41.	Rosemary	रोज़मेरी
42.	Saffron	केसर
43.	Sage	सेज
44.	Savory	सेवरी
45.	Star Anise	स्टारेनाइज़ (आनसफल)
46.	Sweet Flag	स्वीट-फ्लैग (बच)
47.	Tamarind	इमली
48.	Tarragon	टैरागण
49.	Tejpat	तेजपात
50.	Thyme	थाइम (इषार), (अजवायन)
51.	Turmeric	हल्दी
52.	Vanilla	वैनिला

ANNEXURE 1.9

Research Organisations Working on Various Spices

1.Cardamom (Small)

1. Indian Cardamom Research Institute,
   Myladumpara Kailasanadu P.O.
   Nedumkandam (Via),
   Idukki Dist.,
   KERALA-685563

2. Cardamom Research Station,
   Kerala Agricultural University,
   Pampadumpara,
   Kerala-685553.

3. UPASI Research Station,
   Vandiperiyar,
   Kerala.

4. Regional Research Station
   Indian Cardamom Research Institute
   Saklespur,
   Karnataka-573134.

5. Regional Research Station,
   Indian Cardamom Research Institute,
   Thadiyankudisai,
   Tamil Nadu-624212.

6. Regional Research Station,
   (University of Agricultural Sciences),
   Mudigere,
   Karnataka-577132.

7. Horticultural Research Station,
   (Tamilnadu Agricultural University),
   Yercaud,
   Tamil Nadu-636012.

8. National Research Centre for Spices,
Marikannu P.O.,
Calicut,
Kerala-673012.

9. Cardamom Research Centre,
(National Research Centre for Spices),
Appangala,
Madikeri,
Karnataka-571201.

2. Cardamom (Large)

1. Regional Research Station,
Indian Cardamom Research Institute,
Gangtok,
Sikkim-737102.

2. ICAR Research Complex,
Gangtok,
Sikkim.

3. Coriander

1. Dept. of Genetics & Plant Breeding,
S.K.N. College of Agriculture,
(Rajasthan Agriculture University),
Jobner,
Rajasthan-303329.

2. Regional Agriculture Res. Station,
Gujarat Agri. University,
Jagudan,
Gujarat-382710.

3. Regional Agri. Res. Station,
(Andra Pradesh Agri. University)
Lam Farm,
Guntur,
Andhra Pradesh-522034.

4. Dept. of Spices & Plantation Crops,
Faculty of Horticulture,
(Tamilnadu Agricultural University),
Coimbatore,
Tamil Nadu-641003.

4. Cumin

1. Department of Genetics & Plant Breeding,
   S.K.N. College of Agriculture,
   (Rajasthan Agriculture University),
   Jobner-303329.

2. Regional Agricultural Research Station,
   (Gujarat Agricultural University),
   Jagudan,
   Gujarat-382710.

5. Fennel

1. Dept. of Genetics & Plant Breeding,
   S.K.N. College of Agriculture,
   (Rajasthan Agri. University),
   Jobner,
   Rajasthan-303329.

6. Fenugreek

1. Dept. of Genetics & Plant Breeding,
   S.K.N. College of Agriculture,
   (Rajasthan Agri. University)
   Jobner,
   Rajasthan-303329.

2. Regional Agri. Research Station,
   (Gujarat Agri University),
   Jagudan,
   Gujarat-382710.

3. Regional Agri. Research Station,
   (Andhra Pradesh Agri. University),
   Lam Farm,
   Guntur
   Andhra Pradesh - 522034.

4. Dept. of Spices & Plantation Crops,
   Faculty of Horticulture,
   (Tamilnadu Agricultural University)
   Coimbatore,
   Tamil Nadu-641003.

5. Dept. of Vegetable Crops,
   Hissar Agriculture University,
   Hissar,
   Haryana-126004.

7. Ginger

1. High Altitude Research Station,
   (Orissa University of Agri. Tech).
   Pottangi,
   Orissa-764039.
2. Department of Vegetable Crops,
   (Dr. Y.S. Parmer University of
   Horticulture & Forestry),
   Solan,
   Himachal Pradesh-173230.
3. College of Horticulture,
   (Kerala Agriculture University),
   Vellanikkara, Trichur,
   Kerala-680651.
4. National Research Centre for Spices,
   Marikunnu P.O.,
   Calicut,
   Kerala-673012.

8. Nutmeg, Clove, Cinnamon, Allspice

1. National Research Centre for Spices,
   Marikunnu P.O.,
   Calicut,
   Kerala-673012.

9. Pepper

1. Pepper Research Station,
   (Kerala Agricultural University),
   Panniyur,
   Kerala-670141.
2. Pepper Research Station,
   (Andhra Pradesh Agricultural University),
   Chintappali,
   Andhra Pradesh-531111.

10. Turmeric

1. High Altitude Research Station,
   (Orissa University of Agri. & Forestry),
   Pottangi,
   Orissa-764039.

2. College of Horticulture,
   (Kerala Agricultural University),
   Vellanikkara,
   Trichur,
   Kerala-680651.

3. Regional Agricultural Research Station,
   (Andhra Pradesh Agri. University),
   Jagtial,
   Andara Pradesh-505307.

4. National Research Centre for Spices,
   Marikunnu P.O.,
   Calicut,
   Kerala-673012.

5. Department of Spices & Plantation Crops,
   Faculty of Horticulture,
   Tamilnadu Agricultural University,
   Coimbatore,
   Tamil Nadu-641003

Source: Spice India, 1990, 12 (III), 22-24.

ANNEXURE 1.10 **Export of Spices from India by Major Commodity Groups**

(Qty. in M.T; Value in Rs. Lakhs)

Commodity	1988-89		1989-90(P)		1990-91		1991-92(P)		1992-93(E)	
	Qty	Value	Qty	Value	Qty	Value	Qty	Value	Qty	Value
Pepper	36981	16463.16	34482	15296.59	29985	10239.93	20565	7420.82	25480	8317.35
Cardamom (Small)	787	1037.36	180	306.68	400	1086.61	553	1606.74	175	679.59
Cardamom (Large)	464	200.10	787	294.82	1077	490.53	932	476.25	1270	807.85
Chillies	7876	1718.37	11983	2585.31	24534	2755.55	33398	9790.64	16850	6786.55
Ginger	6368	940.82	9037	1268.96	6555	1175.79	13396	2032.45	8220	1569.62
Turmeric	18968	1939.28	16860	1615.28	13624	1548.48	16565	3157.57	18950	4631.65
Coriander	8175	591.04	2664	278.50	3488	405.45	9228	1190.39	13550	1991.48
Cumin	1213	391.63	4030	695.06	1029	304.95	1460	586.53	2080	1176.95
Celery	2997	315.89	3106	373.85	3199	414.03	2782	463.69	2750	418.30
Fennel	1099	208.37	2284	311.25	1163	201.22	1663	362.73	2650	635.80
Fenugreek	3575	366.72	6241	441.43	3748	304.56	4941	424.09	4850	521.20
Other Seeds (1)	1384	188.78	1578	174.05	1035	122.59	1340	280.47	1000	206.95
Garlic	4178	230.15	2241	176.80	4023	256.89	9894	763.25	7700	716.98
Other Spices (2)	2239	465.41	2660	796.32	11740	1049.06	9650	1179.00	13700	2166.00
Curry Powder	3066	566.26	3320	675.42	3144	660.04	3068	863.92	2900	1040.95
Spice Oils and Oleoresins	576	1857.32	717	2285.77	892	3198.74	1132	5602.63	1140	6539.23
Grand Total	99946	27480.66	102170	27576.09	109636	24214.42	130567	36204.17	123265	38206.45

(P) Provisional, (E) Estimated

(1) Include Seed Spices such as Aniseed, Ajwanseed, Dill Seed etc.

(2) Include Tejpat, Cinnamon, Cassia, Kokam, Tamarind, Saffron, Asafoetida etc.

Source: 1988-89 to 1990-91 : DGCI&S., Calcutta/Exporters Returns.
1991-92 : DGCI&S., Calcutta/Shipping bills passed by Customs/Exporters Returns.
1992-93 : Rough estimate based on data from DGCI&S., Calcutta, Shipping bills passed by customs, Quantity graded for export under Agmark, consultations with major exporters etc.

ANNEXURE 1.11 (Tables A — O)

Table: A

Area and Production of Pepper in India

Year	*Area In Hects*	*Production In Tonnes*
1970-71	119960	26160
1971-72	118630	26160
1972-73	119800	26190
1973-74	121720	28700
1974-75	121920	28180
1975-76	111930	25570
1976-77	112240	25500
1977-78	104700	21100
1978-79	84570	21500
1979-80	110720	27700
1980-81	109290	29490
1981-82	111020	29230
1982-83	110440	26610
1983-84	107350	22710
1984-85	109400	18220
1985-86	125120	34000
1986-87	132810	31340
1987-88	149930	48090
1988-89	160740	44160
1989-90	155780	38790

Source : Directorate of Economics & Statistics, Ministry of Agriculture, New Delhi.

Table: B

Area and Production of Cardamom Small in India

Year	*Area In Hects*	*Production In Tonnes*
1970-71	91480	3170
1971-72	91480	3785
1972-73	91480	2670
1973-74	91480	2780
1974-75	91480	2900
1975-76	91480	3000
1976-77	91480	2400
1977-78	91480	3900
1978-79	92760	4000
1979-80	93950	4500
1980-81	93950	4400
1981-82	93950	4100
1982-83	93950	2900
1983-84	93950	1600
1984-85	100000	3900
1985-86	100000	4700
1986-87	100000	3800
1987-88	105000	3200
1988-89	105000	4250
1989-90	81000	3100

Source: Area: Upto 1988-89; Estimates based on reports received from State Governments on Registration of Cardamom estates by Spices Board (Board).

From 1989-90; Based on Complete enumeration Survey conducted by the Board in 1989-90.

Production: Estimates Based on field sample survey and market sales data by the Board.

Table: C

Area and Production of Cardamom large in India

Year	*Area In Hects*	*Production In Tonnes*
1980-81	25685	4000
1981-82	25685	4000
1982-83	25685	3000
1983-84	25685	2100
1984-85	25685	3300
1985-86	23110	3380
1986-87	23210	2900
1987-88	23310	3250
1988-89	25690	3965
1989-90	25690	3260

Source: Area: Upto 1984-85; Estimate by the Board. 1985-86 to 1987-88; Directorate of Eco. & Stat., Ministry of Agriculture, New Delhi. From 1988-89; Estimates by the Board.

Production: Estimates Based on field sample survey and market sales data (Board).

Table: D

Area and Production of Chillies in India

Year	*Area In Hects*	*Production In Tonnes*
1970-71	783400	520400
1971-72	753100	493900
1972-73	682400	411700
1973-74	738800	497000
1974-75	685600	441200
1975-76	739800	526100
1976-77	781500	419400
1977-78	790900	543300
1978-79	826500	565700
1979-80	853900	507600
1980-81	834800	509100
1981-82	806400	514700

Contd...

...Contd.

1982-83	818000	538900
1983-84	808100	566500
1984-85	794800	630500
1985-86	904100	877400
1986-87	834600	629200
1987-88	743200	579800
1988-89	805000	680400
1989-90	892600	783300

Source: Directorate of Economics & Statistics, Ministry of Agriculture, New Delhi.

Table: E

Area and Production of Ginger in India

Year	*Area In Hects*	*Production In Tonnes*
1970-71	21590	29290
1971-72	24590	34710
1972-73	22880	33630
1973-74	24860	38460
1974-75	24140	37910
1975-76	27200	45150
1976-77	25650	43390
1977-78	36020	71700
1978-79	40800	75720
1979-80	41420	71140
1980-81	40450	82440
1981-82	41110	89710
1982-83	43830	94170
1983-84	48960	121310
1984-85	51510	133860
1985-86	53520	138020
1986-87	52630	136010
1987-88	54240	142840
1988-89	51870	152120
1989-90	53020	152890

Source: Directorate of Economics & Statistics, Ministry of Agriculture, New Delhi.

Table: F

Area and Production of Turmeric in India

Year	*Area In Hects*	*Production In Tonnes*
1970-71	80500	150600
1971-72	75900	178400
1972-73	69000	121100
1973-74	74300	133900
1974-75	78100	145700
1975-76	71800	135200
1976-77	66800	109700
1977-78	75700	126300
1978-79	89700	190400
1979-80	105000	235400
1980-81	101500	216900
1981-82	90700	191300
1982-83	85900	173100
1983-84	94300	212500
1984-85	102300	259200
1985-86	109300	367100
1986-87	109900	319900
1987-88	108700	303900
1988-89	123400	390400
1989-90	123900	390000

Source: Directorate of Economics & Statistics, Ministry of Agriculture, New Delhi.

Table: G

Area and Production of Garlic in India

Year	Area In Hects	Production In Tonnes
1975-76	39800	140900
1976-77	35900	129600
1977-78	41500	133300
1978-79	49400	167200
1979-80	59700	205600
1980-81	59300	216000
1981-82	60540	229700
1982-83	63400	245000
1983-84	80700	311000
1984-85	72600	268700
1985-86	57700	189600
1986-87	59600	208200
1987-88	93700	318600
1988-89	85600	313600
1989-90	83500	327000

Source: Directorate of Economics & Statistics, Ministry of Agriculture, New Delhi.

Table: H

Area and Production of Coriander in India

Year	Area In Hects	Production In Tonnes
1970-71	272300	101200
1971-72	358700	114600
1972-73	252800	82900
1973-74	281000	106500
1974-75	246800	103700
1975-76	242400	93700
1976-77	263400	115700
1977-78	508900	231600
1978-79	383900	145300
1979-80	263700	90200

Contd....

...Contd.

1980-81	280100	110800
1981-82	359800	145200
1982-83	422600	189100
1983-84	435500	163500
1984-85	388300	119900
1985-86	382100	117100
1986-87	395200	182500
1987-88	593400	296800
1988-89	380600	181700
1989-90	332700	143100

Source: Directorate of Economics & Statistics, Ministry of Agriculture, New Delhi.

Table: I

Area and Production of Cumin in India

Year	*Area In Hects**	*'Production In Tonnes**
1975-76	86880	28170
1976-77	128426	48798
1977-78	158009	84727
1978-79	180549	79116
1979-80	165887	78376
1980-81	165305	89155
1981-82	80867	43177
1982-83	135576	62740
1983-84	149917	88315
1984-85	102400	54213
1985-86	73629	35475
1986-87	80743	41606
1987-88	110013	49745
1988-89	223493	114440
1989-90	150493	46874

* Include figures for major producing States only.

Source: State Agriculture Departments.

Table: J

Area and Production of Fennel in India

Year	*Area* In Hects*	*Production* In Tonnes*
1975-76	14566	17443
1976-77	18710	21070
1977-78	18418	25720
1978-79	17507	22258
1979-80	12494	14018
1980-81	11785	13239
1981-82	12655	14090
1982-83	12947	13234
1983-84	27908	27849
1984-85	16388	20001
1985-86	9959	10401
1986-87	10084	8648
1987-88	5740	5504
1988-89	13134	16473
1989-90	11700	12150

*Include figures for major producing States only.
Source: State Agriculture Departments.

Table:K

Area and Production of Fenugreek In India

Year	*Area* In Hects*	*Production* In Tonnes*
1975-76	31164	43473
1976-77	32964	49659
1977-78	54764	56773
1978-79	31276	48176
1979-80	41797	57575
1980-81	38478	52636
1981-82	32355	63203
1982-83	32246	45697
1983-84	40630	36429
1984-85	44687	53580
1985-86	30956	31953
1986-87	23866	25949
1987-88	24091	21243
1988-89	38402	37431
1989-90	37635	38806

* Include figures for major producing States only.
Source: State Agriculture Departments.

Table: L

Production of Celery in India

Year	*Production In Tonnes*
1970-71	3500
1971-72	3200
1972-73	2500
1973-74	3200
1974-75	3500
1975-76	4000
1976-77	3600
1977-78	3200
1978-79	4200
1979-80	4000
1980-81	4500
1981-82	3000
1982-83	4000
1983-84	3500
1984-85	4300
1985-86	3600
1986-87	4300
1987-88	3700
1988-89	4400
1989-90	3000

1983-84 to 1988-89 - Estimate based on past trends.

Source : Directorate of Cocoa, Arecanut & Spices Development, Calicut.

Table: M

Area and Production of Clove in India

Year	*Area* In Hects*	*Production* In Tonnes*
1980-81	1399	1000
1981-82	1376	1000
1982-83	1520	1000
1983-84	1626	1100
1984-85	1736	1200
1985-86	1787	1300
1986-87	1674	1500
1987-88	1484	1500
1988-89	1855	1700
1989-90	1943	1800

* Include figures for major producing States only.

Source : State Agriculture Departments.

Table: N

Production of Nutmeg & Mace in India

Year	*Production* In Tonnes*
1985-86	4880
1986-87	5118
1987-88	4770

* Figures refer to Kerala State only.

Source: State Agriculture Department.

Table: O

Area and Production of Saffron in India

Year	*Area In Hects*	*Production In Tonnes*
1970-71	1628	3.90
1971-72	1644	4.00
1972-73	2024	5.50
1973-74	2028	5.60
1974-75	2109	0.96
1975-76	2127	0.61
1976-77	2191	0.84
1977-78	3185	14.75
1978-79	3255	13.09
1979-80	3405	20.04
1980-81	2615	9.83
1981-82	3022	10.13
1982-83	3185	4.49
1983-84	3699	9.02
1984-85	3841	8.84
1985-86	3566	8.64
1986-87	3655	8.50
1987-88	3796	8.54

Source: Directorate of Agriculture, Srinagar, Office of the Financial Commissioner (Statistical Section), Srinagar.

Part - II

2

Flavours and Spices

FLAVOURS and spices are used for similar purposes in the food and flavour industry. Spices, of course, have many other applications, but the quintessence of the spices, the essential oils derived from spices by several methods, their application to flavourings and similarly oleoresins derived from spices by extraction also have many applications. Flavouring materials are often classified as condiments i.e. materials used to give relish to food and enhance the taste.

Flavour is that attribute of a substance (spices and condiments here) which causes a simultaneous reaction or sensation of taste on the tongue and odour in the olfactory centre in the nose. Thus defined, taste and odour are descriptive of a sensation though colloquially taste connotes flavour also.

Flavour is an experience as well as a memory. Though too much emphasis is put on the olfactory (smell) and gustatory (taste) aspects while defining flavours, yet audio, video and tactile senses play an important and unavoidable role. Flavour can be viewed as a division between physical and chemical senses. The former comprises of texture, consistency and appearance while the latter consists of taste, feeling and smell. Nevertheless, the Society of Flavour Chemists has proposed its definition as :

> "Flavour is the sum total of those characteristics of any material taken in the mouth, perceived principally by the senses of taste and smell and also the general senses of pain and tactile receptors in the mouth as perceived by the brain."

Flavour is one of the important quality factors in food acceptance. Consequently, research and development of flavours have been widened due to their increased use in the prepared foods. But flavour evaluation is adequate only when the origin of the flavour is known and differences can be measured by a scientific method based upon units of significant qualities of flavour.

In pursuance of this principle, various physio-chemical tests are described for evaluating these flavours in spice extracts or in their essential oils or in their oleoresins. Before these tests, brief resume's of the technical data about some of the commercially important oleoresins as culled from commercial brochures in India is appended.

A. Oleoresin Ginger

Oleoresin ginger is a dark brown viscous liquid with the odour of ginger and a pungent after-taste. 3 to 4 kgs of oleresin can replace 100 kgs of ginger. Acetone, ethylene dichloride, trichloro ethylene, isopropanol, ethyl acetate or n-hexane, any of these solvents are employed for extration.

The oleoresins generally conform to the following specifications:

i)	Volatile oil	16 to 35 ml/100 gms
ii)	Gingerol content % by mass (Minimum)	15
iii)	Sp. gravity 30/30° C	0.8640 to 0.8758
iv)	Optical rotation @ 30° C	+ 30° to 60°
v)	*Refractive index @ 20° C	1.488 to 1.497
vi)	Residual solvent	
	a) Acetone, ethylene dichloride or trichloroethylene	below 30 ppm
	b) isopropanol or ethyl acetate	below 50 ppm
	c) n-hexane	below 25 ppm

B. Oleoresin Capsicum

Specifications

i)	Capsicum % (minimum)	1.5
ii)	Colour value	400 to 20,000
iii)	Residual solvent	
	a) Hexane	below 25 ppm
	b) Acetone/chlorinated solvents	below 30 ppm
	c) Methanol/isopropanol	below 50 ppm

C. Oleoresin Black Pepper

Specifications

i)	Piperine	35 to 45 %

* Correction factor for refractive index is 0.0004/°C.

ii) Volatile oil	20 to 25 ml/100 gm
iii) Spice equivalent	1:20 to 25
iv) Residual solvents	as above
v) Appearance	natural/decolourised

D. Oleoresin Turmeric

Types	Low Curcumin	C. longa	High Curcumin
Specifications			
i) Organolepticity	Yellowish red viscid fluid with charateristic odour	*Dark yellow viscous liquid with charac-teristic odour	Yellow orange powder
ii) Colour value	5000–5300	7200–7500	14200–14400
iii) Curcumin %	3	33	90 to 95
iv) Residual solvents			
a) acetone, ethylene dichloride or trichloro ethane (ppm)	30	30	30
b) isopropanol, methanol or ethyl acetate	50	50	50
c) Hexane	25	25	25

*No off flavours or off odours due to residual solvent or other causes. Deep yellow to orange red colour of the mass with or without top oily layer (IS:10925-1984).

E. Oleoresin Cardamom

Specifications

i) Organolepticity	Oleoresin shall be a dark green liquid with exquisite warm spicy odour
ii) Volatile oil	55 to 60 ml/100 gms
iii) Residual solvents	As above in turmeric
iv) Spice equivalent	1:20 to 25

F. Oleoresin Nutmeg

Specifications

i)	Organolepticity	Brownish red, fairly viscous liquid combining spicy note and vigorous taste
ii)	Volatile oil	20 to 70 ml/100 gms
iii)	Spice equivalent	2:25 (nutmeg seeds)

General Information :

Oleoresins are packed in 1, 5 and 50 kgs carboys. All oleoresins should preferably be stored in full, tight containers in a cool place, protected from light. Flavour connotes odour as well as taste. Flavour is evaluated by comparing it with a prepared standard oleoresin.

Flavour Assessment of Oleoresins

Procedure

The well pulverised and dried spice is extracted in Soxhlet extractor with ethanol or preferably with the solvent employed by the manufacturer of oleoresin. The extracting solvent is distilled off using high vaccum at the culminating stage.

Taste is compared by weighing out in a beaker 4.5 gms of the neutral soup base containing 9 parts of NaCl, 30 parts of corn flour and 11 parts of castor sugar. The contents are mixed into a smooth cream with 5 ml of cold water followed by 50 ml of boiling water, stirring the contents simultaneously. This soup is boiled for a minute, 10 mgm of the sample is added and mixed by stiring them. A similar control soup is made by mixing it with the standard oleoresins.

Absence of off-taste and flavour means that the material is accepted.

Essential Oil, Herb and Spice Equivalents

Herb or spice	*Essential oil equivalent to 100 kg of corresponding best quality, dry herb or spice, kg*
1	2
all spice (pimental berries)	2.50

(Continued)

Herb or spice	*Essential oil equivalent to 100 kg of corresponding best quality, dry herb or spice, kg*
1	2
almond, bitter	0.50
angelica root	0.75
angelica seed	1.00
anise seed	2.50
basil, sweet reunion	0.15
calamus	2.50
caraway seed	2.50
cardamom seed	3.00
cassia cinnamon	1.50
celery seed	2.00
cinnamon Sri Lanka	0.50
clove	15.00
coriander seed	0.75
cumin seed	3.00
dill seed	4.00
dill weed	1.00
estragon	0.13
fennel seed	5.00
garlic	0.50
ginger	0.25
horse radish	1.00
laurel leaves (bay)	1.00
lovage root	0.50
mace	5.00
marjoram, sweet	0.50
mustard seed	0.25
nutmeg	5.00
onion	0.75
origanum	0.75
parsley seed	3.00
pepper, black	1.00
rosemary	0.50
sage	1.25
savory	0.25
thyme	2.00
valerian root	1.00

3

Spices and Condiments Extracts

LIKE most plant materials, particularly organic matter, spices, condiments and other culinary herbs contain 65% or obove of water. Carbohydrates like cellulose, starch, sugar and crude fibre and proteins form about 10 to 25% of the content. Spices and condiments are poor in fat content (less than 2%). These plant materials are used in very small quantities; hence do not contribute much towards direct nutrition.

Spices and condiments are valued for their aroma, pungency, piquancy. They owe these characteristics to individual essential/volatile oils inherent in them. These oils belong to organic compounds, belonging to the groups of alcohols, ketones, esters, aldehydes, terpenes and sesquiterpenes and are present in varying proportions in them as well as in the same spice due to varying agroclimatic conditions and procedures. In short, it is the collective resultant odour, flavour and fragrance which distinguishes one spice from the other as well as the produce of one area from that of the other. For example, the pungent bite of chilly which is due to alkaloid capsaicin is distinguishable from the equally pungent bite of black pepper, due to piperine and chavicine hydrodlysed by salivic juices to piperidine. Similarly, bird chilli's pungency is predominantly different from that of chilly from Samana and, colourwise, chilly from Kashmir is at variance with Bydgi chilly and Guntur chilly. Similarly, the bitter tastes of saffron, mustard and turmeric are specific to the spice, as also the sour tastes of unripe mango powder, tamarind paste and of pomegranate seeds, though all are acidulants.

Concluding, spices and condiments are used only for the distinct and specific spicy principle. Water and the rest of the organic materials are deemed avoidable impediments.

Traditionally powdered spices were used in foods with the accompanying disadvantage of the loss of flavour (on storage), moisture pick up and spoilage apart from the unpleasant appearance of black specks. Oleoresins and spice oils overcome many of the above defects which are used as flavourings, in the processed foods by dispensing them into carriers like salt, dextrose or rusk powder. These inert carriers do not offer any protection to the loss/deterioration of the flavours. The answer is encapsulation of flavours which protects the active ingredients from loss and or oxidation spoilage.

With the advancement of technology the spicy principle is being isolated thereby discarding the aforesaid organic impediments. The resultant extracts rich in spicy principles and free from the rest of constituents are known in technical parlance as *oleoresins* and *spice oils.*

I. Oleoresins

Oleoresin has two parts :-

(i) Volatile materials, and

(ii) Non-Volatile pungent principles including colours.

Oleoresin is a true concentrate of the spice. It may be a solid or a semisolid pungent resin component, frequently trapping the volatile oils along with their constituents.

Oleoresins are obtained by extraction of the dry powdered spices with solvents like alcohol or acetone in which the flavours as well as the resins are soluble. The solution is carefully concentrated under vacuum to obtain maximum of volatiles, the solvent being removed meticulously. The oleoresin yield from individual spices is generally as follows:

> Chilly — 15%, capsaicin content being 2 to 3%, ginger — 6%, gingerol content being 25 to 30%, black pepper — 11%, containing 40 to 95% piperine and turmeric — 7% containing 35% curcumin.

Obviously a ten fold concentration of the active principle has been brought out in each case.

Oleoresins have several advantages over raw spices and condiments as the former are free from contaminations and are coupled with their consistent quality and strength with regard to their flavour, aroma, pungency and colour. They are easy to mix, easy to transport and equally easy to store by virtue of their occupying less space during storage in comparison to the corresponding whole or even powdered spice. Each unit of the oleoresin fetches higher returns. Even lower grade spices can be profitably employed for the extraction of oleoresins.

The increase in production has accelerated the move to use oleoresins. Consequently, oleoresins and spice oils are being widely preferred in processed meats, fish and vegetables, soups, sauces, cheeses, chutneys, baked foods, confectionary and beverages. Uses of oleoresins in medicines, cosmetics, perfumes, aerosols and hygienic products like dental creams, dentifrices, mouth washes, skin and body care thus going to the beautician's help have been detailed separately under appropriate headings in the book.

Oleoresins are in great demand by the meat processing industries and other aforesaid industries in foreign countries. Consequently, export of oleoresins which was only 460 kgs in 1970-71 rose to 1140 kgs, valued at Rs. 65.39 crores during the period 1992-93.

II. Spice Oils

Spice oils are being increasingly used by the food processing industries in Western countries. Oils of cardamom, pepper and ginger have good export potential as indicated in the above para and the Indians have already started producing them.

Super Critical Extraction

In this field, extraction of flavours employing super critical carbon dioxide has opened a new era of promise. Data has been worked out at Central Food Technological Research Institute (CFTRI), Mysore for extraction of essential oils and resinous pungent materials from pepper and ginger using this new emerging technique. (For details of this process refer author's *Indian Plant Perfumes*, pp 15 to 23). It is pertinent in this context that some of the importing countries have already objected about the safety of chlorinated hydrocarbon solvents in food system(s) and they have already banned the presence of ethylene dichloride in spice extracts.

Encapsuled Spice Flavours

Spray drying technique has been employed for producing encapsuled flavours because these are of a free flowing nature, uniform strength, are convenient to use and the flavour is released instantly on contact with water. These qualities make them specially suitable for processed and convenient foods like soup powders, sausages, meat gravies, snack foods, dairy products and special spice seasonings, dry beverage mixes, bakery and confectionary items etc. The process know how for these is also available at the CFTRI, Mysore.

Spice Mix Slabs

Pending the aforesaid extract's manufacture, powdered spices and their mixes which are prone to insect infestation and deterioration of their volatile flavours during storage, a new process has been developed with whose adoption spice mixes can be converted into stable slab forms with added fats/oils. Slabs can be prepared from curry powders, sambar powders, garam masalas and any other spice mixes. These slabs melt and dispense well in cooked foods.

Oils and Fats from spices

Some of the exhausted spices and condiments (i.e. free of essential oils) yield fixed oils and fats.

A brief resume follows:-

(i) Aniseeds

Yield a dark green – coloured fatty oil suitable for soap making. A hard fraction (yield 20%, mt pt. 28.5°C to 30.1°C) of the oil can be used as a substitute for cocoa butter in confectionaries and pharmaceutical preparations. The fatty oil expressed from the whole fruit possesses the characteristic aniseed flavour.

(ii) Coriander Seeds

Ether extraction of the exhausted (freed of essential oil) fruits of coriander seed yield 19 to 21% of a dark, brownish-green–coloured fatty oil emitting the specific coriander odour. It is a semi-drying oil of Iodine value 93-100, Sap. value 182-190, Sp. gravity @ 15°C lies between 0.9262 to 0.9284 and Refractive Index @ 30°C is around 1.4704. Petroselinic and oleic acids constitute 53% and 32% respectively, palmitic 8% and linoleic 7%. Sodium soap of coriander oil has good lathering and odorous characteristics, soft consistency and leaf–green colour — hence is an acceptable bath soap.

(iii) Cumin White

Ether extract of the exhausted fruits of white cumin seed (freed of essential oil) yield nearly 10% of an aromatically strong, greenish brown, semi-solid drying oil of Iodine value nearly 92.

(iv) Caraway Black

Benzene extract of black caraway seeds, after steam distillation till free of volatile oil, yield nearly 31% of a semidrying, reddish-brown oil of Sap. value 199.6, Iodine value 117.6, Sp. gravity @ 25°C 0.9152 and Refractive Index @ 21°C 1.4662.

(v) Fennel Seeds

Yield between 9% to 13%, oil is of semi-drying nature, Iodine value is 99, Sap. value 181 but an unusual Unsap. matter of about 4%.

Petroselinic acid constitutes 60%, linoleic 14% and oleic acid only 22%, hence can be a good source of essential fatty acids (EFA) so effective for lowering serum cholesterol levels.

(vi) Fenugreek Seeds

Yield though only 7% of the fixed oil but this oil is otherwise a good source of EFA like linoleic and linolenic acids.

(vii) Kokam

Fruit seeds yield nearly 25% fat, w/w basis or about 45% fat on kernel w/w basis, well appreciated as Kokam butter having Iodine value between 25 to 36, Sap. value between 187 to 192 and melting point between 40 to 43°C. Kokam butter has wide applications in pharmacy, cookery, confectionary, candle and soap manufacture as well as for sizing cotton yarn.

(viii) Nutmeg

Kernels yield upto 30% of a highly aromatic fat. For commercial exploitation, only undersized, damaged or worm–eaten kernels which are otherwise unfit as a spice, are employed. Nutmeg butter, melting point 38 to 51°C, yellow or yellowish colour/tinge has Iodine value ranging from 35 to 65, Sap. value 154–199 and an unusually high unsap. matter 8 to 18%. This is due to variation in butter isolation techniques resulting in varying quantums of volatiles and resins.

(ix) Parsley

Parsley fruits yield about 20% of a greenish fatty oil with a peculiar odour and disagreeable sharp flavour. The oil has a high content of petroselinic acid (76%). Hence may find use in making of plastics, synthetic rubber, lubricating oil additives and protective coating.

(x) Poppy Seeds

Poppy seeds are either white or balck. Black variety is easy to cultivate whereas the white variety seed oil is the finest. Unscarified seeds yield more oil. Paradoxically, oil is free from narcotic properties, has high digestibility co-efficient (96%) at 50 gms/day intake level. Yield 50% w/w basis.

4

Essential Oils From Spices

ALL *spice* viz, Pimenta, Jamaican pepper, Pimenta oil (BPC 1949) is yellow or yellowish-reddish oil which darkens with age, with a characteristic odour and a spicy pungent taste, obtained by distillation from pimenta. It contains not less than 60% eugenol; wt/ml 1.03 to 1.045, miscible with alcohol (90%), soluble in 1 to 3 ml of 70% alcohol (Martindale). Richmond reports density 1.018 to 1.048, Ref. Index 1.520 to 1.540 @ 20°C. It has to be stored in a cool place in air tight containers and protected from light.

Dried crushed berries yield 3 to 4.5% of oil. Pruthi reports sp. gravity of oil at 15°C: 1.024-1.055, optical rotation :0.5° to 5.0°, Ref. Index: 1.525-1.536, solubility in 70% alcohol: 1 to 2 vols. Eugenol content: 65 to 80%: Oils of fruit and leaf are covered under BS 2999/28/29:1972. Dried leaves on steam distillation yield 0.7 to 2.9% of oil which is inferior in odour and flavour to that of berry.

Pimenta oil is used as a flavouring agent in cakes, fruit pies, mixed meat, plum pudding, sauces and soups in quantities not more than reasonably required to accomplish the desired effect.

The safety profile of pimenta oil is a weak sensitizer causing dermatitis on local contact. Eugenol is moderately toxic and combustible. Like all essential oils, this too emits acrid smoke and irritating fumes when heated.

2. *Angelica* rhizomes and roots contain 0.3 to 1% and the fruits about 1% of volatile oil (Martindale). Gildemeister and Hoffmann report that fresh angelica root, upon steam distillation, yields 0.1 to 0.37% of essential oil, dried roots 0.35 to 1.00% and fruits 1.2 to 1.3%. Guenther reports that normal dried angelica roots yield 0.40 to 0.5% and aged roots around 0.37% of oil. Pruthi reports that prolonged distillation (upto 24 hours) yields oils containing higher lactones which account for superiority of colour and flavour. The main constituent of the essential oil is β-phellandrene and a recently isolated flavour archengelinone. Prolonged distillation oils have higher Sp.Gr., Ester NO. and Opt.Rot. The root oil

is a pale yellow to amber liquid, with a pungent odour and a bitter sweet taste. It is soluble in fixed oils, slightly soluble in mineral oil, insoluble in glycerine and propylene glycol. It is a flavouring agent in various foods, quantum according to desired effect. Angelica seed oil is a light yellow liquid, sweet to taste, soluble in fixed oils, slightly soluble in mineral oil, insoluble in glycerine and propylene glycol. It is used as a flavouring agent in various foods to have the desired effect.

3. *Aniseed*, according to Martindale, the dried ripe fruits must give more than 2% v/w volatile oil. *Star anise* dried ripe fruits yield about 5% of volatile oil. Star anise (BPC 1934) is bigger than Japanese produce. Japanese seed has a poisonous principle sikimin. Syrian aniseed may yield upto 6%. For prescription anise or aniseed oil is generally used.

Anise oil, Aniseed oil or oleum Anisi (BP; USNF) is a colourless, pale yellow oil obtained by distillation from aniseed or star anise. The oil tastes sweet and aromatic. It contains about 80 to 90% anethole, CH_3- chavicol, p-methoxy phenone, small amounts of terpenes and sulphurous compounds of disagreeable odour. Sp. gr. 0.978 to 0.992, freezing point not below 15°C. The oil is soluble in 1 to 3 ml of 90% ethanol, sometimes with a slight opalescence. It can be cooled considerably below 15°C without getting solidified provided it is not disturbed. Crystallised oil is to be liquified and then mixed before use. Air exposure polymerises and partly oxidises anethole to anisaldehyde and anisic acid.

Storage of anise oil is specific. Storage temperature should be less than 25°C. Dark coloured containers should be completely filled to exclude air and light. Anise oil is soluble in macrogol esters according to K. Thoma and G. Pfaff, *J.Soc. Cosmet. Chem.*; 1976, 27, 221. PVC bottles are softened and distorted fairly rapidly in the presence of anisi oil hence unsuitable (*Pharma J.;* 1973, 1,100).

In pharmacy, anise oil or its preparations are used as an ingredient of cough mixtures and lozenges. The oil is also a flavouring agent and, according to Richmond, it is used in bakery, beverages (alcoholic as well as non-alcoholic), candy, chewing gum, confections, ice-creams, liquors, meat, sweet pastries and soups in doses reasonly required to accomplish the desired effect. The toxicity of oil by oral feeding on rats at LD_{50} levels is 2250 ppm.

4. *Asafoetida* volatile oil is obtained by steam distillation of the gum-resin. Yields upto 20% have been reported. Asafoetida oil has Sp.gr. @ 20°C 0.906 to 0.973; Opt.Rot. at 20°C 9° to 9° 18', R.I. @ 20°C 1.493–1.518 and sulphur content 15.3 to 29.0%. The oil has not attained

commercial viability, hence only tincture's use has been reported elsewhere.

5. *Basil or Sweet Basil* has four types of essential oils, they are;

(i) The European type is obtained from sweet basil (*O.basilicum* Linn). It contains CH_3-chavicol as the principal constituent and linalool but no camphor.

(ii) The Reunion type was originally distilled in Reunion Island but now is produced in Comorros, Malagassy (Madgascar) and Seychelles Island from plants of doubtful nomenclature. The oil contains CH_3-chavicol and camphor but no linalool and hence deemed inferior to (i) above i.e. European oil, reports Pruthi.

Contrary to above, Richmond states that basil oil, Comorros type is obtained from the steam distillation of *O.basilicum* Linn. This oil is a light yellow liquid having a spicy odour, is soluble in fixed oils, mineral oils, slightly soluble in propylene glycol and insoluble in glycerine. It is a synonym of basil oil exotic, Reunion type and is used as a flavouring agent in tomato sauces and vegetables in various quantities to have the desired effect.

(iii) According to Pruthi, this CH_3-cinnamate type is distilled in Bulgaria, Sicily, Egypt, India and Haiti. It contains CH_3-chavicol, linalool and a substantial percentage of CH_3-cinnamate, but no camphor.

(iv) The Eugenol type is distilled in Java, Seychelles, Samoa and the U.S.S.R. It is rich in eugenol.

Richmond reports of another basil oil obtained by the steam distillation of leaves of *O. resilium.* It is a pale yellow liquid, floral, spicy odour, soluble in fixed oils, propylene, glycol, insoluble in glycerine, having nearly 55% CH_3-chavicol and 35% of alcohols calculated as lenatol and other compounds. This oil, according to Richmond, is synonym with European type oil and has oral LD_{50} for rats: 1400 ppm.

Several authors quoted by Pruthi report that European oil has Sp.gr. at 15°C: 0.895 to 0.930, Ref. Index: 1.477 to 1.495, Opt.Rot. 22° to -6°: solubility in 80% ethanol 1 to 2 parts, alcohol content calculated as linalool: 34.5 to 39.66%.

6. *Laurel leaf oil* is obtained from leaves of *Laurel nobilis* Linn. The yield is 1 to 3%. Parry found the Sp.gr. @ 15°C: 0.915 to 0.930; Opt.Rot. at 20°C: -15° to -22°C, R.I. @ 20°C; 1.4670 to 1.4775 and solubility: 1 to 3 volumes of 80% ethanol. Principal constituent is cineol: 25-50%. Geraniol, eugenol, eugenol acetate, methyl eugenol, 1-β

terpineol, l-linalool etc. This oil often called bay oil must not be confused with the genuine bay oil from pimenta acris (*P. racemosa*) which has eugenol and chavicol (55-65%).

Laurel leaf oil is used for flavouring soups, stews, meat game dishes, fish, sauce and pickle, lamb and pork tongues. Use as per dish requirement, but LD_{50} oral rat dose is 1800 ppm. Seeds infusion is prescribed in gonorrhoea, dysentry and chronic diarrhoea.

The bay or laurel (*Laurel nobilis*) berries are listed in Swiss, Argentinian, Australian and Portugese pharmacopoeias. Berries dried and ripe, yield about 25% fixed oil and 1% of essential oil. Berries were reputed to have carminative, emmenagogue and diuretic properties. The oil is sometimes used in stimulating liniments.

7. *Caraway oil* (BP) also enlisted in Austrian, British, Czechoslavakian, German, Hungarian, Indian, Yugoslavian and Roumanian pharmacopoeias. It is a colourless or pale yellow oil with a characteristic odour and taste, obtained by distillation of freshly–crushed caraway. The B.P. specifies that caraway oil must have ketones w/w basis between 53 to 63% as carvone, $C_{10}H_{14}O$; the USNF specifies not less than 50% v/v of *d*-carvone, Sp.gravity: 0.902 to 0.912, Opt.Rot. @ 25°C is between 70° to 85° and Refractive Index at 25°C is between 1.484 to 1.498. Kashmir caraway oil confirms to B.P. standard. The volatile oil contains, besides carvone, *dl*-limonene and traces of carvacrol. Pure carvone is prepared by decomposing the crystalline compound of carvone with hydrogen sulphide. Decarvonised oil has Sp.gr. 0.848 and Opt.Rot. 130°.

Caraway oil is soluble in 7 to 8 vols. of 80% ethanol, also soluble in chloroform and ether. It is to be stored in well filled air tight containers, protected from light at temperatures below 25°C.

Caraway water is prescribed for flatulence, colic of infants and is a vehicle for children mixtures. Dose 0.05 to 0.2 ml. (oil).

Temporary estimated acceptable daily intake of (±) caravone individually or mixed upto 1 mgm/kg body wt. Oil itself has in oral rats feeding LD_{50} = 3500 ppm.

Preparations

(a) *Caraway water*: Concentrated caraway water 2 ml, freshly boiled and cooled water to 100 ml. Concentrated caraway water (cited above) (BPC 1973) also called Aq. Cari. Conc. is prepared with caraway oil 2 ml, alcohol (90%) 60 ml, water to 100 ml; shaken with 5 gms of sterilized talc and filtered. Dose 0.3 to 1 ml.

Caraway volatile oil is used in bakery products, beverages (non-alcoholic condiments) and ice cream products as flavouring agent.

8. *Small Cardamom Oil* (BP) Ol. Cardamom is a colourless or pale yellow oil with an aromatic pungent odour and taste. The oil contains cineol, limonene and terpineol, Sp.gr.: 0.917 to 0.94, soluble in 6 vols. of 70% ethanol. It is to be stored as indicated in the aforesaid volatile oils.

Preparations

i) *Aromatic cardamom tincture* (BP) Arom. Cardam. Tinct., Tincture carminative. Cardamom oil 0.3 ml, caraway oil 1 ml, cinnamon oil 1 ml, clove oil 1 ml, strong ginger tincture 6 ml, ethanol 90% to 100 ml.

ii) *Compound Cardamom Tincture* (BP) (Co. Cardam. Tinct.). Cardamom oil 0.045 ml, caraway oil 0.04 ml, cinnamon oil 0.0225 ml, glycerol 5 ml, with cochineal in alcohol 60% to 100 ml.

iii) *Compound Cardamom Tincture* (USNF) is prepared by macerating cardamom seed 2 gm, cinnamon (USNF) 2.5 gm and caraway 1.2 gm with glycerol 5 ml and diluted with alcohol to 100 ml. The tincture may be coloured. This tincture is to be stored at a temperature below 40°C in air tight containers protected from light.

Cardamom volatile oil has the penetrating odour of cardamom, and a pungent taste. The oil is used as flavouring agent in foods like bakery products, beverages (alcoholic and non-alcoholic), bread, chewing gum, condiments, confections, cookies, desserts, ice cream products, meat pickles, marinades and punches (not fruit) in suitable quantities to have the desired aroma and taste.

9. *Large Cardamom oil* is obtained by steam distillation of freshly collected crushed seeds from the pods. The yield is about 2.5% of a dark-brown mobile liquid with cineolic smell. The physio-chemical data at 29°C of this oil is: Sp.gr.: 0.9142; Ref. Index: 1.4600; Opt.Rot. in chloroform: -18°3'; cineole: 64.94%, terpinene: 10.7% and terpeniol: 7.15% besides other aromatics.

10. *Cassia Oil* (BPC 1949) *Oleum Cassiae*, Cinnamon Oil (USNF), Chinese cinnamon oil etc. is mentioned in Chinese, Hungarian, Indian and Japanese pharmacopocias.

Cassia oil is a mobile yellowish or brownish liquid, with a fragrant pungent odour and a sweetish, spicy, burning taste, obtained by steam distillation from the leaves and twigs of *Cinnamomum cassia* and rectified by distillation. It darkens with age or exposure to light and becomes more viscous. The (USNF) specifies not less 86% v/v of aldehyde and a

Sp.gravity of 1.045 to 1.063. Soluble in 2 vols of 70% ethanol, 1 vol of ethanol, acetic acid. Oil is stored in air tight bottles protected from light exposure at temperatures below 40°C.

(BS 2999/17: 1972) gives British standard for cassia oil.

Cassia oil has properties resembling those of cinnamon oil but the odour is less fragrant and more pungent and the taste is harsher. Cassia oil is soluble in fixed oils, propylene glycol, insoluble in glycerine and mineral oil and is employed as a flavouring agent in various foods within the limitations of oral rat feeding LD_{50}: 2800 ppm. The Tech. Rep. Ser. Wld. Hlth. Org. No. 648, 1980 reported an estimated acceptable daily intake of Cinnamicaldehyde upto 700 ug/kg body weight.

11. *Celery Oil* is covered under BS 2999/2:1965 and has been used as an antispasmodic. Celery seed oil is obtained from the seeds and fruits of *Apium graveolens* Linn. by steam distillation. The oil is a yellow to green-brown liquid of aromatic odour. Sp.gr.: 0.870 to 0.910, soluble in fixed oils, mineral oil, slightly soluble in propylene glycol and insoluble in glycerine. It is used as a flavouring agent in foods like meats, salads, sauce and soups.

Celery oil is much valued both as a fixative and as an ingredient of novel perfumes. Celery oil has Sp.gr. between 0.850 to 0.875, OR: +65° to +82°; Ref. Index: 1.478 to 1.486. The principal constituents are *d*-limonene (60%) and *d*-selinene (10%). But the oil owes its aroma to sedanonic acid anhydride (0.5%) and sedanolide (2.5 to 3%).

Celery green leaf oil (0.1%) has no market viability. Celery chaff oil is harder, coarser in colour and flavour. It is abused as an adulterant in celery seed oil.

12. *Cinnamon Oil* (BP) also known as Cinnam Oil, *Oleum Cinnamoni*, Ceylon Cinnamom Bark oil, *Aetheroleum cinnamoni zeylanici*, *Essence de Canelle* de Ceylon; *zintol; Essencia de Canela.*

Cinnamon oil is listed in Argentinian, Austrian, Belgium, British, Czechoslavian, French, Indian, Mexican, Roumanian, Spanish and Swiss pharmacopoeias. The Argentinian and Mexican oils have not less than 80% v/v aldehydes; Austrian, Czech and Swiss have not less than 65 to 76% w/w; Belgian has 55 to 74% w/w; Spanish has 65 to 75%, v/v; French has 65 to 75% w/w; Indian has 55 to 70% and Roumanian 66 to 76% v/v of aldehydes calculated as cinnamic aldehyde.

Cinnamon oil in Chinese and Japanese pharmacopoeias as well as in USNF is cassia oil.

Cinnamon oil is yellow in colour with the characteristic odour and taste of cinnamon obtained by distillation from cinnamon. It becomes reddish brown on aging. It contains 60 to 80% w/w of aldehydes, calculated as cinnamic aldehyde with eugenol, phellandrene and other terpenes. Sp. gr. : 1.000 to 1.040.

Cinnamon oil is soluble in 3 vols of 70% ethanol with a slight opalescence and in 0.3 vols of 90% ethanol; soluble in propylene glycol and most fixed oils; practically insoluble in glycerol and mineral oils. The oil should be stored in well-fitted air tight containers below 25°C temperatures and protected from light.

Cinnamon spirits (BPC 1949) Sp. cinnam is prepared from 1 volume of cinnamon oil in 10 volumes of 90% ethanol. Dose 0.3 to 1.2 ml.

Cinnamon oil is carminative and is occasionally used as an inhalation and as a spray, but oily solutions are discouraged as they inhibit ciliary movement and may cause lipoid pneumonia. Dose 0.05 to 0.2 ml.

Contra indications for cinnamon oil are there. L.G.M. Uard; *Br. Med. J*; 1973, 1676, reported acute contact sensitivity of the the mouth when tooth paste containing cinnamon oil was used. Each patient also responded to a patch test of cinnamon oil 0.5% in parrafin (soft). V. Kirton and D.S. Wilkinson in *Br. Med. J*; 1973, 2, 115; T.E. Drake and H.I. Maibach, *Arch Derm*: 1976, 112, 202; M.J. Roberts, *Br. Med. J*; 1976, 2, 47 and C.G. Mathias, *Arch. Derm.*; 1980, 116, 74 have also reported sensitivity to cinnamon.

Cinnamon Leaf Oil is also known as Ol. Cinam. Fol: This oil finds mention only in Indian pharmacopoeias. As hinted above, this oil is distilled from the leaves of *Cinnamomum cassia* and other species of *Cinnamomum.* It is a dark brown limpid liquid with a penetrating fragrant odour. Richmond restricts distillation only to *C. Zeylanicum* leaves. The oil smells of spicy cinnamon, clove odour and taste. It contains 70 to 90% eugenol and density 1.05 gm/ml. It is soluble in 3 vols of alcohol 70%. Richmond reports that leaf oil is soluble in fixed oils, propylene glycol, mineral oil also but is insoluble in glycerine. As with other oils, this too should be stored in a cool place, protected from light and in air tight containers.

In India, cinnamon leaf oil is used as a substitute for clove oil though in food industry it is used as a flavouring agent for bakery products, non-alcoholic beverages, chewing gum, condiments, ice cream, meat and pickles.

Britain has given specifications for this oil in BS 2999/3: 1965. Pruthi has reported that this oil is heavier than water, Sp. gr. @ 15.5°C;

1.055, Opt.Rot. @ 20°C -1 to + 3°. R.I. at 20°C: 1.530 to 1.548 containing eugenol upto 95% even. Minor components are cinnamon and benzene aldehyde. Eugenol if cheap is employed to synthesize vanillin.

13. *Clove Oil* (BP; USNF) also known as *Oleum Caryophylli; Ol. Caryoph; Essence de Girofle, Nelkenol; Essencia de clavo.*

The above nomenclature confirms that clove oil is listed in Argentinian, Austrian, British, French, German, Hungarian, Indian, Italian, Japanese, Jugoslavak, Mexican, Netherland, Portugese, Roumanian, Spanish and Swiss pharmacopoeias.

Clove oil is a colourless or pale yellow oil with the characteristic odour and taste of clove, obtained by distillation from cloves. It darkens and thickens with age and on exposure to air; it should not be allowed to come in contact with iron or zinc. It contains 85 to 90% v/v of eugenol and its density is between 1.041 to 1.054, soluble in 2 vols of 70% ethanol, miscible with 90% ethanol, ether and with glacial acetic acid. The oil must not be stored at temperatures above 25°C. It is stored in well filled air tight containers protected from light. PVC bottles get softened and distorted fairly rapidly in the presence of clove oil, so it should not be stored or dispensed with in such bottles (*Pharm. J*; 1973, 1100) and (K. Thoma and G. Pfaff, *J. Soc. Cosmet Chem.* 1976, 27, 221).

Clove oil besides having upto 90% eugenol, also contains eugenol acetate and caryophyllene. Despite their combined percentage in oil is nearly 99%, yet the oil owes its characteristic fresh and almost fruity note of pure cloves buds to CH_3-n-amyl ketone and traces of other compounds.

Clove bud oil is an antispasmodic, carminative and occasionally helps in flatulent colic. Doses: clove 120 to 300 mgm; clove oil 0.05 to 0.2 ml. Applied externally, clove oil is rubefacient, irritant and slightly analgesic. It has been used in liniments with olive oil. Clove oil is a domestic remedy for toothache, a plug of cotton wool soaked in clove oil being inserted in the cavity of the carious tooth; repeated applications sometimes damage gigival tissues. Mixed with zinc oxide it is employed as a temporary anodyne dental filling, though eugenol is preferred.

Dentifrices contain (1-3%) as a flavourant and preservative.

Clove oil is extensively employed in perfumes in scenting soaps and as a cleaning agent in histological work. Eugenol from cloves is used as an imitation carnation in perfumes and synthetic vanilla, Clove bud oil is indispensible for flavouring of meat products, sausages, baked goods, confectionaries, candies, table sauces, pickles etc.

Clove Stem Oil

It is obtained by steam distillation of clove stem. Not yet thoroughly investigated, however, Pruthi reports that stem oil has higher percentage of free eugenol, small quantities of eugenol acetate. Micro quantities of CH_3-n-amyl ketone are there along with still lesser quantities of other odourous substances reminiscent of bud oil, hence stem oil is coarser and flat in odour. As an adulterant in bud oil it is difficult to detect because little chemical changes result. However, organolaptic tests have proved more helpful in spotting adulteration of bud oil with stem oil.

Clove Leaf Oil, too, is similarly obtained by steam distillation of leaves of cloves. It is a pale yellow liquid. Richmond has reported its Ref.Ind. between 1.527 to 1.538, its solubility in propylene glycol and fixed oils. It is insoluble in glycerine and mineral oils. The oil is used as a flavouring agent in foods like bakery products, beverages, cakes, chewing gums, condiments, confections, cookies, fruit punches, fruits (spiced), gelatine desserts, ice cream, marmalades, meat, meat sauces, pickles, puddings, relishes and sauces in amounts reasonably required to accomplish the desired effect, reports Richmond from his studies of Madgascar cloves.

Chemically, leaf oil has a somewhat lower percentage of total eugenol as compared to clove bud oil, eugenol acetate is less like stem oil, CH_3-n-amyl ketone and other micro flavourants are more in leaf oil in comparison to stem oil plus a sesquiterpene alcohol and napthalene reports Pruthi, who further states that as an adulterant leaf oil is like stem oil. According to British standard, specifications for oiis of clove bud are: leaf and stem (BS 2999/20/21/22/1972) and Indonesian clove leaf oil (BS 2999/54: 1975).

Adulteration of clove bud oil with synthetic terpineol or dibenzyl ether is best detected by odours of non-phenolic portions of the oil. Acetins are detected by brine washing of oil or from high saponification number of water soluble material. Clove terpines addition in larger quantities increases the Opt.Rot. and lowers eugenol content, sp.gr. and Ref.Ind. of the oil.

14. Coriander Oil; Oleum Corianderi; Oil. Coriand.

Listed in Argentinian, British, Czechokoslaviak and Indian pharmacopoeias as well as in USNF.

Coriander oil is colourless or pale yellow with the characteristic odour and taste of coriander obtained by steam distillation of coriander seeds. The flavour becomes less pleasant on ageing. The chief constituent of coriander essential oil is coriandrol, i.e. (+)-linalool together with hydrocarbons and oxygenated compounds. Martindale Extra Pharmacopoeia reports coriandrol content ranging from 65 to 80% together with terpenes, whereas, Pruthi reports corianderol content between 45 to 70% and the hydrocarbons about 20%. Indian oil has Sp. gravity @ 15°C : 0.8715 to 0.8760; Ref.Ind. @ 25°C: 1.4569 to 1.4612; OR @ 25°C between + 10° to + 13°. Martindale reports it sp. gr. between 0.863 to 0.870. Richmond reports sp. gr. at 20°C: 0.863 to 0.875 & Ref.Ind. 1.462.

According to BP, coriander oil is soluble in less than one volume of 90% ethanol, 3 vols of 70% ethanol, chloroform and ether. The oil is to be stored at temperatures below 25°C in well fitted air tight containers protected from light.

British standards Institution has published a standard for coriander oil bearing No. (BS 2999/33: 1971)

Coriander oil is aromatic, stimulant and carminative. Dose: 0.05 to 0.2 ml. It is used as a flavouring agent in curry powder, meat, sausages and pickles as well as in spirtuous liquors, cocoa and chocolate industries. It is a valuable ingredient of perfumes; its soft pleasant, slightly spicy note blends into scents of oriental character. Pruthi reports further that coriander oil harmonises well with jasmine imparting life to otherwise dull or too synthetic compositions. Decyldehyde (0.1% of volatile oil), obtained by bisulphite precipitation and separation is also useful in perfuming.

The oil has the advantage of being more stable, retentive of its agreeable odour longer than any other oil of its class. In other words, it does not oxidise easily hence is able to correct the nauseating or gripping qualities of other medicines.

Essential oil of coriander is extensively adulterated with sweet orange oil, turpentine, and anethole or aniseed oil or cedar wood oil.

15. *Cumin Oil* is obtained by steam distillation of dried cumin seeds. It is a light yellow to brown liquid having strong odour, density: 0.925; R. Index @ 20°C is 1.501. The oil is soluble in fixed oils and mineral oil. It is not used as a flavouring agent in foods like cheese, meat, relishes and soups. The oral dose for rats LD_{50} is 2500 ppm.

The bazar cumin seed has 2.5 to 3.6% (average 3.1%) of volatile oil. Pruthi has reported the yield elsewhere between 2.5 to 4.5% of volatile oil having sp.gr. @ 25°C: 0.8923 to 0.9246 (mean 0.8969); Opt.Rot. at 20°C: +3 to +6°30' (mean +3°56'); Ref.Ind. at 20°C. 1.4945 to 1.5060 (mean 1.4968) and aldehyde content between 32 to 42% (average 36.30%).

The chief constituent of the oils is cuminaldehyde (20-40%) which is used in perfumery.

16. *Cumin Black Oil*: It is obtained from steam distillation of dried seeds and is a yellowish brown volatile oil with an unpleasant odour having sp. gravity at 15°C between 0.875 to 0.886; Ref.Ind. @ 20°C: 1.4836 to 1.4844; Opt.Rot. @ 20°C : +1.43° to +2.86°, soluble in 5 volumes of alcohol. Carvone is the ketone present upto 60% with *d*-limonene and cynene. Nigellone has also been isolated which in laboratory tests has been found to be effective in histamine-induced broncho-spasm in pigs. Clinical trials are on for its therapeutic use.

17. *Curry Leaf Oil*: It is obtained from steam distillation under pressure of 6.2×10^5 pascals i.e. nearly 6.124 atmospheres, yield being 2.6% which Pruthi suggests may find application as a fixative for heavy type of soap perfumes. Distillation at ordinary pressure gives very poor yield while distillation with super heated steam (c. 220°C) yields an obnoxious smelling polymerised oil. Simple water distillation yields 1% of a light yellow oil comprising of terpenes like 1-sabinene (34%), 1-α pinene (27%) and others. The oil needs further exploratry studies and is of little technical use at present.

18. *Dill Oil* (BP); *Oleum Anethi, European Dill Seed Oil*

The Indian dill seed oil also called East Indian Dill Seed oil, is obtained from *Anethum sowa*. American dill seed oil also named dill herb oil is obtained from the stalks, leaves and seeds of *Anethum graveolens*. Though this variety is cultivated in England, Germany, Roumania, Turkey and U.S.A. as well as U.S.S.R. yet it finds mention only in BP. The Indian seed oil is listed in IP.

Indian dill seeds on steam distillation yield between 1.5 to 4.0% of volatile oil while European dill grown in India yields between 2.5 to 4.0% of oil. Pruthi has reported a new variety experimentally grown in India which yields about 6.5% of volatile oil. Recent GLC analysis in U.K. has revealed that it is the presence of dill apiole and low carvone content in dill seed oil from Indian species which distinguish it from dill seed oil from European species irrespective of the country of cultivation. The difference is inherent and not geographical.

Dill oil is a colourless or pale yellow liquid which darkens on ageing and has a characteristic odour, resembling that of caraway and a sweet aromatic and subsequently pungent taste. European oil contains 43% to 63% of carvone ($C_{14}H_{10}O$:) and density 0.895 to 0.91. It is soluble in an equal volume of 90% ethanol and 10 vols of 80% ethanol, soluble in propylene glycol, practically insoluble in glycerol. It is stored at a temperature below 25°C in air tight, well filled containers protected from light.

Dill oil is usually used in water solutions as an aromatic carminative, especially in infantile flatulence. The adult dose of dill oil is 0.05 to 0.2 ml. Tentatively (±) - carvones are acceptable upto 1 ppm daily intake.

The American type dill oil is used as a flavouring agent in foods like dips, meat, sauces and spreads in quantities required to have the desired effect.

The dill seed oil is soluble in fixed oils, mineral oils and propylene glycol but is insoluble in glycerine. This oil also has caraway odour and taste, density: 0.890-0.915, R.I.: 1.4836 @ 20°C. In oral feeding of rats LD_{50} is 4040 ppm.

Sowa oil (Indian dill seed oil) is a yellowish liquid having harsh caraway odour and taste. Its density is between 0.925 to 0.980, R.I. @ 20°C is 1.486. Sowa oil is soluble in fixed oils, mineral oils and slightly soluble in propylene glycol; insoluble in glycerine and low in carvone content (19%).

19. *Fennel Oil* (BPC 1949) syn. *Oleum Foeniculi, Aetheroleum Foeniculi; Essencia de Hinojo; Essencia de Funcho.* These are several names found in pharmacopoeias of Argentina, Austria, Czechoslavia, Germany, Hungry, India, Japanese Jugslavia, Netherland, Nordie, Poland, Roumania, Swiss and USNF.

Fennel oil is a pale yellow or colourless liquid with a characteristic aromatic odour and a bitter camphoraceous taste obtained by steam distillation of fennel seeds. It contains anethole (p-propenylanisole, $C_{10}H_{12}O$) 50-70%, and about 20% of fenchone ($C_{10}H_{16}O$) having density between 0.95 to 0.98.

The oil is soluble in equal volume of 90% ethanol. If solid matter gets separated it should be melted and mixed before use. Oil should be stored in a cool place, in air tight containers, in a dark place, protected from light. As aromatic carminative, the dose for adults is 0.03 to 0.2 ml.

It is a flavouring agent in various foods like soups, meat, sauces, bakery products, confections; oral rat feeding has observed LD_{50} = 3120 ppm.

20. *Galanga Major* syn. Greater Galangal; Java Galangal is the dried rhizome of *Alpinia galanga* (Zingiberacea). This oil has antibacterial activity against a variety of Gram positive and Gram-negative organisims, reported A.K. Bhargava and C.S. Chauhan; *I.J. Pharm.*; 1968, 30, 150.

Volatile oil of galangal is a pale yellow to olive brown liquid with a eucalyptus — cardamom — ginger-like odour and warming camphoraceous bitter taste. The green rhizome contains 0.04% essential oil having sp. gr. 0.978 to 0.985; Opt.Rot. : +4.6°; Ref.Ind. : 1.5167. Oil contains CH_3- cinnamate about (48%), cineol (20-30%) and some camphor. Leaves also yield some volatile oil, reports Pruthi.

21. *Garlic Oil* is obtained by steam distillation of *Allium sativum Linn.* It is a clear to yellow liquid, strong odour and garlic taste. The oil is soluble in fixed oils, mineral oils; insoluble in glycerine, alcohol and propylene glycol. It is used as a flavouring agent in meat, sauces and vegetables.

On steam distillation of crushed garlic at atmospheric pressure, allium in garlic gets hydrolysed to diallyl disulphide and other disulphides. It is only allicin produced as a result of enzymatic clevage of allin (the mother prescursor) which is bactericidal.

22. *Ginger Oil* is obtained by steam distillation of ground rhizomes of ginger. It is a yellow liquid with the odour of ginger, density: 0.870 to 0.882; Ref.Ind. @ 20°C 1.488. Ginger oil is soluble in fixed oils, mineral oils and ethanol; insoluble in glycerine and propylene glycol. It is used as a flavouring agent in foods like baked goods, beverages, desserts, meats relishes and sauces.

Pruthi further reports that the average yield is about 2.0%. The aroma of the oil lasts long, but lacks the pungent bite of the spice. Opt.Rot. : 23°58'. Dried ginger is more viable for oil distillation. Nevertheless fresh scrapings of ginger are quite rich for immediate distillation to avoid over night loss of about 80% of v.oil.

23. *Horse Radish Oil*: Roots contain a pungent, acrid and vesicating volatile oil. This oil has sinigrin which under the effect of enzyme myrosinase and moisture yields oil of mustard chemically known as allylisothiocynate. More of it shall be discussed under Mustard oil. The oil is used as an alternative to root for dishes like horse radish cream, sauce or relish.

24. *Juniper Oil* (BPC 1949) syn. *Oleum juniperi*;

Juniper Berry Oil; *Essence de Genievre; Wacholderol*

It is listed in the pharmacopoeias of Austria, France, Hungary, Jugslavia, Roumania and Swiss.

The oil is distilled from the dried ripe fruits of *J. communis*. It is a colourless or pale greenish-yellow limpid liquid with a characteristic odour and a somewhat bitter burning taste of density 0.859 to 0.890. The oil is soluble in 4 vols. of ethanol, becoming less soluble and viscid with age, miscible in most organic solvents, practically insoluble in glycerol and propylene glycol, soluble in fixed oils and mineral oils.

Principal constituents include *d*-α-pinene, camphene, terpineol and other oxygenated constituents. Though used as a flavouring agent in various foods yet has oral rat feeding LD_{50} = 6280 ppm. The oil must be stored in air tight containers in a cool and dark place protected from light.

Junipar oil is carminative and has been used in flatulence and colic. It has been used as a diuretic but it should not be employed during pregnancy or in the presence or renal disease. Dose 0.03 to 0.2 ml.

Therapeutic Preparations

Juniper Spirit (BPC 1949) Sp. Juniper — It is prepared from juniper oil 10 ml + ethanol (90%) to 100 ml. Dose 0.3 to 1.2 ml.

Oleum Juniperi Ligni also erroneously called juniper wood oil. It is a trade name for a fictitious juniper oil supposed to be made from juniper wood but usually a mixture of juniper berry oil and turpentine oil.

The Indian Pharmaceutical Codex specifies that the oil must have sp.gravity @ 20°C from 0.862 to 0.892; Ref.Ind. @ 20°C : 1.476 to 1.484 and Opt.Rot. : +1° to -15°.

Berries are employed for flavouring gin and food products and occassionally articles of food.

25. *Lovage Oil* is obtained by steam distillation of fresh roots of *Levisticum officinale* Linn. Koch. *synonym with* Angelica levisticum *Bailon.*

The oil is yellow to brown liquid of strong odour and taste, density: 1.034 to 1.057, Ref.Ind. @ 20°C : 1.536 to 1.554, soluble in fixed oils, slightly soluble in mineral oil but insoluble in glycerine and propylene glycol.

Constituents include d-α-terpineol, butyl dihydro pthalides, butyl tetra hydro pthalides, coumarin, aldehydes, acetic acid and valeric acid. It is a flavouring agent in various foods but has oral rat feeding LD_{50} = 3400 ppm.

26. *Mace and Nutmeg Oil (BP; USNF);* Oleum Myristicae; Myristica Oil, Essence de muscade; Atherisches Muskatol, Essencia de Moscada; Essencia de Nuez Moscada.

It is listed in pharmacopoeias of Argentina, Austria, Britain, India and Swiss as well as in USNF.

Nutmeg and mace oils are volatile oils obtained by steam distillation of nutmeg and mace respectively. Both the oils are either colourless or pale yellow or pale green liquids with an odour and taste of nutmeg. Nutmeg oil consists cheifly of terpenes including α-pinene and β-pinene and a small portion of myristicin. They are scarcely distinguishable and frequently no commercial distinction is made between the two. The West Indian nutmeg oil has density between 0.860 to 0.880 and the East Indian nutmeg oil has density between 0.885 to 0.915. West Indian oil is soluble in 4 vols of 90% ethanol whereas East Indian oil is soluble in 3 vols. Richmond reports density of West Indian oil between 0.854 to 0.880 and of East Indian oil between 0.880 to 0.930; Ref.Ind. @ 20°C of East Indian Oil between 1.474 to 1.480 and of West Indian oil between 1.469 to 1.480. The oils are soluble in fixed oils, mineral oil, very soluble in hot ethanol, chloroform, ether, slightly soluble in cold ethanol, insoluble in glycerine and propylene glycol.

Pruthi has collated the following physio-chemical properties of mace oils.

Property	*East Indian Mace Oil*	*West Indian Mace Oil*
Yield of oil %	10.4 to 16.4	8.5 to 15.0
Sp.gr. @ 20°C	0.923 to 0.947	0.860 to 0.892
Opt.Rot. @ 20°C	+ 2°42' to +11°48	+21°18' to +41°30'
Ref.Ind. @ 20°C	1.486 to 1.494	1.492 to 1.479

The leaves of *M. fragrans* yield on water distillation 0.41 to 0.60% of a light brown volatile oil of sp. gr. @ 30°C : 0.864 with a pleasing spicy odour. Steam distillation of dried leaves (from East Indies) gave 1.58% of a colourless volatile oil containing 80% of α-pinene and 10% of myristicin.

All these oils are required to be stored in well-filled air tight containers at a temperature less than 25°C protected from light.

British Standards Institution has published (BS 2999/37/38:1971) specifications for East Indian and West Indian Nutmeg.

Mace is the name also applied to a solution of chloroaceto-phenone (a tear gas) in organic solvents but it has no relation with mace-the spice. Only mace is mentioned in the Portugese pharmacopoeia.

27. *Marjoram Oil:* It is the volatile oil obtained by steam distillation of the herb Marjoram hortensis (L). It is a yellow to green-yellow liquid with spicy odour, soluble in fixed oils, mineral oil, partly soluble in propylene glycol, insoluble in glycerine. It is a flavouring agent for meats, fishes, sauces and soups.

There is a Spanish marjoram oil which is obtained by steam distillation of the flowering plant material from the shrub *Thymus mastichina* Linn. The oil is a faintly yellow liquid having density 0.904 to 0.920, R.Index @ 20°C:1.463, soluble in fixed oils, insoluble in glycerine, propylene glycol and mineral oils.

Sweet marjoram oil (yield from fresh flowering herb is less than 0.4% but the dried herb yields upto 3.5%). The persistent odour of marjoram oil reminds of nutmeg and mint. Sweet marjoram oil is often confused with the aforesaid Spanish oil which should actually be understood as thyme oil as well as with origanum oil.

Sweet marjoram oil though not listed in any pharmacopoeia is, however, used as a carminative, expectorant and tonic, leaves and seeds are astringent. An infusion of plant is used as a stimulant, emmenagogue and galactagogue. This oil is also used as an external application for sprains, brusises, stiff and paralytic limbs, toothaches, hot fomentation in acute diahorrea.

28. *Mint Oil* is obtained by steam distillation of shade-dried leaves and flowering tops of *Mentha arvensis Linn. Var. piperascens malinvaud.* The oil is golden yellow. 50% of menthol can be separated out in crystalline form on cooling the oil. The residual oil is used as peppermint oil and this too has been processed to yield further quantities of menthyl acetate (24.4%), free menthol (44.8%), menthone (24.6%) and hydrocarbon (6.2%). Synthetic menthol does not equal in flavour to that of natural one.

M.Arvensis has a harsh flavour and has to be masked to some extent by skillful blending with the Japanese oil. Nevertheless, arvensis is not used where delicacy of aroma and flavour is the prime object.

29. *Japanese Mint Oil* (*Mentha arvensis, var. piperascens*). Yield is 5% from the tetraploid of Japanese mint. The best oil yield is at the flowering stage. Japanese mint is used as a substitute for true pepermint (from *M. piperita*) as the physiochemical constants of the two are nearer to each other.

Japanese mint oil is preferred to peppermint oil for flavouring purposes.

Peppermint oil is colourless or pale yellow liquid having strong odour and taste of peppermint. The oil has Sp.gr. at 25°C between 0.896 to 0.908; Ref.Ind. @ 20°C:1.459. The oil is used as a flavouring agent in bakery products, beverages (alcoholic as well as non-alcoholic), chewing gums, confections, fruit cocktails, gelatin desserts, ice creams, meat, puddings, sauces and toppings. Its addition is, however, limited to oral rat feeding LD_{50}: 2426 ppm.

30. *Onion Oil* is obtained by steam distillation of bulbs of *Allium cepa (Linn)*. It is a clear amber liquid of strong pungent odour and taste of onion. Oil is soluble in fixed oils, mineral oil and ethanol; insoluble in glycerine, propylene glycol. It is used as a flavouring agent in various foods like ketchups and sauces. Oil has Ref.Ind. of 1.041, Opt.Rot. : –5° reports Pruthi. The chief constituent of oil is allyl-propyl disulphide.

31. *Origanum Oil* is obtained by steam distillation of herb *Thymus capitatus (Hoffm) et. Link* (0.15 to 0.40% yield) though erroneously in the BPC 1949, oil of origanum was given as a synonym for Thyme oil. Pruthi states that the source of origanum, the plant *Origanum vulgare (Linn)* is closely related to mint family.

The oil is a yellow to dark red brown liquid having pungent and spicy odour of thyme oil, density between 0.935 to 0.960; Ref.Ind. @ 20°C : 1.502, soluble in fixed oils, propylene glycol and mineral oils, insoluble in glycerine. It is used as a flavouring agent in various foods, the oral rat feeding LD_{50} = 1850 ppm as reported by Richmond.

The oil possesses carminative, stomachic, diuretic, diaphoretic and emmenagogue properties. It is given as a stimulant and tonic in colic and diarrhoea, applied in chronic rheumatism, toothache and earache. Due to spasmolytic action of the oil, like the plant, it is used in whooping cough and bronchitis.

32. *Parsley Oil* syn. parsley herb/seed oil, petroselinum, peter o-siliensaman oil (German) is obtained from steam distillation of ground parts (herb oil) or ripe seed (seedoil) of *Petroselinum (Hoff)*. Parsley oil is a yellow to light brown liquid emitting odour of parsley, density of herb oil: 0.908 to 0.940, of seed oil: 1.040; Ref.Ind. of herb oil: 1.503 to 1.530 and seed oil between 1.512 to 1.522 both @ 20°C.

Parsley oil is soluble in fixed oils, mineral oils, slightly soluble in propylene glycol, insoluble in glycerine. The oil is used as a flavouring agent in various foods, but limited to oral rat feeding LD_{50} = 3300 ppm.

Parsley oil (BPC 1934), syn, *Oleum Petroselini*, parsley seed oil, parsley fruit oil. The Codex describes parsley oil as thick, colourless or yellowish, having density about 1.05. The oil is soluble in 8 volumes of 80% ethanol. The oil must be stored in air tight containers protected from light. It contains apiol ($C_{12}H_{14}O$) which separates in crystals at low temperatures.

British Standards Institution specifications for parsley oil are BS 2999/9 : 1965. Oil has properties similar to apiol.

Apiol (BPC 1934) is mentioned in the Portugese and Spanish pharmacopoeias as a green oil with a peculiar odour and a disagreeable taste obtained by alcoholic extraction from the dried ripe fruits of parsley, *Petroselinum crispum* syn. *Carum petroselinum*. Apiol has density about 1.1, is practically insoluble in water, soluble in alcohol and ether. The emmenagogue properties of apiol are unconfirmed. A very old finding is that acute haemolytic anaemia, thrombocytopenic purpura, nephrosis, and hepatic dysfunction resulted from taking 36 capsules of a proprietary compound, each capsule containing 300 mgm of apiol reported by L. Lowenstein and D.H. Ballow, *Canadian Med. Ass. J.*, 1958, 78, 195.

33. *Pepper Black Oil :* British Standards Institution has published specifications for Pepper Oil (No. BS 2999/12:1965). The distilled black pepper oil is used as a flavouring agent.

White pepper has less of volatile oil hence is less aromatic, otherwise it has same end uses. Martindale has reported volatile oil yield 1.0 to 2.5% while Pruthi reports yield upto 4.8%. For oil distillation low qualities of pepper, damaged or broken fruits and pepper hulls are economically viable raw materials.

Pepper oil is colourless to slightly greenish liquid with a characteristic odour of pepper and also of phellandrene. Sp. gravity of oil @ 15°C: 0.873 to 0.916; Opt.Rot. : -10° to +3°; Ref.Ind. : 1.480 to 1.499; soluble in 10 to 15 vols. of 90% ethanol and 3 to 10 vols. of 95% ethanol.

Siftings gave 1.44% and dust 0.85% of oil having Sp.gr. @ 15°C, 0.991, Opt.Rot. : -1.3°, and -2°; Ref.Ind. @ 20°C: 1.4961 and 1.4980 respectively; phellandrene test is negative in both cases.

Oil of pepper consists chiefly of terpenes, 1-phellandrene and caryophyllene. The characteristic odour of the oil has been attributed to 0.5% of oxygenated compounds according to Pruthi.

Oil of pepper is a valuable adjunt in the flavouring of sausages, canned meats, table sauces and certain beverages and liquors.

Pepper Long Oil is produced in India, Malaysia and Singapore. The dried fruits on steam distillation give 0.7% of an essential oil with spicy odour resembling that of pepper and ginger oils and having Opt.Rot.: 40.1°, Ref.Ind. : 1.4769 and sp.gr. : 0.8484.

34. *Peppermint. Oil* (BP., Eur.P., USNF) is also known as *Menthae Pipentae Aetheroleum; Oleum Menthae* Piperitae Ol. *Menth Pip; Essence de Menthe Poiree; Pfeffer minzol; Essencia de Hortela-Pimenta*

Peppermint oil is listed in the pharmacopoeias of Argentina, Austria, Belgium, Czechoslavia, Europe, Germany, Hungary, India, Italy, Jugslav, Mexico, Netherland, Nordan, Poland, Portugal, Roumania, Russia, Spain and Switzerland. Also in USNF. German phamacopoeia also has a similar oil. Mentha oil (Ind.P.) is from various species of Mentha. Belgium specifies *M.Piperita* or *M. arvensis var. piperascens. Oleum Menthae* (Chin. P.) is from *M. haplocalyx.*

Peppermint oil is obtained by distillation of fresh flavouring tops of *Mentha X piperita* and rectified if necessary. It is a colourless oil, pale yellow or greenish yellow liquid with the characteristic odour of peppermint and a pungent aromatic cooling taste. It contains menthol, menthyl acetate and terpenes; unrectified oil contains dimethyl sulphide.

The BP specifies 4.5 to 10% w/w of esters, calculated as menthylacetate, $C_{12}H_{22}O_2$, not less than 44% w/w of free alcohols calculated as menthol and 15 to 32% of ketones calculated as menthone $C_{10}H_{18}O$. The USNF specifies not less than 5% of esters calculated as menthyl acetate and not less than 50% of total menthol, free as well as esters.

Menthol separates out on cooling to a low temperature especially when seeded with menthol crystals.

Density of oil is between 0.9 to 0.912 and is soluble in 4 volumes of 70% ethanol with slight opalescence and 0.5 volume of 90% ethanol, miscible with dehydrated alcohol.

Richmond further reports that peppermint oil has a strong odour and taste of peppermint, Sp.gr. @ 20°C is 0.896 to 0.908, Ref.Ind. @ 20°C is 1.459. *Pfeferminzol oil* (German) is a flavouring agent in baking products, beverages (alcoholic as well as non-alcoholic), chewing gums, confections, fruit cocktails, gelatin, desserts, ice cream, meat, puddings, sauce and toppings.

Peppermint oil darkens on ageing and becomes viscous on storage, therefore, it should be stored below 25°C in well filled, air tight containers protected from light. However, the Pharmaceutical Society's Department of Pharmaceutical Sciences have reported in *Pharm. J*: 1973, 1,100 along with K. Thoma and G. Pfaff in *J.Soc. Cosmet Chem.* 1976, 27, 221 discussing the solubility of peppermint oil in macrogal esters that PVC bottles get softened and distorted fairly rapidly in the presence of peppermint oil, hence must be avoided for storage and dispension in these bottles.

British Standards Institution has published specifications for peppermint oil under B.S. 2999/39: 1971 and dementholized Mentha arvensis oil under BS 2999/56: 1975.

Adverse effects of Peppermint Oil

Peppermint oil may cause allergy and auricular fibrillation in peppermint sucklers, as reported by J.G. Thomas, Lancet, 1962, 1,222. An acute allergic reaction was traced to peppermint oil incorporated in a tooth paste, reported I.L.F. Smith, *Br. Dent. J.* 1968, 125, 304. Recurrent attacks of muscle pain due to consumption of large quantities of peppermint oil flavoured confections by B. William, *Med. J. of Aust.* 1972, 2,390. Richmond reported that LD_{50} by oral feeding of rats with peppermint oil = 2426 ppm.

Medicinal Uses

Peppermint oil is an aromatic carminative; it relieves gastric and intestinal flatulence and colic. It is employed with purgatives to prevent gripping. It is given in doses of 0.05 to 0.2 ml. It is also used to flavour dental preparations. Water is used as a basis of mixtures. It is essential that the peppermint capsules are entericoated; the use of uncoated capsules may lead to gastric irritation, wrote D. Slagel in his letter to *Pharm. J.* 1979, 2,557.

Preparations

(I) Emulsions

Concentrated Peppermint Emulsion (BP) Peppermint oil 2 ml, polysorbate '20' 0.1 ml, double strength chloroform water 50 ml, freshly boiled and cooled water to 100 ml. When diluted to 40 times its volume with freshly boiled and cooled water it yields a preparation equivalent in strength to peppermint water.

Conc. Peppermint Emulsion (BPC 1973) was prepared from peppermint oil 2 ml, quillaia liquid extract 0.1 ml, double strength chloroform water 50 ml, freshly boiled and cooled water to 100 ml.

(II) Spirits

Peppermint Spirit (BP) syn. Spiritus Menthae Piperitae; Sp. Menthapip; Peppermint Essence; Essence of Peppermint. Peppermint oil

10 ml, ethanol 90% to 100 ml. Clarify if necessary by shaking with sterilized talc and filtering.

APF uses alcohol (95%).

Peppermint Spiri (USP) syn. Essence of Peppermint. Peppermint oil 10% v/v in alcohol in which 1% w/v of coarsely powdered peppermint leaves (previously macerated in H_2O for 1 hour and then expressed) have been macerated for 6 hours. It is stored in airtight containers protected from light.

(III) Waters and Solutions

Concentrated Peppermint water (BP 1973) syn. *Peppermint Water Conc (APF); Aq. Menth. Pip. Conc.* is prepared from peppermint oil 2 ml, alcohol (90%) 60 ml, water to 100 ml; shaken with talc and filtered. It is 40 times as strong as peppermint water. Dose 0.25 to 1 ml.

Diluendum Menthae (Hung. P.); Concentrated peppermint oil solution. Pepper oil 200 mgm, polysorbate '20' 2 gm, alcohol (95%) 20 gms and water 77.8 gms.

Mentha water (Jap. P.) Mentha oil 0.2 ml, water to 100 ml.

Peppermint Water (BP 1973) Aq. Menth. Pip.

Concentrated Peppermint water 2.5 ml, freshly boiled and cooled water to 100 ml.

Peppermint water (USNF) : A saturated solution of peppermint oil in water stored in air tight containers.

(IV) *Colpermin* (Tillots, U.K.) Peppermint oil, available as enteric-coated capsule of 0.2 ml.

35. *Rosemary Oil* (BPC 1973); *Oleum Rosemarini; Oleum Roris Marini; Esseence da romarin; Rosmarinol; Essencia de Romeno;* Essencia de Alecrim are its synonyms.

Rosemary oil is listed in the pharmacopoeias of Argentina, Austria, Belgium, Czechoslavia, Germany, Mexico, Portugal, Spain and Swiss. The oil is obtained by steam distillation of the flowering tops or leafly twigs of rosemary, *Rosmarinus officinalis*. It contains 2 to 5% of esters, notably bornyl acetate ($C_{12}H_{20}O_2$) and 10 to 18% of free alcohols including borneol ($C_{10}H_{18}O$) and linalool also ($C_{10}H_{18}O$). It is a colourless or pale yellow oil with a characteristic odour and a warm bitter camphoraceous taste. Density is between 0.893 to 0.910. Ref.Ind. @ 20ºC is 1.464. Pruthi reports sp.gr. @ 15ºC: 0.895 to 0.920; Opt.Rot. @ 20ºC : -2º to +15º; Ref.Ind. at 25ºC : 1.466 to 1.472.

Chief constituents of the oil are pinene, camphene, cineol, camphor, borneol and bornyl acetate.

The oil is soluble in 10 vols of 80% ethanol with slight turbidity and equal volumes of 90% ethanol with not more than opalescence. The oil is light-sensitive hence is to be stored in dark and cool place in air tight, well filled containers.

British standards Institution has published standard No, BS: 2999/40: 1971 laying its specifications.

Rosemary oil is used as flavouring agent in canned meat, poultry and soups with oral rat feeding limitation of LD_{50} = 5000 ppm. It is also used in cheap perfumery, soaps scenting, hair lotions and denaturing of alcohol.

Medicinally rosemary oil is carminative and mildly irritant. BPC 1973 specifies it for soap lotions.

Rosemary Spirit *(BPC 1949)*. Sp. Rosmarin *It is prepared by rosemary oil 10 ml, ethanol 90% to 100 ml. Dose 0.3-1.2 ml.*

The oil is also used as an ingredient in rubefacient liniments. A 5% tincture is used as a circulatory and cardiac stimulant. The oil is useful in headache, tardy menstruation, is diphoretic and is employed with hot water in chills and colds, reports Pruthi. He further reports the oil to be antibacterial and has protistocidal activity.

36. *Sage oil* is obtained by steam distillation of leaves of *Salvia officinalis* which contain 1 to 2.5% of volatile oil and it is the *Dalmatian sage oil* which contains not less than 50% ketones calculated as thujone. *Spanish sage oil* is obtained from *S. lavandulae* or *S. hispanorium* and has a different odour. *Spanish sage oil* is colourless to yellow, density: 0.909 to 0.932; Ref.Ind. @ 20°C: 1.468, soluble in fixed oils, glycerine, mineral oils and propylene glycol, Spanish oil is used as a flavouring agent in fish, pork, poultry, seasonings and soups. British Standards Institution has published standard No. BS 2999/13: 1965 for oil of Spanish sage.

Dalmatian sage oil is a yellow liquid having thujone odour and taste; density: 0.903 to 0.935; Ref.Ind. @ 20°C 1.457; soluble in fixed oils, mineral oils, slightly soluble in propylene glycol, insoluble in glycerine. Dalmatian sage oil is used as a flavouring agent in fish, pork, poultry, seasonings, soups, etc. Oral rat feeding LD_{50} = 2600 ppm.

37. *Summer Savoy Oil* is obtained by steam distillation of dried leaves of *Satureja hortensis* Linn. The oil is bright yellow to dark brown

liquid, spicy odour, density: 0.875 to 0.954, Ref.Ind. @ 20°C: 1.1486 to 1.505, soluble in fixed oils, mineral oils, insoluble in glycerine and propylene glycol. It is a flavouring agent for salads, sauces and soups. Oral rat feeding LD_{50} = 1330 ppm.

Pruthi provides the additional data that the yield of the oil is 10%; carvacrol — a colourless to pale yellow liquid with a pungent thymol odour is the chief constituent. Opt.Rot. is -0°56' to + 0°4', phenols 30 to 42%, and soluble in 2 vols of 80% ethanol

38. *Sweet Flag Oil* syn. Oil of Calamus. It is extracted from *Acorus calamus* (Linn) and contains asarone, eugenol, esters of acetic acid, heptylic acid. The volatile oil is yellow to yellowish brown liquid (viscid); aromatic odour, bitter taste, Sp. gr. @ 20°C: 0.960 to 0.9707; very slightly soluble in water, miscible with alcohol. The oil must be kept in dark, protected from light and air in air tight containers in a cool place. Under Federal Drug Act, it is prohibited in foods i.e. prohibited from direct addition or use in human foods. The oral rat feeding dose LD_{50} = 777 ppm.

However, the oil finds use in perfumary as a component of the finest perfumes.

39. *Spearmint oil* is obtained by steam distillation of the plant *Mentha spicta* (L) (common spearmint) or of *Mentha cordiaca Gerard OX Baker's (Scotch spearmint)* or *Mentha virdis* (L). The oil contains principally carvone, phellandrene, limonene and either dihydrocarveol acetate or dihydro cuminic acetate. The oil is colourless or greenish yellow liquid having odour and taste of spearmint.

Spearmint Oil (BP; USNF) also known as *Oleum Menthae virdis, Oleum Menthae crispae.* The oil becomes darker and viscous on keeping. The pharmacopoeias specify that carvone ($C_{10}H_{14}O$) should be not less than 55% w/w and density between 0.917 to 0.934. The oil is soluble in an equal volume of 80% ethanol the solution may become opalescent on the addition of more 80% ethanol. The oil is to be stored below 25°C, in well filled air tight containers protected from light.

British Standard for spearmint oil is (BS 2959/14: 1965) published by British Standards Institution.

Spearmint oil has properties similar to peppermint oil. It is used as a carminative and as a flavouring agent in various foods. Dose: 0.05 to 0.2 ml. Oral rat feeding LD_{50} = 5000 ppm.

Concentrated spearmint water (BPC 1959) *Aq. Mentha vir.* : Conc.

spearmint oil 2 ml + 90% ethanol 60 ml, water to 100 ml, shaken with talc and filtered. Dose 0.3 to 1 ml.

Spearmint Water. Concentrated spearmint water 2.5 ml + freshly boiled and cooled water to 100 ml.

40. *Tarragon Oil*, syn. *Estragon oil.* It is obtained from steam distillation of leaves, stem and flowers of *Artemesia dracunculus (Linn).* It is a pale yellow to amber coloured oil, spicy liquorice and sweet basil odour; soluble in fixed oils, mineral oils, insoluble in propylene, glycol and glycerine. It is used as a flavouring agent in various foods. Pruthi reports that its flavour is similar to aniseed. The oil is reported to have sp.gr. @ 25°C: 0.9 to 0.981; Ref.Ind. @ 20°C: 1.5028 to 1.5160; Opt.Rot.: + 2° to +9°, soluble in 6 to 11 volumes of 80% ethanol. CH_3- chavicol is the chief, pellandrène and ocimene are its additional constituents. Oral rat feeding LD_{50} = 1900 ppm.

41. *Thyme Oil* is obtained from steam distillation of flowering plant *Thymus vulgaris* Linn. It is a colourless to reddish brown liquid of pleasant odour and sharp taste. Density of oil is 0.930 @ 25°C; Ref.Ind. at 20°C is 1.495. It is a flavouring agent in foods like appetisers, cheese, sauce and soups with oral rat feeding LD_{50} = 2840 ppm.

Thyme Oil Red is syn. with Spanish Thyme Oil obtained from plants besides *Thymus vulgaris* Linn from *Thymus zygis* Linn (Richmond). This oil is also used as a flavouring agent with oral fat feeding LD_{50} = 4700 ppm.

Thyme Oil (BPC 1949) syn. *Oleum Thymi ; 01. Thym; Esencia de Tomillo; Essencia de Tomilla.* Thyme oil is specified in the pharmacopoeias of Argentina, Austria, France, Mexico, Poland, Romania, Spain and Swiss (all from *T. vulgaris*) as reported by Martindale.

Pharmaceutical grade thyme oil is a yellow or dark reddish brown liquid with a strong pleasant odour and a biting, persistent, cooling taste, obtained by distillation from the leaves and flowering tops of *Thymus vulgaris*, other species of *Thymus* and from species of origanum. As mentioned earlier, frequently oil of organum is called thyme oil also. This oil contains more than 40% v/v of phenols like thymol and carvacrol ($C_{10}H_{14}O$). Density of oil is 0.9 to 0.955; soluble in 2 vols of 80% ethanol and to be stored in a cool place in air tight containers protected from light.

Thyme oil has antimicrobial, antispasmodic and carminative properties. Externally it has been employed in conjunction with olive and other oils as a rubefacient and counter - irritant.

Pruthi's data is at variance with above. He gives the oil yield 2.5%, Sp. gr. at 15°C: 0.905 to 0.930, Opt.Rot. @ 20°C: 0 to 4°; Ref.Ind. at 20°C: 1.480 to 1.498, thymol content (45%). Wild thyme yields 0.5% essential oil containing phenols.

42. *Turmeric Oil* is derived from the crushed turmeric tubers and is an orange yellow liquid, occassionally slightly fluorescent liquid with an odour, reminiscent of tubers. The dried rhizomes yield 5-6% while fresh ones give 0.24% essential oil. About 58% of the oil has turmerones (sesquiterpene ketones) and 9% tertiary alcohols.

43. The expression LD_{50} mentioned frequently in the above paragraphs means a calculated dose of a material which is expected to cause the death of 50% of an entire defined experimental animal population. It is determined from the exposure to the material by any route other than inhalation of a significant number from that population.

The standard tabulation of such studies is as under:

Category LD_{50}	Exposure time (Acute death statistically determined)	Rate of tion exposure all except inhalation	Toxic effects Human/Animal

5

Spices and Condiments in Medicine

The Ayurvedic System and Unani System

DIETETICS in every system of medicine is always an important aspect. In Ayruveda, diet and medicine interact each other. Sometimes a food acts as a medicine. Similarly a medicine is taken as a food also. Out of 86 spices and condiments listed in the nomenclature of Bureau of Indian Standards, the following spices and condiments have been approved in Ayurvedic Formulary of India, issued by the Govt. of India, Part I, First Edition pp. 241-259.

Sanskrit or Popular Name	*Botanical Name*	*English Name*	*Synonyms in Formulations*
1	2	3	4
Ajmoda	Trachyspermum Roxb. (DC) Sprague	Bishop's weed	Dipyaka, Ajamoja
Ahiphena	Papaver somniferum Linn.	Poppy seed	Phaniphena, Nagphena, Karuppu
Amra	Magnifera Indica Linn.	Mango (Unripe)	Amchur
Ardraka (freshform)	Zingiber officinale Roscoe	Ginger (green)	Nagara, Vishvabhesaja, Sringavera, Sunthi, Aushodha, Visvaaushodha
Upakuncika	Nigella sativa Linn.	Black cumin	Kalonji, Sthuljirka, Karvi, Susavi
Kumkuma	Crocus sativus Linn.	Saffron	Kasmira, Kasmira Janma, Ksataja, Valhika
Krsnjirka	Carum carvi Linn.	Caraway seed	Asitajirika, Karunjiraka (Sy)

(Continued)

1	2	3	4
Cinca	Tamarindus indica Linn.	Tamarind	-
Jatiphala	Myristica fragrans Houtt.	Nutmeg and mace	Jatikosa, Jatipatri, Jatikka (S.Y.) Jatipatra
Takkola	Illicium verum Hook f.	Staranise	-
Tulasi	Ocimum sanctum Linn.	Basil	Surasa
Tejpatra	Cinnamomum tamala Nees & Eberm	Indian Cassia	Patra, Patraka, Trayantika, Nalika
Tvak	Cinnamomum zeylanicum Blume	Cinnamon	Coca, Darucini, Varanga
Dadima	Punica granatum Linn.	Pomegranate seeds	Anardana
Dhanyaka	Coriandrum sativum Linn.	Coriander	Kustumburi, Dhanika, Vitunnka
Pippali	Piper longum Linn	Long pepper	Kana, Krsna, Magadha, Saundi, Upakulya, Pippala
Madhurika	Foeniculum vulgare Mill	Fennel	Misi
Marica	Piper nigrum Linn.	Black & White pepper	Vallija, Usana, Usanaka
Methi	Trigonella foenum-graecum Linn.	Fenugreek	-
Yavani	Trachyspermum ammi (Linn) Sprague	Bishop's weed	Ajowan
Lavanga	Syzgium aromaticum (Linn) Merr. & LM Perry.	Cloves	Lavangka, Devapuspaka, Varala, Karayampu, Karampu
Lasuna	Allium sativum Linn.	Garlic	Rasona, Ulli (S.Y.)
Vaca	Acorus calamus Linn.	Sweet flag	Sadgrantha, Ugra, Ugra gandha, Vayambu (S.Y.)
Vrksamla	Garcinia indica Choisy	Kokum	-
Sthava	Anethum sowa Kurz	Indian dill seed	Sata puspa
Sigru	Maringa pterygosperma Gaertn or Cochlearia armoracia Linn.	Horse radish	Sobhanjana, Bahala

(Continued)

1	2	3	4
Sunthi (dried form)	Zingiber officinale Roscoe	Dry ginger	see Adraka above
Svetjirika	Cuminum cyminum Linn.	White cumin	Ajajijiraka
Sarsapa	Brassica campestris var.rapa (Linn) Hartm.	Mustards	Siddharta, Gaura sarsapm.
Suksmaila	Elletaria cardamomum Maton	small cardamom	Truti, Tuti, Ela, Elasuksma
Sthula ela	Amomum subulatum Roxb.	Big cardamom	Bhadra, Bhadraila, Ela.
Haridra	Curcuma longa Linn	Turmeric	Rajani, Nisa, Nisi, Ratri, Ksanada, Dosa paimanjala
Hingu	Ferula foetida Regel	Asafoetida	Ramatha, Vedhi, Sahasra vedhi
Hingupatri	Ferula jaeschkeana Vatka	-do-	Hingra
Himsra	Capparis spinosa Linn.	Caper	Kartotti (S.Y.)

1. Ginger

Let us start from the ***Maha aushadha*** **i.e. 'Great Medicine'** an adjective for ginger.

Ginger, long pepper and black pepper are together called *Trikatu* i.e. 'Three acrids'. As a group, these are ingredients of many digestive formulations. This group is a medicine for cough, obesity, elephantiasis, slackening of digestive capacity, asthama and cold (recent as well as chronic), says *Ashtangahridyam.*

Ginger is sweet at post-digestive stage, cures *vata* and works as a tonic. It cleans body pores, promotes appetite, digestion and virility, one leading to the other. There are many recipes with fresh and dry ginger.

Dry ginger in hot water, hot salt water with jaggery, decoction or as electuary with other mediums is used. In distension of stomach it, is administered with castor oil. It is very effective in *Amavata* with pain in joints. Stomach pain and nausea due to purgatives are relieved if taken with powder of ginger. Fevers accompanied with shivering are brought down through decoctions of dry ginger and covering well, the patient is left to perspire. 5 parts of jaggery with one part of dry ginger is mixed well with one part of melted ghee and is kept as a bolus and taken in the morning or evening relieves cold, cough and headache. Ginger and jaggery fried with sesame seed is the popular *gulasundhi* for cough. Ginger is good to stop diarrhoea and also to remove constipation. Diabetics can relish ripe sweet mango without ill effect if taken with dry ginger powder. Dry ginger powder decoction relieves post delivery *vata* troubles. Ginger powder boiled in 40:40 parts of water: milk, back to milk consistancy and taken daily for 21 days provides wonderful effect in leucorrhoea. 10 gms of ginger powder mixed with sucrose if taken repeatedly in small doses relieves stomach pain. Headaches accompanied with excess *Pitta* are relieved by a ginger powder - sandalwood paste application on the forehead. All *Vata* dominated headaches are cured by applying a paste made of ginger powder, cinnamon, black pepper, cloves and roots of castor plant on the forehead. Cholera caused fatigue, tense muscles, cold hands and feet are cured by covering toes with ginger paste or rubbing dry ginger on the effected limbs. Garlic along with ginger powder can also be used. In unconcious states, collyriums are applied with ginger pastes or powder. In hysteria and insanity, ginger is used as collyriums. In liver suppurations, ginger and ammonia or ginger and cedar in water or cow's and goats' urine are applied. Fresh ginger is diuretic and cold in *Veerya*. Dry ginger is hot in potency while fresh ginger is cooling. For anorexia and indigestion, juice of fresh ginger, lemon juice and rock salt are taken together before meals. A mixture of ginger juice and cow milk in the proportion of 2:7 boiled to half the volume and mixed with sugar candy taken at bed time relieves deliriums due to *Pitta*. Fresh ginger juice and sugar candy twice a day is good for diabetics. Fresh ginger juice is found beneficial in cases of cirrhosis of liver with ascitis and dropsy of the lower limbs.

Ashtanghridyam reports that fresh ginger and jaggery in equal quantities taken daily and increasing the doses from 25 gms to reach 300 gms at the end of month with a diet of vegetable soup and milk cures *gulam* (misperistalsis), *Udara* (ascitis), dropsy, diabetes, asthma, chronic cold, immobility of organs due to obstructed intestinal movements, jaundice, consumption and mental troubles, cough and all *kapha* based ailments.

Sowbhagya Sunthi is another popular recipe of *post partum* stage for improvement in health and complexion.

2. Pepper

It is the second acrid, bitter, light, hot and appetiser according to *Nighantu Ratnakara*. It stimulates digestion. It diminishes semen, is abrasive and emaciative. It is dry, increases *Pitta*, decrease *Kapha* and *Vata* and is wormicidal. Asthama, cough, heart ailments, diabetes and piles are relieved by it.

White pepper is moderately hot and cold. It is the best of all peppers and good for the eye, says Sushruta in *Sutrasthana.* 5 to 10 gms of pepper powder taken with honey, ghee or sugar or jaggery, or 3 to 5 gms of this in any decoction with honey and ghee or with lime juice or sour liquids heal fever. It is good for erratic fever. A decoction of pepper and *Ocimum sanctum* itself could relieve influenza and was prevalent in earlier epidemics. Pepper is a good prophylactic in places where filaria is endemic. In elephantiasis it produces good results. In several skin itchings pepper paste in milk is applied. In gonorrhoea it is given with milk and sugar candy. Inhaling of pepper fumes by epileptics is practised. It is antidote for poison. For nyctalopia, pepper with curd is applied as collyriums.

J.F. Dastur has described black pepper as an aromatic stimulant, carminative, stomachic, nervine tonic, deobstruent resolvent and antiperiodic. It has been used successfully in dyspepsia, flatulence, debility, prolapse of anus, vertigo, paralytic and arthritic diseases besides the diseases mentioned above. It is also useful as an emmenagogue, has a stimulating action on membranes laced with mucous, especially of the rectum and promotes excretion of bile. Black pepper is often given with quinine when the system refuses to respond to it alone. Black pepper powder is applied to the boils as a resolvent and relaxant, so is for sour throat, muscular rheumatic pains. Alopecia and toothache are also relieved by black pepper paste.

A mixture of black pepper, onions and salt is rubbed briskly on the bare patches of scalp caused by ring worms, promoting thereby hair growth. Mixed with ghee and applied to the skin gives relief from urticaria. Powdered black pepper paste in vinegar is a good remedy for snake bite.

3. Long Pepper

It is the third acrid, very useful for all troubles of liver and spleen. It is a rejuvenating medicine also, 5 to 10 long peppers as per the genotype of the man, if taken daily for a year gives full *rasayanic* effect. Long pepper douched overnight in an alkaline solution of Indian coral tree (*Erythrenia variagate*), dried during day, fried in ghee, if taken thrice a day with honey before meals is also *rasayana* as well as a medicine for cough, consumption (pthisis, tuberculosis), breathing problems, traumas, hiccup, throat troubles, piles, dyspepsia, anaemia, erratic fevers, voice troubles, cold, misperistalsis and all diseases due to *Vata* and *Kapha.*

Vardhamana Pippali is another famous *rasayana.* In this, 10 long peppers' powder is made into a paste with milk on the first day. The dose is increased @ 10/day to reach 100. The dose is decreased similarly. So on the 19th day 1000 long peppers have been consumed. Every day, after the digestion of medicine, a diet of *shastika* rice with milk and ghee is given. This effectively cures ascites. It increases semen, prolongs life and improves intelligence.

The ordinary dose of long pepper is 5-15 grams with ghee, honey, and sugar. 10-60 grams with decoctions and milk or with an equal quantity of rocksalt and ghee. It is milder than ginger and black pepper. With ginger it destroys *Vata* and with pepper it destroys *kapha*. Long pepper is used in many ways against lung diseases, beriberi, asthma and bowels troubles.

Dried long pepper is poisonous internally as well as exterenaly if cooked in oil or ghee used for frying fish.

4. Turmeric

According to Ayurveda and Siddha system turmeric is pungent (*Katu*) in *Rasa*, bitter (*Tikta*) in *Rasa* and is hot in potency (*Veerya*). It is dry (*Ruksha*), hence is used to cure wounds, diabetes, anaemia, blood impurities, worms and chronic cold.

It is a recognised aromatic, stimulant, tonic, carminative and anthelmintic. It is antiseptic and is antidote for poisons. It is depilatory but imparts loveliness to complexion. It enters in a number of formulations. For diabetes, it is to be taken every morning with juices of *amla* (*Embellic myrobalans*) and honey. As *Kashayam* (decoctions) and powders' ingredient it cures diarrhoea and amoebiasis. Ladies after delivery smeer turmeric over their bodies and take milk boiled with turmeric to protect them from infection. Turmeric powder taken with cows' urine or applied externally is considered as one of the best medicines for pruritis.

Turmeric with basil is commonly applied in insect bites including scorpion. Cuts and wounds are leached and then sprayed with turmeric powder. In small pox and chicken pox, the paste of turmeric and *neem* (*Margosa indica*) leaves is applied to facilitate the process of scabbing. In the case of sore eye and conjuctivitis, turmeric and tamarind leaves boiled in water are used as a lotion to relieve pain due to swelling. The fumes of the burning turmeric produce a copious discharge giving instant relief to catarrah and coryza. *Rajanyodi* and *Saraswath choorans* and many other recipes contain turmeric intended to promote health and intellect of children.

Turmeric checks bloody bite, dropsical swellings, all types of gonorrhoea and initiation of semen. It acts an antacid in smaller doses and antispasmodic in larger doses. For cough, cold, laryngitis and bronchopneumonia of children it is given with milk. Patients of glaucoma, leuchoma, and purulent opthalmia are benefitted if turmeric paste in goat's butter is applied to the eyes.

It is also used for deep jaundice, stones and maladies of dehydration. It improves vitiated breast milk and checks faults of the female generative system. Turmeric is a good cholagogue, stimulating the contraction of gall bladder.

5. Garlic

Our ancestors called it *Amrit* (ambrosia) with a bad odour. Mythology informs us that garlic was generated when demons, *Rahu* and *Ketu*, tasted ambrosia stealthily and Lord Vishnu punished them by cutting their necks with the celestial disc and the droppings of ambrosia from their mouth became garlic. There are special chapters on garlic in *Kaṣhyapa Samhita* and *Navneethaka* titled *Lasuna Kalpa*.

Garlic is dry and hot in taste. The post-digestion taste is acrid and operative. Garlic increases appetite and helps in digestion. It is highly unctuous, good for heart and semen production. It promotes growth of hair. It provokes *Rakta Pitta* and heals *Kapha, Vata, Gulma,* usual type worms, diabetes, difficulty in breathing, skin diseases, leuchoderma, cough and hiccup.

All *Vata* diseases except those in which blood and *Pitta* are combined can be cured by garlic. Garlic with sesame oil is given in a *rasayanic* way. It is good to cure epilepsy and convulsive *Vata* diseases. It is specially good to contract the uterus after delivery. In hysteria, distension of stomach and sciatica and in all diseases where *Vata* is pressing upwards, decoction of garlic with milk is served. It is diuretic, too. Garlic pearls kept in honey for 41 days and then taken one tea spoon in the morning daily for one year heals leuchoderma and hoarseness of voice. It is also good for treating consumption.

Garlic bulbs have anti-inflammatory activity as well as hypoglycaemic activity. It is highly beneficial against hyperlipemia and blood coagulation changes after early fatty meals. Coagulation time is also increased together with fibrinolytic activity.

6. Pomegranate

Mythology, eastern and western, bestows upon pomegranate fruit fertility, guaranteeing conception to sterile women even. *Dadimadi ghritam*, a ghee preparation with pomegranate, coriander, *Plumbago rosea*, ginger and long pepper is reputed for correcting the bowels, curing anaemia and guarantees conception for women *Dadimashtaka* is a powder carminative and is used for curing diarrhoea and dyspepsia also. Butter milk boiled with rind of pomegranate, turmeric, cumin and Bishop's weed is used in our homes. Seeds of pomegranate have digestive power. The water extract is used in chronic diarrhoea, dysentry and other chronic bowels' complaints, tapeworms, chronic feverishness, consumption, spleen enlargement, piles and locally for relaxed sore throat, vaginal and uterine discharges and ulcers. Cooling effect of seeds helps in fever. Unani system has recommended a compounded pile of its seeds (36 parts), black pepper (18 parts), long pepper (5 parts) and others for dyspepsia.

7. Cardamom small

One of the prime ingredients of the formula known as *Chaturjata.* The other three are *tejpatra* , cinnamon and iron wood tree (*Mesua ferrea*). *Chaturjata* members are used to flavour electuaries and to promote their actions.

It is used in *yogas* to cure dermatological disorders, poisons, colds and inflammation. *Eladigana* cures *vata* and *kapha* diseases, inproves complexion, removes itching and *wrinkles*. It improves digestion, cures vomitting, stimulates diuresis, particularly in snake bite cases.

Cardamom is an ingredient of such standard Ayurvedic formulations like *gandha paka, mustadigana, kameshwara modaka*. Cardamom seeds alongwith saffron, galena and *nealgor* of the collyrium cure catract and other eye ailments like tumours in eyelids, fleshy growth, night blindness, and opthalmia. *Kirtikar* and *Basu* mention cardamom fruits as an emmenagogoue, the only spice to qualify for this. Cardamom is low in sodium (Na^+)content (10 mgm/100 gms) makes palatable food of patients with high blood pressure. Due to low fat content, cardamom helps in fat reduction in obesity and also in urinary complaints. The pharmacopoeias use it as carminative flavour, hiding the bitter taste of the rest.

8. Chilli

Chilli (*Capsicum annum* Linn) is exogenic and its cultivation, as mentioned in introductary part of this book, commenced from Barazilian samplings brought to India by the Portugese, hence is not mentioned in the classical texts.

Nevertheless, recently *Dravyaguna Vijnan (Materia Medica*) by P.V. Sharma has included it.

Being acrid and hot, it relieves troubles of *Kapha* and *Vata*. It is also good to induce sleep, and is prosalivary. It stimulates heart, is diuretic increases vitality, cures fever, particularly erratic ones, but debilitates tissues as it is acrid at post-digestion stage.

Chillies used externally as a paste are a rubefacient and a local stimulant for tonsils in tonsillitis. In dyptheria, their application is reported to hasten the separation of false mucus membranes. When applied locally chillies produce blisters. For counteracting this effect, fresh fruits are made into a paste in combination with mustard. In chronic lumbago, a plaster of chillies with garlic, pepper and liquid amber or storax (*Styrax officinalis*) serves as a good stimulant and rubefacient. Internally also, chillies are an irritant. Larger doses produce gastroenteritis, but when made into a lozenge with sugar candy and tragacanth (*Astragalus virus,* Oliver) it becomes a remedy for hoarseness. Chillies are useful in atonic dyspepsia, loss of appetite and flatulence. Pills made of equal parts of capsicum, rhurbarb, ginger and aloes are used as a carminative.

With asafoetida and camphor, chillies are used in pills for choleric cases. Alternatively, a decoction of chilli fruits with addition of opium and fried asafoetida is administered with equal success in cholera. Chilli vinegar is an excellent stomachic. The whole capsicum plant steeped in milk is successfully applied to reduce swellings and hardened tumours. An infusion with cinnamon and sugar is a valuable drink for patients suffering from delirium tumours as it satisfies the cravings of a dipsomaniac. In cases of snake bite, paste made from chillies fruits is applied directly on the bitten spot. Exposure to fumes emanating from chillies roasted on cow dung cakes smoulders is believed to be beneficial for scabbies.

9. Saffron

Pregnant women use it in milk as they believe that it improves the complexion and beauty of the child. It is pungent, bitter and unctuous. It regulates all *doshas*. It stops vomitting and expells worms, heals headache and wounds. It is good for haemorrhoids. The discoloured face and its pimples are removed by saffron. Saffron and camphor are used as an additive in many oils. It is also good for epilepsy and *kapha* troubles of the children. Saffron along with small cardamom, galena and nealgor of the collyrium are beneficial for cataract, tumour in eyelids, fleshy growth, night blindness and opthalmia. The expectant mothers should use saffron and musk in winter for their warming effect. Contrary to this, both Nadkarni and Chopra et. al. found the dried stigma and style top of saffron as an abortificient.

Saffron is medicinally a stimulant, aphrodisiac and stomachic, slightly analgesic (anodyne) and anti spasmodic. The aphrodisiac properties are attributed to the ability of its essential oil to stimulate the central nervous system. Saffron in small doses is used in fever, melancholia, enlargement of liver and spasmodic cough and asthama. It is given in anaemic chlorosis and seminal debility.

Saffron imparts a yellow colour to urine. It is administered in rheumatism and neuralgia to the children with ghee when the bowels are loose. It also relieves flatulent colic amenorrhoea, dysmenorrohea and leucorrhoea. Saffron is useful in painful affections of the uterus.

Saffron infusion is a tea in the proportion of 1:80 and dose 1-4 ounces.

10. Cloves

It is good for all digestive troubles. The gripping pain of purgatives is removed if taken with cloves. It is also used to stop vomitting, indigestion, headache, toothache and pain due to *vata*.

11. Fenugreek

Fenugreek is particularly useful to cure disturbance after delivery, cures *Vata*. It is applied externally for burns, wounds and swellings. It also helps to cure cough and difficult breathings. In small pox, it is given as a cold drink. It has antibacterial property and and is used to cure diabetes also. It is an ingredient of *Panchajeerakadugam.* Ancient belief was that fenugreek reduced fever, stimulated digestive process, and general metabolism. Seeds relieve colic flatulence, dysentry, diarrhoea, dyspepsia with loss of appetite, dropsy, liver enlargement, spleen enlargement, rickets and gout. They are carminative, tonic and aphrodisiac.

12. Bishop's Weed

Ayurveda uses Bishop's weed to cure *Vata* and indigestion. It is anthelmintic, digestive and antiseptic. Its oil is used for cholera, pain of stomach, dyspepsia, diarrhoea and indigestion etc.

13. Dill

Dill is an important medicine used externally as well as internally. Emulsion of dill oil in distilled water is deemed to be aromatic, carminative, antiflatulent, anticolic and prevents hiccups of infants and children.

14. Anise

Anise paste in *Dhanyamla (veppurkadi)* is very effective to heal *vata* and *Raktavata* swellings. *Navneethka* and other classical texts have special chapters on anise named *Sathahwa Kalpa*. It reduces fever. It is very effective in menstrual troubles of women. It is used in syphyllis, dermatology and piles.

15. Curry Leaf

Curry leaf is used to cure liver diseases. It increases digestive power and is particularly good to expel *garam* or poisonous stuffs stuck fast in the alimentary system. When curries are cooked, curry leaves are put in it which is supposed to protect the curry from poisons. It is antiseptic and heals swellings, fever, skin diseases, intestinal worms, dysentry, diarrhoea and cleans wounds. Curry leaf, bark and root are a tonic, stomachic, stimulant and carminative. Externally, curry leaves cure eruptions, poisnous bites. Roasted curry leaves infusion stops vomitting. Decoction of leaves helps bitters as vermifuge. Chutney with mint leaves (*Mentha arvensis*) checks vomitting. Curry leaves root juice is taken to relieve pain associated with kidney.

16. Mint

Mint is used as a carminative and also as a chutney. Mint oil finds wide application in medicine, especially in ointments for headache, rheumatism and other pains, in cough drops, inhalation and mouth washes. Oil and the dried plant are antiseptic, carminative, refrigerant, stimulant, diurectic. Dried plant lacks the good taste, yet is an expectorant, emmenagogue, tonic to the kidney, useful in diseases of liver, spleen, asthma, jaundice, vomitting and spasms.

17. Spice Mixtures

Most of the troubles connected with piles are cured by use of ginger and other spices. Bleeding piles is cured by the use of ginger and cinnamon; black pepper with cumin seeds and dry ginger are prescribed for excited wind. Cardamom, cinnamon bark, black pepper and ginger are useful for piles, loss of appetite or digestive powers, chest diseases, throat troubles, asthma, cough etc.

Cloves, cardamom, nutmegs, cinnamon and dry ginger are used to cure wind borne piles, diarrhoea, abdominal turmours, lienteric dysentry, asthama, cough, hiccup and diseases of the chest.

For intestinal worm trouble, turmeric, coriander and cumin seeds are given using ginger juice as a vehicle (*anupan*). Turmeric, ginger and black pepper are prescribed for chlorosis, anaemia and jaundice. Cloves, cumin seeds, cardamom, cinnamon, dry ginger, nutmegs and big cardamom go to the succour of pthiasis and asthma paticnts.

Turmeric, black pepper, grapes, old treacle, *Vanda* Roxb, long pepper and *Curcuma zerumbet*; pulv. of equal proportions and mustard oil are brought to the shape of a snuffy powder which is claimed by Ayurvedic physicians as an excellent cure for hiccup and even fatal asthma.

The mixture of Bishop's weed, pomegranates, 25 gms each added to common salt, cumin seeds, bark of cinnamon, 100 fruits of long pepper, 200 berries of black pepper and 450 gms of sucrose is a good cure for disgust for food, pains in the sides of chest, stoppage of stools, urine, epitaxis, cough, asthma, lienteric dysentry and piles.

Dry ginger, coriander seeds and *Tinospora cardifolia* each 25 gms are taken to make an aqueous concentrate which cures all sorts of tubercular leprosy and leuchoderma. For all types of gonorrhoea — cardamom seeds, *silajit*, long pepper and Cactus ambainious; pulv. of equal parts is used.

Aphrodisiac is a special mixture of spices nutmeg, clove, camphor and black pepper are the ingredients of Ayurvedic aphrodisiac, *Chandrodaya Makardhwaja*. This preparation is a general tonic which increases virility, retention of semen during coitus, increases the quality of ejaculation and semen by increasing its spermatogenticity. The aforesaid spices are employed in other preparations of this group with micro quantities of metals like gold, silver, mercury, iron, tin, sulphur etc.

Fenugreek, coriander seeds, liquorice, sesame seeds, fennel seeds, nutmegs, ginger, black pepper, cumin seeds, leaves of *Cinnamon tamala* and cardamom are employed in the preparation called *Kameshwara-Modaka*

Spices like ginger, coriander seeds, cumin seeds, cardamom seeds, black pepper, liquorice, nutmeg flowers, cloves, cinnamon and saffron are also employed. The following spices have been reported to be abortificient or emmenagogue or both as tabulated here.

S.No.	Name of plant	Part used	Authors recording Abortificient	Authors recording Emmenagogue	Authors recording both the properties
1.	Cinnamon Camphore Nee & Eburm	*	–	–	Chopra et. al.
2.	Cinnamon Cassia BL	Bark of young root	Nadkarni	Kirtikar & Basu	–

(Continued)

S.No.	Name of plant	Part used	Authors recording Abortificient	Authors recording Emmenagogue	Authors recording both the properties
3.	Cinnamom Zeylanicum Bl.	Oil	–	Kirtikar & Basu	–
4.	Crocus Sativa L.	Dried stigma & style top	Nadkarni & Chopra et. al.		–
5.	Cuminium cyminium L.	Fruit Basu	Kirtikar & and Nadkarni	Kirtikar & Basu	–
6.	Curcuma Longa L.	Rhizome	–	Kirtikar & Basu	–
7.	Elletaria, cardamom (Maton)	Fruit	–	Kirtikar & Basu	–
8.	Piper nigrum L.	*	Kirtikar & Basu	–	–
9.	Sesamum indicum D.L.	Seed	–	Nadkarni, Chopra et. al.	Kirtikar & Basu &Chopra *et.al.*

* Not indicated in the original text

Source: *I.J. Med Res.* (1961) 49, 130–151.

18. Coriander

Coriander is chiefly used to conceal the odour of other medicines. An infusion of coriander seeds with cardamom and caraway is useful in flatulence, indigestion, vomitting and other intestinal disorders. Nadkarni reports its use in bleeding piles, mucous diarrhoea, rheumatism, neuralgia, cephalalgia and locally in eye ailments. Coriander seeds are helpful in lessening the intoxicating effects of spirtuous liquors.

19. Cumin

Cumin seeds are accepted as a stimulant and carminative. They are stomachic, astringent and useful for diarrhoea and dyspepsia.

20. Tejpat

Tejpat i.e. Indian cassia leaves are carminative and are used in colic and diarrhoea.

21. Fennel

Indians, Chinese and Egyptians have been using fennel seeds as a remedy for snake bite since ancient times. Fennel seeds are aromatic, stimulant, carminative and beneficial in diseases of chest, spleen and kidneys. Fennel is also used to cure headaches, flatulence, colic, diarrhoea, dysentry of children, painful micturition, suppression in menses and general heat of the body, jaundice, haemoptysis and epistaxis, hence is an ingredient of early gripe mixtures in Europe. Fennel fruits are aromatic, stimulant and carminative. A corrective for less pleasant drugs like senna and rhubarb. Infusion of fennel fruits, 8-12 gm/500 ml of water, is employed as an enema for infants for the expulsion of flatus. Hot infusion accelrates lacteal secretion and sweating.

22. Nutmeg and Mace

Nutmeg and mace, both are the produce of the same tree. Both are considered more as drugs than as spices. Nutmegs are stimulant, carminative, astringent, aphrodiasiac and also used in pharmaceutical preparations for dysentry, stomach-ache, flatulence, nausea, vomitting, malaria, rheumatism, sciatica and early stages of leprosy. Nutmeg oil is used in the treatment of inflammation of the bladder and urinary tract. Nutmeg butter is used as a mild external stimulant in ointments, hair lotions, plasters, and has useful applications in conditions of rheumatism, paralysis and sprains. Excesive doses have a narcotic effect, hence advised cautious use. Hippies, Beatniks and jail inmates continue to use nutmegs as a hallucinogenic drug for kicks. Only 2-3 table spoons of nutmeg powder suffice. Like other fags nutmeg also produces serious hangovers, headaches, nausea and other toxic effects.

Nutmeg and mace spiced food was deemed beneficial for expectant weds. These are still ingredients of sacrificial fire as advised by Swami Dayanand Saraswati in his *"Sanskar Vidhi"*.

23. Asafoetida

Asafoetida is an important ingredient of the famous formulation *Hingashtak chooran.* It stimulates the intestinal and respiratory tracts and nervous system. It is beneficial in relieving spasms, indigestion and colic by applying it externally on the stomach to stimulate intestines. It cures asthma, chronic bronchitis and whooping cough and acts as an enema for intestinal flatulence.

24. Basil (Sweet)

Basil (sweet) plant is considered an expectorant, anthelmintic, antipyretic, stimulant and pectoral, diphoretic, carminative and alexipharmic. The juice of leaves is deemed beneficial for treating cough and harsh sounding in breathing of children. It cures laryngeal obstruction. It is slightly narcotic but reduces throat irritation. Basil infusion gargle removes foul breath, cures cephalalgia and gouty joints. Nasal douch and as a nostrum for earache are other applications of this plant.

Its seeds are diuretic, diaphoretic, stimulant, demulcent and have cooling properties. It is prescribed for piles and habitual constipation. Seed poultices calm sores and sinuses. The roots, bark and basil leaves are cynagenetic. The infusion of its seeds is good for gonorrhoea, dysentry and chronic diarrhoea.

25. Large or greater Nepal Cardamom (Amomum subulatum Roxb)

The seeds are a good tonic for heart and liver, an appetiser and relieve wind through belching. They are astringent to the bowels and a hypnotic. With melon seeds these are diuretic in cases of gravel of the kidneys. Seeds are used in gonorrhoea and an aphrodisiac, useful in neuralgia in large doses (30 grams) in conjunction with quinine, antidote to snake and scorpion venom, fragrant adjuncts to other stimulants, bitters and purgatives.

The outside covering of seeds is good for headache, teeth and stomatitis but its decoction is preferred.

26. Cumin black (Nigella sativa)

The seeds are considered carminative, stimulant, diuretic, emmenagogue, galactogogue and antipyretic in mild puerperal fever. They are externally applied for skin eruptions, scorpion bite. Its seeds are scattered between the folds of garments to ward off insect damages.

27. Galangal

Galangal rhizomes are prescribed for early catarrhal affections, specially bronchial catarrh. It is depressant of the cardio vascular system. Rhizomes are helpful in rheumatisim, and are carminative and stomachic.

28. Horse radish

Sigru of vedic lore, horse radish is deemed as a stimulant, diaphoretic, diuretic and digestive. It is also used as a counter irritant in lumbago and similar painful affections.

29. Hyssop

Hyssop's tea or infusion is reported to be effective against nervous disorders, toothache, pulmonary, digestive and urinary ailments, a stimulant, carminative, pectoral hot fomentation for wounds, sprains and strains, muscular rheumatism; removes bashing spots from skin. It is also used as a salve in catarrhal opthalmia. Its leaves have similar properties. Leaf juice expels round worms and acts as a resolvent.

30. Kokum

Kokum fruit is anthelmintic and cardiotonic and is useful in piles, dysentry, tumours, pains and heart complaints. Kokum syrup is beneficial in billious affections. Kokum butter is considered as nutritive, demulcent, astringent and emollient, suitable for pharmaceuticals.

31. Marjoram

Marjoram is understood to be a tonic, expectorant and carminative; its leaves and seeds are astringent and provide relief in colic. An infusion of the plant is used as a stimulant, emmenagogue and galactogogue, in asthma, paralysis and hysteria. Oil finds external application for stiff and paralytic limbs, toothache, bruises, sprains and as a hot fomentation in acute diarrhoea.

32. Onion

Onion is reported to be diuretic, expectorant, stimulant and is used in flatulence and dysentry. Fresh juice is moderately bactericidal.

33. Parsley

Parsley is reported to have diuretic, carminative, ecbolic, emmenagogue and anti-pyretic properties and is useful in uterine troubles. Fresh leaf juice is an insecticide. Bruised leaves are applied to bites and stings of insects. Mericarps are used to get rid of lice and skin parasites.

34. Peppermint

Peppermint herb is considered aromatic, stimulant, stomachic, carminative. It allays nausea, flatulence and vomitting. Bruised leaves are applied locally for pains and headache. A hot infusion allays stomach ache and colicky diarrhoea.

35. Poppy seeds

Poppy seeds are demulcent, emollient and are specific against obstinate constipation and in catarrah of the bladder. Poppy seed oil is used against diarrhoea, dysentry and scalds.

36. Rosemary

All parts of the plant are astringent, nervine tonic and excellent stomachic. Plant infusion with borax is a hair-wash to prevent premature baldness. Plant useful in atonic dyspepsia. Rosemary tea causes temporary sterility. Flowering tops and leaves are considered carminative, diphoretic, diuretic, aperient, emmenagogue, stimulant and stomachic. These are also used for vapour baths to relieve rheumatism, paralysis and incipient catarrah. Dried leaves of rosemary are smoked for asthma. The decoction of the leaves is an abortificient. Leaf juices possess a strong antibacterial affect against *Straphylococcus aureus, Eschenichia coli* and *Bacillus subtilis*.

37. Sage

Sage is a mild tonic, astrigent, and carminative. The cold infusion of its leaves cures sore throats, while hot infusion is diphoretic. Concentrated infusion dries breast milk to help child weaning and cures female disorders by virtue of estrogenic substances present in dried leaf tops. Dried leaves are used as a fumitory and a good dentifrice, in poultices, hair tonics and dressings.

38. Staranise

Staranise is stomachic and carminative, useful in flatulence, spasmodic affections of the intestinal canal and dysentry. The plant is useful for colic, constipation and insomnia.

39. Tamarind

The ripe fruits of tamarind are appetising, laxative, heart tonic and anthelmintic. It cures *vata* and *kapha*, heals wounds and fractures, a refrigerant, digestive, useful in deranged bile ailments viz. burning sensation of the body and intoxication from liquors or *dhatura*. A gargle of tamarind water is recommended for sore throat. Its unripe fruits are indigestible, astrigent to bowels, cure vata, cause biliousness, cough and blood troubles.

40. Thyme

Thyme is recommended to cure weak vision, complaints of stomach and liver, suppression of urine and menstruation. An infusion of the herb is prescribed in convulsive coughs, whooping coughs, catarrh and sore throat. It is good for nervous or hysterical headaches and flatulence. The herb itself has a sharp pleasant taste; it is emmenagogue, alexiteric, anthelmintic and is good for liver complaints, pain in the spleen, liver or chest. It is useful in asthma and bronchitis. It thins phlegm and blood. The leaves are laxative, stomachic, tonic and are good for the kidney and eye. The leaves also purify blood. The seeds are given as vermifuge. Its infusion is also used in skin eruptions/diseases.

The following spices and condiments have been approved in National Formulary of Unani Medicine issued by the Govt. of India, Part-I, First Edition pp 257-275.

Popular Name	*Botanical Name*	*English Name*	*Synonyms in formulations*
1	2	3	4
Amba Haldi	Curcuma amada (Roxb)	Mango ginger	-
Abhal	Juniperus communis Linn	Juniper berries Mountain Cyperus	Aarar
Adrak	Zingiber officinale	Ginger	-
Ajwayin	Trachyspermum ammi (Linn) Sprague syn. Ptychotis ajowan (D.C.)	Bishop's weed	Nankhwah
Anar	Punica granatum (Linn)	Pomegranate	-
Amba	Mangifera indica (Linn)	Mango	Aam
Anisoon	Pimpinella anisum (Linn)	Anise, Aniseed	-
Badiyan	Foeniculum vulgare (Mill)	Fennel	Saunf
Bibasa	Myristica fragrans	Mace (Houth)	Javetri
Darchini	Cinnamomum zeylanicum (Blume)	Cinnamon	-
Faranj Mushk	Ocimum basilicum (Linn)	Sweet basil	-
Filfil Daraz	Piper longum (Linn)	Long pepper	-
Filfil (Safed/Siyah)	Piper nigrum (Linn)	Pepper (white/black)	-
Fitrasaliyun	Petroselinium cripsum (Mill)/Nym. ex - A.W. Hill. syn. P. sativum (Hoffm)	Parsley	Karafas-e-Kohi
Habb-ul-ghaar	Laurus nobilis (Linn)	Laurel	-
Hasha	Thymus serphyllum (Linn)	Thyme	-
Heelkalan	Amomum subulatum (Roxb)	Greater cardamom, wild cardamom	Elaichikalan, Moti elaichi

(Continued)

1	2	3	4
Heel Khurd	Elettaria cardamom (Maton)	Lesser cardamom	Elaichi-Khurd, Choti elaichi
Hilteet	Ferula foetida (Regel)	Asafoetida	Hing
Hulba (Methi)	Trigonella foenum graecum (Linn)	Fenugreek	Methi
Jauzbuwa	Myristica fragrans (Houtt)	Nutmeg	Jaiphal
Kalonji	Nigella sativa (Linn)	black cumin	-
Karafs	Apium graveolens (Linn)	Celery	-
Khardal	Brassica nigra (Linn) Hook	Black mustard, Rai	-
Khash Khassh (Safaid/Siyah)	Papaver somniferum (Linn)	Poppy seeds	-
Khulanjan	Alpinia galanga (Linn)	Galangal, Siamese ginger	-
Kishniz	Coriandrum sativum	Coriander	Dhania
Marzanjosh	Oliganum vulgare (Linn)	Marjoram	-
Nana	Mentha arvensis (Linn)	The Marsh mint, Pudina weed	
Nankhwah	Ptychotis ajowan	Bishop's weed (D.C.)	Ajwayin Ajowa seeds
Piyaz	Allium cepa (Linn)	Onion	-
Qaranful	Syzgium aromaticum (Merr & L.M. Perry)	Clove	Loung
Qirfa	Cinnamomum cassia (Blume)	Cassia, Chinese Cinnamon	Taj (Saleekha)
Raihan	Ocimum sanctum (Linn)	Holy basil	-
Saleekha	Cinnamomum cassia (Blume)	Cinnamon	Taj (qirfa)
Sarson	Brassica campesteris	Mustard	-
Satar Farsi	Satureja hortensis (Linn)	Savory	-
Sazaj Hindi	Cinnamomum tamala (Nees & Eberm)	Indian Cassia, Lignea	Telispattar, Zarnab
Seer	Allium sativum (Linn)	Garlic	Lahson
Sosambar	Ocimum basilicum	Black basil	Kali Tulsi
Tamar Hindi	Tamarnidus indica	Tamarind	Imli
Waje Turki	Acorus calamus (Linn)	Sweet flag	-

(Continued)

1	2	3	4
Zafran	Crocus sativus (Linn)	Saffron	-
Zanjabeel	Zingiber officinale (Rosc)	Ginger	-
Zardchob	Curcuma longa (Linn)	Turmeric	-
Zeerah Siyah	Carum carvi (Linn)	Black caraway	-
Zufa	Hyssopus officinalis (Linn)	Hyssop	-

Spices in Allopathic Medicine

1. All spice, Pimento, Jamaican pepper, Pimenta

(BPC 1934), dried ful-grown unripe fruits of Pimento officinalis containing 3 to 4.5% of volatile oil. Pimento oil has been used as carminative flavouring agent, stimulant, bactericidal, fungicidal and an antioxidant. (BPC 1949):

All spice is used as an adjunct to tonics and purgatives. It is an anodyne against rheumatism and neuralgia, an aromatic stimulant in digestive problems. All spice powder finds use in diarrhoea, flatulence and dyspepsia.

2. Angelica

Angelica has diphoretic and expectorant properties. It was administered as a powder in doses of 0.6 to 2.0 gm, or as an infusion (1 in 20).

3. Aniseed

Aniseed and star anise are employed as carminatives and mild expectorants.

a. *Anise water: Concentrated anise water* + 2.5 ml freshly boiled and cooled water to 100 ml or 2 ml of anise oil, 70 ml of 90% alcohol, water to 100 ml; shaken with 5 gms of sterilized talc and filtered. The fruit is considered stimulant, diuretic, diphoretic, anti colic, flatulent and is used in the preparation of asthma powders.

b. *Aqua Anisi* or *Aqua de Badiana* is according to Argentinian Pharmacopoeia: star anise 10 gms + 200 ml water, distilled to 100 ml distillate.

c. *Sifrapus Anisi* (Arg.P.) *Jarabe de anisi*. Sucrose 85 gms, *aqua anisi* to 100 ml.

R.N. Patel, *Ind. J. of Pharm.* 1968, 30, 43 has reported upon the antimicrobial activity of star anise.

Aniseeds yield a fixed oil 8 to 23% which has 17.1% of linoleic acid which is good for growth and skin nutrition, affording protection against X-ray radiation, maintenance of capillary pressure in the sub-cutaneous blood vessels and for lowering serum cholesterol levels.

The volatile oil of aniseed is an old known medicine used to relieve flatulence and cough. It is a mild expectorant and antiseptic, hence is a good choice for gripe mixture formulations. Aniseeds perfumed water, *arqe-saunf* or *badian* of Northern India bazars, is used to relieve dysentry, gastro-intestinal disorders and resulting headaches. Aniseed oil is extensively used as an insecticide against lice, mites and vermin. It is a fungicide, too.

4. *Asafoetida*

Asafoetida (BPC 1949), Gum asafoetida, Devil' dung; Asant. It is also used in Portugese and Spanish Pharmacopoeias. It was formerly used in the treatment of flatulence and bronchitis and for its supposed effect in nervous disorders. It has been given in doses of 0.3 to 1 gm. V.W. Rahlfs and P. Mossinger; *Dt. Med. Wschr*, 1979, 104, 140 reports use of asafoetida in patients with irritable colon.

Asafoetida Tincture (BPC 1949) is prepared by macerating 1 gm in 5 ml of 70% ethanol. Dose is 2 to 4 ml.

5. *Basil oil*

Basil oil possesses insecticidal and insect repellant properties. It is effective against house-flies and mosquitoes. Bactericidal, the Rideal-Walker coefficient against *Salmonella typhoxi is 12*. Aqueous extracts of seeds are active against Gram positive bacteria and mycobacteria.

Basil (sweet). Alcoholic extracts of leaves and aqueous as well as alcoholic extracts of flowers possess antibacterial activity against *Micrococcus pyogenes var. aureus* by inhibiting their coagulase activity. Aqueous extracts of seeds also are active against Gram positive bacteria and mycobacteria. Basil oil possesses insecticidal and insect repellant effect. It is effective against house flies and mosquitoes. It is bactericidal. The Rideal Walker coefficient against *Salmonella typhoxi* is 12.

6. *Chillies*

Chillies tincture is an adjunct to bitter tonics and other stimulants. Chillies with cinchona are useful in intermittant fever and lethargic affections, atonic gout and advanced stages of rheumatism. It has a powerful affect on the mucous membrane and sore throat. In putrid throat, a gargle made of chillies (14 dracham in a bottle containing boiling water) is found particularly beneficial. In the West Indies, it is used to relieve the sinking feeling at the epigastrum by drunkards. Capsicum wool, also known as calorific wool, made by dissolving the capsicum oleo-resin in ether and pouring it on an absorbant cotton wool, has been reported useful in rheumatic affections.

Capsicum tincture is indicated in a general enfeebled atonic condition. In cases of acute alcholism and delirium, tremors where digestive powers are weak and absorption of food or medicine is practically impossible, 10 to 15 drops of the tincture in a cup of hot beef tea or any hot liquid food is of great service. Regular use of this tincture helps greatly in overcoming the desire for alcoholic stimulants. In cases of cardiac weakness that attends delirium tremors, this tincture is most useful as it assists in quieting the stomach and promoting sleep.

Capsicum tincture is very useful in diarrhoea and dysentry when the stools are frequent, small, accompanied with mucous and blood and there is tense rectum and bladder and excessive burning in the anus. Chilli has been of great service in malaria fever when the liver and spleen are enlarged, especially when the spleen is sensitive, swollen, indurated and large amounts of quinine have already been administered. It is also useful in acute inflammatory condition of the pharynx and larynx. Many people employ it internally and for gargling too.

Phlegmonous inflammation, particularly when it is deep and abscess is threatened, abscess of the mastoid, nostalgia in a typical capsicum patient with red cheeks, insomnia, hot feeling in the face, gonorrhoea with frequent and ineffectual efforts to urinate with tenesmus and stranguary, impotency when there is a general relaxation of the genital organs and other diseases are curable by capsicum thereapy. It has some reputation in nephritis and pyelitis also. 'It antidotes the effect of alcohol, coffee, opium, quinine fever after a bout of cold feeling in limbs, swelling of belly and muscles lame.

C. Herrung (1971) *"The Guiding symptoms of our Materia Medica" Vol. III, p. 336.*

Capsicum oleoresin (BPC 1973), Capsaicin, Capsicum Extract, also included in Indian and Belgium Phamacopoeias.

It is made by extracting capsicum with hot acetone or alcohol (90%) and evaporating the solvent, extracting the residue with cold 90% ethanol and removing ethanol by evaporation. It is a thick, dark, reddish-brown liquid with an intensely pungent taste containing not less than 8% capsaïcin:

Soluble in alcohol, acetone, ether, chloroform, voatile oils and fats; soluble with opalescence in fixed oils. It must be stored in air tight containers. If it gets separated it should be warmed and mixed before use.

Capsicum oleoresin is highly irritant. Use a dilute solution of pot. permanganate on the skin and of cocaine eye drops for the eyes to allay the irritation. Dose is 0.6 to 2 mgm.

Preparations

i) Dressings

a) *Capsicum cotton wool* (BPC 1973); *Capsicum cotton.* Absorbant cotton wool impregnated with capsicum oleoresin (equivalent to approx. 0.05% capsicum), CH_3-salicylate (c.1%) and an orange brown dye.

b) *Capsicum Self-adhesive Plaster* (BPC 1963), *Capsicum Plaster*: Cotton or rayon or cotton and rayon cloth of plain weave spread evenly with a self adhesive plaster mass containing about 1% of capsaicin oleoresin. The cloth may be perforated and the adhesive surface is covered by a protective layer of muslin or any other suitable material.

c) Gauze and capsicum cotton tissue (BPC 1973), Capsaicin tissue Capsaicin cotton wool enclosed in tubular absorbant gauze which is tinted orange-brown.

ii) Ointments

a) *Capsicum ointment* (BPC 1973), *Unquentum Capsaici* Capsicum oleoresin 1.5 gm, emulsifying wax 5 gm and simple ointment 93.5 gm. Belgium Pharmacopoeia has 2.0% in an emulsified basis.

b) *Compound capasaicin ointment* (BPC 1949); Ung Capsic Co; Chilli Paste: Capsicum oleoresin 2 gm, menthol 10 gm, chloral hydrate 10 gm, camphor 10 gm and yellow soft parraffin 68 gms.

c) *Capsolin (Parke Davis)* Capsicum oleoresin 1.2%, Camphor 5.25%, terpentine oil 9.75% and eucalyptus oil 2.5%.

iii) Tinctures

Capsicum tincture (BPC 1973) is prepared by macerating capsicum oleoresin 320 mgm with alcohol 90% to 100 ml. Dose 0.3 to 1 ml. A tincture prepared from capsicum, usually 1 in 10, is included in some pharmacopoeias.

G.T. Walker, *Mfg. Chemist*; 1968, 39, 35 has described the properties, reactions and uses of capsicum. J.G. Smith *et.al; J. Invest. Derm*, 1970, 54, 170 *per J. Am. Med.Assn*; 1970, 211, 1726, reported that capsaicin caused erythema and burning, but not vasication, when applied to skin. H.G. Desai *et.al., Gut,* 1973, 14, 974, reported that intragastric infusion of powdered red chillies (0.8 or 1.6 gm per hour) caused a rapid and marked increase in the DNA content of gastric aspirate, indicating exfoliation of epithelial cells from the gastric mucosa.

F.P. Anita in her book *"Clinical Dietetics and Nutrition,* (1986), *OXFORD UNIV. Press, Delhi*, advises that chillies in large amounts produce gastritis and even predispose to a bout of haematemesis. Chillies are not tolerated by those who have suffered from dysentry and have an irritable colon and pungent food usually provides a burning reminder during defaecation on the next day. Chillies also produce recurrance of bleeding in person suffering from piles.

Anita continues to state that the role of chillies and spiced foods in the production of liver damage has not been assessed. Many people in tropical countries are used to eating heavily spiced foods, particularly chillies, a taste inconceivable to Europeans. It is likely that active principles in spices, when absorbed from the intestine damage liver cells and this may be a contributing factor in the development of cirrhosis, so extensively seen in the tropics.

On the other hand, Hans Glatzel *et.al.* in Germany have made the following observations about the effect of spices on human physiology:

Addition of spices induced an increase of salivary quantity and contained substances not obtained in unspiced foods. These are amylase, the enzyme responsible for converting polysaccharides of the food into sweet digestible disaccharide sugars like maltose. The other aforesaid substances are neuraminic acid and hexo-samines. Neuraminic acid protects against infections; pathogenic micro-organisms like *Pneumo-coccus* and influenza virus are able to surmount by means of *neuroaminidase* — the protecting layer of the mucous membrane and these organisms and viruses are able to penetrate in cell, therefore, it is necessary to curb this *neuraminidase* activity of the organism. Neuraminic acid-rich saliva does this very function, hence spices aid in inhibiting infections besides increasing the digestive capacity of the user.

Glatzel arranged the spices and condiments in the following order of their increasing intensities regarding saliva production: (a) Acidulants like tamarind, mango powder; (b) chillies, curry powder, ginger, capsicum, pepper, mustard and allspice. Here allspice has lesser amylase activity and low hexosamines concentration than other spices.

It was further concluded that the inner individual differences of the intensity of response on the same spice stimulus range vary widely. One individual may react very strongly, while another may do so slightly. The place of spice within a spice group is not always the same *vis a vis* all the persons because an individual may respond more strongly to pepper than to chilli; the other may react more strongly to chilli than to pepper. But as a rule the homogenity of the groups is not disturbed.

Another important observation made in this connection is that the effect of a spice on the saliva is bound to the immediate touch with the saucy organs of the mucous membrane of the mouth, pharynx and nose. This was confirmed when the spice to be tested was taken in a capsule and no effect was observed. In other words, the receptors of the activating spice stimuli are situated in the space of the mouth, pharynx and nose.

That the spices act as aphrodisiacs and or tonics has already been stated. Modern medicine supported this observation when the relation between the quality of spices in food and adrenocortical function was examined. The latter was judged by measuring the plasma 17-OH corticosteroids and urinary 17-OH corticosteroids.

Spices added to food enable the physicians to effect the required changes in stroke efficiency, systolic blood pressure and pulse pressure which according to Glatzel cannot be produced by any of the known medicaments.

Spices also decrease the thrmobocyte number and fibrinolytic activity sometimes five times more than unspiced food. It is further confirmed that this effect is not due to ascorbic acid. Spices are better than even nicotinic acid as fibrinolytic agents because the acid increases the clotting disposition of the blood and after long dispensing looses its effectiveness. On the other hand, chillies inhibit the clotting and as far as possible do not loose their effectiveness.

Some spices assist the heart of a sportsman for higher performance while some others assist a sickman whose heart must be discharged. Black pepper, white pepper, cardamom and ground ginger all have low Na^+ content (10, 10, 10 and 30 mgm/100 gms respectively) that these can be used to spice the food of patients suffering high blood pressure, making the food more palatable and nutritive yet causing him least trouble usually caused by other similar foods due to their high Na^+ and oxalate contents as found out by C.A. Elvehjam and C.H. Burns of Wisconsin University.

It is curious that spices and condiments are consumed more in hot tropical climates than in colder regions. This is partly due to food being seasonal and monotonous in the Tropics. Poor transport also contributes to this. Nevertheless, spices should be used to bring out the best flavour of food and make it more appetising rather than to give the food a pungency which irritates the mouth and masks the original flavour.

F.P. Anita in her book (p. 290-294), quoted earlier, teaches following *contra indications*:

(i) Alimentary tract

Condiments and spices irritate mucous membranes, hence should be avoided in all inflammatory diseases of the digestive tract. In stomatitis, spices produce a sense of intense burning and they are also best avoided in gastritis, peptic ulcer and diarrhoea. Some apparently healthy individuals get loose stools after eating spiced food because the irritation may activate a latent colic infection. The habit of 'purging with pleasure', the consumption of highly spiced food to relieve constipation is to be condemned.

(ii) Liver and Gall Bladder

Spices, on digestion and absorption reach the liver. It is possible that these products of absorption are an aetiological factor in hepatic cirrhosis so frequently seen in the Tropics. Spices produce flatulence in sufferers from gall bladder disease.

(iii) Urinary Tract

Infections of the urinary tract like pyelitis, cystitis and urethritis tend to relapse with spiced foods. The probable explanations are (a) irritation of the intestinal mucous membranes by spices produce hyperaemia and favours absorption of intestinal bacteria which are excreted by the kidney.

(b) Small amounts of spices may be absorbed into the blood stream and irritate the urinary tract as they are excreted in the urine.

(iv) Gout

Persons suffering from metabolic disorders like gout may get an attack after eating spiced foods.

7. Caraway

Caraway (BP; USNF) is listed in Austrian, British, German, Hungarian, Indian, Polish, Portugese, Roumanian and Swiss pharmacopoeias. BP specifies not less than 3.5% v/w of volatile oil. Powdered caraway (BP) (Carvi pulvis) contains not less than 2.5% v/w of volatile oil. The oil should be kept at a temperature below 25°C in a dry place; the powdered drug must be kept in air tight containers protected from light.

8. Small Cardamom

Small Cardamom (BP) Cardamom Fruit is listed in British, Indian, Japanese and Portugese pharmacopoeias, whereas Argentinian and USNF specify cardamom seed recently removed from the fruit. Nevertheless, only the seeds are used in the preparations of cardamom, they are removed from the fruit when required for use. Seeds yield more than 4% v/w of oil provided fruits are kept in a cool dry place.

9. Large Cardamom

Large Cardamom seeds have been found useful in neuralgia taken in large doses (30 grains), in conjunction with quinine and as fragrant adjunct to other stimulants, bitters and purgatives. No pharmacopoeia mentions it.

10. Cassia Bark

Cassia Bark (BPC 1949) is listed in Chinese, Hungarian, Indian, Japanese and Roumanian pharmacopoeias. The dried bark of *Cinnamomum cassia* contains not less than 1% v/w of volatile oil while powdered cassia (BPC 1949) contains not less than 0.7% v/w of oil. Powdered drug is kept in air tight containers in a cool dry place.

11. Celery

Celery (BPC 1949), Apium,; celery fruit; celery seed, is not listed in any other pharmacopoeia. The dried ripe fruits of cultivated plants of celery, *Apium graveolens*, contains a minimum of 1.5% v/w of volatile oil.

Celery seeds are stimulant, carminative, nervine, sedative and tonic. A domestic remedy for rheumatism, celery seeds are antispasmodic and nervine stimulant. They have been successfully employed in rheumatoid arthritis and probably act as an intestinal septic. The root is deemed an alterative, diuretic and given in colic.

12. Cinnamon

Cinnamon (BP; USNF) *Cinnam; Cinnamoni Cortex*, Cinnamon bark,

Ceylon Cinnamon; Ceylonzimt etc. is mentioned in Belgian, British, Brazilian, French, Indian, Mexican, Netherland, Portugese, Roumanian, Spanish and Swiss pharmacopoeias.

USNF and Mexican pharmacopoeias specify not less than 2.5% v/w of volatile oil, Austrian and Brazilian not less than 1.5%. Swiss not less than 1.4%, Argentinian not less than 1.3%, Netherland not less than 1.2% and Belgian not less than 0.7%. USNF specifies *Cinnamomum loureirii* having not less than 2.5% of volatile oil. The BP specifies dried inner bark of the shoots of capriced tree of Ceylon cinnamon (C. zeylanicum) containing not less than 1.2% v/w of volatile oil.

Powdered cinnamon (BP) contains not less than 1% v/w of volatile oil. Cinnamon powder is to be kept in a cool, dry place in air tight containers protected from light. Dose 0.3 to 1.2 gm.

Cinnamon Waters

(i) *Distilled Cinnamon Water* (BPC 1949) Aq. Cinnam., Dest.. Cinnamon 10 gms + 200 ml. water; distillate 100 ml. Dose 15 to 30 ml.

ii) *Concentrated Cinnamon Water* (BP 1949) Aq. Cinnam. Conc.: Cinnamon oil 2 ml, ethanol (90%) 60 ml, water to 100 ml, shaken with 5 gms of sterilized talc and filtered.

iii) *Cinnamon Water* : Concentrated cinnamon water (ii) above 2.5 ml, freshly boiled and cooled water to 100 ml.

Cinnamon Tincture (BPC 1949): Tincture Cinnam.: It is prepared by percolating cinnamon with 5 times of ethanol 70%. Dose 2 to 4 ml.

Cinnamon Syrup also called Syrupus Cinnamoni (Argen. P.) and Jarabe de Cavella is prepared from sucrose 85 gm in distilled cinnamon water.

Cinnamon oil in a 9% emulsion, when used upon on hands, completely sterlizes them. A 7 to 8% emulsion is equivalent to 1% solution of corrosive sublimate. The former is certainly more agreeable to use. Similarly, oil of thyme in an 11% solution is equivalent to a 7% solution of cinnamon oil.

13. Clove

Clove (BP) also known as Caryophyllum; Caryoph; *Clou de Girofle, Giroflien, Gravinbo* and *Cravo da India*

Clove is listed in Austrian, British, French, Hungarian, Indian,

Japanese, Netherland, Portugese and Swiss pharmacopoeias.

The dried flower buds of clove must have 15% minimum of volatile oil and this oil, too, must have 85 to 92% of eugenol. Powdered clove (BP) contains not less than 12% v/w of volatile oil. Clove has a strong, characteristic aromatic spicy odour and an aromatic pungent taste. Cloves must be stored in a cool dry place, the powdered drug should be kept in air tight containers protected from light.

Clove oil is a good disinfectant solution for household use. For moth extermination, pepper and clove oil are good. A coarse powder made from cloves, cinnamon, mace, black pepper and orris roots, all in equal proportion, keeps moths away.

Preparations

i) *Concentrated clove water* (BPC 1934), Aq. Caryoph. Conc. is prepared from 2 ml of clove oil, 60 ml of alcohol (90%) and 100 ml of water, shaken with talc and filtered. Dose 0.3 to 1 ml.

ii) *Clove Water*: Concentrated clove water 2.5 ml freshly boiled and cooled water to 100 ml.

iii) *Concentrated clove Infusion* (BPC 1954) Inf. Caryoph Conc. is prepared from clove buds 1 part macerated with 5 parts of 25% ethanol. Dose 2 to 4 ml.

iv) *Clove Infusion* is prepared by diluting 1 vol. of (iii) above to 8 vols. of water.

v) *Toothache Drops are also called Odontalgium.* It is prepared from 25 gms of chlorbutol+clove oil to 100 ml.

14. Coriander (BP)

Coriander; Coriander fruits, seed, *Fruto de Cilantro.*

Coriander fruit i.e. its seed is standardised in Austrian, Belgian, British, French, Hungarian, Indian, Polish, Portugese and Spanish pharmacopoeias. The seeds should have volatile oil content v/w not less than 0.3%.

Powdered coriander (BP) (Coriander pulvis) contains not less than 0.2% v/w of volatile oil. Like other essential oils this, too, needs to be stored at less than 25°C temperature in dry, air tight containers.

15. Cumins

No pharmacopoeia mentions any of them, white as well as black.

16. Dill

Dill (BPC 1954), *Anethum*, Dill fruit.

The European and not the Indian variety is enlisted in the Indian pharmacopoeia. The dried fruits (*Anethum graveolens*) must have a minimum of 2.5% v/w of volatile oil.

Powdered Dill (BPC 1954) contains not less than 2% v/w of volatile oil. Seeds as well as powders are stored in dark, air tight, completely filled containers kept in cool and dry places.

Concentrated Dill Water (BPC 1973), *Aq. Anethi Concentrata*

Dill oil 2 ml, ethanol (90%) 60 ml, water to 100 ml; shaken with 5 gm of sterilized talc and filtered. Dose 0.3 to 1 ml.

Dill Water: Concentrated dill water 2.5 ml, freshly boiled and cooled water to 100 ml.

17. Fennel

Fennel (BPC 1973); *Foeniculum,* Fennel Fruit; Fennel seed; *Fenouil, Fenouil Donx; Fenchel; Fruto de Hinojo; Funcho.*

All these names have been collected from Austrian, Belgian Chinese, Czechoslavakian, French, German, Hungarian, Indian, Japanese, Netherland, Polish, Portugese, Roumanian, Russian Spanish and Swiss pharmacopoeias. Specifications for volatile oil content range from 1.4 to 4%.

Fennel under (BPC) is the dried fruits of cultivated plants of *Foeniculum vulgare var. vulgare, Syn. F. copillaceum; F. dulce*, containing not less than 1.2% v/w of volatile oil. *Powdered Fennel* (BPC 1973) contains not less than 1% v/w of volatile oil. This drug is stored in a cool dry and dark place in air tight containers.

Preparation

i) Concentrated Fennel Water

Concentrated Fennel Water (BPC 1934) also called Aq. Foenic. Conc. It is prepared from fennel oil 2 ml, ethanol 90% 60 ml + water to 100 ml; shaken with talc and filtered. Dose 0.3 to 1 ml. Hungarian Pharmacopoeia has a similar preparation with 2% of polysorbate "20".

ii) Fennel Water

Concentrated fennel water 2.5 ml + freshly boiled and cooled water to 100 ml.

18. Fenugreek (BPC 1949)

Foenum graecum; Semen Foenugraeci, Semen Trigonellae; Bockshornsame. Fenugreek is listed in pharmacopoeias of Austria, China, Poland and Switzerland.

Fenugreek are the dried leaves of *Trigonella foenumgraecum* containing not less than 30% of water soluble extractives.

Fenugreek is still a widely used spice. Recent studies in England found diosgenin from fenugreek a starting steroid for the synthesis of oral contraceptives and sex hormones. Its cheapness compared to Mexican dioscorea makes it a viable economic source of diosgenin production.

19. Galangal

Galangal (BPC 1934) is also known as Chinese root; Chinese Ginger; East Indian Root; Lesser Galangal; Rosne.

Only Indian and Swiss pharmacopoeias mention it. The dried rhizome of the lesser galangal *(Alpinia officinarum) (Zingiberaceae)* contains about 0.5 to 1.5% v/w of volatile oil. Galanga is aromatic, carminative and similar in its effects to ginger.

Galanga MAJOR also called Greater Galangal; Java Galangal are the dried rhizomes of the greater galangal *Alpinia galanga* (Zingiberaceae). Galanga has been used in India as an aromatic carminative and in rheumatism and catarrhal affections.

20. Garlic

Garlic (BPC 1949), Allium; Ajo is listed in pharmacopoeias of China, Spain and Swiss. They accept the fresh bulb of *Allium sativum* Linn (Lilaceae). It has a very strong and disagreeable odour and a strongly pungent and persistent taste. It yields 0.1 to 0.3% of a volatile oil having allyl propyl disulphide and diallyl disulphide. If stored in a cool dry place with free access of air it may be kept for about 6 months after harvesting.

Garlic has expectorant, diphoretic, disinfectant and diuretic properties and has been used in doses of 2 to 8 gm. The juice was used formerly alone, or in a syrup, in the treatment of pulmonary conditions. Administration of garlic preparation to children is dangerous and sometimes it has proved to be fatal.

The larvicidal properties of garlic, active against the cutex mosquito, were found to be due to dially di and tri- sulphides. Natural and synthetic samples proved larvicidal at 5 ppm level, reported S.V. Amonkar and A. Bannerje, *Science*; 1971, 174, 1343. A report of allergic contact dermatitis to garlic E. Bleumink *et. al. Br. J. Derm.*; 1972, 87, 6.

Garlic juice and the essential oil of garlic prevented the hyperlipaemia and blood coagulation changes following fat ingestion in 5 healthy subjects as written in a letter to *Lancet,* 1973, 1491, 2, by A. Bordia and H.C. Bansal as well as in *Lancet* letter 1976, 2, 575 by G.S. Sainani et.al.

An extract of garlic called allicin possessed anti-fungal activity against *Candida, Cryptococus, Trichophyton, Epidermophyton* and *Microsporum Spp. in vitro* - Y. Yamada and K. Azuima in *Antimicrob. Aq Chemother;* 1977, 11, 743. Also refer V.D. Sharma *et. al. I.J. Expl. Bio.;* 1977, 15, 466.

Application of thin slices of garlic bulb was reported to aid healing during repair of perforations of the eardrum in 17 out of 18 patients at a Chinese hospital — *Br. Med. J.* 1977, 2, 324.

The notion that garlic and onion are useful in ischaemic heart disease was not corroborated in 27 countries from the work of *C.Buck et.al. Lancet* (letter) 1979, 2, 104.

Evidence of a platelet aggregation inhibitor in garlic — T. Ariga *et.al.* (letter) *Lancet,* 1981, 1, 150 and D.J. Baull in (letter) *ibid,* 776.

In 5 consecutive cases of hypertension, garlic reduced the blood pressure to satisfactory levels — *V. Srinivasan* (letter), *Lancet*, 1969, 2, 800.

Preparations

Preparations (BPC 1949) also known as *succus Allici*. Bruise garlic 80 gm and express for juice; mix the mass with 20 ml water and again express the liquid; repeat the operation untill the volume of the mixed juice and washings amounts to 80 ml and add alcohol (90%) 20 ml; allow to stand for 14 days and decant or filter. Dose 2 to 4 ml.

Garlic syrup (BPC 1949) Syr. Allici. Garlic juice 20 ml, sucrose 80 gm, acetic acid (6%) 20 ml, water 10 ml. Dose 2 to 8 ml.

Influence of garlic antibiotic on malignant tumours, human as well as animal, has been found to be useful. Transplanted tumours of *Jensen saxcoma* in rats regressed and in some cases, completely disappeared after the injection of 1-3 mgm of allicin given either intramuscularly or directly into the tumour; but all types of tumours do not respond well, reports Pruthi who makes the following observation :

"There is an increase in the intestinal synthesis of Vitamin B1 on the administration of garlic to human subjects as alli-thiamine was found by the reaction of thiamine (Vit. B1) and allicin, which was also absorbed faster than thiamine in the intestine. This appears to be the fundamental scientific basis for the therapeutic use of garlic and also for the utilization of food ingredients."

Garlic from recent developments in therapeutics is found useful in pulmonary tuberculosis by inhaling its fresh juice. It is recommended for intestinal use as a tonic and vermifuge. Preparations of garlic are given in pulmonary pthiasis bronchiectasis, gangrene of the lung and whooping cough. Garlic juice finds application in the treatment of laryngeal tuberculosis, lupus and duodenal ulcers, atonic dyspepsia, flatulence and colic. Dymock recommends garlic as a powerful restorative. Garlic juice diluted with water can be used as a lotion for washing wounds and foul ulcers. Essential oil of garlic is deadly against aedes and culex family of mosquitoes which are responsible for spreading yellow fever and filaria. Garlic finds use as an ingredient of several allopathic drug formulations. Garlic has antibacterial action against *Eberthella typhose, Escherichia coli, Acid fast bascilli, Aerobacter aerogenes, staphylococcus auerus* and *Shigella sonnei,* various Gram-positive and Gram-negative organisms in dilutions as low as 1:85,000 to 1:125,000. and its effectiveness against *L. caseii* and *S. faecalis* have been experimentally demonstrated.

21. Ginger

Ginger (BP) also known as *Zingiber; Zingib; Gingembre,; Ingwer; Gengibre.* Listed in the pharmacopoeias of Austria, Belgium, Britain, China, India, Japan, Mexico, Portugal and Swiss. The BP specifies scraped or unscrapped rhizome of ginger - (*Zingiber officinale Roscoe - Zingiberaceae*) known in commerce as unbleached Jamaican ginger and containing zingiberene, gingerol and terpene derivatives.

It contains not less than 4.5% of ethanol (90%) soluble extractive and not less than 10% of water soluble extractive.

Powdered Ginger (BP) is light yellow or yellowish-brown. Ginger rhizomes must be stored in a cool dry place, the powdered drug should be kept in air tight containers. For further study *The Chemistry of pungent principles of ginger* by N. Pravatoroff in *Manufacturing Chemist,* 1967, 38 (March), 40.

Uses

Ginger has carminative properties and has been added to purgatives in the belief that it prevents gripping. Ginger is also used as a flavouring agent in medicines. Dose 0.25 to 1 gm; the *Reduction of Motion Sickness by Ginger* by D.B. Mowrey and D.E. Clayson, *Lancet,* 1982, 1, 655).

Preparations

i) *Ginger Oleoresin* (BPC 1968):Oleores; Zingib; Gingerin. The acetone-soluble matter of ginger is stored in air-tight containers. Dose 15 to 60 mgm.

ii) *Ginger Syrup* (BPC 1973), APF, Ind. P), also known as Syrupus Zingiberis. Strong ginger tincture 5 ml, syrup to 100 ml. Dose 2.5 to 5 ml.

iii) *Strong Ginger Tincture* (BP) also called Tinct. Zingib Forte; Ginger Essence; Essence of Ginger. It is prepared by percolating 50 gm with 90% ethanol to 100 ml. Indian P. has a similar tincture; Belgian P. and Mexican P specify 1:5.

iv) *Weak Ginger Tincture* (BP) Weak Ginger Tinct.; Tinct. Zingib Mit; Ginger tincture is prepared from strong Ginger Tincture (iii) above, 20 ml. plus 90% ethanol to 100 ml.

22. Juniper (BPC 1934)

Juniper (BPC 1934) *Juniper berry, juniper fruit, Beccae Juniperi, Juniperi Fructus; Genievre; Wacholder Beeren; Zimbro*. These names are from the pharmacopoeias of Austria, Belgium, Czechoslavia, Germany, Hungry, Portugese, Roumania, Russia and Swiss.

All these pharmacopoeias define it as the dried ripe fruit of *Juniperis communis* (*Cupressaceae*). It contains 0.5 to 2% of volatile oil and about 10% of resin. Fruits possess carminative, stimulant and diuretic property and are useful in different forms of dropsy. They have been used in disorders of the urino-genitary tract such as gonorrhoea, gleet and leucorrhoea and certain cutaneous diseases.

23. Nutmeg (BPC 1973) Myristica, Nux Moschata; Muscade; Nuez Moscada; Noz Moscada;

Nutmeg is listed in the pharmacopoeias of India, Portugal, Spain and Swiss. The dried kernels of the seeds of *Myristica fragrans (Myristicaceae)* contain not less than 5% v/w of volatile oil. It contains about 35% of solid fat, the chief fatty acid constituents are myristic acid (60%) and smaller amounts of palmitic, oleic, linoleic and lauric acid.

Powdered *nutmeg* (BPC 1973) contains less than 4% v/w of volatile oil. The powdered nutmeg should be stored in a cool place in air tight containers.

Nutmeg taken in large doses may cause nausea and vomiting, flushing or sometimes shivering, dry mouth, tachycardia, disorientation, stupor or stimulation of central nervous system possibly with epileptic form convulsions, miosis sometimes followed by mydriasis and euphoria and hallucinations. The hallucinogen in nutmeg is believed to be myristicin according to D.J. Panayotopoulas and D.D. Chisholm in *Br. Med.* J.; 1970, 1,754 later on corroborated by R.A. Faguet and K.F. Rowland in *Am.J. Psychiat*; 1978, 135, 860.

Nutmeg powder 1 teaspoonful 4 times/day proved beneficial in intractable diarrhoea due to Crohn's disease unresponsive to conventional therapy, reported by I. Shafran and others in *New Engl. J. Med.*; 1977, 296, 694. Nutmeg powder 1 teaspoonful 9 times daily was found more beneficial in a 41 year old woman with medullary carcinoma of the thyroid and diarrhoea probably due to elevated plasma-prostaglandin concentrations, persistent diarrhoea following thyroidectomy — J.A. Banoman *et.al.; Br. Med. J.*; 1975, 3, 11.

24. Onion

Onion has been reported to reduce platlet aggregation and to enhance fibrinolysis as reported by I.S. Menon, *B.Med. J.;* 1969, 1,845; 1970, 2,421; H.J. Goldsmith, *Lancet*, 1971, 2,738; K.I. Baghurst *et.al. Lancet* 1977, 1,101; C. Phillips and N.L. Poyser, *Lancet*, 1978, 1,1051.

Hypoglycaemic effect in animals has been reported by R.C. Jain *et.al. Lancet*, 1973, 2,1491; *B.Med. J.*, 1974, 2,730.

The antihypertensive action of onions was associated with prostaglandin A1, 1 ppm — T.H. Maugh, *Science,* 1979, 204, 293.

25. Origanum

Originum is mentioned in Czechoslavic pharmacopoeia wherein it is stated that origanum is the fresh or dried flavouring tops of marjoram, *Origanum vulgare (Lapiate)* containing a volatile oil.

Origanum has been used as an aromatic carminative and in cough syrups. It has also been employed externally in healing lotions for wounds, usually in conjunction with other herbs.

Pruthi, however, reports that origanum grown extensively in Mexico is also known as Mexican sage. The herb's taste is fragrant, spicy, warm, pungent and bitter. Some opine that the properties of Mexican herb resemble those of sage rather than those of marjoram.

26. *Parsley syn. Petroselinum; Persil, Petroselinum crispum; P. sativum; Apium petroselinum; Carum petroselinum*)

Parsley is mentioned in the Czechoslavic pharmacopoeia which specifies the root. Portugese P. specifies the root and the fruit. Both the root and fruits of parsley have been used medicinally as diuretics and emmenagogues.

Pruthi reports that in a series of experiments conducted on hearts of frogs, cats and rabbits, it was noted that small dose (2 drops) of 1% solution of leaves increased the amplitude and slowed down cardiac contraction, large doses (5-10 drops) of 10% leaf infusion were followed by desperation of cardiac activity. Intravenous administration of the infusion as well as of the extract caused fall in blood pressure and dialation of blood vessels.

27. Pepper (Black) (BPC 1949) Piper Nigrum; *Pepper; Piper.*

Pimenta is mentioned in Austrian and Portugese pharmacopoeias. These are the dried unripe fruits of *Piper nigrum* containing a pungent resin, chavicine, with piperine, piperidine and 1 to 2.5% of volatile oil. Black pepper should be stored in a dry and cool place.

Black pepper stimulates the taste buds, producing a reflex increase in gastric secretion. It has diphoretic and diuretic properties.

28. Pepper Long

It has 4-5% of alkaloid piperine and piplartine and two unnamed alkaloids. This is closely related to pellitorine producing marked salivation, numbness and tingles mucous membrane. One of the unnamed alkaloid showed significant antitubular activity against *Mycobacterium tuburculosis H-37 RV strain*; it inhibited the growth of the bacillus in 20 ug/ml concentrations.

Alcohlic extracts of the dry fruits and aqueous extracts of the leaves showed activity against Micrococus phygenes var. aureus and Eocherichia coli. Ether extract of the fruits showed larvicidal properties, according to Pruthi.

29. Pomegranate's rind contains alkaloids pelletierene and its isomers. These alkaloids are effective vermifuges. The bark and root alkaloids are astringent, anthelmintic and specific in tapeworms. Pomegranate pulp is cardiac and stomachic. Its seeds are reported to have estrogenic activity as they contain steroidal estrogens. Gujral *et.al I.J. Med. Res.* 1960, 46-51, have found that by oral feeding of pomegranate to female rats, their fertility is reduced.

30. Poppy Seed Oil

It is a fixed oil, soluble in carbon disulphide, chloroform, ether and light petroleum. Occassionally used as a substitute for olive oil for pharmaceutical purposes.

Nevertheless, poppy seed oil has a specialised application in Medicine as Iodised Oil Fluid Injection (BP) also well known as Ethiodized Oil Injection (USP). This iodised oil is listed in the pharamacopoeias of Britain, U.S.A. and the French includes *Huiled' Oeillette Iodle.*

It is sterile iodine addition product of the ethyl esters of the fatty acids obtained from poppy-seed oil. The BP specifies 37 to 39% w/w of combined iodine. USP specifies 35.2 to 38.9% of combined iodine. It is a straw coloured or amber coloured, clear, oily liquid which has not more than a slight alliaceous odour and a bland oily taste of density 1.28 to 1.30. It decomposes in air and sunlight and develops dark brown colour. Further details Martindale p. 440.

31. Rosemary plant

All parts of this plant are astringent, nervine tonic and an excellent stomachic. An infusion of rosemary plant with borax is employed as a hair wash to prevent baldness. Rosemary infusion causes temporary sterility as practised in Central America.

Flowering tops are considered carminative, diphoretic, diuretic, apperient, emmenegogue, stimulant and even stomachic, reports Pruthi, though no pharamacopeia lists the plant as such for medicinal purposes.

32. Saffron *(Er. P; BPC 1949)* Crocus; Croci Stigma; *Safran;* Eastigmas de Azafran; Azafran; Acafrao; Ci Natural Yellow, *Colour Index No 75100.*

Saffron is listed in the pharmacopoeias of Argentina, Austria, Belgium, Europe, France, Germany, Japan, Yugoslavia, Mexico, Netherland, Portugal, Roumania, Spain and Switzerland.

The dried stigmas and tops of the styles of *Crocus sativus* containing crocines, crocetins and picrocrocine. Saffron spice needs protection from light.

Saffron is used as a food dye and flavouring agent. It was once widely used as a glycerin syrup and tincture for colouring medicines, but now it is largely replaced by the solutions of Sunset yellow FCF and tartrazine. But early reports indicate that the chief toxic symptons following poisoning with saffron are flushing of the face, epistaxis, vertigo, vomiting and bradycardia. Profuse metrorrhagia and menorrhagia may occur. Abortion occurs rarely.

Preparations

Tincture de Safaran (Bel. P; Fr.P) Saffron 1 gm in 10 ml of alcohol prepared by maceration. Belgium P. specifies ethanol 60% whereas French P. Specifies 80% ethanol.

33. Sage (BPC 1934) Salvia, Feuilles de sauge: Salbeiblatter

It is mentioned in the pharamacopoeias of Austria, Germany. Hungary, Yugoslavia, Poland, Portugal, Roumania, Russia and Switzerland. Czechoslavia includes sage herb. German P. also specifies *Salvia triloba.*

Sage has carminative properties and is used as a flavouring agent for meat. It is a mild tonic, astringent and has also been used in tooth and mouth washes, gargles, poultices, hair tonics and dressings.

34. Summer Savory (Satureja hortensis Linn)

The dried leaves of savory are used as carminative, stimulant and an antioxidant. Fish, salad, stews, sauces and vegetables take on a new flavour when the tiny leaves of summer savory are used instead of parsley or chives.

35. Sweet Flag Root, Calamus Rhizome (BPC 1934); Acore Vrai; Kalamus.

It is mentioned in the pharmacopoeias of Austria, Hungary, Yugoslavia, Poland, Russia and Switzerland.

The dried rhizome of sweet flag, *Acorus calamus (Araciae).* It contains 1.5 to 3.5% v/w of a bitter aromatic oil. The rhizome is a bitter and a carminative; it has been used to flavour alcoholic beverages.

36. Tarragon

Its aromatic leaves are credited with apperient, stomachic, stimulant and vermifuge properties.

37. Thyme

It has carminative properties due to its volatile oil. The liquid extract has been used as an ingredient of cough linctuses. It is a flavouring agent. D.R. Somerset, *Practitioner*, 1972, 208, 577 has reported a success rate of 85% achieved in 6 weeks in 17 children aged 3 to 18 with enuresis by administration of a small wine glass ful of distilled thyme tea at bed time.

Thyme Liquid Extract (BPC 1949) syn. *Ext. Thym; Liq. Thyme.* 100 gms is exhausted by percolation first with a mixture of glycerol 10 ml, alcohol 90% 25 ml and water 65 ml and then with a mixture of ethanol 90% : H_2O::1:3; the first 85 ml of percolate is reserved; the remainder of the percolate is evaporated to a soft extract, dissolved in the reserved portion and diluted to 100 ml with the second menstrum. Dose 0.6 to 4 ml. A similar preparation is included in some pharmacopoeias.

Wild Thyme Syn. *Herba Serpylli; Mother of Thyme; Serpolet; Qhuendel.*

It is mentioned in French, Hungarian, Roumanian and Swiss pharamacopoeias. The dried leaves and flowering tops of *Thymus serpyllum* contain about 0.6% of volatile oil. Wild Thyme has properties similar to thyme. Pruthi reports that wild thyme is given in weak vision, complaints of stomach liver, suppression of urine and menstruation in Punjab.

The herb is emmenagogue, alexiteric, anthelmintic, good in liver complaints. The seeds are vermifuge.

38. Turmeric (BPC 1949); Curcuma; Indian saffron; CI Natural yellow 3; Colour Index No 75300. The dried rhizome of Curcuma longa.

Turmeric is listed in the pharmacopoeias of China and India specifying a volatile oil content of not less than 4%. *Temoe-Lawaq* (Fr. P.) and *Javanische Gelb Wurz* (German P) are the rhizomes of *Curcuma zanthorrhiza* containing not less than 5% (French) or 3.5% (German) of volatile oil.

Turmeric contains curcumin — a yellow pigment which dissolves in alcohol to form a deep yellow solution; alkalis change its colour to reddish brown.

Curcumin showed the same amount of inhibition of induced oedema in rats as similar doses of cortisone and phenylbutazone, but its action was much reduced in adrenalectomised rats. In mice, larger doses were required of curcumin than of cortisone for the same effect. No fatalities were noted in mice receiving a total dose of 2000 ppm and it has no antipyretic or analgesic action as reported by R.C. Srimal and B.N. Dhawan *J. Pharm. Pharmac* ADDENDUM 1973, 25,447.

Spices in the Homeopathic System

Allium Cepa

(Red Onion)

A picture of coryza, with acrid nasal discharge and laryngeal symptoms, eye secretion bland; singers' cold, worse in warm room and towards evening; better in open air, is presented by this remedy. Specially adapted to phlegmatic patients; colds in damp cold weather. Neuralgic pains, like a fine thread, following amputations or injuries to nerves. Traumatic chronic neuritis. Burning in nose, mouth, throat, bladder and skin. Sensation of glowing heat on different parts of the body.

Head — Catarrhal headache, mostly in forehead; worse in warm room towards evening. Thread-like pains in face. Headache ceases during menses; returns when flow disappears.

Eyes — Red. Much burning and smarting lachrymation. Sensitive to light. Eyes suffused and watery; profuse, bland lachrymation, better in open air. Burning in eyelids.

Ears — Earache, shooting in eustachian tube.

Nose — Sneezing, especially when entering a warm room. Copious, watery and extremely acrid discharge. Feeling of a lump at root of nose. Hay-fever. (Sabad; Sil.; Psor.) Fluent coryza with headache, cough, and hoarseness. Polypus.

Stomach — Canine Hunger. Pain in pyloric region. Thirst. Belching. Nausea.

Abdomen — Rumbling, offensive flatus. Pain in left hypogastrium. Colic sitting, moving about.

Rectum — Diarrhoea with very offensive flatus. Stitches in rectum; itching and rhagades in anus. Glowing heat in rectum.

Urinary — Sensation of weakness in bladder and urethra. Increased secretion of urine with coryza. Urine red with much pressure and burning in urethra.

Respiratory — Hoarseness. Hacking cough on inspiring cold air. Tickling in larynx. Sensation as if larynx has split or torn. Oppressed breathing from pressure in middle of chest. Constricted feeling in the region of epiglottis. Pain extending to ear.

Extremities — Lame joints. Ulcers on heel. Painful affections of fingers about nails. Neuralgia of stump. Bad effects from getting wet feet. Limbs, especially arms, feel sore and tired.

Sleep — Yawning with headache and drowsiness. Gaping in deep sleep. Dreams. Wakes at 2 a.m.

Modalities — Worse, in the evening, in warm room. Better, in open air, and in cold room.

Relationship — Compare; Gels.; Euph.; Kali hyd.; Aconite; Ipecac.

Complementary: Phosphor.; Thuja; Puls.

Antidotes: Arn.; Cham.; Verat.

Dose — Third potency.

Allium Sativum

(Garlic)

Acts directly on intestinal mucous membrane increasing peristalsis.

Colitis, with pathological flora. It has vasodilatory properties. Arterial hypotension begins usually in 30 to 45 minutes after 20 to 40 drops of the tincture.

It is adapted to fleshy subjects with dyspepsia and catarrhal affections, high livers. Patients who eat a great deal more, especially meat, than they drink. Pain in hip, pain in psoas and iliac muscles. Pulmonary tuberculosis.

Cough and expectoration diminishes, temperature becomes normal, weight is gained, and sleep becomes regular. Haemoptysis.

Head — Heavy; pulsation in temples; catarrhal deafness.

Mouth — Much sweetish saliva after meals and at night. Sensation of a hair on tongue or throat.

Stomach — Voracious appetite. Burning eructations. Least change in diet causes trouble. Constipation, with constant dull pain in bowels. Tongue pale, red papillae.

Respiratory — Constant rattling of mucous in bronchi. Cough in the morning after leaving bed room, with mucous expectoration, which is tenacious and difficult to raise. Sensitive to cold air. Dilated bronchi, with fetid expectoration. Darting pain in chest.

Female — Pain in swelling of breasts. Eruption in vagina and on breasts and vulva during menses.

Relationship — Allium Sat., according to Dr. Teste, belongs to the Bryonia group, including Lycopod. Nux. Colocy, Digital, and Ignatia which affect deeply all flesh eating animals and hardly at all vegetarians, hence is their special applicability to meat eaters rather than to exclusive vegetarians.

Compare — Capsicum; Arsenic; Senega; Kali nit.

Complementary: Arsenic.

Antidote: Lycopod.

Dose — Third to sixth potency. In tuberculosis, dose, four to six grammes in moderate state of dessication daily, in divided doses.

Apium Graveolens

(Common Celery)

Contains a soporific active principle. Obstinate retention of urine, throbbing headaches and heartburn have been produced by celery. Swelling of throat, face and hands. Rheumatic pain in muscles of neck, also in sacrum. Growing pains. Hungry for apples. Dysmenorrhaea, with sharp, short pains, better flexing legs.

Head — Depressed; energetic; feeling of fidgets; cannot sleep from thinking. Headache; better eating. Eyeballs feel sunken. Itching in eyes. Itching and smarting in inner canthus of left eye.

Abdomen — Sore; sharp sticking pain as if stool was coming on; diarrhoea, sharp pain in left iliac region going over to right. Nausea increases with pain.

Female — Sharp sticking pain in both ovarian regions, left, better bending over, by lying on left side, with legs fluxed; nipples tender.

Respiratory — Tickling, dry cough. Intense constriction over sternum, withdrawing feeling through the back on lying down. Throat swollen, dyspnoea.

Skin — Itching blotches; burning creeping sensation. Profuse discharge from granulating ulcers. Urticaria with shuddering.

Sleep — Unrefreshed; sleepless. Wakes from 1 to 8 a.m. Eating does not help sleep. Not fatigued from loss of sleep.

Dose — First to thirtieth potency.

Capsicum

(Cayenne Pepper)

Seems to suit especially persons of lax fiber, weak; diminished vital heat. A relaxed plethoric sluggish, cold remedy. Not much reactive force. Such persons are fat, indolent, opposed to physical exertion, averse to go outside of their routine, get homesick easily, general uncleanliness of body, abstainers from accustomed alcoholics. It affects the mucous membranes, producing a sensation of constriction. Inflammation of petrous bone. Burning pain and general chilliness. Older people who have exhausted their vitality, especially by mental work, and poor living; bleareyed appearance; who do not react. Fear of slightest draught. Marked tendency to suppuration in every inflammatory process. Prostration and feeble digestion of alcoholics. Myalgia, aching and jerking of muscles.

Mind — Excessive peevishness. Homesickness, with sleeplessness and disposition to suicide. Wants to be let alone. Peppery disposition. Delirium tremens.

Head — Bursting headache; worse, coughing. Hot face. Red cheeks. Face red, though cold. (Asafael.).

Ears — Burning and stinging in ears. Swelling and pain behind ears. Inflammation of mastoid. Tenderness over the petrous bone; extremely sore and tender to touch. (Onosmod.) Otorrhoea and mastoid disease before suppuration.

Throat — Hot feeling in fauces. Subacute inflammation of Eustachian tube with great pain. Pain and dryness in throat, extending to the ears. Sore throat of smokers and drinkers. Smarting in; constriction. Burning constriction worse between acts of deglutition. Inflamed uvula and palate; swollen and relaxed.

Mouth — Herpes labialis. (Apply one drop of the mother tincture). Stomatitis. Disagreeable smell from mouth. Fetid odor from mouth.

Stomach — Burning in the tip of the tongue. Atonic dyspepsia. Much flatulence, especially in debilitated subjects. Intense craving for stimulants. Vomiting, sinking at the pit of stomach. Much thirst; but drinking causes shuddering.

Stool — Bloody mucous, with burning and tenesmus; drawing pain in back after stool. Thirsty after stool, with shivering. Bleeding piles, with soreness of anus. Stinging pain during stool.

Urine — Strangury, frequent, almost ineffectual urging. Burning in orifice. Comes first in drops, then in spurts; neck of bladder spasmodically contracted. Ectropion of meatus.

Male — Coldness of scrotum, with impotency, atrophied testicles, loss of sensibility in testicles, with softening and dwindling. Gonorrhoea, with chordee, excessive burning, pain in prostate.

Female — Climacteric disturbances with burning of tip of tongue. (Lethyrus.) Uterine haemorrhage near the menopause, with nausea. Sticking sensation in left ovarian region.

Respiratory — Constriction of chest; arrest breathing. Hoarseness. Pain at apex of heart or in rib region, worse touch. Dry, hacking cough, expelling an offensive breath from lungs. Dyspnoea. Feels as if chest and head would burst to pieces. Explosive cough. Threatening gangrene of lung. Pain in distant parts on coughing — bladder, legs, ears, etc.

Extremities — Pain from hips to feet. Sciatica, worse bending backward; worse, coughing. Tensive pain in the knee.

Fever — Coldness, with ill-humor. Shivering after drinking. Chill begins in the back. Must have something hot in the back. Thirst before chill.

Modalities — Better, while eating, from heat. Worse, open air, uncovering, draughts.

Relationship — Antidote; Cina; Calad.

Compare: Pulsat.; Lycop. Bell.; Centaurea (surging of blood homesickness; intermittent fever).

Dose — Third to sixth attenuation. In delirium tremens, dram doses of tincture in milk or tincture of orange peel.

Cinnamomum

(Cinnamon)

Cancer where pain and fetor are present. Best when skin is intact. Its use in haemorrhages has abundant clinical verification. Nosebleeding. Haemorrhages from bowels, haemotysis, etc. A strain in loins or false step brings on a profuse flow of bright blood. Post-Partum haemorrhage. Flatulency and diarrhoea. Feeble patients with languid circulation.

Female — Bearing-down sensation. Menses early, profuse, prolonged, bright red. Sleepy. No desire for anything. Fingers seem swollen. Uterine haemorrhages caused by overlifting, during puerperal state; menorrhagia.

Relationship — Compare: Ipec.; Sil.; Trill.

Antidote: Acon.

Dose — Tincture to third potency. For cancer strong decoction, one-half pint in a day. Oil of cinnamon in aqueous solution best local disinfectant. 3-4 drops in two quarts of water as a douche, whenever a germicide and disinfectant is needed. Three drops of sugar for hiccup.

Cochlearia Armorcia — Armoracia Sativa

(Horse-radish)

Frontal bone and sinus, antrum and salivery glands are specifically affected by this drug. Bloated sensation. It raises vital forces and is used as a gargle in scorbutic gums and sore throat. Hoarseness and in relaxed conditions of the fauces. Internally in gonorrhoea. It is useful as a condiment in enfeebled states of stomach. An infusion of the root in cider, for dropsy, causes copious diuresis. It locally cures dandruff.

Head — Thinking is difficult. Anxiety, driven to despair by pain. Pressing, boring pain as if frontal bone would fall out. Violent headache with vomiting. Impaired hearing.

Eyes — Sore and scrofulous; traumatic inflammation of eyes, bleared-ness and cataract. Copious running from eyes.

Stomach — Pain towards back; worse, pressure on dorsal vertebrae. Belching and cramps. Colic with backache. Violent cramp from stomach through both sides around to back. Griping around navel.

Back — Pain in back as from incarcerated flatulence from abdomen to back and down into sacrum.

Respiratory — Dry, backing, laryngeal cough, also post-influenzal cough, dry or loose, worse lying down. Chest painful to touch. Coryza, with hoarseness. Mucous asthma. Oedema of lungs. Throat feels rough and hoarse.

Urinary — Burning and cutting at glans penis before, during, and after urination. Frequent urination.

Modalities — Worse evening and at night.

Relationship — Compare: Cannab; Sinapis; Caps.

Dose — First to third attenuation.

Crocus Sativa

(Saffron)

Saffron is a remedy often useful in haemorrhages that are black and stringy. Tingling in various parts. Chorea and hysterical affections. Frequent and extreme changes in sensations and mental conditions. Anger with violence followed by repentance. Laughing mania. Drowsiness and lassitude; better by literary labor.

Mind — Vacillating; pleasant mania; sings and laughs. Happy and affectionate; then angry. Sudden changes from hilarity to melancholy. Vivid recollection from music heard. (Lyc.).

Head — Throbs, pulsates, during climacteric; worse during menses.

Eyes — Appearance as of electric sparks. Must wipe eyes as if mucus or water were in them. Feeling in eyes as after violent weeping. Sensation as if she had been looking through too sharp spectacles. Eyes feel as if in smoke. Pupils enlarged and react slowly. Lids heavy. Ciliary neuralgia, pain in eyes and spreads to top of head. Sensation as if cold air was rushing through eye. (Fluor, ac.; Syph.). Asthenopia with extreme photophobia. Threatened glaucoma; embolism of arteria centralis retinal.

Nose — Epistaxis, Dark, stringy, clotted. Strings of dark blood hanging down the nose.

Abdomen — Obstinate constipation due to portaı stagnation. Constipation in infants. Crawling and stitches in anus. Sensation of something alive in abdomen, stomach, etc., especially on left side. (Calend.) Abdomen swollen, feeling of something heavy.

Female — Threatened abortion, especially when haemorrhage is dark and stringy. Urging of blood to genitals. Menses dark, viscid, too frequent and copious, black and slimy. Uterine haemorrhage; clots with long strings; worse from least movement. Jerking pain in interior of left breast, as if drawn toward back by means of thread. (Crot. tig.) A bounding feeling, as if something alive in right breast.

Respiratory — Wheezy cough, with frothy expectoration containing threads like fine twine; worse, lying down. Breath has offensive, sickly smell. Feeling as if the uvula is elongated in hysterical patients.

Back — Sudden feeling of coldness in back as if cold water were thrown over him; icy-cold extremities.

Extremities — Spasmodic contractions and twitchings of single set of muscles. Chorea and hysteria, with great alterations of feeling. Whole upper extremity falls asleep. Cracking in hip-joint and knees. Weakness in knees and legs. Pain in ankles and soles.

Modalities — Worse, lying down, hot weather, warm room, in morning, fasting, before breakfast, looking fixedly at an object. Better, in open air.

Relationship — Antidote: Opium; Bell.

Compare : Ipec.; Trillium; Plat.; China; Sabina.

Dose — Tincture, to thirtieth attenuation.

Granatum

(Pomegranate)

As a vermifuge for the expulsion of tapeworm, and homoeopathically for the following symptomatic indications. Salivation, with nausea, and vertigo. Spasm of the glottis.

Head — Feels empty, Sunken eyes; pupils dilated; weak sight. Vertigo very persistent.

Stomach — Constant hunger. Poor digestion. Loses weight. Vomiting at night.

Abdomen — Pain in stomach and abdomen; worse about ambilicus

(Cocc.; Nux m.; Plumb.); ineffectual urging. Itching at anus. Dragging in vaginal region, as if hernia would protrude. Swelling resembling umbilical hernia.

Chest — Oppressed, with sighing. Pain between shoulders; even clothing is oppressive.

Skin — Itching in palms. Sensation as if pimples would break out. Jaundiced complexion.

Extremities — Pain around shoulders, as if heavy load had been carried. Pain in all finger-joints. Tearing in knee-joint. Conclusive movements.

Relationship — Compare: Pelletierine (one of its constituents, anthelminitic, especially for tapeworm); Cina; Kousso.

Doses — First to third potency.

Illicium

(Anise)

Should be remembered in the treatment of flatulent conditions. So-called three-months' colic, especially if it recurs at regular hours; much rumbling in abdomen. One symptom is worthy of special remembrance — pain in region of third rib, about an inch or two from the sternum, generally on right side but occasionally on left side, too. Frequent cough with this pain. Purulent tracheal and gastric catarrh of old drunkards. Old asthmatics. Vomiting, epileptiform convulsions with biting of tongue.

Nose — Sharp stitches beneath lip. Acute catarrh. Burning and numbness of inner lower lip.

Respiratory — Dyspnoea. Pain near third intercostal cartilage. Cough, with pus-like phlegm. Palpitation, with aphthae. Haemoptysis.

Dose — Third potency.

Juniperus Communis

(Juniper Berries)

Catarrhal inflammation of kidneys. Dropsy, with suppression of urine. Old persons, with poor digestion and scanty secretion of urine. Chronic pyelitis.

Urinary — Strangury; bloody, scanty urine, violet odor (Tereb.). Weight in kidney region. Prostatic discharge. Renal hyperaemia. (Evcalyptol).

Respiratory — Cough with scanty, loaded urine.

Relationship — Compare: Sabina; *Juniperus virginianus* — Red Cedar — Violent tenesmus vesical. Persistent dragging in *back*; hyperaemia of the kidneys; pyelitis and cystia dropsy of the aged with suppressed urine. Dysuria burning cutting pain in urethra when urinating. Constant urging apoplexy, convulsions, strangury, uterine haemorrhage. Tom binthina.

Dose — Best form is the infusion. One ounce to a pint of boiling water. Dose, one-half to two ounces, or tincture, one to ten drops.

Mangifera Indica

(Mango Tree)

One of the best general remedies for passive haemorrhages, uterine, renal, gastric, pulmonary and intestinal. Rhinitis, sneezing, pharyngitis, and other acute throat troubles, suffocative sensation as if throat would close. Relaxation of mucous membrane of alimentary canal. Catarrhal and serous discharges, chronic intestinal irritation. Varicose veins. Drowsiness. Atonic conditions, poor circulation, relaxed muscles.

Skin — Itching of palms. Skin as if sunburnt, swollen white spots, intense itching. Lobes of ears and lips swollen.

Relationship — Compare: Erigeron; Epilobium.

Dose — Tincture.

Mentha Piperita

(Peppermint)

Stimulates the cold-perceiving nerves so just after taking it a current of air at the ordinary temperature seems cold. Marked action on respiratory organs and skin. Useful in gastrodynia flatulent cold.

Abdomen — Bloated, disturbing sleep. Infantile colic with great accumulation of gas.

Respiratory — Voice husky. Tip of nose sore to touch. Throat dry and sore, as if pin crosswise in it. Dry cough, worse from air into larynx, tobacco smoke, fog, talking; with irritation in suprasternal fossa (Rumex.) Trachea painful to touch.

Skin — Every scratch becomes a sore. Itching of arm and hand when writing. Vaginal pruritus. Herpes zoster. (Ars.; bulb.).

Relationship — Compare: Rumex; Laches.; Mentha pulegium — European pennyroyal — (pain in bones of forehead and extremities). Mentha viridis — Spearmint — (scanty urine with frequent desire).

Dose — Tincture, 1 to 20 drops, to thirtieth potency. Locally, in pruritus vaginae.

Menthol

The stearopten from the essential oil of Mentha. Mucous membrane of naso-pharynx and spinal nerve plexus, producing neuritic pains and parethesias. Menthol has proved curative in acute nasal catarrh; in acute eustachian catarrh; pharyngitis; laryngitis; neuralgias, etc. Itching, especially pruritus vulvae.

Head — Frontal headache, pain over frontal sinus, descends to eye-balls. Mental confusion. Supra orbital pain over left eye. Pain in face above zygoma with numbness. Pain in eye-balls. Coryza with post-nasal dripping. Cold sensation in hot. Eustachian tubes feel blocked and some deafness.

Respiratory — Tickling in the fauces. Stabbing pains in the precordia, radiating over entire chest. Short, dry cough, worse smoking. Asthmatic breathing, with congestive headache.

Extremities — Muscular pain in cervical region. Soreness of lumbar muscles.

Relationship — Compare: Kali bich.; Spigel.

Dose — Sixth potency. Externally for itching, use 1 per cent solution or ointment.

Nux Moschata

(Nutmeg)

Marked tendency to fainting fits, with heart failure. Cold extremities, extreme dryness of mucous membranes and skin. Strange feeling, with irresistible drowsiness. Indicanuria. General inclination to become unconscious during acute attacks. Lypothymia. (Ignatia.) Staggers on trying to walk.

Mind — Changeable; laughing and crying. Confused, impaired memory. Bewildered sense, as in a dream. Thinks she has two heads.

Head — Vertigo when walking in open air; aches from eating a little too much. Feeling of expansion, with sleepiness. Pulsating in head. Cracking sensation in head. Sensitive to the slightest touch in a draught of air. Bursting headache better hard pressure.

Eyes — Objects look larger, very distant or vanish. Moles before eyes. Mydriasis.

Nose — Oversensitive to smell; nosebleed, dark blood; dry, stopped up.

Mouth — Very dry. Tongue adheres to roof of mouth.

Origanum

(Sweet Marjoram)

Acts on nervous system generally, and is effective in masturbation and excessively aroused sexual impulses. Affections of the breasts. (Bufo) Desire for active exercise impelling her to run.

Female — Erotomania; powerful lascivious impulses, leucorrhoea, hysteria ideas and lascivious dreams.

Relationship — Compare: Ferula glauca (in violent sexual excitement in women; icy coldness in occiput); Plat.; Valer.; Canth; Hyos.

Dose — Third potency.

Petroselinum

(Parsley)

The urinary symptoms give the keynotes for this remedy. Piles with much itching.

Urinary — Burning, tingling, from perineum throughout whole urethra; sudden urging to urinate; frequent, voluptuous tickling in fossa navicularis. Gonorrhoea; sudden, irresistible desire to urinate; intense biting, itching, deep in urethra; milky discharge.

Stomach — Thirsty and hungry, but desire fails on beginning to eat or drink.

Relationship — Compare: Apiol — the active principle of Parsley — (in dysmenorrhoea); Canth; Sars.; Cannab.; Merc.

Dose — First to third potency.

Piper Nigrum

(Black Pepper)

Sensation of burning and pressure everywhere.

Mind — Sad, apprehensive. Unable to concentrate, starts at any noise.

Head — Severe headache, as if temples were pressed in; pressure in nasal and facial bones; eyes inflamed and burning. Red burning face. Bursting aching in eyeballs. Nose itches; sneezing; nosebleed. Lips dry and cracked.

Throat — Sore, feels raw, burns. Burning pain in tonsils.

Stomach — Gastric discomfort. Full feeling. Great thirst. Flatulence. Tympanites. Colic and cramps.

Chest — Dyspnoea, cough with pain in chest in spots, feels as if spitting blood. Palpitation, cardiac pain, slow intermittent pulse. Great flow of milk.

Urinary — Burning in bladder and urethra. Difficult micturition. Bladder feels full, swollen; frequent inclination without success. Priapism.

Dose — Low attenuations.

Salvia Officinalis

(Sage)

Controls excessive sweating when circulation is enfeebled; of less use in phthisis with night-sweats and suffocating tickling cough. Galactorrhoea. Exerts a tonic influence on the skin.

Respiratory — Tickling cough, especially in consumption.

Skin — Soft, relaxed, with enfeebled circulation and cold extremities. Colliquative perspiration.

Relationship — Compare: *Chrysanthemum leucanthemum* — Os-eye Daisy. Has specific action on sudoriparous glands. Quiets nervous system like Cypripedium. Right sided tearing pain in bones of jaw and temple. Pain in teeth and gums, worse touch, better warmth. Irritable and tearful. Here use 12x. Insomnia and night-sweats. For colliquative sweating and hyperaesthesia of nervous system. Material doses of tincture Phelland; tuberc.; Salvia sclerata (tonic influence on nervous system; dose, teaspoonful to one pint hot water, as inhaled for sponging. Rubia tinctorum — Madder — A remedy for the spleen. (Ceanothus.) Chlorosis and amenorrhoea; tuberculosis. Anaemia; undernourished conditions; splenic anaemia. Dose 10 drops of tincture.

Dose — Tincture, in twenty-drop doses, in a little water. The effects manifest themselves quickly two hours after taking a dose and they persist for two to six days.

Sinapis Nigra — Brassica Nigra

(Black Mustard)

It is used in hay-fever, coryza, and pharyngitis. Dry nares and pharynx, with thick, lumpy secretion. Small-pox.

Head — Scalp hot and itches. Sweat on upper lip and forehead. Tongue feels blistered.

Nose — Mucous from posterior nares, feels cold. Scanty, acrid discharge. Stoppage of left nostril all day, or in afternoon and evening. Dry, hot, with lachrymation, sneezing; hacking cough; better lying down. Nostrils alternately stopped. Dryness of anterior nares.

Respiratory — Cough is relieved by lying down.

Throat — Feels scalded, hot, inflamed. Asthmatic breathing. Loud coughing-spells with barking expiration.

Stomach — Offensive breath, smelling like onions. (Asaf.; Armorac.) Burning in stomach, extending up oesophagus, throat, and mouth, which is full of canker sores. Hot sour eructations. Colic; pains come on while bent forward; better sitting up straight. Sweating gets better when nausea comes on.

Urinary — Pain in bladder, frequent copious flow day and night.

Back — Rheumatic pain in intercostal and lumbar muscles; sleeplessness from pain in back and hips.

Relationship — Compare: Sulph.; Capsic.; Colocy.; Sinapis alba — White Mustard — (Throat symptoms marked, especially pressure and burning, with obstruction in oesophagus; sensation of a lump in oesophagus behind the Manubrium Sterni and with much eructation; similar symptoms in rectum). Mustard oil by inhalation (acts on the sensory nerve endings of the trigeminal. Relieves pain in middle ear disease and in painful conditions of nose, nasal cavities, and tonsils.).

Dose — Third potency.

Thymus Serpyllum

(Wild Thyme)

Respiratory infections of children; dry nervous asthma, whooping-cough, severe spasms but little sputum.

Ringing in ears with feeling of pressure in head. Burning in pharynx, sore throat worse empty swallowing; blood vessels distended, dark.

Dose — Tincture.

Thymol

(Thyme Camphor)

A remedy having a wide field in genito-urinary diseases. It is indicated in pathological emissions, priapism and prostatorrhoea. The provings show an action limited to the sexual organs, producing a typical sexual neurasthenia. Specific for hook-worm disease. (Chenopodium).

Mental — Irritable, arbitrary, must have his own way. Craves company. Energy gone.

Back — Tired, aching throughout lumbar region. Worse mental and physical labor.

Male — Profuse, nightly seminal emissions with lascivious dreams of a perverted character. Priapism. Urinary burning and subsequent dribbling of urine. Polyuria. Urates increased. Phosphates decreased.

Sleep — Awakes tired and unrefreshed. Lascivious and fantastic dreams.

Relationship — Compare: Carbon Tetrachloride as a remedy for Hookworms, according to Dr. Lambert, Suva, Fiji, who employed it in 50,000 cases.

"1. Carbon tetrachloride is a vermifuge and vermicide of great potency, and has shown itself to be the best vermifuge for the treatment of hookworm in a country where the disease predominates.

"2. It gives little discomfort to the patient, is palatable, required no preparation of the patient, and when pure is apparently not toxic — all of which features are of advantage in a popular campaign.

"W.G. Smillie, and S.B. Pessoa, of Sao Paulo, Brazil too have found carbon tetrachloride to be extremely efficient in removing hookworms. A single dose of 3 ml. given to adults has been proved to remove 95 per cent of all the hookworms harbored."

Modalities — Thymol. Worse, mental and physical labor.

Dose — Sixth attenuation.

Zingiber

(Ginger)

States of debility in the digestive tract, and sexual system and respiratory troubles, call for this remedy. Complete cessation of function of kidneys.

Head — Hemicrania; sudden glimmering before eyes; feels confused and empty. Pain over eyebrows.

Nose — Feels obstructed and dry. Intolerable itching; red pimples.

Stomach — Taste of food remains long, especially of bread and toast. Feels heavy, like from a stone. Complaints from eating melons and drinking impure water. Acidity. (Calc.; Robinia.) Heaviness in stomach on awakening with wind and rumbling, great thirst and emptiness. Pain from pit to under sternum, worse after eating.

Abdomen — Colic, diarrhoea, extremely loose bowels. Diarrhoea from drinking bad water, with much flatulence, cutting pain, relaxation of sphincter. Hot, sore, painful anus during pregnancy. Chronic intestinal catarrh. Anus red and inflamed. Haemorrhoids hot, painful, sore. (Aloe.).

Urinary — Frequent desire to urinate. Stinging, burning in orifice. Yellow discharge from urethra. Urine thick, turbid, of strong odor, suppressed. Complete suppression after typhoid. After urinating, continues to ooze in drops.

Male — Itching of prepuce. Sexual desire excited; painful erections. Emissions.

Respiratory — Hoarseness. Smarting below larynx; breathing difficult. Asthma, without anxiety, worse in the morning. Scratching sensation in throat; stitches in chest. Cough dry, hacking copious morning sputa.

Extremities — Very weak in all joints. Back lame. Cramps in soles and palms.

Relationship — Compare: Calad.

Antidote: Nux.

Dose — First to sixth potency.

Source of the aforesaid role of spices and condiments in the Homoeopathic system is "Pocket Manual of Homoeopathic Materia Medica by William Boericke, Ninth Edition, published by Indian Books & Periodical Syndicates, New Delhi: 5.

Homoeopathic Tincture Analysis

Asafoetida

Part used : Gum resin

Preparation

(a) Mother tincture ϕ(phi) Drug strength 1/1

i) Asafoetida in coarse powder 100 gms

ii) Strong alcohol in sufficient quantity

To make 1000 ml of the mother tincture

b) Potencies:- 2x and higher with *dispensing alcohol*

History and Authority:

Allen's Encyclop. Materia Medica vol. I, 560.

	Specifications	(Mother Tincture)
i)	Alcohol content	87.8 to 91.0% v/v
ii)	pH	Between 5.00 to 6.00
iii)	Sp. gravity @ 25°C.	From 0.828 to 0.870
iv)	Total Solids	Not less than 0.30% by w/v
v)	λ Max.	324 nm

Identification

TLC of mother tincture using n-hexane: CH_3OH::98:2 (v/v) as mobile phase. The chromatogram when sprayed with iodine vapours, six spots appear at Rf. 0.06, 0.09, 0.15, 0.28, 0.36 and 0.98.

Black Pepper

Part used:- Dry Unripe Fruit

Preparation

(a) Mother tincture ϕ(phi) Drug Strength 1/10

i) Piper nigrum, in coarse powder 100 gms

ii) Strong alcohol, in sufficient quantity

To make 1000 ml of the mother tincture

b) Potencies: 2x and higher with *dispensing alcohol*

History and Authority:

Proved by Houat, *Hahn. Month* 11, 369, 1867 and Berridge, Month. Hom. Rev., 1870, 14, 108; Allen's Encyclop. Materia Medica, Vol. VII, 552; Clarke: A *Dictionary of Practical Materia Medica Vol. III, 833.*

Specifications		(Mother tincture)
i)	Alcohol content	91.0 to 95.0 % v/v
ii)	pH	Between 5.50 to 6.50
iii)	Sp. gravity at 25°C	From 0.810 to 0.830
iv)	Total Solids	Not less than 1.10% w/v
v)	λ max.	260, 305 and 340 nm

Identification

TLC of the concentrated mother liquor is carried out using $CHCl_3$: CH_3OH::9:1 (v/v) as mobile phase. In ultra violet light six spots appear at Rf. 0.08 (red), 0.28 (red), 0.76 (blue), 0.85 (blue), 0.88 (yellow) and 0.95 (blue); with Dragendorff's reagent one spot appears at Rf. 0.88 (orange)

Celery

Part used - Fruit

Preparation

(a) Mother tincture ϕ(phi)Drug strength 1/10

i) *Apium graveolens* in coarse powder 100 gm

ii) Strong alcohol in sufficient quantity

To make 1000 ml of the mother tincture

b) Potencies : 2x and higher with *dispensing alcohol*

History and Authority:

Proved by Beckwich, Allen's Encyclop. Materia Medica, Vol. I, 422; A *Dictionary* of *Practical Materia Medica*, Clarke, Vol. I, 145.

Specifications		(Mother Tincture)
i)	Alcohol content	91.0 to 95.0% v/v
ii)	pH	Between 5.50 to 6.50
iii)	Sp. gravity at 25°C	From 0.800 to 0.830
iv)	λ Max.	288, 318 nm

Identification

20 ml of mother tincture is evaporated on water bath and alcohol removed. The aqueous layer is extracted with 3x20 ml $CHCl_3$. Extract is concentrated to 2 ml and its TLC is carried out on silica gel G plate using

$CHCl_3$:CH_3OH::9:1 v/v as mobile phase. With antimony trichloride ($SbCl_3$) as spray reagent two spots appear at Rf. 0.28 (brown) and 0.72 (pink).

Chilli

Part used : Ripe Fruit

Preparation

(a) Mother tincture ϕ(phi) Drug strength 1/10

i) *Capsicum annum moist magma* containing solids 100 gms + plant moisture 50 ml.

ii) Strong alcohol 958 ml.

To make 1000 ml of the mother tincture.

b) Potencies: 2x and higher with *dispensing alcohol*

History and Authority:

Introduced by Hahnemann in 1805; Allen's Encyclop. Materia Medica Vol. II, 540 x, 432; Herings: Guiding symptoms, Vol. III, 321.

	Specifications	*(Mother Tincture)*
i)	Alcohol content	87.5 to 91.5% v/v
ii)	pH	Between 4.70 to 5.70
iii)	Sp. gravity at 25°C	From 0.850 to 0.880
iv)	Total solids	Not less than 1.10% w/v
v)	λ Max.	272 nm

Identification

TLC of mother tincture using CCl_4:CH_3OH::9:1 (v/v) as mobile phase. The chromatogram when sprayed with iodine vapours, four spots appear at Rf. 0.11, 0.24, 0.58 and 0.83 (corresponding with standard capsicum).

Garlic

Part used: The Mother Bulb

Preparation:

(a) Mother tincture ϕ(phi) Drug strength 1/10

i) *Allium sativum moist magma* containing solids 100 gms + plant moisture 300 ml.

ii) Strong alcohol 730 ml.

To make 1000 ml of the mother tincture

b) Potencies: 2x to contain 1 part tincture, 2 parts purified water and 7 parts strong alcohol.

3x and higher with *dispensing alcohol*

Old Method

Class III, p. 248

History and Authority

Allen's Encyclop. Materia Medica Vol. I, 160.

	Specifications	*(Mother tincture)*
i)	Alcohol content	66.0% to 70.0% v/v
ii)	pH	Between 6.00 to 6.70
iii)	Sp. gravity at 25°C	From 0.850 to 0.898
iv)	Total Solids	Not less than 0.80% w/v
v)	λ Max.	260 nm

Identification

i) Colour Test: To 1 ml of mother tincture is added a few drops of $AgNO_3$ solution, a black precipitate, insol. in dil. HNO_3 is formed.

ii) Solvent system of CCl_4: CH_3OH:H_2O::60:30:3 (v/v) is shaken in a separating funnel. The lower layer of CCl_4 gives one black spot with vanillin-H_2SO_4 reagent. Chromatogram heated to 105°C for 15 minutes, at Rf. 0.22. The plate develops from upper layer gives one yellow spot at Rf. 0.74 on spraying with ammonical $AgNO_3$ solution, chromatogram heated to 105°C for 15 minutes.

Ginger

Part used : Dried rhizome

Preparation

(a) Mother tincture ϕ(phi) Drug strength 1/10

i) *Zingiber officinale moist magma* containing solids 100 gms + moisture approx. 12.5 gms.

ii) Strong alcohol in sufficient quantity

To make 1000 ml of the mother tincture

b) Potencies: 2x and higher with *dispensing alcohol*

History and Authority:

Proved by Franz, stapf. and Bute. Allen's Encyclop. Materia Medica, Vol. X, 225; Hering's Guiding symptoms Vol.X. 562; Clarke' A Dictionary of Practical Materia Medica, Vol. III, 1608.

	Specifications	*(Mother Tincture)*
i)	Alcohol content	89.0 to 93.0% v/v
ii)	pH	Between 5.80 to 6.80
iii)	Sp. gravity @ 25°C	From 0.800 to 0.830
iv)	Total solids	Not less than 0.50% w/v
v)	λ Max.	272 nm

Identification

20 ml of mother tincture is evaporated on a water bath to remove alcohol. The aqueous residue is extracted with 3x20 ml of $CHCl_3$. The $CHCl_3$ layer is concentrated to 2 ml. TLC is carried out on silica gel 'G' plate using $CHCl_3$:CH_3OH::9:1 (v/v) as mobile phase and $SbCl_3$ as spray reagent. Four spots appear at Rf. 0.32 (violet), 0.65 (violet), 0.72 (brown) and 0.84 (brown)

Juniper

Part used: Ripe Berries

Preparation

(a) Mother tincture φ (phi) Drug strength 1/10

i) *Juniperus communis, moist magma* containing solids 100 gms and moisture nearly 150 ml.

ii) Strong alcohol 867 ml

To make 1000 ml of the mother tincture

(b) Potencies: 2x and higher with *dispensing alcohol.*

History and Authority:

Materia Medica with Repertory, Boericke, 360. American Homoeopathic Pharmacopoeia, 265.

	Specifications	*(Mother Tincture)*
i)	Alcohol content	79.0 to 83.0% v/v
ii)	pH	between 5.50 to 6.50
iii)	Sp. gravity at 25°C	0.850 to 0.870
iv)	Total solids	Not less than 2.0% w/v
v)	λ Max.	276, 338 nm

Identification

20 ml of mother tincture is evaporated on water bath to remove alcohol. The aqueous layer is extracted with 3x20 ml of $CHCl_3$. The extract is concentrated to 2 ml. TLC of this concentrated extract is carried out on silica gel G plate using $CHCl_3$:CH_3OH::9:1 (v/v) as mobile phase. The plate when kept in iodine chamber, 4 spots appear at Rf. 0.46, 0.58, 0.88 amd 0.93.

Onion

Part used: The Red Mature Bulb

Preparation

(a) Mother tincture ϕ (phi) Drug strength 1/10

i) *Allium cepa moist magma* containing solids 100 gms + plant moisture 567 ml.

ii) Strong alcohol 468 ml

To make 1000 ml of the mother tincture

(b) Potencies : 2x to contain 1 part tincture, 4 parts purified water and 5 parts strong alcohol

3x and higher potencies with *dispensing alcohol.*

Old Method

Class III, p. 248.

History and Authority

Hering Guild. Symp. 3; Allen's Encyclop. Materia Medica Vol. I, 146.

	Specifications	(Mother tincture)
i)	Alcohol content	41.0 to 45.0% v/v
ii)	pH	Between 5.00 to 6.00
iii)	Sp. gravity at 25°C	From 0.960 to 0.975
iv)	Total solids	Not less than 2% w/v
v)	λ Max.	255 nm

Identification

i) Colour tests: To 1 ml mother tincture are added a few drops of $AgNO_3$ solution, a black ppt. insoluable in dilute HNO_3 is formed.

ii) TLC of mother tincture is done using CCl_4: CH_3OH:H_2O::60:30:3 v/v (upper layer) as mobile phase and ammonical $AgNO_3$ as spray reagent. One brown coloured spot appears at Rf. 0.34.

Nutmeg

Part used: The Seeds

Preparation

a) Mother tincture ϕ (phi) Drug strength 1/10

i) *Myristica fragrans* in coarse powder 100 gms

ii) Strong alcohol in sufficient quantity

To make 1000 ml of the tincture

b) Potencies: 2x and higher with *dispensing alcohol.*

Old Method

Class IV, page 248

History and Authority

Introduced into Homoeopathic practice by Dr. Helbig in 1883. Allen's Encyclop. Materia Medica vol. VII, 61.

	Specifications	Mother tincture
i)	Alcohol content	87.0 to 91.0% v/v
ii)	pH	Between 4.80 to 5.20
iii)	Sp. gravity at 25°C	From 0.810 to 0.830
iv)	Total solids	Not less than 10% w/v
v)	λ Max.	274 nm

Identification

TLC of $CHCl_3$ extract is carried out using $CHCl_3$:CH_3OH::9:1 (v/v) as mobile phase. Under ultraviolet light four spots appear at Rf. 0.31, 0.64, 0.70 (all blue) and 0.96 (yellow).

Peppermint

Part used: Whole plant, excluding roots.

Preparation

(a) Mother tincture ϕ (phi) Drug strength 1/10

i) Mentha piperita moist magma containing solids 100 gm + moisture 400 ml. 500 gms

ii) Strong alcohol 632 ml

To make 1000 ml of the mother tincture

b) Potencies: 2x to contain one part mother tincture, three parts purified water and six parts strong alcohol. 3x and higher with *dispensing alcohol.*

History and Authority:

Proved and introduced into Homoeopathic Materia Medica by Demeures, J.d.1. Sec. Gal IV, 115. Allen's Encyclop. Materia Medica, Vol. VI, 180, X, 578.

	Specifications	*Mother tincture*
i)	Alcohol content	56 to 61.0 % v/v
ii)	pH	Between 5.70 to 6.70
iii)	Sp. gravity at 25°C	From 0.890 to 0.925
iv)	Total solids	Not less than 1.00% w/v
v)	λ Max	284, 324 nm

Identification

20 ml of mother tincture is evaporated to remove alcohol. The solute is extracted with 3x20 ml of $CHCl_3$. The $CHCl_3$ extract is concentrated and TLC carried on silica gel 'G' plate using $CHCl_3$:CH_3OH::9:1 (v/v) as a mobile phase. With $SbCl_3$ reagent five spots appear at Rf. O. (violet), 0.36 (violet), 0.51 (black) 0.62 (violet) and 0.98 (violet green) (Corresponds to menthol).

Sacred Basil

Part used: Whole plant excluding roots

Preparation

(a) Mother tincture ϕ (phi) Drug strength 1/10

i) *Ocimum sanctum, Moist magma* containing solids 100 gm + plant moisture 233 ml.

ii) Strong alcohol in sufficient quantity

To make 1000 ml of the mother tincture

b) Potencies: 2x and higher with *dispensing alcohol.*

History and Authority

Mentioned in "Drugs of Hindoosthan" by Dr. Ghose.

	Specifications	*Mother tincture*
i)	Alcohol content	72.0 to 76.0 % v/v
ii)	pH	between 5.20 to 5.80
iii)	sp. gravity at 25°C	From 0.830 to 0.860
iv)	Total solids	Not less than 0.50 % w/v
v)	λ Max.	255, 275 and 315 nm

Identification

TLC of the chloroform extract is carried out using $CHCl_3$:CH_3OH::95:5 (v/v) as mobile phase. Under ultraviolet light six spots appear at Rf. 0.43 (red), 0.66 (red), 0.75 (red), 0.78 (blue), 0.90 (blue) and 0.95 (red).

Black Mustard

Part used: Seeds

Preparation

a) Mother tincture ϕ (phi) Drug strength 1/10

i) Sinapis nigra in coarse powder 100 gms

ii) Strong alcohol in sufficient quantity

To make 1000 ml of the mother tincture

b) Potencies: 2x and higher with *dispensing alcohol*

History & Authority

Proved and introduced by Catell and Butler, Allen's; *Encyclop. Materia Medica.* Vol. IX, 46;

Hering:- Guiding Symptoms, Vol. IX, 426.

Cinnamon

Part used: Inner bark

Preparation

a) Mother tincture ϕ (phi) Drug strength 1/10

i) Cinnamon in coare powder 100 gms

ii) Strong alcohol in sufficient quantity

To make 1000 ml of the mother tincture

b) Potencies: 2x and higher with *dispensing alcohol.*

History and Authority

Allen's Encyclop. Materia Medica, Vol. III, 333; X, 470, 654; Hering's Guiding Symptom Vol. IV, 214.

Parsley

Part used: Whole Plant

Preparation

(a) Mother tincture ϕ (phi) Drug strength 1/10

i) *Petroselinum sativum moist magma* containing solid 100 gm + moisture 450 ml.

ii) Strong alcohol 586 ml.

To make 1000 ml of the mother tincture

b) Potencies: 2x to contain 1 part mother tincture, 4 parts purified water, 5 parts strong alcohol; 3x and higher with *dispensing alcohol.*

History and Authority

Proved and introduced by Bethman. Archiv. XVIII, 3, 34, (1841); Allen's Encyclop. Materia Medica Vol. II, 333; Hering's Guiding Symptoms Vol. VIII, 295.

Star-Anise

Part used: Seeds

Preparation

(a) Mother tincture ϕ (phi) Drug strength 1/10

i) Illicium anisatum in coarse powder 100 gms

ii) Strong Alcohol in sufficient quantity

To make 1000 ml. of the mother tincture

b) Potencies: 2x and higher with *dispensing alcohol.*

History & Authority

Introduced and proved by Franz in 1838, Archiv, XVII 3; 175, Allen's Encyclop. Materia Medica Vol. V, 91; Clarke: A Dictionary of Practical Materia Medica Vol. II, 16.

Turmeric

Part used: Rhizome

Preparation

(a) Mother tincture ϕ (phi) Drug strength 1/10

i) Curcuma longa moist magma containing

solids 100 gms + plant moisture 250 ml.

ii) Purified water 150 ml

iii) Strong alcohol 635 ml

To make 1000 ml of the mother tincture

b) Potencies: 2x to contain 1 part of mother tincture, 3 parts of purified water and 6 parts of strong alcohol. 3x and higher with *dispensing alcohol.*

History and Authority

Introduced and proved by Arya, Bala Chandran and Augustine, Hahnemannian Gleanings, XLIV No. 7, 1977, 320-30.

White Mustard

Part used: Ripe seeds

Preparation

(a) Mother Tincture ϕ (phi) Drug Strength 1/10

i) Sinapis alba, bruised 100 gms

ii) Strong alcohol in sufficient quantity

To make 1000 ml of the mother tincture.

b) Potencies: 2x and higher with dispensing alcohol.

History and Authority

Proved and introduced by Bojanus; Allen's Encyclop. Materia Medica, Vol. IX, 40; Clarke: A Dictionary of Practical Materia Medica, Vol. III, 1192; Herring: Guiding symptoms, IX, 429.

6

Nutritive Value of Spices and Condiments

SINCE spices, condiments and herbs are consumed in very small quantities every day, their contribution by way of the macro elements of nutrition, namely carbohydrates, proteins and fats, cannot obviously be of any significance. Occasionally, however, an exceptionally high level of a mineral, or even more so of a vitamin, which are two micronutrient groups could have some meaning in nutrition. This is especially true where the material is one which is used in fair amount in cooking.

Thus, use of these materials in every day cooking in reasonable amounts cannot but contribute cumulatively towards the needs of vitamins and minerals of the human body.

NUTRITIVE VALUE OF SPICES AND CONDIMENTS

Name of Spice/ Condiment	Moisture %	Calories %	Protein %	Fat %	Carbo-Hydrate %	Calcium %	Phosphorus %	Iron ppm	Sodium %	Potassium %	Copper ppm	Magnesium ppm	Vit.A I.U./ 100 gm	Thiamine ppm	Niacin ppm	Riboflavin ppm	Ascorbic Acid (Vit.C) ppm	Vit. D I.U./ 100 gm	Remarks
1	2	3	4	5	6	7	8	9	10	11	12	13	14	15	16	17	18	19	20
1. All Spice	8.8	380	6	6.6	52.2	0.8	0.1	75	0.01	1.1			1445	1	29	0.6	392		
2.. Amchur	90	39	0.7	0.1	8.8	0.01	0.08	45					150		300		80		
3. Anardana	78		1.6	0.1	14.5	0.01	0.07	3	0.009	0.133	200	0.012	NIL	0.06	3	1	140		
4. Aniseed	9-13		18	8-23	8.5														
5. Basil	6.1	325	11.9	3.6	20.5	2.1	0.47	400	0.04	3.7			290	1.5	69	3.2	613		
6. Bay/Laurel Leaves	4.5	410	7.6	8.8	50.2	1	0.11	5300	0.02	0.6			545	1	20	4.2	466		
7. Red Chilli	10	246	15.9	6.2	31.6	0.16	0.37	23000					576				500		
8. Paprika	7.9	390	13.8	10.4	41.1	0.2	0.3	2300	0.02	2.4			4915	6	153	13.6	588		
9. Caraway Seeds	4.5	465	7.6	8.8	50.2	1	0.11	90	0.02	1.9			580	380	8100	380	1200		

Contd...

...Contd

1	2	3	4	5	6	7	8	9	10	11	12	13	14	15	16	17	18	19	20
10. Cardamom (Large)	8.49		6	2.31															
11. Cardamom Seeds (Small)	8.3	263	10.3	2.9	45.4	0.3	0.21	120	0.01	1.2			175	1.8	23	2.3	120		
12. Cassia	6.5-11.9		3.1-3.4	0-2.1	6.9-32														
13. Celery seed	5.1	450	18.1	22.8	40.9	1.8	0.55	4500	0.17	1.4			650	4.1	4.4	4.9	172		
14. Celeriac Leaves	81.3		6	0.6	8.6	0.23	0.04	63					5800-7500				620		
15. Celriac Stalk	93.5		0.8	0.1	3.5	0.03	0.04	48					Nil				60		
16. Cinnamon	9.9	355	4.6	2.2	59.5	1.6	0.05	40	0.01	0.4			175	1.4	19	2.1	398		
17. Clove	5.4	430	6.3	15.5	57.5	0.07	0.11	100	0.25	1.2			175	1.1	15	0.4	809		
18. Coriander seeds	6.3		1.3	19.6	24.0	0.08	0.44	60	0.02	1.2			175	2.6	32	2.3	120		
19. Coriander Leaves	87.9		3.3	0.6	6.5	0.14	0.06	100					10460		8	600	1350		
20. Cumin Seeds	6.2	460	17.7	23.8	35.5	0.9	0.45	4800	0.16	2.1			175	7.3	25	3.8	172		
21. Curry Leaves	66.3		6.1	1	16	0.81	0.6	31000					12600	Nil		Nil	40		

Contd...

...*Contd*

1	2	3	4	5	6	7	8	9	10	11	12	13	14	15	16	17	18	19	20
22. Fennel Seeds	6.3	370	9.5	10	42.3	1.3	0.48	100	0.09	1.7			1040	94	60	3.6	120		
23. Fenugreek seeds	6.3		9.5	10	42.3	1.3	0.48	110	0.09	1.7			1040	4.1	60	3.6	120		
24. Garlic Powder	5.2	380	17.5	0.6	71.4	0.1	0.42	40	0.01	1:1			175	6.8	7	0.8	120		
25. Ginger	6.9	380	8.6	6.4	66.5	0.1	0.15	110	0.33	1.4			175	6.8	0.5	19	120		
26. Horse Radish	73.4		3.2	0.2	21.4												302		
27. Leek	78.9	77	1.8	0.1	17.2	0.05	0.07	23					30	2.3			110		
28. Mace	15.9		6.5	24.4	47.8	0.18	0.1	126					175	3.7	12	5.6	120		
29. Marjoram	7		14.31	5.6		21.2	9.1	67000	0.65			57500							
30. Mint	84.9	48	4.8	0.6	5.8	0.2	0.062	15.6						5	10	2.6	270		
31. Mustard Seeds	8.5	541	20	39.7	23.8	0.49	0.7	79			8.3	25.6		6.5	40	2.6			
32. Nutmeg	14.3		7.5	36.4	28.5	0.12	0.24	46			7.1	17.8		3.3	14				
33 Onion	4.6	370	10.6	0.8	74.1	0..3	0.29	20	0.04	1	1.8	1.8	175	4.2		0.6	147		

Contd...

...Contd

1	2	3	4	5	6	7	8	9	10	11	12	13	14	15	16	17	18	19	20
34. Origanum	8	360	11.7	6.4	53.9	1.7	0.2	500	0.02	1.7			1010	3.4	62	4.1	120		
35. Parsley	68.4		5.9	1	19.7	0.39	0.2	179					3200	0.4		Trace	2810		
36. Pepper (Black)	18.2	304	11.5	6.8	49.2	0.46	0.2	124			14.2	41.4		0.9	14	1.4			
37 Pepper Seeds	4.3	408	21.7	19.3	36.8	1.58	0.43	159			6.3	43.1		9.5		9.7			
38. Rosemary	5.7	440	4.5	17.4	47.4	1.5	0.7	300	0.04	1			175	5.1	10	0.4	613		
39. Salforn	15.6			5.63	13.35														
40. Sage	5.7	415	10.2	14.1	46.3	1.8	0.09	300	0.01	1			2395	7.5	57	3.4	398		
41. Savory	9.1	355	7.1	5.2	54.6	2.2	0.14	400	0.02	1.1			865	3.7	41	0.4	120		
42. Spearmint	83		4.8	0.6	8	0.2	0.08	156			1.8		2700	50	80				
43. Tamarmid Pulp	18.2	283	2.8		38.2	0.17	0.11	110					100		20				
44. Tarragon	4.7	365	24.2	7.3	44.7	1.3	0.31	340	0.07	3.2			175	20	89.4	13.4	120		
45. Thyme	7.1	340	6.8	4.6	44	2.1	0.2	140	0.08	0.9	2.5		175	510	49	4			

Contd...

...*Contd*

1	2	3	4	5	6	7	8	9	10	11	12	13	14	15	16	17	18	19	20
46. Turmeric	5.8	390	8.6	8.9	63	0.2	0.26	500	0.01	2.5			175	0.9	48	1.9	498		
47 Vanilla Beans	28.6		3.7	5.7	8.1	19.7	9.5	3000	6.7	16.2									
Adult Daily Requr.						0.5	0.5	240						1400	19000	1700	40000		

7

Refrigeration of Spices

PRESERVATION of fresh fruits and vegetables in cold storage is a must and is a routine practice in the advanced countries. It is catching up well in developing countries also. The Cold Storage Order, (1980) being enforced by the Directorate of Marketing and Inspection, Government of India, is overseeing the functioning of cold storages for preservation of farm and animal produce since early seventies, yet the department has not specified storage temperatures and humidity percentages for storage of spices and condiments, the produce of our immediate interest.

Spices and condiments are usually stored in serviceable jute bags at temperatures between 45 and 50°F and at a relative humidity of 80%. This is empirical and no scientific data is available in India for enforcement. Under the circumstances we can take a cue from ASHRAF Hand Book 1982 — Applications; issued by the American Society of Heating, Refrigerating And Airconditioning Engineers, Inc, 1791, Tullie Circle, NE, Atlanta, GA. 30329. Various data worked out by the aforesaid society are tabulated here and table number (in brackets) refer to the above text.

Table I: (41.2)

Approximate Heat Evolution Rates (Btu/Ton/hour) at Different Temperatures (English Values)

Commodity	*32°F*	*40°F*	*50°F*	*60°F*
Celery	1600	2400	4300	8100 to 6000
Garlic	700 to 2400	1300 to 2200	2000 to 2200	2400 to 6000
Horseradish	1800	2400	5800	7200
Onions	500	700 to 700	1600 to 1500	2400
Peppers, sweet	NA	NA	3200	5000

Table 2 (41.4)

Storage Requirements and Properties (English Values)

Commodity	*Storage Temper-ature F°*	*Approximate Storage life (days)*	*Water Content %*	*Highest Freezing Tempa-rature F°*	*Specific Heat above Freezing Tempa-rature Btu/lb F°*	*Specific Heat below Freezing Tempa-rature Btu/lb F°*	*Latent Heat Btu/lb*	*Relative Humidity %*
Garlic Dry	32	180–210	61	30.6	0.69	0.40	89	65 to 70
Horseradish	30 to 32	300–360	75	28.7	0.78	0.42	104	95 to 100
Onions Dry & SETS	32	30–240	88	30.6	0.90	0.46	126	65 to 75
Parsley	32	30–60	85	30.0	0.88	0.45	122	95
Peppers Dried	32 to 50	180	12	NA	0.30	0.24	17	60-70
Peppers Sweet	45 to 50	14 to 21	92	30.7	0.94	0.47	132	90-95

Table 2a (41.8)

Storage Requirements and Properties (Metric Values)

Commodity	*Storage Temper-ature C°*	*Relative Humidity %*	*Water Content %*	*Highest Freezing Tempa-rature C°*	*Specific Heat above Freezing Tempa-rature J/Kg° C*	*Specific Heat below Freezing Tempa-rature J/Kg° C*	*Latent Heat J/Kg*	*Approximate Storage life (days)*
Celeriac	0	95 to 100	88	-0.9	3.785	1.943	293.52	90 to 120
Celery	0	95	94	-0.5	3.986	2.018	313.54	30 to 60
Garlic Dry	0	65 to 70	61	-0.8	2.880	1.604	203.46	180 to 210
Horseradish	-1 to 0	95 to 100	75	-1.8	3.349	1.779	250.16	300 to 360
Onions Dry & Onions Sets	0	65 to 75	88	-0.8	3.785	1.943	293.52	30 to 240
Parsley	0	95	85	-1.1	3.684	1.905	283.52	30 to 60
Peppers Dried	0 to 10	60 to 70	12	N.A.	1.239	0.998	N.A.	180
Peppersweet	7 to 10	90 to 95	92	-0.7	3.919	1.993	306.87	14 to 21

Celery (0°C and rh 95%)

Celery is a relatively perishable commodity, and for storage of one to two months, it is essential that a commodity temperature of 0°C be maintained. The rh should be high enough to prevent wilting (90 to 95%). Considerable heat is given off because of respiration, and for this reason the stacks of crates should be separated and dunnage be used to allow cold air circulation under and over the crates and between the bottom crates and the floor. Forced air circulation should be provided; otherwise there may be a 1.7 to 2.2°C temperature differential between the top and the bottom of the room.

Celery can be precooled by forced air cooling, by hydro-cooling, or by vacuum cooling. Hydro-cooling is the most common precooling method; temperatures should be brought to as near 0oC as possible. In practice, temperature reduction is often only 4 to 7oC. Vacuum cooling is widely used for celery packed in corrugated cartons for long distance shipment. (Para 33.10)

Garlic, Dry (0°C and 65 to 70% rh)

Garlic should be kept at 0°C for six to seven months, if it is in good condition and is well cured when stored. Garlic cloves sprout most rapidly at 4°C; therefore, prolonged storage at this temperature should be avoided. In California it is frequently put in common storage, where it can be held for three to four months or sometimes longer if the building can be kept cool, dry, and well ventilated. (Para 33.11)

Onions (0°C and 65 to 70% rh)

A comparatively low rh is essential for successful storage of dry onions. However, humidities as high as 85% and forced air circulation have given satisfactory results. At higher humidities, at which most of the other vegetables keep best, onions are disposed to root growth and decay; at too high a temperature, sprouting is encouraged. Storage at 0°C with 65 to 70% rh is recommended to keep them dormant.

Onions should be adequately cured either in the field in open sheds, or by artificial means before they are stored. The most common method of curing in northern areas is by forced ventilation during storage. Onions are considered cured until they rustle. If not cured, onions are likely to decay in storage.

Onions are stored in 22.7 kg bags, in crates, in pallet boxes that hold loose onions, or in bulk bins. Bags of onions are frequently stored in pallets. Bagged onions should be stacked to allow proper air circulation.

Modern air-cooled storages have forced ventilation systems. Air is introduced through floor racks beneath the bins of onions. The air can be heated if necessary. Onions in bins are stored about 3.1 m deep. Soft onions at the bottom of the bin may be distorted when they are stored in this manner. Onions should not be stored with other products that tend to absorb odors.

When onions are removed from storage in warm weather, they are apt to sweat because of moisture condensation. This may favor decay. By warming onions gradually, this difficulty can be avoided.

In the northern onion growing states, onions of the globe type are generally held in common storage because average winter temperatures are sufficiently low to permit common storage. They should not be held after early March unless they have been treated with maleic hydrazide in the field to reduce sprout growth.

Refrigerated storage is often used to hold onions for marketing late in the spring. Onions to be held in cold storage should be placed there immediately after curing. A temperature of 0°C will keep onions dormant and reasonably free from decay, provided the onions are sound and well cured when stored. Sprout growth indicates to a high storage temperature, poorly cured bulbs, or immature bulbs. Root growth indicates that relative humidity is too high.

Globe onions can be held for six to eight months at 0°C. Mild or Bermuds types can usually be held at 0°C for only one to two months. Onions of the Spanish type are often stored; if well matured, they can be held at 0°C, at least until January or February. In California, onions of the sweet Spanish type are held at 0°C until April or May.

Onions are damaged by freezing, which appear as water-soaking of the scales when cut after thawing. Onions that have been slightly frozen may recover with little perceptible injury, if allowed to thaw slowly and without handling.

Onion sets require practically the same temperature and humidity conditions as onions, but because they are smaller — in size they tend to pack more solidly. They are handled — in approximately 11.3 kg bags and should be stacked to allow the maximum air circulation. (Para 33.12 and 33.13)

Parsley (0°C and rh 95%)

Parsley can be kept for one to two months at °C and for a somewhat shorter period at 2 to 4°C. High humidity is essential to prevent desiccation. Package icing is often beneficial. (Para 33.13)

Peppers, Dry Chilli or Hot

Chilli peppers, after drying to a moisture content of 10 to 15%, are stored in nonrefrigerated warehouses for six to nine months. The moisture content is usually low enough to prevent fungus growth. A relative humidity of 60 to 70% is desirable. Polyethylene-lined bags are recommended to prevent changes in moisture content. Manufacturers of chilli pepper products hold part of their supply of the raw material in cold storage at 0 to 10°C, but they prefer to grind the peppers as soon as possible and store them in the manufactured form in airtight containers. (Para 33.13)

Peppers, Sweet (7 to 10°C and rh 90 to 95%)

Sweet peppers can be stored for a maximum of three weeks at 7 to 10°C. They are subjected to chilling injury if they are stored at temperatures below 7°C. The symptoms of this injury are surface pitting and discoloration near the calyx, which develops in a few hours after removal from storage. At temperatures of 0 to 2°C, peppers usually develop pitting in a few days. When stored at temperatures above 10°C, ripening (red color) and decay development are rapid. Peppers are often waxed commercially, which reduces chafing in transit and moisture loss. (Para 33.13)

8

Analysis of Spices and Condiments

I. Moisture Determination

Importance

MOISTURE in agricultural products plays a very vital role in their preservation. Less and excess, both are not conducive to maintain their quality, especially in the case of spices and condiments. The loss in moisture is usually due to its evaporation, which in the case of spices is accompanied by loss due to volatilization of the flavouring compounds. The commercial demand of spices and condiments is by virtue of their flavouring compounds. Absence of aroma and flavour dilutes the consumer's acceptability of the product. On the other hand, excess moisture ferments the starch and then produces off flavours, fungus and mould leading to non-acceptance of these spices and condiments by the consumer and consequently by the trade. Exposure to excessive heat, solar or thermal, results in evaporation of moisture in a spice and also of its volatile oil and prolonged exposure to humidity results in fungus and mould growth, despite the presence of volatile compounds whose function is prophylactic against micro-organism attack. This aspect is better illustrated as under:-

In the kiln drying process for small cardamom it is the controlled temperature and humidity which helps in maintaining the appropriate moisture content of the capsules thereby retaining the aroma, flavour and green colour of the dried capsules; an advantage lacking in the other two processes — the gudu and sun drying. In the sun drying process, the humidity is provided by exposure to dew in the night and drying is carried out in the sun on the following day. Both these processes defy operative control. Consequently the green colour of the pods is not uniform and splitting of fruits also occurs abundantly.

The green colour is considered a criteria for good quality and freshness of pods in most markets especially of the Middle-East countries where a premium upto 25% is offered for the green colour alone of this capsule. Experimentally it has been determined that for an efficient retention of green colour of the skin of the cardamom capsule during storage, the capsules need to be dried to a 10% moisture level, neither more nor less, and this moisture level is preserved by packing the capsules in 300 gauge high density polythene (H.D.P.E.) lined gunny bags. The green colour under these conditions remains green for about ten months.

Similarly, proper drying and storage have a direct bearing on the quality of red chillies. when the chillies are dried by spreading on tin roofing then chilli pods become brittle and break into several pieces due to over drying. In damp godowns the pods get rancid and musty. The best storage temperatures have been worked out so that chilli pods have moisture around 10%. It was reported, in a trial, that for bailing whole chilli pods for transportation to distant markets, the level of 39% relative humidity, 88°C temperature and a pressure of 295 kg/sq. cm is ideal. The bailed chilli fruits had a moisture content of 8% with a total loss of 4.8% (2% in moisture and the remaining included seed droppings).

Similar is the case of powdered spices and condiments. The morphological changes are more marked in them because of manifold increase of active surface area.

Theory

Generally, the moisture is determined by drying the weighed test material in an air oven. The loss in weight due to evaporation is accepted as the moisture content. But this simple method is not of universal application. Spices, condiments, flavouring materials and essential oils contain volatile compounds. Some materials themselves or some of their components are thermo-labile at 100°C ± 2°C. Subjecting such materials to the oven drying method shall entail loss of volatile and thermo-sensitive constituents as well as moisture. Obviously a higher moisture content than the factual shall get recorded. Pearson has suggested drying (preferably at 70°C in a vaccum oven). Although volatile oil is lost during drying by this method also, yet the results obtained are often sufficiently accurate for comparison purposes. The advantage in this routine method is that for preliminary screening of spices, several samples can be analysed simultaneously. The alternative to the oven method is the method of Dean and Stark.

In the Dean and Stark method the apparatus has been designed by these two workers, hence named after them. Toluene of C.P. quality and of b. pt. 110°C ± 1°C is used as the media for distilling water and volatile oil vapours. The vapours after condensing separate the liquid aromatic phase from the water phase, water being heavier percolates through the toluene column and settles at the bottom of the graduated tap and the volatile oils, mostly terpenes, being immiscible with water flow back with toluene into the boiling flask. In this way a true moisture percentage is obtained but only on volume/weight (v/w) basis.

The various advantages in using toluene are:-

(i) that the boiling point of toluene (110° ± 1°C) is slightly above but not very far from that of water. This ensures complete removal only of moisture present in the sample, without carbonizing or damaging the other components of the sample.

(ii) that toluene does not mix with water and being lighter than water assists its gravitation and flow back to continue the cycle.

(iii) that toluene does not decompose on boiling for long hours.

(iv) that toluene being a hydrocarbon does not react chemically with the sample material.

(v) that toluene can be recovered in a pure form hence can be used again making this system cheaper.

(vi) that the test does not require highly skilled personnel to perform it.

The following points, however, need to be kept in mind regarding this test.

(i) The test remanents of the sample material should not be used for other tests.

(ii) The glass assembly must be scrupulously clean and dry, otherwise the moisture sticking to the apparatus shall interfere in obtaining the correct moisture content.

(iii) The test materials being hygrosopic should be transferred immediately to distillation flask after opening the packet and immediately weighing the required quantity and instantaneously covering it with toluene to ward off moisture vapourisation or absorption.

(iv) Toluene must be subjected to a blank determination whenever a new batch is employed for test purposes.

Procedure

"The Manual of Methods of Tests and Analysis for commodities graded under Agmark" released by Central Agmark Laboratory, Nagpur (1988) (Agmark Manual) stipulates the following steps for preparation of sample for analysis:

(i) Unless specified, spice powder must pass through 500 micron sieve.

(ii) ingredients must not absorb moisture;

(iii) the sample shall have the least dead space;

(iv) it should be ground quickly and uniformly;

(v) net be caused undue heating;

(vi) contact with outside air is to be avoided.

Approximately 40 ± 0.01 gms of the sample, accurately weighed is transferred to the distillation flask and is immediately covered with toluene and swirled to mix. The Dean and Stark apparatus is assembled and the receiver is filled with toluene by pouring it through the condenser unit until it begins to overflow into the distillation flask. A loose cotton plug is inserted in the top of the condenser to ward off the condensation of atmospheric moisture within the condenser tube. Alternatively the condenser tube is attached to a small calcium chloride tube. The flask is heated and water circulated in a way that distillation rate is 100 drops/minute. When the greater part of the moisture has been distilled over then distillation rate is doubled. This is continued till no more moisture is collected. Occasionally 5 ml of toluene is poured through the condenser to wash down any sticking moisture.

The water is separated by rotating up and down the copper wire in the condenser as well as receiver. Refluxing is stopped when the last moisture drop has been distilled half an hour ago. Some more toluene is run down the condenser, scrubbing down the adhering water droplets with copper wire spiral. On cooling the receiver at room temperature the volume of water collected is read off. The distillate should not be more than 4.5 ml.

Calculation :

Moisture percentage v/w = 100 v/w and

Moisture percentage by weight = 100 vd/w

Where v = volume in ml of water,

d = sp. gravity of water at the volume recording temperature and

w = weight in gms of the sample taken for the test.

Diagram of Dean and Stark Apparatus —

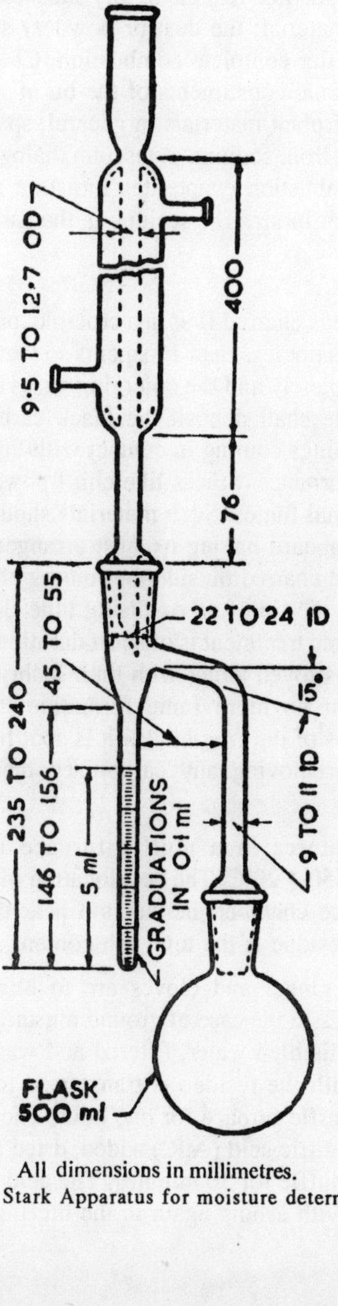

All dimensions in millimetres.

Dean and Stark Apparatus for moisture determination

II. Ash Determination

Introduction

Ash is the incombustible residue of any substance i.e. the remains of a completely burnt material; the dust or powdery substance to which a material is reduced after complete combustion. Chemically ash consists of non-volatile inorganic constituents of the burnt substance. The major constituents of ash of plant materials in general, spices in particular, are calcium, phosphorus, iron, sodium, potassium, halogens, silica or sand or silicious matter. Combustion evaporates moisture and oxidises the organic matter to vanish in air. The residue is the ash of the material.

Procedure

The spice sample is charred first in a crucible, preferably dish, whose bottom surface area is not less than 15 sq.cms so that the organic material gets carbonized completely and the emerging gases escape which if done directly in the muffle shall deposit the black carbon soot on its face. Apart from soiling things coming in contact with this soot it also gives a shabby look to the furnance. Spices like chilli powder when carbonized emit pungent/lachrymal fumes. Such materials should be charred preferably in a fuming cupboard having exhaust arrangements. Alternatively, such materials can be charred outside the fuming chamber also by igniting their fumes with the tip of an oxidising blue flame impinged inside the crucible. This flame treatment is of short duration because the vapours catch fire and get destroyed along with their lachrymacy. After carbonization, evident from no more fume formation, the flame should be impinged on the sides of the crucible till it is soot free so that tongs may be applied without removing any carbonized material of the sample under test.

Ashing temperatures in a muffle furnace must be within the prescribed range of 550 ± 20°C. The best location of the crucible is in the middle of the furnace chamber, neither too near the thermocouple nor near the door. The residue is the total ash content.

Nutmeg, mace, ginger and cloves are to be ashed in the muffle furnace at 600 ± 25°C. In the case of ground mustard, the carbon-free ash is leached with hot distilled water, filtered and washed thoroughly. The filter paper along with the residue is transferred to dish/crucible, dried and ignited in the muffle furnace for one hour. The crucible is cooled, 5 to 10 drops of conc. nitric acid (A.R.) added, dried again on a water bath and ashed again in muffle for 30 minutes. The acid treatment is repeated once again, ending with ashing again in the muffle for 1 hour.

Turmeric powder yields an ash of white colour, chillies of a greyish spongy type, coriander and cumin yield a brownish spongy type.

If the temperature crosses 570°C then some of the inorganic salts in the ash get fused. Though such a fusion does not effect the total ash content of a sample yet it certainly effects the other ashes like water soluble, water and or acid insoluble ashes etc. Over-heated ashes reflect a metallic tinge of the cations present. Copper imparts a greenish, iron imparts a brownish and alkali metals a greyish tinge. Incomplete ashing gives a black tinge. The best sign of complete ashing is the total absence of ember like glow in the ash when the crucible is seen immediately after taking out of the furnace.

Ashing at temperatures beyond 570°C results in fusion of the ash components i.e. the inter molecular space is completely reduced. The ashed material changes from the molecular to the polymerised state, so boiling with 1:9 HCl does not remove the acid soluble constituents of the total ash because of inability of the acid to act on the entire periphery of each molecule. Consequently numerous ash molecules, though soluble in boiling 1:9 HCl remain unreacted thus unremoved from the ashed mass and the very purpose of digestion in HCl gets defeated. When such an ash is ignited in the muffle the quantity of ash which ought to have been dissolved in HCl and subsequently washed out with hot water, stays back and accepted erroneously as acid insoluble ash yielding results on the higher side.

Materials having low ash percentages have to be taken in more than routine quantities for determination of their ash percentages. In such determinations (sample weighing more than 2.5 gm) some of the sample material in the middle of the ash heap may remain unashed. Therefore the partially ashed sample crucible should be taken out of the muffle and cooled till ember glow vanishes. With the pointed end of a glass-rod this semi-ashed mass should be upturned so that the unashed portion gets thorough exposure to heat during the repeat ignition in the muffle. If even after this treatment the ashing is incomplete then the ash crucible should be again withdrawn and cooled and a few drops of H_2O added. This well moistened mass be dried on a low flame/heat to avoid crackling. The dried material is reintroduced in the muffle for final ashing. Ashing and cooling has to be continued till difference between two successive readings does not vary by more than ± 0.0001 gm.

The total ash is digested in (1:9) HCl. The centents in the acid medium should just simmer and not boil for a prolonged period otherwise the concentration of (1·9) HCl will increase with the result that some of the acid insoluble ash may unwarrantedly pass into solution and the result shall be lower than factual. Choose the crucible of a capacity sufficient enough that it provides ample space along its walls after adding HCl so that the tong's pincers do not touch the acid. This shall preclude the chances of dissolution of the tong's metal from its tips.

Chrome plated steel tongs are in use in most laboratories, but the best buy in this case shall be a Teflon or platinum tipped tong. Teflon and platinum are stable to acid corrosion to a temperature of 300°C.

Always use hot distilled water in small portions for several washings till the filtrate is chloride free. Do preferably a spot test of filtrate with dil. $AgNO_3$. Similar adherance is required in respect of Whatman No. 42 or 44 filter papers, these being ashless hence of grávimetric grade.

Siliceous matter is found in certain silica-rich soils. Plants from such soils may absorb silicates from it provided it is available in the soluble form as sod. silicate. However, it is certain that silica has no role in plant nutrition and the high silica content i.e. high acid insoluble ash owes its presence generally to dust, dirt, stones and lumps of earth reaching the spices and condiments during processing or are present in the parent material.

A subtle distinction of siliceous matter is called grit which the Technical Dictionary defines as "siliceous sediment, loose or indurated, the component grains being angular in contrast to sand and sand stone in which the grains are rounded".

Grit determination has its utility only when the materials are not subjected for acid insoluble ash percentage determinations. For example, spices like celery, coriander, fenugreek, fennel and anise seeds are so tiny in size that siliceous matter present on their coats cannot be separated mechanically, therefore, a non-polar organic solvent like CCl_4 is employed. This method indicates the extent of extraneous siliceous matter present in the sample but does not include the inherent siliceous matter which is also accounted in the acid insoluble ash. Obviously, it would be judicious to prescribe grit determination for samples of the above seeds as well as for caraway, cardamom and poppy seeds when tested in their whole form. But grit has no analytical value when these spices are in the pulverised form and their acid insoluble ash is being determined simultaneously because to emphasize again the acid insoluble ash shall cover total siliceous matter, inherent and extraneous, as evidenced from the following analytical results:

Commodity	*Acid insoluble ash percentage (1:9) HCl*	*Grit percentage*
Turmeric powder	0.65	0.45
"	0.70	0.46
Chilli powder	0.90	0.43
Curry powder	0.61	0.25
Coriander powder	0.60	0.45
Amchur powder	1.00	0.96

The irrelevance of grit percentage in spices and condiments, where acid-insoluble-ash is also determined, is evident from the fact that A.O.A.C has prescribed this test for grain and stock feeds only and not in spices and condiments. For these materials a test has been laid to find out the type of filth.

The opinion of the Public Analyst that even a small % grit i.e. siliceous sediment present in spices is injurious to health, is not corroborated by pathological evidence. Firstly spices and condiments are food additives and not food themselves. Thus the daily intake of all these additives i.e. powderd spices and condiments is hardly 5 to 6 gm/adult in an upper class family. On the basis of 1% grit even the daily intake shall hardly be 50 mgm/50 kg. body weight adult which during cooking gets converted to either silicic acid or its salts.

Sallmann quotes Goldwater who observed the urinary concentration of silica as SiO_2 in men, not exposed to silicosis, ranging from 0.25 mgm/100 gm. Page *et. al.* quoted by Sallmann calculated that on the average about 16.2 mgm/day of SiO_2 is excreted through the urine. Experimentally he observed that if a fine quartz suspension is administered by stomach tube, the urinary excretion is promptly increased, silicate absorbed by oral administration of silicic acid or sod. silicate or magnesium-trisilicate passes rapidly in the urine without material increase of the silicate level of the blood.

Differentiating, lesions due to silicosis which are caused by inhaling regularly and for long periods silica dust particles of less that 10 microns size: no lesions are formed due to deposit of silicate particles in human tissue absorbed orally. By way of information the silicate content of various human tissues normally ranges from 10 to 200 mgm/100 gms. of dry weight. The spleen contains 15 mgm/100 gms. dry weight of silica and 140 mgm/100 gms. in normal lungs and more than 200 mgm in silicosis lungs when the concentration is still higher, only then lesions are formed in the lungs. Thus silica particles when of less than 10 micron size are inhaled resulting in lesions of lung etc. are injurious to health and not when taken in cooked food in the particle size of 300 to 500 microns size. The dietary silicates are promptly passed into urine. Spectroscopic studies have shown that normal human blood cannot hold more 0.1 mgm per 100 gm of silicate.

In grit determination, advantage is taken of the sp. gr. of CCl_4 (1.58 to 1.60). The powdered spices are lighter than CCl_4 hence float whereas the gritty matter is heavier than CCl_4 hence gravitates towards the bottom of the containing vessel. The grit free floating test material is laddled out, CCl_4 decanted and the residue is washed free of traces of CCl_4, the H_2O washed residue is dried and weighed to find out the grit percentage.

Based on these facts a court case was dismissed in favour of the vendor. The turmeric sample had acid insoluble ash of 2.64% and its grit was determined as 0.8%. The defence plea was that acid insoluble ash minus grit is the inherent ash present in the parent plant material in its whole form which cannot be removed by physical means including water washing. Therefore 2.64 - 0.80 = 1.84% is the inherent acid insoluble ash which is erroneous because limit for genuine turmeric powder is only 1.5%.

Recently, indigenously fabricated silica crucibles have appeared in the Indian market. Silica crucibles in general and these indigenous ones in particular, actually made from quartz, loose little weight after regular use, therefore, it is advisable to check the tare weight of each crucible after each determination and take into consideration even these little variations. The necessity for this advice is not far to seek. Usually 2 gms of the sample is taken for ash determinations. Consequently the ash weight obtained is multiplied with 50 to get its percentage. Even a 1 mgm difference shall produce a difference of 0.05% and this 0.05% has its importance in the border cases.

A basic precaution usually ignored by analysts to curtail maximally the hygroscopic moisture absorption by the ashes is the absence of moisture absorbents in the balance chamber, which too should have moisture free environs. This can be done by placing silica gel or kieslghur pouch or $CaCl_2$ in a small glass container. In the absence of these arrangements the weight of the ashed material goes on increasing as the ash goes on absorbing moisture from the water vapours in the balance chamber. The variation is sometimes to the tune of 5-6 mgms and this explains for variation in results of the same sample analysed by different chemists. Weighing time can also be curtailed to curtail the moisture absorption by placing macro weights before hand. Soon after the crucible is placed then only marginal micro adjustments be made as quickly as possible.

The best crucible is of platinum, but due to very high initial cost and problem of its safe custody forsakes its use in ordinary laboratories.

The loss in weight in silica or quartz crucibles may be also due to scrubbing of the crucible with pointed glass rods to dislodge sticking unashed particles of the sample as well as suspected ash particles.

Procedure

About 2 gms of the sample is accurately weighed in a previously weighed crucible. The material is charred slowly either on a low flame or on an electric hot plate. After charring it is ashed in a closed muffle furnace at 550°C ± 20°C. The ash must be carbon free. The crucible is taken out, cooled on a clean asbestos pad. When still warm it is transferred to a desiccator containing a fresh desiccant (usually fused calcium chloride lumps). The cooled crucible is weighed accurately and this weight recorded separately. The crucible is returned to the muffle furnace for heating at 550°C ± 20°C for half an hour, cooling and weighing as before till the difference in weight between two successive weighings is less than one mgm.

Total ash, per cent by weight = $100 (W_2 - W)/W_1 - W$

Where

W_2 = Wt in gm of total ash and crucible.

W_1 = Wt in gm of sample for test and crucible.

W = Wt in gm of empty crucible.

The ashed sample in the same crucible is boiled with dil. hydrochloric acid (1:9). The cooled contents are filtered through an ashless Whatman No. 42/44, filter paper. The filter paper is washed with hot water until the washings are chloride free. The filter paper is returned to the dish, dried carefully on low heat, charred, ignited and finally weighed as done in total ash.

Acid insoluble ash, per cent by weight = $100 (W_3 - W)/W_1 - W$,

Where

W_3 = Wt in gms of acid insoluble ash + crucible.

Crude Fibre

Mangold defines crude fibre as the sum of all those organic components of the plant cell-membrane and supporting structures which after chemical analysis remain after the removal of protein, fat, starch and water-soluble components. Thus crude fibre is composed of cellulose, hemicellulose and some of the materials that encrust the cell walls such as lignin and pectic substances. When we chew arecanut or fennel seed or cardamom (small) capsule it is experienced that even after prolonged chewing a fibrous residue is left in the mouth which is tasteless, spongy and voluntarily suggests to spit out as being of no virtue, this is the crude fibre as intelligible to the lay man.

Cellulose owes its name to Anseline Payer, a French agriculturist, who investigated the constituents of plant cell-walls (1837-1842). Cellulose constitutes approximately half of the cell wall material of the wood and other plant products. Wood celluloses always occur in association with hemi-cellulose of related structures and with lignin, a non polysaccharide. Cellulose itself is composed of filaments and alpha-cellulose is the most abundant form in the cell walls.

Cellulose fibres show crystalline regions that are explained on the basis of the miscelle theory; this postulates that the crystalline supermolecular unit is made up of bundles of parallel oriented chains (miscelles). The remarkable mechanical strength and chemical stability are considered to be the result of this misceller structure. The width of a misceller unit is only 60 A° and length only 600A°. Cellulose swells to some extent in water or in a dilute alkali since the crystal lattice is not destroyed hence this effect is deemed to be inter misceller. For these reasons, human beings and carnivora are unable to utilize cellulose as food. Further they lack the enzymes required for hydrolysis. On the other hand ruminants (cud chewing animals) have, within their specially constructed alimenatry systems, enzymes which enable them to digest it and use it as a food.

Cellulose is tasteless, insoluble in water and is a nonreducing carbohydrate, mostly due to its extremely high molecular weight. Like starch, cellulose has the formula $(C_6H_{10}O_5)_n$ and these D-glucose units in a chain are joined by a glucoside linkage to C4 of the next. These linkages are of beta type like the cellobiose. X-ray analysis and electron microscopy indicate that these long chains lie side by side in bundles, undoubtedly held together to form ropelike structures which themselves are grouped together to form the fibres we see. The cellulose 'ropes' are embedded in lignin to give a structure that may be compared to reinforced concrete and not as Payer thought that cellulose is united chemically with other cell wall constituents (lignin, hemicellulose and fats etc.)

Hemicelluloses lie in complexity between disaccharides and

cellulose. They appear to be an intimate mixture of cellulose and pentosan poly saccharides yielding pentoses on hydrolysis. The more common is xylan, yielding xylose. Hemicelluloses are soluble in alkalies.

Starch is the reserve carbohydrate in the majority of plants. It is completely hydrolysed by mineral acids to glucose (For more details see starch determination in spices).

Lignin (from the Latin-*Lignum*-wood) is after cellulose the principal constituent of wood. Lignums are insoluble in water, strong mineral acids and hydrocarbons but soluble in aqueous alkalies.

Plant food products comprise of fats, proteins, carbohydrates (cellulose, hemicellulose, starches etc.), plant pigments, minerals, vitamins and other trace components characteristic of the particular plant product.

For determining crude fiere (CF) the material is first pulverised to a fineness of atleast 300 microns. This helps in reducing mechanically the length of cellulose filaments and size of starch and pectin granules.

In the Soxhlet's extractor, which is a continuous process, ether soluble substances i.e. fats comprising saponifiable glycerides, sterols, turpenoids, plant pigments, waxes, fat soluble vitamins, if any, alkaloids etc. are removed. The fatty film is completely dissolved there by rendering the defatted residue receptive to the ensuing acid and alkali attack. Apparent crude fibre is lowered by defatting.

On refluxing with 1.25% H_2SO_4, the fat present within the cell walls gets dislodged. The acid acts more as a softening agent for cell walls and less as a destructive agent. Starches are hydrolysed to soluble saccharides. The soluble minerals are washed out. Some of the proteins are also hydrolysed to soluble forms. Washings with hot H_2O are carried on till the washings are free of acid.

Treatment with 1.25% NaOH results in the hydrolysis of remaining proteins. This treatment removes tannin and fats also, disgorged from the cell walls during acid digestion. The fats form soaps and are washed out during hot H_2O and alcohol washings. The unreacted alkali and the sodium soaps (pseudo) must be completely removed and this fact be ascertained by checking with phenolphthalein or litmus paper, otherwise, during ashing free alkali gets converted to alkaline oxides leaving black residues even after ignition in the muffle furnace.

The accuracy of the results depends upon:-

(i) proper strength of the acid and alkali and the use of boiling H_2O,

(ii) exact period for reaction where frothing etc. is completely absent,

(iii) thorough washing with H_2O and complete transfer of the washed material,

(iv) crude fibre determinations are greately affected by particle size, the finer the material is ground, the lower the determined crude fibre content,

(v) filtering after each digestion must be completed within a given time. Delay in filtering after acid or alkali digestion lowers the results because some of the cellulose also on prolonged digestion gets converted into soluble low molecular weight materials.

The residue from a crude fibre determination contains about 97% cellulose and lignin. It, however, does not reflect all the cellulose and lignin present in the material.

Crude fibre reflects succulence of spices and condiments. Over mature products have an increased level of crude fibre.

Formula for CF determination on dry weight basis:-

The crucible dried in the oven contains the insoluble inorganic matter + CF + asbestos.

Let its weight be = W_1

The muffle ignited residue when cooled contains inorganic salts + absestos only, let its Wt. = W_2

Weight of the material taken = W

percentage of CF on wet wt. basis = $100(W_1-W_2)/W$

Suppose the moisture % age is = X

then the percentage of CF on dry wt. basis =

$$100(w_1-w_2)\times 100/w(100-X)$$

Excess of CF percentage reflects that the manufacturer has voluntarily added branches, twigs or saw dust for malafide gains. In the stone grinding machines it gets sieved out as fibres, i.e. cellulose filaments which are long. However, with regular use of pulverisers the metallic hammers chop these filaments into small bits defying sieve separation and detection, therefore, this chemical method is of great utility for detecting adulteration with powdered cellulose.

Procedure

About 2.5 gm. of the sample is accurately weighed in No. 1 filter paper. The contents are encapsuled in this sheet and transferred to a thimble and subjected to extraction for about an hour with pet. ether (60° - 80°C) using a Soxhlet apparatus. The defatted and dried material is transferred to a one litre digestion flask. 200 ml of boiling 1.25% (w/v) sulphuric acid is added to the flask, reflux condenser connected and enough heat applied so that the contents of the flask begin to simmer within one minute. The flask is swirled periodically to keep the entire defatted material always in contact with the acid. This reaction is carried out exactly for half an hour. The flask is removed, the contents filtered through a linen cloth (18 threads/cm) or coarse acid washed hardened filter paper spread inside a Büchner funnel connected to a suction pump. The residue is washed with hot water till acid free.

The residue on the linen cloth is washed back in the same flask with the help of an exact 200 ml of boiling 1.25% sod. hydroxide solution and the same reflux condenser connected. The flask is heated like before exactly for half an hour. The flask is removed and the contents filtered through a Gooch crucible having an ignited asbestos powder bed which though compact should be thin. The residue is washed with hot water till free of alkali, followed by 3 x 15 ml of 95% alcohol and 15 ml of pet. ether successively. The crucible is dried alongwith the contents at 105 ± 1°C in an air oven for 3 hours, cooled and weighed. This process of drying for 30 minutes, cooling and weighing is continued till the difference between two successive readings is less than one mgm.

The dried Gooch crucible along with contents is incinerated in the muffle furnace at 550 ± 20°C till complete combustion of the carbonaceous matter is achieved. The Gooch crucible containing the ash is cooled in a desiccator and weighed.

IV. Starch Determination

Introduction

Starch and cellulose are the soul and body of any plant. Starch, the white tasteless carbohydrate present in the seeds, tubers and other parts of the plants serves as food for the growing plants, whereas, cellulose the stable polymer of glucose is the chief constituent of the cell walls of plants and also constitutes its supporting framework. Starch and cellulose both are built from (+) glucose molecules but in a different way, hence these are different in their physical and chemical properties.

Starch when ingested is broken down into the original (+) glucose units and is carried by the blood stream to the liver to be recombined into glycogen or animal starch. When need arises, glycogen is broken down once more into (+) glucose. The blood stream carries (+) glucose to the tissues also where it is ultimately oxidised to CO_2 and H_2O with the release of energy originally supplied as sun light during photo synthesis. Some of the (+) glucose is converted to form amino acids, which in turn are combined to form proteins that comprise up a large part of the animal body.

In short, starch is a valuable food for and from the plants but when cheaper or different starch bearing materials are added in turmeric for monetary gains they become adulterants. These added starches can be detected chemically by finding quantitative increase in starch content and microscopically are precisely located. Presently, the chemical method is discussed.

Plant starches are water soluble, easily hydrolysed and readily digested. Starches occur as granules, only the size and shape of the granule is characteristic of the plant from which the starch has been obtained and this characteristic is utilized in the microscopic examination. When intact, starch granules are insoluble in cold water, however, if the outer membrane is raptured by grinding then the granules swell in cold water and form a gel, but when the intact granule is treated with warm water then a soluble portion of the starch diffuses through the granule wall. Finally, when the same granule is treated with hot water it swells further and bursts.

Principle

In general, starch contains about 20% of water-soluble fraction called amylose and 80% of water insoluble fraction called amylopectin. Both, amylose and amylopectin are made up of (+) glucose units but differ in their respective molecular sizes and shapes though denoted by the same general formula $(C_6H_{10}O_5)_n$. Upon treatment with acids the components of starch are hydrolysed progressively via dextrin and maltose to the final product (+) glucose. Precisely for this reason the acid hydrolysis is carried out for at least 2.5 hours so that the entire starch of the test material gets hydrolysed to this final product i.e. (+) glucose and this is the basis of result calculation as detailed later in this chapter.

Procedure

(a) Defatting

To effect complete hydrolysis the material needs to be defatted. Soxhlet's apparatus is the best answer, but it is time consuming. Instead, in most laboratories, the pulverised material is washed down on a No. 1

filter paper with pet. ether thrice, each time using 10-15 ml of the solvent till the washing is free from fat. In the case of turmeric powder, the absence of the yellow colour is an indication based on the fat soluble curcumin. Since there is no curcumin there is no fat left in the ether-washed turmeric sample. The fat-free and ether-free residue is washed down with dil. HCl (20 ml of HCl + 200 ml of H_2O) through a hole pierced at the bottom of the filter paper, into an one litre flask for completing the acid hydrolysis along with all the shreds of the shredded filter paper.

Experience has shown that the quickest way to defat the turmeric sample for starch purposes is to pulverise it to 300 micron size if not already done and transfer 3 gms of this powder in a 100 ml clean and dry beaker. Fat is lixiviated with petroleum ether (40-60°C) till the decanted ether has become free of the orange yellow curcumin. For quick and thorough leaching of the fat it is better to mix thoroughly the solute and solvent with the rounded end of a glass rod and resting the beaker in a tilted position. While transfering the decanted ether into another container for repeat use, care should be taken not to disturb the settled material.

(b) Starch Inversion

The defatted turmeric powder should be freed from the traces of entrapped ether, otherwise the ethereal film encircling the material particles will not permit complete reaction to take place. This can be achieved by warming the 1 litre flask containing the defatted turmeric powder + HCl solution till the vapours stop emitting ethereal smell. Refluxing can be done by using a 1 metre high air condenser also but a Liebig's condenser is always better. Two precautions are essential during the progress of hydrolysis.

Frothing needs to be avoided by regulating the heat intensity so that the contents just keep simmering. Occasional frothing can be subdued by injecting cool air with an anaesthetic bulb. The aim is to have a thorough hydrolysis of the sample's starchy content otherwise it shall remain sticking on the flask's walls unreacted.

Secondly the excess of HCl needs to be neutralized. Solid Na_2CO_3 is the best answer. It produces little exothermic heat as would happen if NaOH is used. The bulk of reactants is not much increased but produces frothing due to exit of CO_2. This frothing can be quitely subdued if not altogether stopped by adding Na_2CO_3 in pinches and not spoon fulls and also by lightly swirling the flask and not shaking it vigorously.

Fehling's solutions (Herman Fehling: 1812-85)

Method of Preparation

(i) *Fehling's Solution* A is prepared by dissolving 34.639 gms of $CuSO_4.5H_2O$ in water, 0.5 ml of conc. H_2SO_4 of sp. gravity 1.84 added and the volume made up to 500 ml. in a volumetric flask.

(ii) *Fehling's Solution* B is prepared by dissolving 173.0 gms of *Rochelle's salt* ($KNaC_4H_4O_6.4H_2O$) and 50 gms of NaOH in water diluted to 500 ml in a volumetric flask. The solution is allowed to remain like that for 2 days. It is then filtered through prepared asbestos.

A general consideration for complex formation, as mentioned by Walton (1966) is that to form a neutral chelated compound with a metal ion, an organic molecule must have a dual character. On the one hand this molecule should be acidic in nature i.e. it must have displaceable hydrogen atom(s) and on the other hand it must also be basic i.e. it must have a pair of unshared electrons available for coordination. Further the acidic and basic groups must be so spaced that the chelate ring when formed is completely free from strain or nearly so. The (OH) group is a universal complex former by virtue of its dipole moment and unshared electrons. It can compete with the solvent i.e. water molecules only if chelation is possible. The (alpha-OH) acids like citric and tartaric are better to hold tripositive ions in solution at pH 7.

In the present case the ion to be held is di-positive, therefore pH is not kept at 7 and tartaric acid is not used as such but as its pot. sod. salt. The solutions are kept separate, otherwise (Cu^{++}) will precipitate as $Cu(OH)_2$ as soon as it contacts the strong base NaOH but Na, K tartarate chelates Cu^{++} much quicker.

The end-product of acid hydrolysis is deemed to be glucose; the aldose having the terminal — CHO group reduces the strongly basic solution of $CuSO_4$ chelated through sod. pot. tartarate to Cu_2O. The chelate provides the small concentration of Cu^{++} which in turn imparts a blue colour.

$$\underset{\text{Reducing sugar}}{R\text{—}CHO} + \underbrace{2CU^{++} + Na^{+} + 5OH^{-}}_{\text{Fehling's solution}} \rightarrow RCOONA + \underset{\text{Cuprous red ppt.}}{Cu_2O\downarrow} + 3H_2O$$

Fehling's solution serves as the mutual comparison between the reducing sugar (glucose) produced as a result of acid hydrolysis of starch and dextrose — the standard analytical comparator, therefore, volume accuracy to a fine drop must be adhered to in respect of Fehling's solution measurement and its transfer into the flask while doing the determinations to avoid erroneous results.

To the accurately delivered 10 ml of the Fehling's (A+B) solutions, nearly 25 ml of the 0.2 % dextrose solution can be added straightway through the burette. The contents need to be simmered for 2 minutes, adding the dextrose solution drop by drop but continuously. As soon as the Cu_2O colour appears to be rising then only add 4-5 drops of methylene blue indicator and continue titration. When the blue colour completely vanishes as seen from the film of rising bubbless then only the end point is reached and the bright metallic Cu_2O colour appears clear and shining.

Repeat titration while increasing the volume of dextrose for the initial straight bulk run, thereby narrowing the gap between this first bulk volume and the final titration volume to 2-3 drops only. In the case of inverted starch the first run can be of 35 to 36 ml. Like before the gap in this case also has to be narrowed down to 2 or 3 drops.

Usually starch percentage ranges between 47 to 53. Lesser percentages are possibly due to weevilled turmeric rhizomes, the weevils thriving on starch thereby consuming some of it from the turmeric. However, such samples have higher total ash and consequently higher acid insoluble ash percentage. If the starch percentage is beyond 54 then it is necessary to examine the material microscopically for the presence of other starches. Detailed characteristics of these starches are appended.

(i) *Wheat:* The granules are flat and circular, have a clear circular outline and very fine concentric striae which can often be seen on careful examination. They are usually divisible into two classes: (a) large circular granules, (b) small, may be circular granules or very often distinctly irregular or polygonal and often showing a hilum. These must not be mistaken for rice granules. Their appearance is studied in a large unraptured parenchymatom cell containing large and small granules. Minimum dia. is between 35 to 45 micron with polarized light, a cross is observed.

(ii) Barley granules are very similar to wheat but the texture of granules is coarser and the smallest granules are not found. They are occassionally circular like wheat. Their dia. is less than 35 micron. under polarised light a cross is seen.

(iii) Rye is similar to barley. The granules have very often an irregular central hilum, dia. upto 60 micron with polarised light. The cross is distinct in comparison to wheat cross.

(iv) Rice granules are small, irregular, polygonal with a small central star-shaped hilum, typically collected in groups of 5 or 6, dia. 6 to 9 micron and with polarised light exhibit cross.

(v) Maize granules are larger than rice, irregularly polygonal with a distinct central hilum. Granules are separate, dia. 15 to 20 micron. The cross is well defined with polarized light.

(vi) Oat has polygonal granules which are intermediate in size between rice and maize. Like rice these are in groups of 5 to 6. Commonly their dia, is 10 to 11 micron. No cross with polarized light.

(vii) Tapioca granules appear microscopically as (a) circular granules with a very distinct hilum, circular or split, (b) doubly truncated spheres. The hilum is usually nearer the curved side. Concentric striae are usually present, dia. between 15 to 25 micron and the centre is dark.

(viii) Sage has large granules with an oval hilum. They are oval shaped or truncated (often irregular) at one end. Concentric striae are usually seen and the dia. is between 20 to 60 micron. Dark petals appear in the centre.

(ix) Potato has large, oval, oyster—shell shaped granules, some are large and some small. Potato granules have a distinct circular hilum situated near the

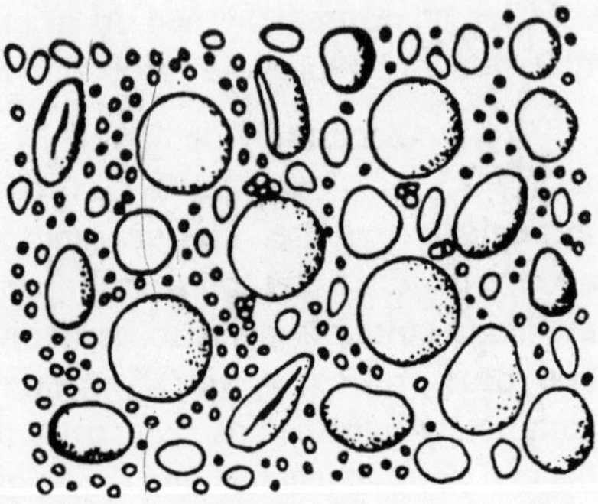

Wheat starch

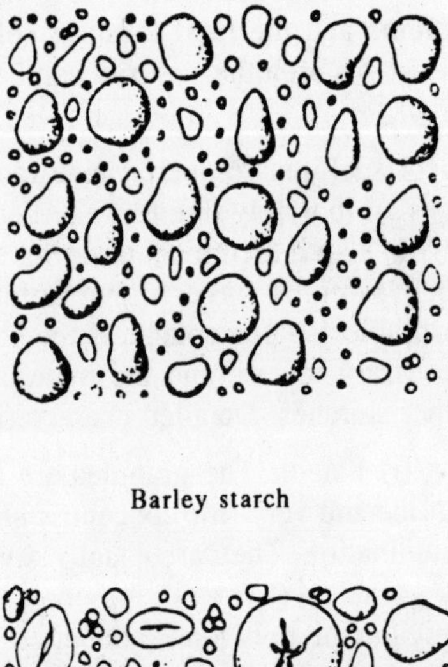

Barley starch

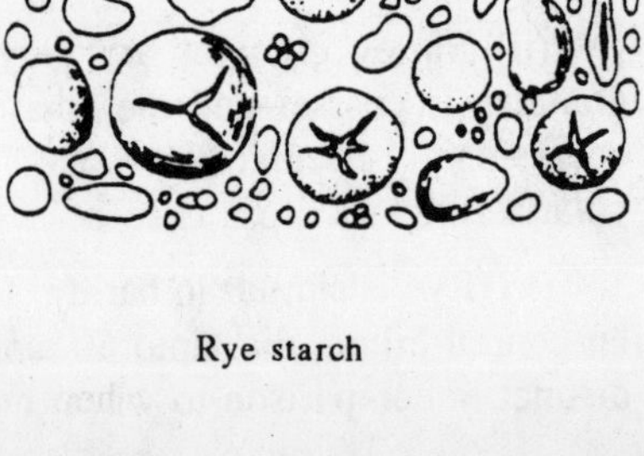

Rye starch

Rice starch

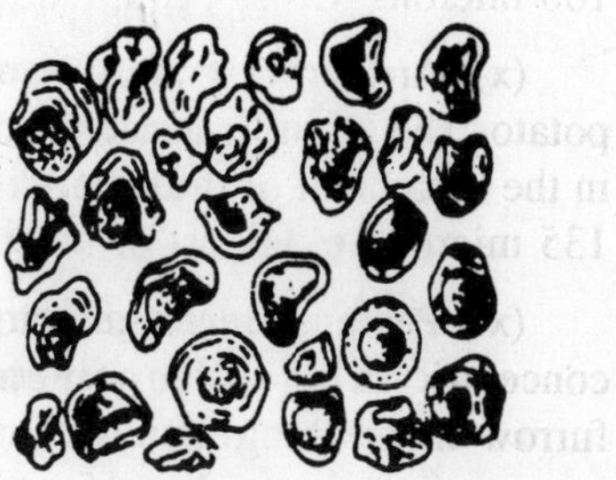

Tapioca

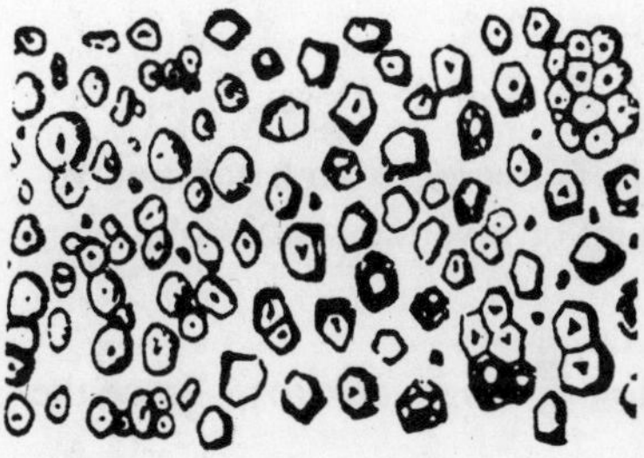

Maize starch (Corn flour)

Potato starch

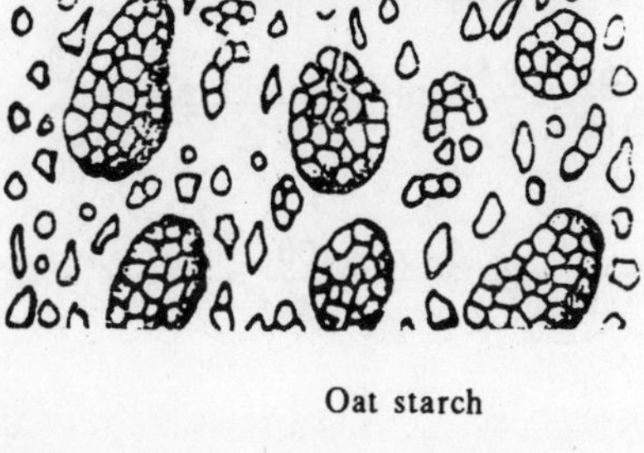

Oat starch

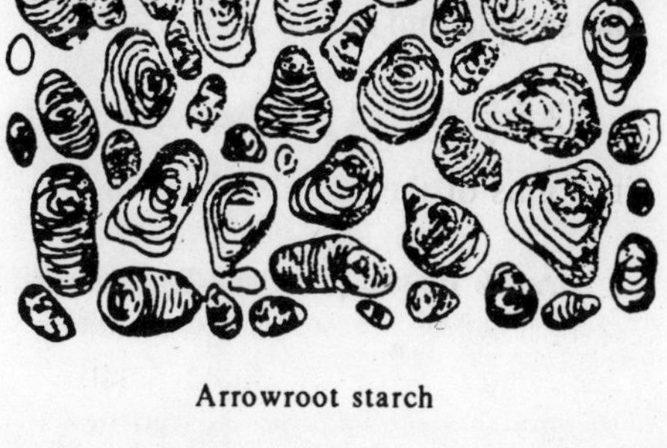

Arrowroot starch

narrow end. The concentric striae are very distinct. In some Indian potato starches the hilum appears at the broad end resembling arrow root. Dia. 100 microns. Cross central at hilum with polarized light.

(x) Arrowroot granules are large, oval but not shell shaped as of potato. The hilum is usually broken, shaped like a flying bird and placed in the broad half of the oval. Concentric striae are very distinct, their dia. 135 micron i.e. largest of all starches.

(xi) Pea and Beans granules are usually elliptical with very distinct concentric striae. Hilum centrally longitudinal, resembling an irregular furrow in the long axis. Indian pulse has many granules with distinct concentric striae and a central hilum, two granules being occasionally joined by a common fiat face, length 57 microns.

Generally rice bits are well mixed with semi pulverised turmeric rhizomes and again pulverised to yield a homogeneous but adulterated turmeric powder.

Formula derivation for starch determination

In a 0.2% dextrose solution 1 ml = 2 mgm of dextrose.

Suppose x ml of dextrose and y ml of inverted starch solution reduces 10 ml of Fehling's solution then y ml of inverted starch solution = 2 x mgm of dextrose.

then 1 ml of inverted starch solution = $\frac{2x}{y}$ mgm dextrose. Since the dilution is 5 times, therefore,

the original solution $=250 \times \frac{2x}{y} \times 5$ mgm $= 2.5\frac{x}{y}$ gms dextrose.

Dextrose ($C_6H_{12}O_6$) mol, wt. 180 has been formed from

$C_6H_{10}O_5$; mol. wt. 162 + by the extraneous H_2O, mol. wt. 18, therefore,

∴ 180 gms of dextrose correspond to 162 gms of starch present in the sample and

$2.5\frac{x}{y}$ gms of glucose correspond to $\frac{162}{180} \times \frac{2.5x}{y}$ gms of starch present in 3 gms of the sample, therefore,

∴ % of starch in the test material $= \frac{162}{180} \times \frac{2.5x}{y} \times \frac{100}{3} = 75\frac{x}{y}$

Determination of Crude Starch

Weigh 2 to 5 gms of sample depending on its starch content, wash on a filter paper with several portions of ether (about 5 successive portions of 10 ml each of ether) and allow the ether to evaporate off completely. Wash with several portions of 10% (by volume) of ethyl alcohol using about 150 ml in all. Transfer all the washed residue to a 500 ml graduated bottle, add 20 ml HCl (sp. gr. 1.125), place a funnel in the neck of the flask to prevent evaporation, and heat in a boiling waterbath for 3 hours. Cool, nearly neutralise with NaOH solution and make up to 500 ml. Filter and determine the reducing sugar in the solution by titration with Fehling's solution using methylene blue internal indicator by Lane & Eynon volumetric method. Express the result as dextrose.

Dextrose x 0.90 = starch

NB: With some spices the resulting solution after HCl digestion is very dark in colour which interferes with Fehling titration (as in the case of black-pepper). In such cases the following procedure of clarification is suggested. Nearly neutralise the digested acid solution with dilute NaOH, clarify in cold with 3 ml of a saturated aqueous solution of neutral lead acetate, make up to 500 ml and filter. Remove the excess lead from the filterate with a little potassium oxalate and refilter through a dry filter into flask. Titrate the clear filtrate with Fehling's solution as usual.

The above method gives the value of crude starch, and it is sufficiently accurate for spices containing appreciable quantity of starch like turmeric, pepper, ginger, nutmeg, mace, etc. But in spices like chilli, allspice, clove etc. which contain little or no true starch, the above acid digestion will give unduly high result. In such cases the diastase digestion may be followed.

Preparation of malt extract

Digest 5 gms of ground, clean, new barley malt of known efficacy with 100 ml water at room temperature for 2 1/2 hours with occasional shaking, and filter. A few drops of chloroform may be added to prevent the growth of moulds.

The residue left after washing with ether and alcohol as mentioned in the above acid-digestion method, is transferred into a beaker with the aid of 50 ml water. Immerse the beaker into boiling water stirring constantly until all starch is gelatinised (about 15 minutes). Cool to 55° C, add 20 ml of the malt extract and maintain at 55°C for 1 hour or until the solution does not show any blue colour with iodine. Cool, make up to 250 ml and filter. Place 200 ml filtrate in a flask, add 20 ml HCl (sp. gr. 1.125) put a funnel in the neck of the flask and heat in a boiling water bath for 2.5 hours. Cool, nearly neutralise with 10% NaOH solution and dilute to 500 ml in a volumetric flask. Filter and determine dextrose as described ablove.

Detection of Foreign Starch

Microscopic Examination

Microscopic examination is carried out on all samples of ground herbs and spices. The prepared slides are observed firstly under low power objective (2/3 in) and then under high power (1/6 in). Also it is preferable to have a set of authentic samples available for comparison purposes.

A "water slide" is prepared by dispersing the sample with a drop of alcohol, and then adding one or two drops of glycerol solution (30% in water) before sliding on the cover slip. The water slide is particularly useful in detecting starch. The presence of starch is confirmed by adding a drop of very dilute iodine solution, which produces the usual dark blue colour.

V. Heavy Metals Determination in Spices

Heavy metals determination in spices is very important because they produce toxic effect by replacing the essential metal ion existing in the chelates present in the body. For example the high toxicity of cadmium is due to its replacing zinc in the body. Zinc is essential in the body to break down the fats, therefore, by replacement of zinc by cadmium the fats accumulate in the circulating system leading to high blood pressure and heart disease.

The body contains adrenaline, cortisone, citric acid etc. that may form chelates with metals. It is generally believed that heavy metals produce their toxic effect by binding with these substances, thereby preventing their normal functioning. The antidotes also for heavy metal poisoning are based on this property. Chelating agents, administered as cures, combine with the harmful metal ion in a way to make it inaccessible to body tissues. In this form the chelated heavy metal is eventually excreted from the body.

Turmeric is used as an ingredient in the manufacture of curry powders. Lead bearing turmeric thus contaminates the curry powder also. The Indian statutory specifications of purity have specified the maximum limits of this metal in them as 2.5 and 10.0 ppm respectively.

Apparent modes of turmeric contamination with lead and other heavy metals are:

(i) Industrial effluents containing heavy metals like lead, mercury, cadmium etc. enter the food chain through aquatic organisms like algael cells. Mercury enters water bodies as organo-mercury pesticides or mercury slimicides used in the paper industry or in mercury paints etc. Bacteria in the presence of oxygen convert metallic mercury through mercurous ion into either methyl mercury or dimethyl mercury. These alkyl mercury compounds get absorbed at the bottom of the chain by photo-plankton and zoo-plankton and further get magnified as evidenced by the presence of mercury in apprcciable concentrations in the littoral flora and fauna like in the Toy river estuary of U.K.

Similarly cadmium is directly absorbed in the elemental form by phyto-plankton and other higher organisms. Lead also accumulates in bacterial and algael cells without harming them. It accumulates in the submerged plants also. These patterns occur in marshy lands near coastal industrial towns as well as near those industrial towns where industrial wastes are drained in channels primarily meant for irrigation.

(ii) Atmospheric dust normally contains substantial amount of lead, sometimes to the extent of several thousands ppm, hence rainfed rhizomes of turmeric and other spices crops get contaminated with lead.

(iii) Polishing of sub-standard turmeric rhizomes with lead chromate-oil emulsion.

(iv) Cooking of rhizomes in waters containing mild doses of lead acetate or in vessels which have been tinned, the tin used is often contaminated or adulterated with lead.

(v) Turmeric bulbs and fingers are pulverised with steel hammers. The machinery parts particularly the ball bearings which invariably contain lead contaminate it during pulverisation.

Lead Estimation

Dithizone reaction mechanism

The dithizone chelation method is usually employed for qualitative and quantitative determination of lead in foods. Direct ashing of sample alone results in the evaporation of lead, therefore, all cations including lead are converted into their sulphates by heating with H_2SO_4. HNO_3 oxidises sulphites to sulphates. The difficulty in wet oxidation is the presence of appreciable amounts of lead in the acids, therefore, only acids certified free from lead should be used. Pearson opines that dry ashing with or without an acid (moistening with H_2SO_4) at a temperature not exceeding 500°C is generally satisfactory. Manual of Methods of Tests and Analysis of Food by Director-General Health Services, Govt. of India (p. 164) also prescribes the incineration of the material in a platinum or silica basin by heating at first over a low flame in order to char the mass completely. Ashing is done at a temperature not exceeding 500°C preferably in a muffle furnace.

To isolate heavy metals, chelation is effected through citric acid which also helps to mask the presence of stannic and ferric ions in solution at pH 7. While describing Fehling's solution it was mentioned that citric acid has a dual role of an acid as well as of a base because it has a displaceable hydrogen atom and simultaneously a pair of unshared electrons available for coordination. Further the H^+ and OH^- groups are so spaced that the chelate ring formed is nearly free from strain. Like tartaric acid, citric acid being an (-OH) acid is a better holder of (+++) ions in solution at pH 7. It is for this reason that 2 gms of citric acid is added and the excess of this acid is neutralized with liquor ammonia solution. Conc. ammonia does not increase much the volume also of the reactants.

Further addition of 1.5 ml of liquor ammonia is done to raise the pH of the reactants between 9 to 10. A 10% KCN solution in small quantity (2 ml) is added to mask effectively all heavy metals except lead, otherwise dithizone in $CHCl_3$ or CCl_4 will form metallic complexes with any metal.

The extracted dithizonates are devoid of solvent and again reacted with conc. H_2SO_4 followed by conc. HNO_3. The 2N H_2SO_4 is capable of decomposing almost any metal complex and 0.005M HNO_3 is used to gain selectivity in determining traces of lead in biological materials.

The colloidal sulphates are coagulated by adding 15 ml of ethyl alcohol and 10 ml water to the cooled contents and keeping for overnight. Next day the coagulated $PbSO_4$ is filtered through a Whatman No. 41/44 filter paper, the residue washed with a solution comprising of 1 part of H_2SO_4, 10 parts of ethyl alcohol and 20 parts of water. The residue is washed down in a Nessler's cylinder with *hot* lead acetate. Only hot (*not boiling*) ammonium acetate solution forms lead acetate.

Lead acetate solution is again made more alkaline with 1.5 ml of liquor ammonia to raise its pH between 9 to 10. When KCN solution is added to this solution, like before, all cations except lead are masked. A dilute (0.5%) solution of sod. sulphide (Na_2S) is added to form lead sulphide (PbS) (dark coloured). The detpth of the colour is measured colourmetrically against a standard solution of lead nitrate $Pb(NO_3)_2$ in 50/100 ml Nessler's cylinders forming the matching dark colour when treated with Na_2S solution.

This quantitative estimation of lead is long and tedious also. Incidently the qualitative tests prescribed for spices suffer from one serious draw back. They are all characteristic tests for chromates only and none for lead. Since the element chromium has been reported as a constituent of natural turmeric occurring in it to the extent of 3 to 5 ppm, the chromate tests are inadequate for the detection of lead.

Formula derivation

100 ml of stock solution contains	160 mgm	$Pb(NO_3)_2$
1 ml of " "	1.60 mgm	"
2 ml of " "	3.20 mgm	"
∴ 100 ml standard solution contains	3.2 mgm	"
1 ml of " "	0.032 mgm	"
x ml of " "	0.032x mgm	"

Mol. wt. of $Pb(NO_3)_2 = 208 + 2(14+48) = 332$

Thus out of 332 parts of $Pb(NO_3)_2$ the wt. of lead = 208 parts.

In 0.032x mgm of $Pb(NO_3)_2$ the wt. of lead present

$$= \frac{208}{332} \times 0.032x \text{ mgm}$$

This much lead is present in w gm of the sample.

∴ Lead present in 1 million gms (ppm)

$$= \frac{208}{332} \times 0.032x \times \frac{10^6}{5} \text{ mgm} \qquad (w = 5 \text{ gm})$$

$$= \frac{208}{332} \times 0.032x \times \frac{10^3}{5} \text{ gms}$$

$$= \frac{208 \times 32x}{332 \times 5} = \frac{1664x}{415}$$

$$= 4x \text{ ppm}$$

(x = ml of diluted $Pb(NO_3)_2$ solution used for colour comparison)

Mathew et. al. (1975) have suggested the following simple and rapid method which can measure lead even in trace amounts.

Limit Test for the Detection of Lead in Turmeric and Curry Powder

Reagents

1. Purified Chloroform

The chloroform is purified as follows:

Shake the chloroform 2 to 3 times with 5% of its volume of con. H_2SO_4 in a separating funnel. Wash thoroughly with distilled water until the chloroform layer is clear. The chloroform is then dried over anhydrous calcium chloride and distilled. Add 1 to 2 ml of distilled alcohol per 100 ml of chloroform and the reagent is stored in a cool place in amber coloured bottles.

2. Dithizone - Stock Solution

Dissolve 1 gm of the commercial reagent in 50 to 75 ml of purified chloroform and filter. Shake in a separating funnel with four 100 ml portions of metal-free aqueous ammonia (1:99). Filter the aqueous extract into a large separating funnel through a cotton plug and extract the precipitated dithizone with two to three 20 ml portions of purified chloroform. Combine the $CHCl_3$ extracts and wash 2 to 3 times with water in the separating funnel. Draw off the chloroform layer into a beaker and evaporate the solvent on a water bath avoiding spattering as the solution goes in a desiccator containing freshly fused $CaCl_2$ overnight.

Dissolve 0.1 gms of the purified dithizone in purified chloroform in a 100 ml volumetric flash and make up with chloroform. This solution can be stored in a refrigerator and is convenient for use in making dilutions.

3. Ammonical sulphite-cyanide solution

Mix together the following : 340 ml of ammonia (sp.gr. 0.88); 75 ml of 2% w/v of sodium sulphite (Na_2SO_3) 30 ml of 10% w/v of pot. cyanide and 605 ml of water.

Method

Take 1 gm of the sample in a test tube and add 1 ml of boiling conc. HCl. Titurate well with glass rod and add 20 ml of distilled water, shake well and filter. Make the filterate alkaline (pH 9.5) with ammoniacal sulphite-cyanide solution (Reagent No. 3).

Pipette 0.2 ml of dithizone solution (Reagent No. 2) and dilute to 10 ml with purified chloroform.

Add 0.5 ml of this solution of dithizone followed by 1 ml of purified chloroform to the filterate. Shake well and note the colour of the chloroform layer. A pink colour indicates the presence of lead in the sample. Conduct a blank experiment also.

Take 2.5 ml, 5 and 10 ml of the standard lead nitrate solution containing 2.5 ug, 5 ug, and 10 ug of lead in separate test tubes. Make the solutions alkaline with ammonical sulphite-cyanide solution. Add to each test tube 0.5 ml of dithizone solution followed by 1 ml. of purified chloroform. Shake well and compare the colour produced in the chloroform layer with that of experimental solution and report the results accordingly.

Arsenic Estimation

Gutzeit Method (Theory)

Arsenic is estimated, besides other methods by Gutzeit method. This method is based on the liberation of arsine from an arsenic solution. The arsine subsequently reduces $HgBr_2$ on a prepared strip of paper with production of stains and if the method is followed as prescribed in detail then then stains are in direct proportion to the amount of arsenic.

Lead acetate is used to eliminate any H_2S that may have been generated along with arsine, otherwise the results may get vitiated as a result of H_2S, reducing $HgBr_2$ also.

The method is empirical and requires strict adherence to all minute details even. Even generation of hydrogen is assured by adopting Gladstone suggestion i.e. use of short zinc rods treated in a way to expose a constant surface area for relatively even evolution of hydrogen gas.

Apparatus

(i) 60 ml wide mouth bottle measuring 45 x 98 mm.

(ii) (a) Glass tube A measuring 120 x 10 mm, having a perforated stopper

(b) A constriction at a distance of 50 mm from the top end

(c) Glass wool wad (small) in the constriction covered with about 4 gms of clean dry sand, moistened with 10% (w/v) solution of lead acetate

(d) Excess lead acetate is removed by light suction

(e) Lead acetate paper in the lower portion of the tube.

(iii) (a) Glass tube B measuring 100 x 2.7 mm.

(b) A constriction at a distance of 40 mm from the lower end.

(c) $HgBr_2$ strip placed in the upper 60 mm portion

(d) This tube is fitted in a rubber cork fitted in the upper end of tube.

Reagents

(i) *Standard stock solution of arsenic*

1.320 gms of AS_2O_3 $\left(\frac{2x75+3x16}{2x75}=1.32\right)$ is dissolved in 25 ml of 20% NaOH Solution w/v. The resultant solution is saturated with CO_2 and diluted to 1000 ml with recently boiled (to exclude CO_2 and other dissolved gases) H_2O. 1 mg of this solution contains 1 mg of arsenic.

(ii) *Stannous chloride Solution*: 40 gms of arsenic-free $SnCl_2.2H_2O$ is dissolved in conc. HCl (sp. gravity 1.16) and the volume made up to 100 ml with HCl.

(iii) *Mercuric Bromide Paper*: Whatman No. 40 filter paper strips measuring 120x2.5 mm are soaked for one hour in a fresh 5% solution of $HgBr_2$ in 95% ethanol and then dried and stored in a dark bottle covered with black paper to be used at the earliest.

(iv) *Standard Dilute Solution of Arsenic*: 40 ml of the stock solution (i) is diluted to 1000 ml and thoroughly mixed. 50 ml of this solution is further diluted to 1000 ml — 1 ml of this diluted solution contains 0.002 mgm of arsenic and is used for the preparation of standard stains.

Procedure

Prepared Solution

50 to 100 gms of the composite sample is weighed accurately and transferred to a 500 ml Kjeldahl flask, wetted with 25 to 50 ml of conc. HNO_3 (sp. gr. 1.42) and 10 to 20 ml of conc. H_2SO_4 (sp. gr. 1.84) added. The flask is heated on a low flame very cautiously. Oxidation of the material is accelarated by adding conc. HNO_3 dropwise and intermittantly. The total volumes of HNO_3 + H_2SO_4 added are noted. Complete oxidation is understood when the solution has become colourless. Then only 20 ml of H_2O is added and contents reboiled to fuming. The cooled contents are diluted with 50 ml. of H_2O in a graduated flask.

An aliquot of less than 30 ml of this solution, estimated to contain 0.01 to 0.03 mgm of arsenic is placed in the 60 ml Gutzeit bottle. Sufficient conc. HCl is added so that total 5 ml of the acid is present. To the cooled reactants is added 5 ml of KI solution (15% w/v) and 4 dropof $SnCl_2$ solution at (ii) above followed by 2 to 5 gms of granulated zinc. $HgBr_2$ strips are inserted in the narrow-tube B (60x2.7 mm) and the entire apparatus is immersed in a water bath maintained between 20 to 25°C within 2.5 cms of the top of the tube B for 90 minutes.

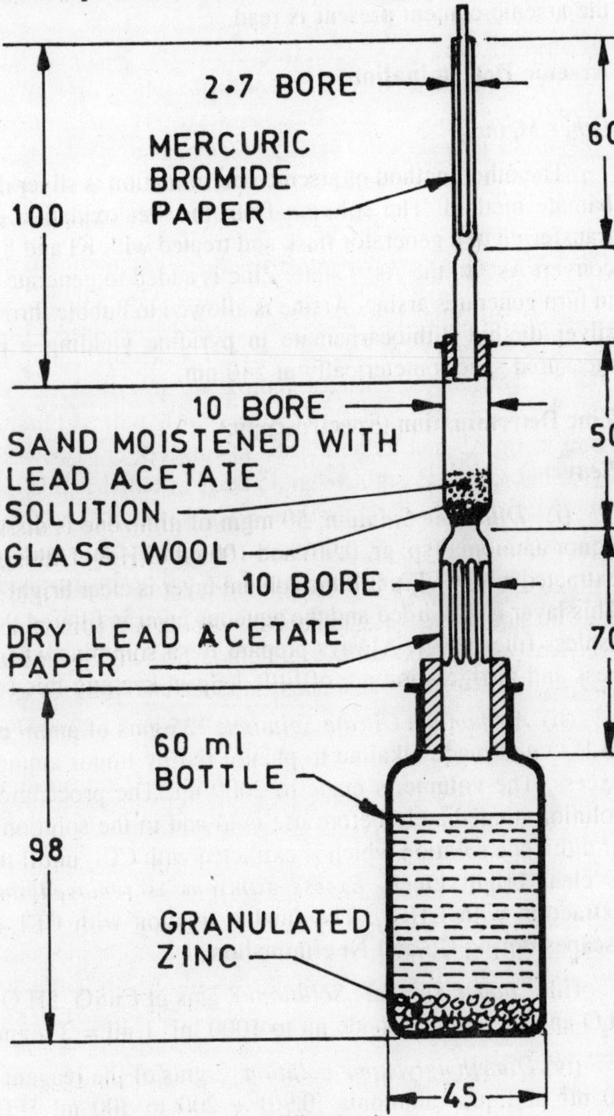

(All dimensions in millimetres)

Apparatus for Arsenic Estimation

The graph is prepared by running known quantities of the standard dilute solution (iv) above, by the above method, X-axis- length of stain Y-axis mgms of arsenic present. Blank done in positive results. The strips are removed and the average length of the stains (mm) on both sides is found out. The length of the unknown is located on a standard graph and the arsenic content present is read.

Arsenic Determination

Other Method

The other method of arsenic determination is silver diethyl-dithiocarbamate method. The solution from the wet oxidation of the sample is transferred to a generator flask and treated with KI and $SnCl_2$ solutions to convert As^{++} to the As^{+++} state. Zinc is added to generate hydrogen which in turn generates arsine. Arsine is allowed to bubble through a solution of silver diethyl dithiocarbamate in pyridine yielding a pink colouration measured spectrometerically at 540 nm.

Zinc Determination (Spectroscopic)

Reagents

(i) *Dithizone Solution*: 50 mgm of dithizone is dissolved in 2 ml of liquor ammonia (sp. gr. 0.90) and 100 ml of H_2O. Dithizone is repeatedly extracted with CCl_4 untill the solvent layer is clear bright-green in colour. This layer is discarded and the aqueous layer is filtered through a washed ashless filter paper. Always prepare fresh solutions when needed. Darkness and refrigeration are of little help in keeping this solution stable.

(ii) *Ammonium Citrate Solution*: 225 gms of amm. citrate dissolved in H_2O and made alkaline to phenol red by liquor ammonia + 75 ml in excess. The volume is made to 2000 ml. The procedure to extract this solution immediately before use is to add to the solution a slight excess of dithizone solution which is extracted with CCl_4 untill the solvent layer is clear bright green. *Excess dithizone is removed* through repeated extraction with $CHCl_3$. The final extraction with CCl_4 otherwise zinc escapes during Co and Ni elimination.

(iii) *Copper Sulphate Solution*: 8 gms of $CuSO_4.5H_2O$ is dissolved in H_2O and the volume made up to 1000 ml. 1 ml = 2 mgm of copper.

(iv) *Dimethylglyoxime Solution*: 2 gms of the reagent is dissolved in 10 ml of liquor ammonia (0.90) + 200 to 300 ml H_2O. The filtered solution is diluted to 1000 ml with H_2O.

(v) *alpha-nitroso-beta-napthal Solution*: 250 mgm of alphanitrosobeta napthal is dissolved in $CHCl_3$ and diluted to 500 ml.

(vi) *Zinc Standard Solution*

(a) *Stock Solution*: 500 mgm of pure zinc is dissolved in slight excess of 0.04 N HCl and diluted to 1000 ml. 1 ml = 500 ug of Zn.

(b) *Working Solution*: 10 ml of stock solution is diluted to 1000 ml with 0.04 N HCl. 1 ml = 5 ug of Zn.

Procedure

Wet Ashing

25 gms of the representative sample is accurately weighed into a 300 to 500 ml Kjeldahl flask. Liquid sample is evaporated to small volume. Conc. HNO_3 is added and the contents heated continuously until first vigorous reaction has subsided followed by the addition of 2 to 5 ml of conc. H_2SO_4. Heating is continued accompanied with addition of small portions of conc. HNO_3 as required to prevent charring till the reactants get clear and colourless. This is followed by evolution of dense fume of H_2SO_4 and removal of entire HNO_3.

Contents are cooled, then diluted with approx. 25 ml of H_2O, filtered, if needed through pre-washed fast filter paper. The filterate is diluted with H_2O to 100 ml.

Dry Ashing

25 gms of the representative sample is accurately weighed in a clean platinum/silica dish, charred and then ashed at temperatures less than 500°C. The carbon free ash is dissolved in minimum volume of HCl (1:1), 20 ml of H_2O added and evaporated to dryness on a steam bath. 20 ml of 0.1N HCl is added, the contents heated for 5 minutes and filtered through a pre-washed fast filter paper as above into a 100 ml measuring flask. The dish is washed with 5x10 ml of 0.1N HCl through the filter paper. The contents are cooled and the volume made up with 0.1N HCl.

Isolation and Zinc Estimation

To a suitable aliquot of ash solution of sample is added 2 drops of methyl red indicator and 1 ml of $CuSO_4$ solution and neutralized with liquor ammonia (sp.gr. 0.90). Nearly 0.5 ml of (1:1) HCl is added so that the resultant solution is 0.15N with respect to HCl (50 ml aliquot). The pH of this solution is adjusted between 1.9 to 2.1 as reflected in the glass electrode. A steady stream of washed H_2S gas is passed untill precipitation is complete. The precipitate is filtered through Whatman No. 42 or

44 filter paper washed before hand with (1:1) HCl followed by H_2O, the filterate being collected in a 250 ml beaker. The flask and filter paper are washed thrice with small portions of H_2O. The filterate is boiled gently to drive away H_2S smell completely. 5 ml of saturated bromine water is added and boiling is done untill it is bromine free and then cooled. The contents are neutralized to phenol red with liquor ammonia, slightly acidified with HCl (excess of 0.2 ml of HCl 1:1) and diluted to a known volume so that optimum conditions of measurement i.e. the solution should contain 0.2 to 1.0 ug of zinc/ml are attained.

20 ml aliquot of the above prepared solution is taken in a 125 ml separating funnel. 5 ml of ammonium citrate solution, 2 ml of dimethyl glyoxime solution and 10 ml of alpha-nitroso-beta napthal solution is added successively and thoroughly reacted by shaking the funnel for 2 minutes. The solvent layer is discarded and the remaining are extracted with 10 ml of $CHCl_3$. The solvent is again discarded. This eliminates nickel and cobalt present, if any, in the solution.

The solution now in the funnel has pH between 8.0 to 8.2. 2 ml of dithizone solution and 10 ml of CCl_4 are added and contents shaken for 12 minutes. On complete separation the aqueous layer is withdrawn to the maximum by the pipette attached to vaccum line. The sides of the separating funnel are washed down with nearly 25 ml of H_2O and without shaking the aqueous layer is again drawn off. 25 ml of 0.04N HCl is added and contents shaken for 1 minute and solvent is discarded, carefully dislodging solvent drops floating on surface also. 5.0 ml of ammonium citrate solution is added to the acidic solution followed by addition of 10.0 ml of CCl_4 (pH of solution at this point should be 8.8 to 9.0).

The volume of dithizone to be added is determined and added. The contents are shaken for thorough mixing for 2 minutes. Exactly 5.0 ml of solvent layer is pipetted into a clean and dry test tube, diluted with 10.0 ml of CCl_4, mixed well. Absorbance 'A' is determined at 540 nm and then converted to ug of zinc from standard curve, finally calculating the zinc content of the sample.

Determination of Volume of dithizone to be added.

Zinc standard solution equivalent to 20 ug zinc is diluted to 25 ml with 0.04 N HCl, 5.0 ml of ammonium citrate solution, 10.0 ml of CCl_4 and dithizone reagent in 0.1 ml increments is added, contents shaken briefly after each addition of 0.1 ml dithizone untill a faint yellow colour is there in the aqueous layer indicating a minimum excess of it present there. The consumed volume of dithizone x 1.5 is the volume of dithizone to be added (nearest to 0.05 ml) to all samples.

Preparation of Standard Curve

0, 5, 10, 15 and 20 ug of zinc diluted to 25 ml with 0.04N HCl is taken in separate and marked separating funnels each of 125 ml capacity. 5.0 ml of citrate solution, 10.0 ml of CCl_4 and determined volumes of dithizone solution (determined for samples as above) are added to each separator and contents shaken for two minutes. 5.0 ml of solvent layer is pipetted into clean dry test tube, diluted with 10.0 ml of CCl_4, contents mixed well and absorbance 'A' is read at 540 nm.

A graph is plotted of 'A' against concentration and a smooth curve is drawn through points.

Mercury Estimation

I. Chemical Method

Special Apparatus in this estimation is Gas inlet adopter, 24/40 standard taper (Kontes Glass Co.) No. k-181000 or equivalent.

Reagents

(i) *Mercury Standard Solutions.*

a) *Stock Solution*: 1000 ug/ml; prepared by dissolving 0.1354 gm of $HgCl_2$ in 100 ml H_2O.

b) *Working Solution*: 1 ug/ml; prepared afresh daily by diluting 1 ml stock solution to 1000 ml with 1 N H_2SO_4.

(ii) *Reducing Solution*

50 ml of H_2SO_4 is slowly mixed into 300 ml of H_2O, mixture cooled to room temperature. 15 gms of NaCl, 15 gms of hydroxylamine sulphate and 25 gms of $SnCl_2$ is dissolved in dil. H_2SO_4 solution and the final volume is made upto 500 ml.

(iii) *Diluting Solution*: 58 ml of conc. HNO_3 + 67 ml of conc. H_2SO_4 is added to about 400 ± 100 ml H_2O in a 1000 ml flask and the volume made up.

Procedure

Preparation of Sample

5.0 gms of the sample is digested with 25 ml of 18N H_2SO_4 + 20 ml of 7N HNO_3 and 1 ml of 2% sodium molybdate solution, adding 5 or 6 boiling chips in a digestion flask, using a water condensor, and gently heated for one hour. The contents are cooled for 15 minutes. 20 ml of HNO_3: $Mg(ClO_4)$:: 1:1 is added through the condenser, water circulation stopped and reactants boiled vigorously untill white fumes appear in the flask. Heating is continued for another 10 minutes.

10 ml of H_2O is added gently to the cooled contents, mixed by gently swirling of the flask liquid. The digestion flask is again heated to boil contents for 10 minutes, recooled and the condenser is washed with 3x15 ml of H_2O. The contents are again cooled to room temperature and then completely transferred with H_2O to a 100 ml measuring flask and diluted with H_2O to volume.

Determination

25.0 ml aliquot of digested solution of each sample is transferred to another digested solution in a 100 ml measuring flask and the volume made up with diluting solution.

The pump output is adjusted to approx. 2 litre air/minute by regulating speed through variable transformer. The apparatus is assembled as shown diagramatically except for gas inlet adopter. Spectrophotometer is zeroed, the pump is operated, 20 ml of reducing solution is added to diluted aliquot, gas inlet adopter connected and the contents aerated for approximately 3 minutes to ensure maximum absorbance. The absorbance 'A' is recorded, pressure removed on outside of pump and vent of filter flask opened thereby flushing the system.

Preparation of Standard Curve

0, 0.2, 0.5, 1.0, 1.5 and 2.0 ug of Hg is added to series of correspondingly marked digestion flasks for preparing reagent blank and standard curve. 100 ml. of diluting solution is added to each of the above flasks, finally reducing solution is added and aerated like done for samples earlier.

Standard curve from least square linear regression of absorbance against ug of Hg is plotted and ug of Hg in aliquot is calculated from the curve. In case the quantum is outside the calibration range the determination is repeated with lesser aliquot of the sample solution to bring ug of Hg into the region of standard curve. Total Hg content is calculated in the original sample.

Hg content of sample in ppm = ug of Hg/gm of sample.

II. Mercury Analyser Method

Principle

Sample is digested with HNO_3 + H_2SO_4 under reflux in a special apparatus. By reduction mercury vapour is generated and measured using Mercury Analyser Model MA 5800 C/D of Electronic Corporation of India.

Mercury Analyser MA 5800 C/D is basically a cold vapour atomic absorption spectrophotometer wherein mercury atoms absorb resonance radiation at 253.7 nm. A low pressure mercury vapour lamp emitting the desired 253.7 nm line, a filter, an absorption cell, a detector with desired electronic gadgetry and a systemised vapour generator. The mercury free air, also called carrier gas, bubbling through the vapour generation system carries mercury in the elemental form from the solution and then passes through the absorption cell.

Reagents (AR/GR grade only)

(i) Mercury Standard Stock Solution

135.4 mg of $HgCl_2$ is dissolved in H_2O, 1 ml of 1% $K_2Cr_2O_7$ is added and the volume made up to 100 ml with 2.0% HNO_3.

Dilute Standard Solution: (100 ug/ml) is prepared from the stock solution.

(ii) 20% $SnCl_2$ (w/v) in 10% HCl

20 gm of $SnCl_2$ is dissolved in 10 ml conc. HCl (sp. gr. 1.16) while warming. After dissolution it is boiled for 1 minute, cooled and diluted with H_2O to 100 ml. 1 to 2 gms of tin metal (pellets) is added and blank is examined for presence of Hg. If Hg is there, pure N_2 gas is bubbled through the solution for 1/2 hour. This solution containing metallic tin stays stable atleast for a month. Turbid solution is useless.

(iii) 1.0% w/v $KMnO_4$ in 10% H_2SO_4

1.0 gm of $KMnO_4$ dissolved in H_2O is carefully added to 10 ml of H_2SO_4 and the volume made upto 100 ml.

Estimation

Suitable aliquot of sample, standard and blank are reacted with 10% HNO_3 to have a total volume of 10 ml. 2 ml of $SnCl_2$ (ii) is added, the reactants are stoppered and stirred vigorously and continuously for

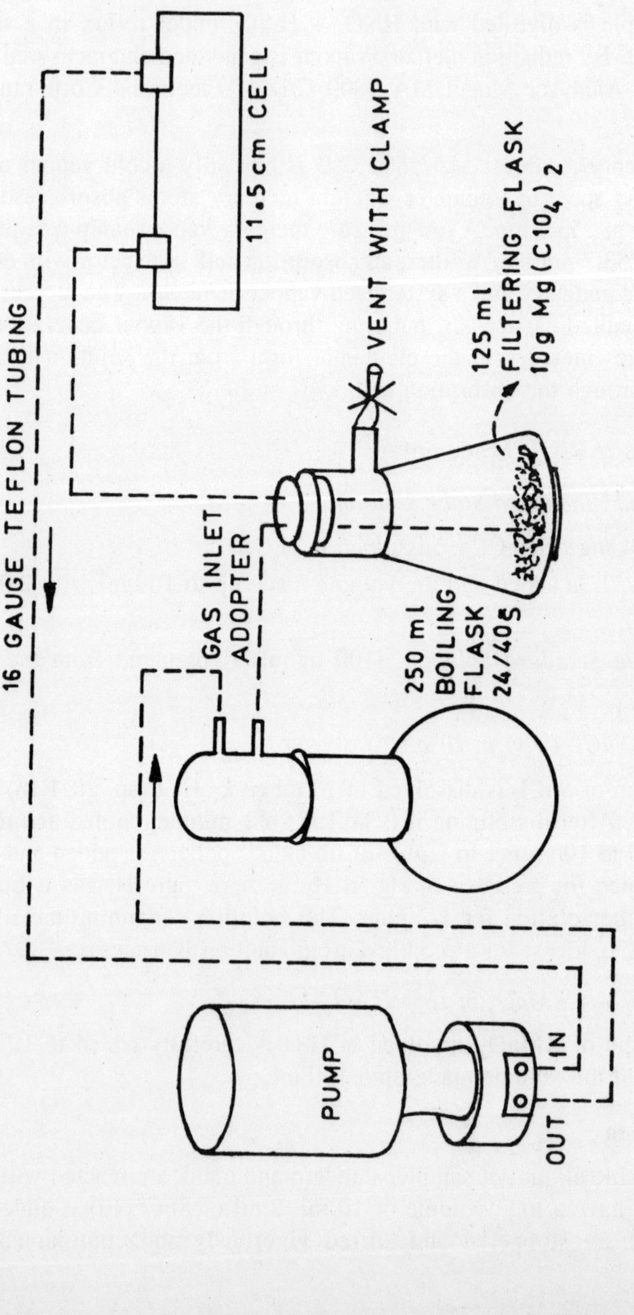

Apparatus for Flameless Atomic Absorption Analysis of Mercury

5 minutes by using an electrical magnetic stirrer. 'O' and '100% T' are adjusted, pump is started and mercury free air is permitted to purge through the reaction vessel. The mercury-free air is effected by passing it through a trap containing 20 ml of 1.0% $KMnO_4$ solution in 10% H_2SO_4. The absorbance is recorded immediately (less than 60 seconds) in the 'Hold' mode of operation, the system reswitched to 'Normal' mode back again. The magnetic stirrer as well as the pump is switched. The 'O' and '100T' is adjusted *before each arrangement.* Before reaching the absorption cell the air along with the mercury vapour from the reaction vessel is passed through the trap containing 4 ml of 20% w/v NaOH and then through another trap containing 4 ml of H_2SO_4 (1:1). The first trap absorbs acid vapours whereas the other trap absorbs moisture. Mercury vapour loaded air leaving the absorption cell is passed through the trap containing 20 ml of 1.0% $KMnO_4$ in 10% H_2SO_4 to arrest the mercury vapours, preventing the surrounding from contamination with mercury vapour.

Standard Curve

The measurements are repeated for standards 30, 60, 90, 120 & 150 ug Hg and a calibration graph is drawn by plotting absorbance against concentration of mercury, from this curve the mercury concentration is calculated.

Cadmium Determination

This is accomplished by colourimetric dithizone method.

Principle

The sample is digested with H_2SO_4 + HNO_3. The pH of the solution is adjusted to 9.0. Cadmium alongwith dithizone metals is extracted from aqueous solution with dithizone - $CHCl_3$ solution. Cd is separated from Cu, Hg and most of any Ni or Co present, by tripping $CHCl_3$ solution with dil. HCl solution leaving Cu, Hg, Ni and Co in organic phase. Aqueous layer is adjusted to 5% NaOH and extracted with dithizone - CCl_4 solution. At this alkalinity Zn, Bi and Pb do not extract whereas cadmium dithizonate is relatively stable. Cd is finally estimated photometrically at 510 nm.

Reagents

i) Stock Solution

a) 1 mgm of Cd/ml is obtained by dissolving 1.0 gm of pure Cd in

20 to 25 ml of dil NHO_3 (1:9) and evaporated to dryness. 5 ml of $HCl:H_2O$ :: 1:1 is added and re-evaporated to dryness. This residue is dissolved in 1000 ml H_2O.

b) *Intermediate Solution* - 10 ml of stock solution is diluted with H_2O to 100 ml. This solution had Cd 100 ug/ml.

c) *Working Solution* - 20 ml of Intermediate solution (b) above plus 15 ml of HCl are diluted to 1 litre with H_2O. This solution has acidity approximately 0.2 N and contains 2.0 ug of Cd/ml.

ii) Dithizone Solutions:

a) 20 mg/litre in CCl_4

b) 1 mg/ml in $CHCl_3$

iii) Thymol blue Indicator

100 mgm of indicator is triturated in agate mortar with 4.3 ml of 0.05N NaOH and diluted to 200 ml in glass stoppered flask with H_2O.

Procedure

A suitable quantity of sample is wet digested with H_2SO_4 (1:1) plus HNO_3. Charred material is oxidised with H_2SO_4 and digestion effected thoroughly with HNO_3 as needed. Fat bearing samples may bump and froth during digestion. Partial digestion of such large samples is effected with warm HNO_3 untill only insoluble part remains. This solid fat is filtered off the cooled contents. The residue is washed with H_2O. The combined filterate is made to suitable volume and the required aliquot is digested as above.

The digest is diluted with 25 ml H_2O, filtered if deemed necessary and transferred to a 125 ml separating funnel using additional 10 ml H_2O portions for rinsing and effecting transfer. 1 to 2 gms of diammonium citrate, and 1 ml of thymol blue indicator are added, pH at 8.8 adjusted by adding ammonia solution slowly while cooling the reactants intermittently, untill solution changes from yellowing-green to greenish-blue. The 125 ml volume is made up with H_2O. This is extracted vigorously with 5 ml portions of dithizone --- chloroform solution until the chloroform layer remains green. Final extraction is done with 3 ml of $CHCl_3$.

The combined chloroform extracts are transferred to a prewetted separating funnel with 3 ml $CHCl_3$. 40 ml of 0.2N HCl is added, contents shaken vigorously for more than 60 seconds and the layers allowed to separate. The chloroform phase is drained, remaining dithizone droplets are removed by extraction with CCl_4 (1 to 2 ml portion) till the bore or stem of the separating funnel is free of acid.

The aqueous phase is adjusted to 5.0% alkalinity by adding 10 ml of 28% NaOH aqueous solution. Cadmium is extracted by shaking vigorously not less than 60 seconds with 25 ml dithizone solution. The extract is transferred to another prewetted, like before, separating funnel. Extractions are repeated with additional 10 ml portions of dithizone solution untill CCl_4 layer become colourless. Cadmium upto 100 ug is completely removed by third extraction.

To preclude that pale-pink colour persisting after third extraction is not due to zinc, a known extract is transferred to another separating funnel containing 5.0% NaOH solution and shaken vigorously with dithizone solution. A colourless CCl_4 layer reflects that original pink was due to zinc hence further extractions are uncalled for. However, if pink persists, confirming the presence of cadmium, the extract is added back to the third separating funnel and extractions are continued.

Cadmium and zinc dithizonates in the third funnel are converted to chlorides by adding 40 ml of 0.2N HCl and shaking the reactants vigorously for a minute. CCl_4 layer is carefully drained and discarded. Droplets of dithizone from aqueous phase are removed by rinsing with 1 to 2 ml of CCl_4, draining CCl_4 carefully to the last drop but even a single drop of the acid layer is not allowed to pass the bore of the separating funnel. The alkalinity is readjusted to 5% by adding 10 ml NaOH solution (28% w/v). A precise 25 ml volume of dithizone is added and the reactants shaken vigorously for one minute and then left to separate the layers for not less than three minutes. The separator stem is wiped dry with cotton. The organic layer is filtered through a pledget, first 5 ml is discarded.

The absorbance of cadmium-dithizone complex solution is read at 510 nm and quantity of cadmium in ug is calculated from standard curve or by substituting absorbance in the linear equation.

Preparation of Standard Curve

6 standards containing 25, 20, 15, 10, 5, 0 ug of cadmium are prepared in duplicate in separate and marked separating funnels, 40 ml of 0.2 N HCl, 10 ml of 28% w/v NaOH solution and 25 ml of dithizone solution is added to each of the above separating funnels. All are shaken for 60 seconds and allowed to stand for not less than 180 seconds. The organic layer is filtered through a pledget, first 5 ml is discarded. Absorbance 'A' is determined at 510 nm and a standard curve is plotted.

Estimation of Copper

Special Reagents

i) sodium diethyl dithiocarbamate solution — 0.1% (w/v) in H_2O

ii) standard copper solution — 100 mgm of pure copper turnings are accurately weighed and carefully dissolved in the minimum volume of dil. HNO_3 (1:1 of sp. gr, 1.42). The contents are cooled and diluted to 1 litre in a graduated flask. 10 ml of this solution is pipetted in a 100 ml graduated flask and diluted to the mark.

1 ml of this solution contains 10 ppm of copper.

Procedure

10 ml aliquot (from arsenic prepared solution) is transferred to a separating funnel. 1 gm of citric acid is added and dissolved by shaking. The solution is made alkaline to litmus by adding liquor ammonia in small measures. 5 ml of the sodium diethyl dithiocarbamate solution is added, the contents are thoroughly shaken and extracted with 5 ml portions of CCl_4 until the final extract is colourless. The extracts are combined and dried by shaking thoroughly with anhydrous Na_2SO_4. The dried extract is filtered and the residual copper complex is removed by washing the filter paper with CCl_4. The filterate volume is made up to 25 ml with CCl_4 and absorption of this solution is measured at 437 nm by means of spectrophotometer.

H_2O is used instead of prepared solution for blank determination.

Series of standards are prepared by treating aliquots of the standard copper solution (ii) above in the aforesaid procedure. From the absorption of the standard solutions, a standard curve of absorption values against concentration is plotted. From the curve, the quantity of copper present in the sample is estimated.

Chromate Test

Lead chromate resembles turmeric powder in colour and is immediately soluble in water. These similarities are abused by unscrupulous traders. The hazardous lead chromate is, at times, employed to uplift the faded colour of old rhizomes and also to hide weevil's bores or black mouldy spots on them. At the same time the element chromium is a constitutent of natural turmeric occurring to the extent of 3 to 5 ppm (Robert, 1968). Earlier it was thought that the absence of chromate also confirms the absence of lead which is untrue. Several samples of turmeric powder give a negative chromate test but still have lead content of more than 60 ppm. Thus both the tests have their individual importance. The PFA Act stipulates that lead chromate test must be negative in turmeric.

Procedure

Ash about 2 gms of the sample material, dissolve this ash in 4 to 5 ml of (1:7) H_2SO_4 in a test tube and then add 1 ml of diphenyl carbazide solution (0.2%, w/v in alcohol 95% v/v). The presence of chromate is indicated by the production of violet colour.

Strong acid solutions of chromate react with diphenyl carbazide (DPC) and give a violet colouration even though only traces of chromium VI are present. It is claimed that the colour reaction involves an action that has not been observed in other cases, the CrO_4 in acid solution oxidises (DPC) initially to colourless diphenyl carbazone and then to light yellow diphenyl carbadiazone.

However, in distinction to all other known redox reactions of the chromate ion, there is no production of chromic ions, rather chromous ions are formed and the latter yield a red violet inner complex salt V by action with the enol form IV of the carbazone.

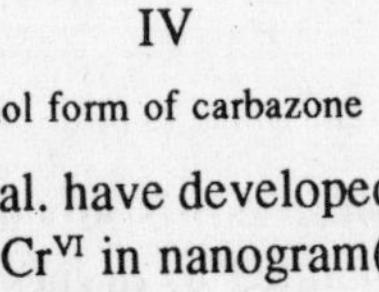

IV

enol form of carbazone

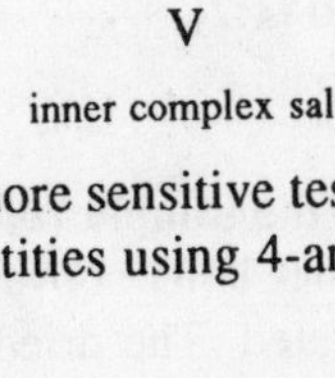

V

inner complex salt

Negi et.al. have developed a still more sensitive test for detecting the presence of Cr^{VI} in nanogram(ng) quantities using 4-amino antipyrine of 0.05% w/v strength.

A drop of faintly acidic test solution containing Cr^{VI} is placed on a spot plate or test paper with a micrometer syringe followed by the addition of a drop of the reagent solution. If Cr^{VI} is present a violet colour develops instantaneously.

F^-, Cl^-, Br^-, I^-, CH_3COO^-, NO_3^-, SO_4^{2-},PO_4^{3-}, BO_3^{3-}, CNS^-, oxalate, citrate, thiourea, Pb^{++}, Ba^{++},Ca^{++}, Sr^{++}, Mg^{++}, Cd^{++}, Zn^{++}, Sn^{++}, Be^{++}, Ag^+, Bi^{+++}, As^{+++}, Sb^{+++}, Al^{+++}, do not interfere even when present in large excess (not more than 500 times). The serious interference by Fe^{3+}, Cu^{2+}

and Mn^{7+} can be reduced considerably by masking Fe^{3+} with hydroxylamine hydrochloride, Cu^{2+} by thiourea and Mn^{7+} is reduced to Mn^{2+} by hydrazoic acid. Though the sensitivity is slightly reduced but Cr^{VI} is present in 10^{-6} gm quantity while the 4-amino antipyrine reagent detects Cr^{VI} even in 10^{-9} gm quantities, therefore it is suitable for the purpose.

CaO Determination in Bleached Ginger

Certain grades of ginger are bleached with lime, partly as claimed to ward off attacks of insects and partly to improve the appearance. Indian ginger is expected to have CaO content below 2.0%.

Estimation (Agmark Method)

Reagents Required

i) Conc HCl (sp. gr. 1.16)

ii) Dil HCl (2:5 of (i)

iii) Saturated solution of Amm. Oxalate.

iv) Dil. ammonia (1:1 of Liquor ammonia sp. gr. 0.90)

v) Dil H_2SO_4 (1:4 of conc. H_2SO_4 of sp. gr. 1.84)

vi) $KMnO_4$ (0.1N)

vii) Bromo cresol green indicator (0.04%). It is prepared by grinding 100 mgm of bromo cresol green accurately weighed with 14.3 ml of NaOH solution (0.IN) in an agate mortar. The contents are transferred to a 250 ml volumetric flask with H_2O and the volume made up.

viii) Acetic acid (1:2)

Procedure

2 to 4 gms of the sample (accurately weighed) is ashed. The ash is digested with dil. HCl (ii) above and evaporated to dryness. Digestion and drying is repeated. The dried residue is treated with 5 to 10 ml of conc. HCl (i) above and about 50 ml of H_2O is added. The contents are kept on a water bath for few minutes and filtered in a 250 ml beaker through a filter paper. The residue is washed with hot H_2O, the washings collected in the same beaker. 0.5 ml of bromo cresol green (vii) above is added to the collected washings followed by dil. ammonia (iv) above till the solution becomes distinctly blue. The pH is adjusted between 4.4 and 4.6 by adding dil acetic acid (viii) above till the reactants are again distinct green. These are filtered, the filter paper washed with hot H_2O. The washings are collected in the same beaker and are boiled. Liquor

ammonia is added drop by drop in the hot solution till precipitation continues plus an excess. The contents are again boiled and then set aside for not less than 3 hours. Clear solution is decanted through an ashless filter paper. The precipitate is freed of its water soluble constituents by washing and decantation as before. The filter paper residue is washed with dil HCl into the original beaker followed by hot water washings. Reprecipitation is effected by boiling and addition of ammonia plus little of amm. oxalate solution (iii) above and are again set aside for not less than 3 hours. The contents are filtered through the same ashless filter paper and made chloride free by repeated hot water washings.

The precipitate is washed down through a pierced hole in the filter paper into the beaker used earlier for precipitation with dil H_2SO_4 (v) above and titrated at more than 70°C with $KMnO_4$solution (vi) above.

Calculation

Calcium oxide (CaO) % by mass = 2.8 VN/M where
V is ml of $KMnO_4$ (vi) used for titration
N is exact normality of (vi) and
M is gms of sample taken for the test.

VI. Salt Determination in Spices

Curry powders and other spice mixtures advertised for use in speical culinaries contain common salt. Statutory restrictions have been laid about the maximum content of common salt in curry powders and spice mixtures covered under curry powder. Under the head "Spices and Condiments" the PFA Act 1954 and the PFA Rules 1955 define salt as NaCl and nothing else when determined volumetrically by titrating the salt-containing extract with silver nitrate ($AgNO_3$). Pot. chromate (K_2CrO_4) is employed as the indicator in direct titration method. In the other method excess of $AgNO_3$ (1:4) should be boiled to eliminate lower nitrogen oxides is added and the unreacted $AgNO_3$ is titrated back against ammonium thiocyanate (NH_4CNS), using alum ($FeNH_4(SO_4)_3$.12 H_2O as indicator.

The accurately weighed sample is ashed as usual. During ashing the proteinous sulphur escapes as SO_2, CO_3^{2-}, HCO_3^- if any decomposes with the exit of CO_2. The ash contains phosphates as well as the alkaline oxides. Even sample to which common salt has not been added give precipitate when $AgNO_3$ is added and this is usually deemed to be Ag-halides which, in view of this author, is not correct. A good deal of literature on this aspect has been gone through but there is no report about the presence of halides in most virgin spices. At the same time it is known that Ag_3PO_4 is an odourless yellow powder, sparingly soluble in water (soluble in 15500 parts of H_2O) and its solubility further decreases in the presence of $AgNO_3$. Therefore it is deduced that the precipitate with $AgNO_3$ is of Ag_3PO_4 and not of Ag halides. This aspect is discussed briefly here.

The phosphorus content of common spices that constitute curry powders is:

Bishop's weed = 0.30%; basil = 0.47%; chilli powder = 0.37% caraway = 0.11%; cardamom seed = 0.21%; cardamom capsule = 0.15%; celery seed = 0.55%; coriander seed = 0.44%; cumin seed = 0.45%; fennel seed = 0.48%; fenugreek seed = 0.48%; dehydrated garlic powder = 0.42%; marjoram = 0.57% plus (chloride from 1.51 to 2.05%); nutmeg = 0.24%; onion powder = 0.29%; poppy seed = 0.79% to 0.89%; turmeric = 0.26%.

(Source: "Spices and Condiments" by J.S. Pruthi.)

Most of these spices, therefore, on the average contain 0.42% phosphorus. We know that Ag_3PO_4 precipitates out in alkaline solutions, whereas Ag halides only in acidic medium. Even neutral solutions precipitate Ag_3PO_4 but acidic solutions certainly do not precipitate Ag_3PO_4. The solubility product of Ag_3PO_4 is 3.4×10^{-14}, of AgCl is 1.56×10^{-10} and of $Ca_3(PO_4)_2$ is 1.0×10^{-25}. Deeming that PO_4^{3-} is present as $Ca_3(PO_4)_2$ in the ash then on the addition of $AgNO_3$, Ag_3PO_4 will precipitate out first in preference to AgCl.

Further, Ag_3PO_4 contains silver 77.31%; phosphorus 7.4% and oxygen 15.29% i.e. silver content is more than 10 times of phosphorus. On weight basis this 0.42% of phosphorus shall consume around 4.4% of silver to form Ag_3PO_4 (mol wt. 418) which shall be reported as NaCl (mol. wt. 58.5). In other words, what is actually a precipitate of Ag_3PO_4 shall be deemed due to NaCl as AgCl. Thus 0.42% phosphorus shall be reported as

$$0.42 \times \frac{77.31}{7.4} = 4.4\%$$

of Ag^+ in Ag^3PO^4 and in terms of NaCL

$$= \frac{4.4 \times 58.5}{418} = 0.61\%$$

This explains the enigma of the innocent manufacturer who adds common salt less than 5% (the statutory limit) but finds reported higher after analysis or his unsalted spice mixture or curry powder is reported to contain NaCl upto 0.8%. Therefore, it is better, rather scientific, to leach out the added salt in the sample with hot H_2O. There shall be no transfer of pigment colour in the water extract because these pigments are mostly carotenoids and only anthocyanins impart colour to water solution. The water extract be acidified with dil. HNO_3 then titrated against $AgNO_3$ using K_2CrO_4 as indicator like before.

The weight of sample taken for salt determination and the volume of aliquot is so adjusted that the volume of $AgNO_3$ (0.1N) consumed does not exceed 8 ml because $AgNO_3$ is a costly chemical.

Standardisation of primary standard 0.IN NaCl.

Usually NaCl (AR) is marketed as 500 gms pack in glass bottles. Very little quantity is required at a time. Consequently the pack gets exposed to atmospheric humidity absorbing moisture hence NaCl needs dehydration every time. For 250 ml of (0.1N) solution we need 1.4625 gms of NaCl.

A clean dried beaker is accurately tared. The above quantity +10 to 15 mgm of NaCl is placed in an air oven for dehydration. After an hour or so, the beaker is taken out, cooled at room temperature, weighed quickly but accurately and contents dissolved in H_2O. The desired final volume is made up and its normality is calculated. This procedure eliminates hygroscepic moisture absorption thus leading to accurate results.

Calculations

wt. of the sample material = w gms

Volume of 0.1N $AgNO_3$ used for complete precipitation of salt = x ml

Now 1000 ml of 0.1N $AgNO_3$ is equivalent to 58.5/10 = 5.85 gms NaCl

$$x'' \quad '' \quad '' \quad '' \quad '' \quad '' = \frac{5.85x}{1000} \text{ gms NaCl}$$

This is present in w gms of sample, therefore,

$$\therefore \quad \text{Percentage of NaCl} = \frac{5.85x}{1000} \times \frac{100}{w} = \frac{0.585x}{w}$$

(N = normality of $AgNO_3$)

VII. Non-Volatile Ether Extract (NVEE)

As the subject title denotes, it is the fixed i.e. the non-volatile ether extractable matter of the plant foods. It is the body of the plant foods. Chemically, NVEE contains the entire fixed oil, saponifiable as well as unsaponifiable matter (USM). The USM contains, sterols, pigments, waxes, fat soluble vitamins, if any and alkaloids. This etheral extract is desolventised under reduced pressure and the residue, the NVEE, constitutes the body of the oleoresin.

The quantitative determination of NVEE is partly helpful in detecting already extracted materials if pulverised along with wholesome spices to increase their weight with ulterior motives of profit. It is, as mentioned above, partly helpful, because the quantity alone of the extract has partial utility, the important factor is the quantity of the active principles of the extract. To illustrate this point let us take the case of chilli.

Chilli owes its importance to the quantitative presence of its alkaloid capsaicin responsible for its pungent taste as well as the pigment capsanthin, alpha and beta carotene and other carotenoids like copsrubin, zeaxanthin, cryptoxanthin, cutein and a few unidentified xanthophylls. The alkaloid is present from 0.2 to 1.0% and the pigments are present from 0.407% to 0.54%. The fixed oils, sugars, and resins have secondary importance though they constitute the bulk of NVEE. These materials of secondary importance are found paradoxically more in seeds and less in pericarp. On the other hand the above active and important principles of pungency and colour are found maximum in pericarp and least in the seeds and stalks. This is evidenced from the following table:

Distribution of Extractions (Sannam Variety) Chilli

Component part	*%age in whole chilli*	*Total extractions (NVEE%)*	*Capsaicin %*	*Total colour, beta carotene, (ug/gm) i.e. (ppm)*
Whole	100	14.8	0.23	1700
Pericarp	40	10.3	0.52	4000
Seeds	54	23.3	0.05	20
Stalks	06	5.2	nil	nil

Thus seeds alone shall yield nearly 100% more of NVEE's statutory requirement of a minimum of 12.0% whereas the consummer get only 20% (approx) of the pungent principle-capsaicin and 1.2% of the total carotenoids — the colouring principle in the chilli.

Some manufacturers however polish the colourless spent chilli powder or even colourless husks with an emulsion of *ratanjot* i.e. alkanet (*Alkanna tinctoria*) in a cheaper oil or with oil soluble colours. The theory of the analytical method employed to detect these has been dealt later and so also of the Scoville test which ascertains the pungency organoleptically and colour value colourimetrically.

There is no restriction to the maximum permissible particle size of pulverised chillies as has been done in the case of turmeric powder. Chillies are occasionally fragmented by pounding and are marketed under the variety "*mirch kutti*". These fragmented chillies have ready acceptability for use in pickles and certain dishes. It is pertinently advised that the analyst should pulverise the material to a fineness of 300 microns or to get a bulk density of 400-450 gm/litre without raising temperatures during pulverising. This shall remove chances of getting low erroneous results.

The approved solvent is diethyl ether (IS: 1797-1961). In the market diethyl ether, hydrated over H_2SO_4 is branded as 'ether sulphuric' or 'ether solvent'. Pet. ether of b. pt. 40-60°C, or 60-80°C, $CHCl_3$ of b. pt. 59.5 to 61.5°C, n-hexane of b. pt. 62°C, ethylene dichlorlde of b.pt. 84°C give reproduceable results corresponding to ether solvent. All these solvents have NVEE not more than 0.002%, still a blank of the solvent batch may be worked out and substracted to find accurate results. Ethanol is unsuitable because 50% of the colouring principle is reduced and the extract is a semisolid instead of the usual free flowing oil. Any solvent having moisture is not suitable for this purpose because soluble saccharides and salts are also leached out and during drying in the oven when water is driven off as steam, these solutes of water become erroneously as part of NVEE.

Desolventization can be carried out also by removing the distilled colourless solvent in batches from the Soxhlet's extractor by disengaging and then tilting it slightly just to raise the ether level slightly above the constriction inside the tube, placing the lower end removed from the 250 ml flask into the receiving container. Traces of solvent can be removed by blowing gently warm air. Check complete removal of the solvent by smelling the flask at room temperature for the complete absence of the characteristic smell of these solvents.

The spent chilli meal usually contains phosphorus = 28%, carbohydrates = 36% and fibre = 29% hence a limit of 30% for crude fibre in chilli.

Procedure

2.0 to 2.5 gms of the ground spice is extracted continuously with diethyl ether in a Soxhlet extractor for 19 hours. The ether is removed by distillation followed by blowing with a stream of air in the flask on a boiling water-bath and dried in an air oven at 110 ± 1°C till the loss in weight between successive weighings is less than 2 mgm. The residue is shaken with 2 to 3 ml of diethyl ether at room temperature, allowed to settle and the ether decanted. These extractions are repeated until no more of the residue dissolves. The flask is dried again until the loss in weight between two successive weighings is less than 2 mg. The lowest weight is noted.

Calculation

$$\text{NVEE\% by wt. on dry weight basis} = \frac{100(W1-W2)}{W(100-W3)}$$

where

W = Weight of the material taken for the test

W1 = Weight of the flask + NVEE

*W2 = Weight of the flask with ether insoluble residue after decantation.

W3 = Moisture % of the sample

* It is evident that NVEE is the material which can be extracted with ether and is soluble in it also. The ether insoluble matter is not accepted as NVEE hence has to be substracted from the total etheral extract.

VIII. Alcohol Soluble Extract

For spices expected to have volatile oil more than 5%, complete extraction with 90% ethanol is necessary. Let it be V%, then

Real Alcohol Extract = V-W3.

Procedure

The sample (2 gms ± 1 mgm) accurately weighed is transferred with 93% v/v of ethyl alcohol to the 100 ml volumetric flask. The flask is filled to the mark. The stoppered flask is shaken at 1/2 hour interval for 4 hours. After this operation, the flask is kept undisturbed for atleast 16 hours. The contents are filtered and a 50 ml aliquot is evaporated to dryness on a water bath followed by heating in an air oven maintained at 103 ± 2°C to constant mass, the difference between the succeeding readings not exceeding 1 mgm after one hour of heating.

IX. Cold Water Soluble Extract

The procedure is similar except that 1/2 hour interval shaking is done for 8 hours instead of 4 hours and the difference between succeeding weight reading is not more than 2 mgm.

Calculation

$$\text{Extracts\% by wt. on dry basis} = \frac{100W1}{W(100\text{-}W2)}$$

where

W = wt. in gms of test material

W1 = wt. in gms of dried extract

W2 = moisture % of the sample.

X. Volatile Oil Determination

The components responsible for the characteristic aroma of a plant material constitute its volatile oil. The volatile oil is an equally important constituent of the plant's oleoresin and is responsible for its top note. Chemically these compounds are mono-and di-sesquiterpenoids and their oxygenated derivatives like alcohol, aldehyde or ketone obtained from the sap and tissues of the plants. For example, aniseed owes its flavour to anethole, Indian basil to methyl cinnamate, linalool and methyl chavicol, cardamom to cineole and caraway to carvone and so on. The di-and tri-terpenoids are not steam volatile hence become constituents of the non-volatile extracts.

The term volatile oil connotes only those constituents which volatilize and get distilled with water vapour at ordinary pressure. The special apparatus meant for the quantitative determination of the volatile oil in spices and condiments is called Clevenger's apparatus which is a slight variation of the Dean and Stark apparatus. The distilling media (water vapours) returns to the main kettle and the volatilized oil, synonymous with essential oil rises to the top. Since the content is generally below one per cent (v/w), therefore atleast 50 gms of the well pulverised sample must be taken for the determination in a 500 ml, preferably one litre flask. The glass assembly, particularly the receiver must be scrupulously clean to facilitate the smooth rise and collection of the volatile oil. The material for distillation in the flask must be adequately under water to avoid bumping, caking and carbonizing. Glass beads of 3 mm dia or pumice stone should be added before the commencement of this distillation.

The distilled volatile oil provides a vivid inner built up, through olfaction, of the spice mixture composition. The flavour of the major dominant note reveals much more than is possible by chemical analysis. For example, turmeric which is not a costly spice contains 5 to 6% of volatile oil (v.o.) and is frequently added to increase the v.o.% of curry powders instead of ginger which contains on the average only 2.0%, cardamom (big) having 1.0 to 1.2% or the more costlier spices like cardamom (small) or cloves or cinnamon. Coriander powder is often used to adulterate cumin powder or fennel powder the former being though poorer in v.o.% (0.04 — 0.8% — Indian variety) yet is much cheaper. Even among the same species, greater cardamom seeds are used for adulterating small cardamom seeds.

Another case is of cinnamon species. In the Indian bazars the most important aromatic barks sold commercially are true cinnamon (*C. zeylanicum*), *jangli dar-chini* (C. inners), *tezpat* or *tamal patra* or Indian cassia, Lignea (*C. tamala*) and *tezpat* or *Ram tezpat* (*C. obtusifolium*). Now *Jangli dar-chini* bark yields 0.5% of volatile oil. *Tejpat* bark has a little use in the flavour industry, instead the bark and oil is used as an adulterant in true cinnamon whose bark is smoother than that of tezpat. The bark oil is also adulterated with cinnamon leaf oil

Evidently it is not enough to determine merely the percentage of volatile oil present in a spice(s) mixture sample. It is equally imperative to examine the characteristics of the volatile oil, the very basis for its acceptability with regard to quality and the corresponding price. For example, greater cardamom oil emits a strong camphoraceous as well as cineoleic odour and taste while small cardamom leaves a flat cineoleic odour with blends of mild notes of limonene and δ-terpineol. Similarly *Cinnamon inners (Jangli dar chinis')* bark oil emits an odour of cloves and musk but *C. tamala* bark oil is of pale yellow colour and contain 70-85% cinnamic aldehyde. True cinnamon's volatile oil has a light yellow colour when fresh and red on storage. This oil contains cinnamic aldehyde 60-75%, eugenol and benzaldehyde. Cinnamom leaf oil, the adulterant in true cinnamon oil is of yellow to yellowish brown hue and contains eugenol 70-95%, cinnamic and benzaldehyde. Indian coriander oil is a pale yellow liquid which causes irritation when is in contact with skin for a long time. The major constituents of the coriander volatile oil are d-linalool or corianderol 45-70%, and the rest about 20% are hydrocarbons. While cumin seed oil has cuminaldehyde 20-30% and Indian fennel seed volatile oil has 70% of anethole and 6% fenchone. All these three oils are of pale yellow colour.

The verification through the characteristic study of volatile oil shall also help in confirming the descending order of the various spices displayed on the package under obligation of Rule 32 of P.F.A. Rules 1955. Often the consumer is misled in this context.

The Central Agmark Laboratory, Nagpur in its annual report

(1984-85) has reported that microscopical examination fails to detect the presence of *Carum carvi (L)* and *Carum bulbocastanum* in each other and the laboratory has employed successfully TLC analysis of their essential oils for differenciating them. Silica gel is the absorbent, pet. ether and benzene (1:1) is the developing solvent and 1% vanillin in 100 ml ethyl alcohol + 1 ml H_2SO_4 as spray agent.

The laboratory claims that adulteration upto 1% can be easily detected.

Similarly presence of cumin in the above two spices is detected by employing carbon tetrachloride, n-hexane, formic acid in the proportion of 60:45:1 respectively as developing solvent.

Volatile oil in mustard seed is estimated (method based on AOAC) by weighing 5 gms of mustard powder in a 200 ml flask and adding 100 ml of H_2O, stoppering the flask air tight. Maceration is continued for 2 hours at 37°C, 20 ml of alcohol 95% is added and about 60 ml of the distillate is collected from distilling the above into a 100 ml volumetric flask containing 10 ml dilute ammonia (1 ml conc. NH_4OH + 2 ml water), taking care that the condenser tip dips into the liquid in the volumetric flask. 20 ml of N/10 $AgNO_3$ is added to the distillate, allowed to stand overnight, heated on a water bath to coagulate Ag_2S, cooled and diluted to 100 ml with H_2O and filtered. The filterate (50 ml) is acidified with 5 ml of conc HNO_3 and titrated with N/10 NH_4 CNS using 5 ml of 10% ferric ammonium sulphate as indicator. 1 ml N/10 $AgNO_3$ = 0.004956 gms of allyl isothiocyanate.

Resuming, the apparatus is cleaned before each distillation by washing successively with acetone and water, then inverting it, filling it with chromic-sulphuric acid mixture allowing to stand, and finally rinsing with water.

When fully assembled, the apparatus is totally enclosed. When air-vent is required it should be arranged at the stopper K.

Method-I

The powdered spice is placed, together with the distillation liquid and a few pieces of porous earthenware in the distilling flask which is then connected to the still-head. The stopper K is removed and water is run into the tubulure K until it overflows at B.

The contents of the flask are heated, with frequent agitation, until ebullition commences, and the distillation is continued at a rate that leaves the lower part of the condenser cold at the point G. The flask is rotated occasionally to wash down any material adhering to the upper part of the walls.

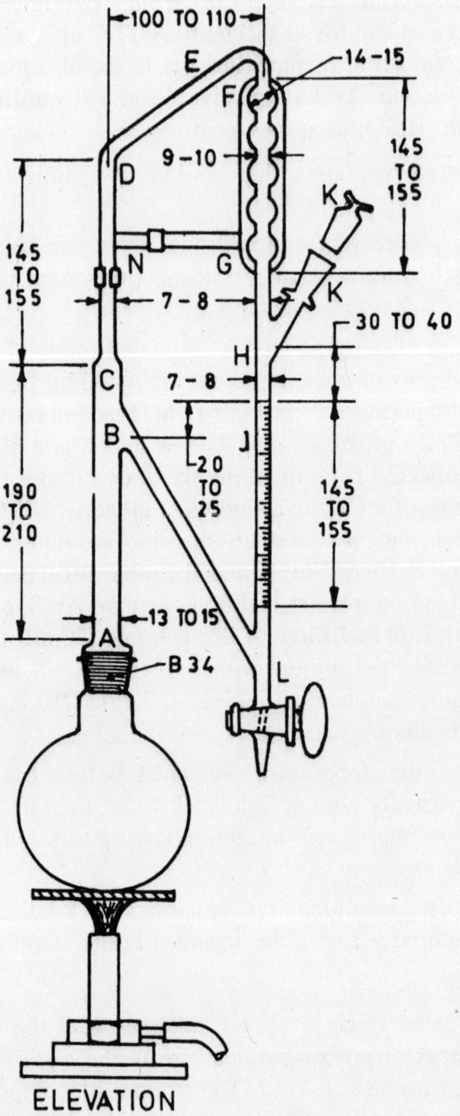

(All dimensions in millimetres)
Clevenger's Apparatus for Essential/Volatile Oil Content

At the end of the specified time, heating is discontinued and, after at least five minutes, the volume of oil in the graduated portion of the tube is read off.

The distillation is then continued for a further period of one hour and the volume of oil is again read off as before. If necessary, the distillation is again continued until successive readings of the volume of oil taken to be the content of volatile oil in the spice are the same.

Method - II

The distillation liquid, and a few small pieces of porous earthenware, are placed in the flask, which is then connected to the still head. The stopper K is removed, and water is run into the tubulure K until it overflows at B. 1 ml of xylene is introduced at K by means of a pipette, the tip of which is inserted into the lower part of the tubulure K. The liquid in the flask is heated until ebullition commences, and the distillation is continued at AD in the flask, which is then connected to the still head. The liquid induction is conducted as described under Method I. The volume of the oily layer and the remainder is taken to be the content of volatile oil in the spice.

Table

Spice	*Weight to be taken in gm*	*Distillation liquid ml.*		*Method*	*Approx. Time of Dist. Hrs.*
Caraway	20	Glycerol	150	I	4
		Water	150		5
Cardamom	20	-do		I	
Cinnamon	40	Water	300	II	5
Clove	40	Glycerol	150	II	4
		Water	150		
Coriander	40	-do-		I	3
Fennel	25	-do-		II	4
Nutmeg	15	Water	300	I	3

XI. Determination of Piperine

Theory

Two methods have been prescribed. The Kjeldahl's method estimates nitrogen expressed as piperine. Obviously variations due to other nitrogen containing compounds shall occur i.e. this method lacks detection of the presence of extraneous nitrogenous substances.

The spectrophotometric method is more reliable by virtue of non-interference of other nitrogenous substances present in the oleoresin. Consequently, in case of dispute, spectrophotometric method will be accepted as the referee method, therefore, only this method has been detailed below.

Procedure

Nearly but accurately weighed 0.5 gm of black pepper powder sample passing through a 500 micron sieve is taken in a 250 ml volumetric flask. 100 ml of 95% alcohol is added and the contents are boiled on a water bath for 3 hours with occasional swirling. The cooled contents are made up to flask volume with 95% alcohol. About 10 ml of the well mixed alcoholic suspension is filtered and out of it 1 ml of the extract is transferred to each of the two 25 ml flasks. A third flask for blank contains 1 ml of the above 95% alcohol + 0.5 ml of 20% chromotropic acid. The above chromotropic acid solution is prepared by dissolving 20 gms of 4, 5 dihydroxy 2,7-naphthalene disulphonic acid in 100 ml of slightly warm water. If a black sediment is present then filtered through a sintered glass filter or centrifuged. Approximately 10 ml of conc. H_2SO_4 is added to all the three flasks, rotating them during the acid addition to wash down the sides and the contents well mixed by swirling. The flasks are heated in a water bath for half an hour. The glass stoppers are seated loosely during the first minute but during the later period are tightened. The flasks are cooled at room temperature and the volumes made up with conc. H_2SO_4 and the contents mixed up thoroughly by inverting these flasks several times. Using 1 ml cell, the absorbance of the solutions is measured at 580 mu.

Precautions

The extract must be filtered again and again till it is clear. Some heating occurs during the first addition of H_2SO_4 and the alcohol approaches the boiling point. However, the volumetric flask shape prevents spattering. No heat is evolved when H_2SO_4 is added to adjust the solution volume. While transferring the solutions to the absorbance cell, avoid excess contact with moist air to prevent striations. If striations do occur, wait a minute or two before measuring the absorbance.

$$\text{Percentage of piperine} = 10.81 \times \frac{(A-B)}{W}$$

Where

A = absorbance of sample solution + Chromotropic acid solution against the second flask containing H_2SO_4 also.

B = absorbance of sample solution but no chromotropic acid against blank of conc. H_2SO_4.

W = weight of the sample.

The constant (10.81) in the above calculation is based on an absorbance of 0.660 for chromotropic acid — formaldehyde complex derived from 1 micromole of piperine formaldehyde or in 25 ml of H_2SO_4.

$$\text{Constant} = \frac{\text{Mol. wt.} \times 10 \times \text{dilution factor} \times 100}{B}$$

where B is the absorbance of 1 cm. cell solution containing 1 micro mole of piperine in 25 ml of solution. This value may vary from lab. to lab., therefore should be standardised with diethoxy methane (formaldehyde diethyl acetal) or pure piperine.

XII. Determination of Scoville Heat Units in Oleoresin Capsicum

(i) 0.200 gm of the oleoresin is weighed into a 50 ml volumetric flask. 95% alcohol is added to volume and the mixture thoroughly shaken. The insolubles present are allowed to settle.

(ii) 22 ml of sugar syrup is diluted to 140 ml with water and 0.15 ml of alcohol solution (i) above is added. After thoroughly mixing, 5 ml of this solution is given to each of 5 panel members. Each panelist swallows the solution and notes whether a pungent/or stinging notion is perceived in the throat. A sensation which is just perceptible at an addition is = 240,000 Scoville units. If this sensation is very strong, further dilution is necessary.

IS: 9345-1979 though has the same working principle but is at variance in quantities used for estimation as seen below.

Procedure

200 mgm of oleoresin is washed down with 95% alcohol into a 50 ml measuring flask and finally the volume is made up with the alcohol. The contents are thoroughly mixed and kept for sedimentation.

140 ml of 5% sugar solution plus 0.15 ml of 95% alcohol are shaken for thorough mixing. 5 ml of this solution is swallowed. A bite or stinging sensation in the throat which is just perceptible at this dilution corresponds to 240,000 Scoville units.

Very strong biting solutions need further dilution.

(iii) The following chart indicates the dilution ratio of the standard solution and its corresponding Scoville units value. The volume of the standard solution in column A is mixed with the volume of sugar solution in column B to yield the total volume of testing solution in column C;5 ml of this solution is given to each of 5 panelists. Each panelist notes whether the pungent or stinging notion is perceptible as outlined above in para (ii). The sugar solution in column B is prepared by diluting 22 ml of syrup to 140 ml with water.

ml standard solution (i) (A)	*ml sugar solution (ii) (B)*	*Total volume of testing solution (mll) (C)*	*Scoville units*
20	0	20	240,000
20	10	30	360,000
20	20	40	480,000
20	30	50	600,000
20	40	60	720,000
20	50	70	840,000
20	60	80	960,000
20	70	90	1,080,000
20	80	100	1,200,000

Comments

(a) The stinging sensation in para (ii) and (iii) above must be at a perceptible level; various dilutions should be made until this point is reached.

(b) Where value is known, initial dilution should be made accordingly.

(c) 3 out of 5 members of the panel must agree to the pungency at the indicated level.

(d) In some cases where the oleoresin is extremely pungent it is recommended that the test be repeated after an interval of at least 1.5 hours to reproduce the results.

(e) Only thoroughly experienced persons should be co-opted in the panel.

The Essential Oil Association of India has specified a Scoville heat value of 480,000 units for 'very hot' chillies and 240,000 for 'hot' chillies. In the trade the former is called *oleoresin capsicum* and the latter as *oleoresin red pepper*. The market values depend upon these heat units.

Limitation of the Scoville Method

Though easy and quick yet it has inherent defects of variability and rapid fatigue of human judgement of the sensonic factor. An individual cannot evaluate efficiently more than two samples a day. Evaluations vary vastly on grounds of individuality and different environments. This was amply demonstrated at trials conducted at CFTRI, Mysore, the findings of the Institute are as under:

Sample of Oleoresin	*Scoville value as reported by US Lab.*	*Scoville value at CFTRI Lab.*
American	1,000,000	480,000
Bahamian	950,000	600,000

Therefore it is better to determine the capsaicin content frequently. Heat value of pure capsaicin = 15,000,000 Scoville units.

XIV. Detection of Colouring of Chilli Powder with Vegetable Tannin

Often chilli powders of poor colour are polished with *ratanjot* i.e. alkanet (*Alkanna tinctoria*) extract in an oily medium. The oil used is generally of *taramira* (*Eruca sativa* (Mill) seeds which is cheap and has its own pungency to enhance that of chilli powders. The ether extract is treated with 10% NaOH solution and a violet colour confirms the presence of such tanning agents.

XIII. Extractable Colour in Chilli

It is done by measuring the absorbance of chilli's alcoholic extract at 450 mu.

Procedure

100 mgm of finely powdered chilli sample is taken in a 250 ml conical flask, 100 ml of isopropanol is added and the flask is stoppered tightly. The contents are swirled and kept for at least 3 hours at 70°C or overnight (16 hours at room temperature). In the former case (3 hours) the extract is cooled to room temperature and filtered through Whatman No. 12 filter paper. The first 10 ml of the extract is discarded. 25 ml of ensuing extract is transferred into a 50 ml volumetric flask and the volume made up with isopropanol. The thoroughly mixed solution is transferred to the cell and its absorbance determined at 450 mu.

Calculation

$$\text{Absorptivity of standard} = \frac{\text{Absorption of std. } K_2Cr_2O_7 \text{ solution at, } 450\ m\mu}{\text{Cell lengh (cms) x Conc. (mg/ml)}}$$

it is denoted by 'A'

$$\text{Extractable colour as per ASTA units} = \frac{\text{Absorption of extract at 450 } m\mu \times 200}{\text{Cell length (cms)} \times A}$$

If the concentration of $K_2Cr_2O_7$ and the sample is 0.500 mgm/ml and the same length cells are used, the extractable colour as per ASTA units is calculated as:

$$\frac{\text{Absorbance of chilli extract at 450 mu} \times 200}{\text{Absorbance of } K_2Cr_2O_7 \text{ solution at 450 mu}}$$

(Note: Spectrophotometer band width should not exceed 20 mu and the least cell size should be 1 cm.)

Bureau of Indian Standards IS: 9345-1979 method estimates objectively by measuring colour at 485 nm.

10 mgm of oleoresin is diluted to 100 ml with acetone. Using a tungsten lamp source and an acetone blank, absorbance of the above oleoresin solution is measured and multiplied with 61.00 to obtain the colour value.

IV. Detection of Argemone in Mustard Powder

Procedure

10 to 15 ml of NVEE of sample is extracted with 125 ml of ethyl ether in a closed conical flask for 24 hours with occassional shaking. The extract is filtered through Whatman filter paper No. 1 into a flask and the residue is washed well with 2x50 ml ether. This filterate is collected into the earlier filterate. This total NVEE is evaporated and the residual oil is dried at $100\pm1^{\circ}C$ till it is moisture free.

5 ml. of the above filtered oil in a test tube is reacted with 2 ml of conc. HCl (sp.gr. 1.19, AR) and 0.4 ml of rectified spirit by shaking the contents for 30 seconds for thorough mixing. The test tube is put in a boiling waterbath for 2 minutes to separate the oil and acid layer. The test tube is gently tilted and 1 ml of $FeCl_3$ solution prepared by dissolving 10 gms of $FeCl_3$ crystals in 10 ml of conc. HCl (sp.gr. 1.19, AR) and then adding 90 ml of H_2O; hazy solutions are filtered and then added. The test tube is gently rolled in the hand and never shaken at all in the vertical

position to mix well all the solutions. The test tube is again placed in the boiling water-bath for 10 to 15 minutes.

The presence of argemone is indicated by an orange red precipitate in light flocks floating in the acid layer. Microscopic examination of the precipitate reveals that it is crystalline, needle shaped (large as well as small). Curved needles connote the presence of safflower or linseed seeds powder in the mustard powder.

XVI. Moisture content in Tamarind Pulp

Methods

Moisture content in tamarind pulp is determined both by (i) Dean and Stark method as well as (ii) drying in a vaccum oven maintained between 60 to 70°C at a pressure not exceeding 50 mm of mercury.

Oven Method

Apparatus

(i) Dish, 7-8 cms dia x 2.5 cms deep (approx.)

(ii) Glass rod, short with widening flat end.

(iii) Sand, not finer than 180 micron and not thicker than 500 micron. It must be digested with conc. HCl, washed free of chloride, dried and ignited in dull red heat.

(iv) Air oven capable of being thermostatically maintained between 60 to 70°C at a vaccum not exceeding 50 mm of Hg.

Procedure

20 gms of sand along with the glass rod in the dish is ignited and then cooled in an efficient desiccator for not less than 40 minutes. The contents are weighed accurately. 2 gms of the sample is accurately weighed in the dish. The contents are homogenised thoroughly by adding 5 ml of H_2O and mixing thoroughly with glass rod. The contents are spread evenly in the dish. The dish is placed in a boiling water-bath for about 30 minutes, then removed, its bottom cleaned and transferred back to the efficient desiccator, cooled and weighed. The process of drying in oven, cooling in the desiccator and accurate weighing is continued till the difference between two successive weighings is not more than 0.5 mgm i.e. 0.0005 gms. The moisture content is calculated as usual.

XVII. Tamarind Concentrates Tests

1. Determination of Head Space

There are two methods.

a) Refree Method

The lid on the edge of the end plate is cut out with a sharp rotary cutter partially. The cut portion is carefully lifted to avoid any alteration in the shape of the end plate.

Six similar wooden measuring sticks are kept ready. Each stick must be clean, straight, not wider than 6.4 mm and thicker than 3.2 mm, length more than the height of the can containing the concentrate.

One such measuring stick is introduced in the can ascertaining that the stick has gone straight and not slanted at all and has touched and is rested flat against the bottom of the can and against the body plate. The stick is rested for a short time to prevent capillary rise of fluid contents as well as to have proper measuring eliminating the surface tension effect on the stick surface of the can fluids. The wet length is accurately measured. The can is completely emptied into a clean and dry beaker. The can is now filled completely with water, another similar stick is introduced and the wet length of this stick is measured accurately. The difference between these two readings gives the gross head space, the net head space is less 5 mm only. The remaining four sticks are used similarly but at different places in the can. The average is the final.

(b) The Routine Method

The lid on the edge in cut as before, however, the measurement from the top of the double seam to the surface of the liquid is instead taken straight away by using a ruler. The average of four readings taken at different places, is the final.

2. Determination of total soluble solids

It is done with either a hand or Abbe's refractometer preferably at 20°C. Nevertheless, no temperature correction is called for at room temperature.

3. Determination of Total Insoluble Pulp

20 gms of sample is boiled with 100 ml H_2O for about 35 minutes. The extract is filtered through a dried and weighed filter paper. The residue is washed with hot water and filter paper is dried at 100 ± 1°C to

constant weight. The difference between the two weights of filter paper is the weight of total insoluble pulp.

4. Determination of Total Tartaric Acid

2 gms of the sample concentrate is dissolved in 30 ml of hot H_2O, contents cooled and acidified with 2 ml of conc. HCl. 65 ml of alcohol (96%) is added while stirring and the precipitated pectin is filtered. Filterate is concentrated on a boiling water bath and after cooling is neutralized with 30% aqueous KOH solution. Reacidified with 2 ml of glacial acetic acid. 80 ml of alcohol (95%) is added while stirring the reactants and are refrigerated overnight. This precipitates the bitartarate which is filtered off over a 9 cms filter paper (Whatman No. 42). The residue is washed with ice cold 3x15 ml alcohol (80%). The filter paper is transferred back along with the precipitate to the precipitation flask, boiled with H_2O to dissolution and titrated against 0.1N NaOH using phenolpthalein as indicator.

The results are expressed as % of tartaric acid.

1 ml of 0.1N NaOH = 0.015 gms of tartaric acid.

XVIII. Microbiological Specifications & Tests

Cans are incubated at 37°C and 55°C for not less than 7 days. It is a statutory requirement that the cans under above test shall be devoid of microbiological activity of any type. The incubated cans shall be deemed to have undergone microbiological spoilage if any can either (i) bulges during incubation and stays bulged after being cooled or after incubation even OR

(ii) leaks

XIX. Detection of colophony

When incisions are made in the bark of pine trees an oleoresin is exuded which on steam distillation gives a distillate consisting of turpentine and the residue is known as resin or colophony. Colophony is a complex mixture of acids, most of which have the formula $C_{19}H_{29}COOH$. The most important acid of colophony is abietic acid. It does not apparently occur naturally but is formed from labile precursors during the collection, storage and steam distillation of the oleoresin. The lessor known acids of colophony are agathic, labdanolic and catavic. These three are bicyclic whereas abietic acid is tricyclic.

Asafoetida (*hing*), musk and soaps are the important articles of commerce abused of adulteration by colophony addition which, however, is usually detected by the following two tests (i) Acetic anhydride — H_2SO_4 test (ii) Copper acetate test; both are detailed below:

Colophony resin in Hing

(i) Sulphuric acid — Acetic anhydride Test

Macerate 2 gms of the well mixed powdered sample with 10 ml of acetic anhydride with the aid of a glass rod in a porcelain basin, applying gentle heat during the process. Cool and add one drop of concentrated sulphuric acid; a bright purplish-red colour, rapidly changing to violet, is produced in the presence of colophony resin.

(ii) 2 gms of the sample is triturated with 10 ml of pet. ether for about 5 minutes and the contents filtered. To 5 ml of the filtrate is added 10 ml of 0.05% aqueous solution of copper acetate in a glass stoppered test tube and the contents shaken well for a minute. On standing, the two layers separate completely. A bluish green colour in the upper layer of petroleum ether shows the presence of colophony. Yellow or light yellowish green colour is to be ignored. The colour is stable for several hours which permits the test for quantitative estimation by colourimetry.

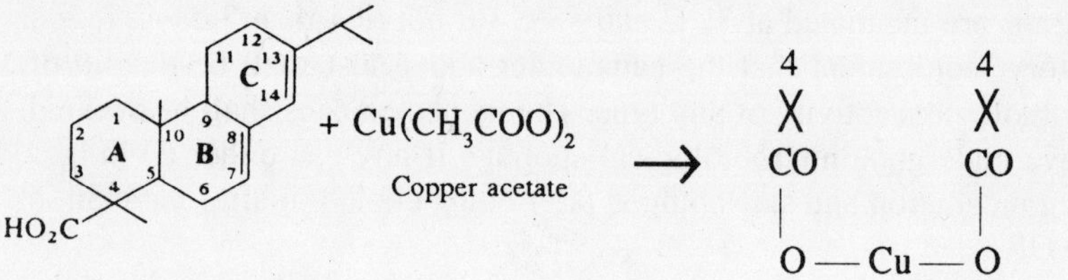

Abietic Acid

($C_{20}H_{30}O_2$)

Cupric abietate (bluish green)

Basic copper acetate $Cu(CH_3COO)_2$ cannot be used because most of the basic acetates are insoluble and this one also known as verdigris is already an insoluble pigment.

For quantitative estimation, different mixtures are prepared from the certified pure material with colophony concentrations of 10,5,2,1,0.5 and 0.25%. The above explained copper — resin coloured compounds are formed by taking as before 2 gm of the material for test.

The permanent colour standared is prepared by taking a little of 0.35% $CuSO_4$ solution in a test tube, diluting it suitably and adding a few drops of 0.01% aqueous solution of metanil yellow dye to develop the yellow tinge of the natural product. This colour mixture should impart a tinge matched by a 10% colophony: 90% pure asafoetida mixture.

The colour solution is diluted and colour standards prepared by matching with 5,2,1,0.5 and 0.25% colophony: asafoetida mixtures by adding, if needed, drops of metanil yellow solution. These $CuSO_4$ — metanil yellow colour standards keep well for a long time.

The colour of the test sample is matched with the above $CuSO_4$ colour standards to approximation. This colour matching is done by transmitting light against a white background in test tubes having same uniform colour tinge of glass and have same diameter and length.

Commercial asafoetida is frequently adulterated with ammonia, common gum, wheat flour, slices of potatoes and inorganic substances like gypsum red, clay and chalk, reports Wealth of India (Raw Materials) part IV, p. 20. The TLC method developed by Verma et. al. to detect colophony in asafoetida is:

The control is prepared by spreading on a clean white tile a good sample of asafoetida, its greyish-white or yellow tears picked up by fine forceps. When this sample is boiled for some minutes with HCl and the solution made alkaline with ammonia solution and diluted, a blue fluorescence is produced. There is no fluorescence in the adulterated samples.

Alternatively, when a fragment of this sample is heated with H_2SO_4 and then diluted with a large volume of water, filtered and made alkaline, a purple-blue fluorescence is produced. Adulterated samples lack this characteristic also.

1 gm of test sample as of the control were dissolved in fluorescent free 95% alcohol by trituration. These were spotted. Also were spotted abietic acid, colophony resin (CR), and umbelliferone (UMB) on usual plates of silica gel G and solvent used was n-hexane: $CHCl_3$: CH_3OH: : 50:50:1(v/v) for saturation and running the chromatogram.

After development, the plates were dried at approx. 30°C. The developed plates were exposed to iodine vapours in a closed chamber at the same temperature. The tabulated details of Rf are appended.

Of the 8 samples (A1 to A8), 4 were found adulterated with abietic acid, 6 with CR and one with UMB. The authors have recommend this as a quick and convenient method for detection of these adulterants in asafoetida.

Comparison of TLC results of commercial asafoetidas (A1 to A8), asafoetida control (AS), colophony resin (CR), abietic acid (AA) and free umbelliferone (UMB)

Sl No.	AA	CR	UMB	A1	A2	A3	A4	A5	A6	A7	A8	AS (Control)
1.	-	-	0.34	-	-	-	-	-	-	-	-	-
2.	0.055	-	0.055	0.055	-	-	-	-	-	-	-	
3.	-	0.13	-	0.13	0.13	0.13	0.13	0.13	-	0.13	-	-
4.	-	-	-	0.16	0.16	0.16	0.16	0.16	0.16	0.16	0.16	0.16
5.	-	0.22	-	-	-	0.22	0.22	0.22	0.22	-	-	-
6.	-	-	-	0.25	0.25	0.25	0.25	0.25	0.25	0.25	0.25	0.25
7.	-	0.44	-	0.44	0.44	0.44	0.44	-	0.44	-	-	-
8.	-	-	-	0.48	0.48	0.48	0.48	0.48	0.48	0.48	0.48	0.48
9.	-	-	-	0.52	0.52	0.52	0.52	0.52	0.52	0.52	0.52	0.52
10.	0.56	-	-	-	0.56	0.56	0.56	-	0.56	-	-	-
11.	-	0.91	-	-	0.91	0.91	0.91	0.91	0.91	-	-	-
12.	-	-	-	0.94	0.94	0.94	0.94	0.94	0.94	0.94	0.94	0.94
13.	-	0.97	-	0.97	0.97	0.97	0.97	0.97	0.97	-	-	-

XX. Detection of Coal Tar Dyes in Spices

Coal tar dyes are divided into two classes.

1) Oil soluble dyes and

2) Water soluble dyes which may be acidic or basic in nature.

(a) Detection of Oil Soluble Dyes

Preliminary Test

Take about 5 gm of the sample and add 10 ml of pet. ether, shake well and filter. To the extract add about 5 ml of 13 N H_2SO_4 or 1:4 HCl. If the acid layer shows the presence of oil soluble dye, it may be confirmed by reverse phase chromatography.

To the coloured concentrated ether extract of the sample, sufficient quantity of sillca gel (column chromatography grade) is added and stirred with a glass rod. The colours are adsorbed on silica gel which settles down to the bottom of the beaker. The coloured silica gel is washed several times with petroleum ether till the oil is removed completely. The colour is then eluted with methanol and concentrated. The concentrated solution and some known oil soluble colours are spotted on a reversed phase chromatogram prepared by soaking the paper (Whatman No. 1) in 5% paraffin in petroleum ether and then dried. The paper is then allowed to run in the ascending manner in 80% ethanol developing solvent system.

(b) Detection of water soluble colours

The residue left after filteration of ether (for detection of oil soluble dyes) is dried. Then about 100 ml of 80% alcohol is added and kept overnight. The extract is then filtered and residue washed with 80% alcohol two to three times so that all the colours are extracted. The filterate is then concentrated till alcohol is removed and sufficient water added. This process extracts both acid and basic dyes. Alternatively, acidulated or alkaline water can also be used for extracting basic or acidic dyes respectively, if no interference is expected in wool dying. The method of wool dying consists in absorbing the colour in acid or base form aqueous solution on white wool strands in boiling condition and washing the wool and stripping the dyed wool fibre with an alkaline or acidic eluent. The extract is chromatographed by ascending way on paper (Whatman No. 1) with any of the following solvent systems using known dyes as control.

1) Iso - amyl alcohol : ethanol : water : NH_3 :: 4:4:4:1
2) N - butanol : acetic acid : water :: 2 : 1 : 1
3) 2% Sodium citrate in 5% NH_3 solution

All the three solvents should be tried for unambiguous detection as some colours do not separate in one solvent or can have the same mobility.

The method adopted now-a-days, for detection of water soluble colours is by TLC using n-Al_2O_3 as the adsorbent.

Extract the sample (5-10) gm with 25 ml water and few drops of NH_3. Cork the flask and let it remain for 10 minutes for extraction. Shake. Filter and concentrate the extract to 2-3 ml. Spot the sample along with standard colours on n-Alumina plate. Run the plate upto 10 cms in the developing chamber using Methanol; NH_3 (9:1) as the development solvent. Remove the plate and dry.

Colour Reaction of Water Soluble Acid Dyes Produced on Dyed Fibres by Various Reagents

S. No.	*Name of Dye*	*Shade*	*Conc. HCl*	*Conc. H_2SO_4*	*10% NaOH*	*Liquor Ammonia*	*Chemical Class*
1	*2*	*3*	*4*	*5*	*6*	*7*	*8*
1.	PONCEAU 4R	Red	Red	Violet Red	Yellowish Brown	Orange	AZO Red
2.	CARMOISINE	Violetish	Little	Deep change	Red violet	Red	"
3.	FAST RED E	Red	Slightl	Violet change	No	No change	" change
4.	ERYTHROSINE	Yellow	Slightly	Slightly	" Darker	" Darker	Xanthene
5.	AMARANTH	Violet	"	Violet to	Dull Brownish Brownish	Little change to orange Red	AZO
6.	TARTRAZINE	Yellow	"	Slightly	No Darker	No change	Pyrazolinev change
7.	SUNSET YELLOW FCF	Orange	"	Slightly Redder	Brown	"	A-ZO
8.	INDIGO CARAMINE	Blue	"	Darker	Greenish	Greenish yellow	Indigoid blue

XXI. Detection of Foreign Resins, Galbanum, Ammoniacum

Foreign Resins

Add a few drops of 9% aqueous ferric chloride solution to 5 ml of the alcoholic extract. Appearance of olive-green colour in the minxture indicates absence of most foreign resins.

Galbanum

Add dilute HCl dropwise to 10 ml of the alcohol extract until a faint turbidity appears. Appearance of a bluish green colour in the mixture which fades on standing indicates the presence of galbanum.

Ammoniacum

Mix well 4 gms of the powdered sample with 90 ml of water in a mortar, filter and make up the filtrate to 100 ml. Prepare fresh sodium hypobromite reagent by dissolving 20 g of NaOH in 75 ml of water, adding 5 ml of bromine and making upto 100 ml with water. Mix 2 ml of the asafoetida extract with 5 ml of water in a test tube and add 5 ml of the hypobromite reagent cautiously down the side of the test tube so as to form a separate layer. Non-appearance of red colour in the mixture shows the absence of ammoniacum.

Saffron Analysis

Saffron being a costly spice, therefore, general methods of testing spices and condiments are not always suitable because they require large test portions, hence the following tests specific to saffron are employed. These tests are applicable to saffron in any of the forms, viz. whole filaments as a loose, supple, elastic and hygroscopic mass or in powder form.

5 gms is the minimum saffron filament needed to do the tests in single. In disputed cases, when required to do in duplicate, 2x5 gms is essential. The sample is divided into 3 gms and 2 gms portions.

3 gm portion is subjected to refraction, regrouped, pulverised till 95% passes through 500 micron sieve. 100 mgm is enough for microscopy and 2.5 gms for determination of moisture by air oven method. The same dried mass is used for total ash as well as acid insoluble ash estimation.

From 2 gm portion, 600 mgm (approx) is used for ultraviolet method for the determination of crocine, picrocrocine and safranal and TLC analysis. Apart 1.4 gms is still left for other determinations or incidents of analysis, if any.

Microscopy

Microscopic examination of saffron powder is carried out to determine that the sample consists exclusively of vegetable elements belonging to *Crocus sativsus* (L). The sample is examined in H_2O, NaOH or KOH solution (5%, m/v) and in iodine water. All reagents to be of AR/GR quality. The microscope should provide X400 magnification.

Observation under H_2O enables to see all the elements of the powder. The scalpel tip or a lanceolate needle transfers the test portion to H_2O drop and mixed in H_2O drop placed on the slide before hand till the powder is thoroughly wet. It is covered with a cover glass by pressing gently. The H_2O quantity is accordingly adjusted lest H_2O come out of the slide.

Observation in the aqueous solution of NaOH or KOH is clear because these alkali solutions destroy totally or partially the major part of the cellular contents, particularly starch, consequently the seclerous elements, the vessels, the fibres and the epidermis are visible more clearly. Thc mineral elements are not altered. Here little wait is practised to enable the medium to become clear.

Observation in iodine water enables the viewer to see the starch grains stained either blackish-blue or blackish violet.

Essential microscopic features characterising saffron:

i) fragments of the top extremity of the stigmas having big papillas elongated like hair capable of reaching a length of 150 micron.

ii) round pollen grains (dia. 85 to 100 microns) having a thick and smooth membrane and with a finely riddled exine.

iii) epidermis debris of stigmas having small round papillas.

Further the debris of (a) epidermis of the style consisting of long, thin walled and slightly sinuous cells (b) of thin vascular bundles and (c) of parenchymatous is also observed. It is pertinent to remember that saffron powder does not have either sclerous cells or fibres or covert hair or starch grains. The contents of the cells dissolve in water making orange yellow in colour. Concordance only of various slides yields judicious conclusions.

Determination of the main characteristics of Saffron

The main characteristics of saffron are safaranal, picrocrocine and crocine contents both for filaments as well as for powder. Saffron owes its colouring power to crocine, bitter flavour to picrocrocine and fragrance to safaranal. These are determined quantitatively by measuring optical density of the aqueous extract of the saffron sample at ambient temperatures by using a filtering membrane, made of cellulose acetate, of 50 mm diameter and porosity of 0.45 micron.

Procedure

About 500 mgm of the untreated sample is weighed accurately to the nearest mgm on a watch glass and transferred quantitatively into a 1000 ml measuring flask. 900 ml H_2O added, flask stirred with a magnetic stirrer @ 1000 rpm for 90 minutes, away from light. The magnetic bar is removed, the volume made up accurately, flask is glass stoppered and shaken to homogenize the contents.

20 ml is diluted to exactly 200 ml with H_2O in a separate flask and like before, contents are homogenised by using again a glass stopper. 20 ml is filtered through a membrane. The filterate must be clear. Optical density of this solution is recorded between 220 nm and 480 nm using H_2O as the reference liquid. Optical density at the maxima of absorption of about 257, 330 and 440 nm is also recorded.

Calculations

Colouring Power	$E^{1\%}_{1cm}$	at 440 nm
Better flavour	$E^{1\%}_{1cm}$	at 257 nm
Flavour	$E^{1\%}_{1cm}$	at 330 nm

Identification of Saffron Pigments

TLC Method

Special Reagents

i) Napthol yellow i.e. monosodium salt of dinitro-2, 4 apthol-1.

ii) Sudan Red G. i.e. hydroxy-2 (methoxy-2 phenyl azo-1 napthalene.)

iii) *Reference Solution*: Prepared by dissolving 5 mgm of (i) above in 5 ml of methanol and adding a solution of 5 mgm of (ii) above in 5 ml of $CHCl_3$.

iv) *Elution solvent*: ethylacetate: isopropanol: H_2O::65:25:10

v) *Revealing solvent*: anisaldehyde: methanol: H_2O ::10:90:10

(i) Corresponds to colour index No. 10315 and

(ii) to No. 12150.

Procedure

About 50 mgm of saffron powder from 2 gms portion is weighed accurately to the nearest mgm and transferred quantitatively to a test tube (60 x 7mm). It is moistened with H_2O drop, 1 ml of methanol is added after about 3 minutes and contents kept aside for 29 minutes protected from light, later on filtered on a small glass wool plug.

Plates are covered with silica gel followed by fluorescence GF 254. On these plates is deposited separately with a micro-syringe or micropipette 5 ul of the solution under examination as well as 5 ul of the reference standard solution (iii) above. It is developed in a chromatographic cell with elution solvent (iv) above, until the solvent front has progressed 10 cms. The solvents are allowed to evaporate.

The chromatogram is examined in ultraviolet light at 254 nm, then in day light. 10 ml of revealing solution (v) is sprayed. The plates are heated at a temperature of 107.5°C ± 2.5°C, examining the chromatogram simultaneously.

Interpretation of the results

a) Observation in day light

The chromatogram shows in its bottom third three yellow spots. The spot of the bottom strip is of more intense colour and corresponds in colour and in size to the napthol yellow spot. It characterises crocin.

b) Observation in ultra-violet light

This chromatogram at a wave length of 254 nm shows 4 main fluorescent spots, 3 corresponding to the spots observed in day light and the 4th with a higher Rf value (c. 0.55), which characterises picrocrocine.

One or two fluorescent spots are faintly visible at the level of the Sudan red G characterising -OH cyclocitral and safaranal. After revelation with the anis aldehyde solution (v) above, the crocine becomes greyish green in colour, while picrocrocine becomes violet in colour.

Nevertheless, the chromatogram should not show any other colour spots (particularly yellow-orange or red spots) before spraying, particularly at the starting point; these would correspond to a deterioration of the crocine and/or presence of foreign colouring matter.

XXII. Curcumin in Turmeric

Introduction

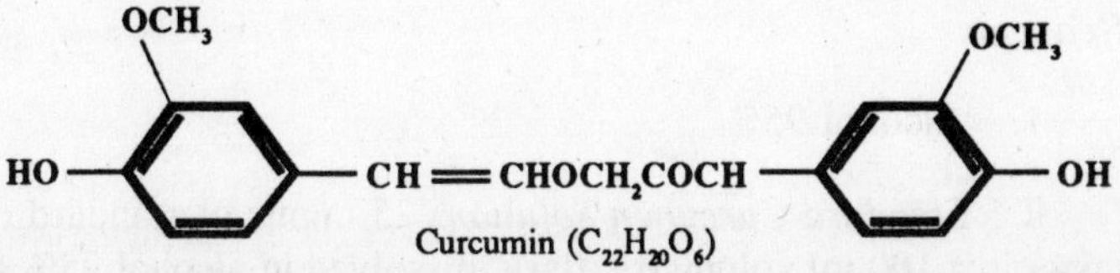

Curcumin ($C_{22}H_{20}O_6$)

Curcumin is an orange yellow crystalline powder soluble in methanol, ethanol, acetone, dichloroethylene and glacial acetic acid and is sparingly soluble in water and diethyl ether. Curcumin in alcohol has yellow colour and light-green fluorescence. Nagaraja et. al. (*Indian Spices, 1988, Vol. 4 and 1989, 1, 9*) quote Y.S. Lewis who reported curcumin content of different varieties of Indian turmerics as follows:

Alleppey (5.5%); Cuddapah (2.5%); Erode (3.0%); Gadhvi (3.5%); Kuchipudi (4.1%); Nanded (3.0%); Rajpuri (3.5%) and Waigon (3.5%).

Other curcuma spices like *C. aromatica, C. zadoria* and *C. Xanthorriza* have very low curcumin content.

Nagaraja et.al. have determined the curcumin content of Indian turmeric rhizomes, bulbs and fingers separately. There is no appreciable difference in the curcumin content of bulbs, finger and rhizomes. The difference is only due to agro-climatic factors.

Indian standards, mandatory as well as voluntary, have not yet adopted curcumin content as a parameter for quality and purity of the turmeric. As suggested by Nagaraja, it can be a very valuable tool in identifying substandard turmerics because curcumin content gets appreciably lowered. The common adulterants in turmeric powder are rice bran, arrow root starch, rice starch, other starches, metanil yellow, lead chromate. Insect infestation also lowers considerably curcumin content.

Determination of Curcumin in Turmeric

(ASTA (1968) Method)

Apparatus

1. Spectrophotometer or Bausch and Lamb Spectronic 20, capable of accurately measuring absorbance at 425 nm.

2. Condenser, West type, with water cooled drip tip and TS 24/40 ground joint, 30-40 cm length.

3. Flask, flat bottomed, 100 ml.
4. Volumetric flasks, 100 ml.

Reagents

1. Alcohol 95%

2. *Standard Curcumin Solution:* 25 mgms of standard curcumin is taken in a 100 ml volumetric flask, dissolved in alcohol 95% and volume made up. 1 ml aliquot is transferred to another 100 ml volumetric flask and volumed made up with alcohol again. This standard solution gives an absorbance of 0.42 at 425 nm. (25 mgm/100 ml).

Procedure

Around 100 mgm (well ground and accurately weighed) turmeric sample is extracted with 30 ml of alcohol by refluxing for 2.5 hours. The entire extract is cooled and filtered thoroughly into the same flask with ethanol and thc volume made up. 5 ml of the filtered extract is pipetted into another 100 ml volumetric flask and volume made up with alcohol. Contents are thoroughly homogenised.

The absorbance of this diluted extract is measured in 1 cm cell against alcohol blank.

Calculation

$$\text{Curcumin \%} = \frac{0.00025 \times 100 \times 100 \times \text{absorbance of sample}}{0.42 \times \text{sample wt. (gm)} \times \text{aliquot}}$$

$$= \frac{5.952 \times \text{absorbance}}{\text{Sample wt. (gms)} \times \text{aliquot)}}$$

N.B. The 95% alcohol used for extraction should be in the pH range below 6.5. If the pH of alcohol is above 7 then the results are erroneous.

XXIII. Estimation of Capsaicin Content

Introduction

Capsaicin is the major alkaloid present in chilli fruits. Other allied pigments present in chilli fruits contributing to over all pungent notes are capsanthin, α, β-carotene, carotenoids like capsrubin, zeaxanthin, cryptoxanthin, cutein and other unidentified xanthophylls. Capsaicin distribution is 0.23% in whole, 0.52% in pericarip, 0.05% in seeds and nil in stalks (based on Sanaam variety of chilli).

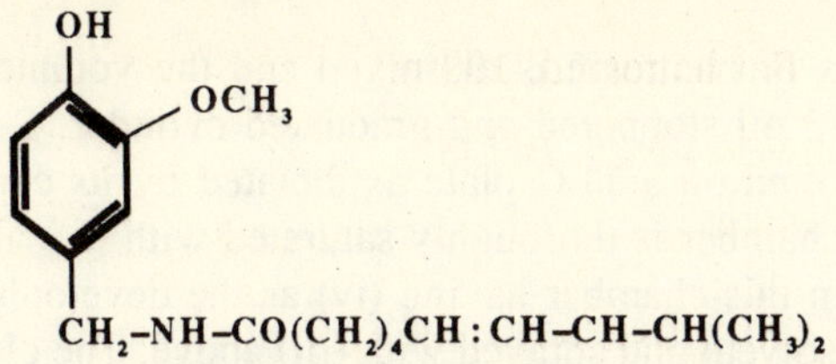

Capsaicin

(Vanilylamide of isodecenoic acid)

is present maximum in the longitudinal dissepiment. In *C. frutescens* it is upto 1.5%, average 0.5% while in *C. annum* it is only .01 to 0.03%.

Capsaicin is crystalline and imparts pungency to water when diluted to 1:10 million. Pungency of capsaicin and capsicum is not affected by alkali but is destroyed with oxidising agents.

Two methods are available and both are equally suitable.

(i) TLC Method

Capsaicin and the aforesaid allied pigments are separated from the rest of the constituents by thin layer chromatography (TLC) on silica gel. Pungent constituents are reacted with Folin-Dennis reagent to obtain the blue complex and this is quantified colourimetrically.

The major equipments are: a TLC complete set, spectrophotometer or colourimeter having region of 660 to 690 nm.

The major reagents are:

(i) TLC grade silica gel

(ii) Vanillin (AR/GR)

(iii) Phosphomolybdic — phosphotungstic Acid (Folin — Dennis Reagent). This is prepared by refluxing for two hours 20 gms of phosphomolybdic acid, 100 gms of sodium tungstate, 50 ml of phosphoric acid with 750 ml H_2O. The refluxed contents are cooled and the volume made to one litre with H_2O.

(iv) Developing solvent is a mixture of 5 ml of methanol and 80 ml of benzene.

Procedure

(a) 30 gm of silica gel having calcium sulphate as binder is mixed with 60 ml H_2O. 6 plates, each measuring 20 cm² x 150um are prepared and air dried for 4.5 ± 0.5 hrs, later activated by drying in an air oven maintained at 103 ± 2°C for half an hour and preserved in a desiccator.

(b) 5 gms of oleoresin is dissolved and the volume made up with acetone in a 10 ml stoppered and graduated cylinder. 5 to 20 ul of this solution is spotted on a TLC plate as dictated by its capsaicin content. The all glass chamber is thoroughly saturated with (iv) above. The plate is developed in this chamber having (iv) as the developing solvent. The plate is rid of solvent and sprayed with (iii) above. The clear blue capsaicin spot is marked (Rf 0.16) with a small stainless steel spatula/scooper in the form of a circle enclosing the spot and an area of 2.5 mm radius. The entire silica gel of the above spot area is scooped out into a clean butter paper and transferred in a test tube. 3.5 ml H_2O is added and the contents shaken well. 0.5 ml of (iii) is pipetted out into the test tube, again well mixed and kept aside for 3 minutes. 1 ml of a saturated aqueous Na_2CO_3 solution is added, again well mixed for not less than 5 minutes and again set aside for one hour.

Using a silica gel from the same blank area a reagent blank is prepared. Solids are separated preferably through a centrifuge. Optical density at 725 nm is recorded in a spectrophotometer or between 660 to 690 nm in a colourimeter using a glass filter.

Different volumes of a standard aqueous solution of vanillin are reacted with (iii) and the corresponding optical density recorded for preparing a standard graph with optical density against vanillin content. The standard aqueous solution of vanillin should contain 10 ug/ml. 1 to 3.5 ml of this reacted with 0.5 ml of reagent (iii) plus 1 ml of the saturated aqueous solution of Na_2CO_3, the total volume made upto 5 ml with H_2O.

The amount of capsaicin (Z) in the spot is determined from a standard graph of concentration of pure vanillin against optical density, the value multiplied with 2 (mol. wt. of capsaicin = 2 x mol. wt. of vanillin).

Calculation

Capsaicin % by mass = $Z \times 2 \times 10^5/r$

where Z = gms of capsaicin and r is optical density

(ii) *Paper Chromatography Method*

Reagents (Special)

i) Methanol Buffer pH 9.6 (60 + 40 v/v) as developing agent.

ii *Gibba Reagent* is a 0.1% solution of 2,6-dichloro-p-benzoquinone, 4-chloroamine in acetone as the chromogenic reagent.

iii) Buffer - 3.1 gms of boric acid and 3.7 gms of KCl in 100 ml H_2O, adjusted to pH 9.6 with 1N NaOH.

Procedure

The extractives or the oleoresin is dissolved in ethyl acetate so that the capsaicin content is nearly 2 gms/litre. Volume corresponding from 10 to 50 ug of capsaicin i.e. from 4 to 20 ul is applied as a thin streak covering the entire width of a 2 x 20 cm strip of Whatman No. 3 paper. This strip is developed by ascending chromatography in methanol-buffer solvent to a height of 15 cms. This takes about an hour. The strip is air dried again. Capsaicin develops as a faint, visible, blue spot near the solvent front. This faint blue colour is further developed by spraying with buffer (iii) above on both sides of the paper and transferring it to a dark cupboard for half an hour for full colour development and drying.

The blue spot is cut out and eluted with methanol in the dark to a convenient volume of 5 to 10 ml, its optical density observed at 615 nm in a spectrophotometer against a blank eluted from the similar strip area run simultaneously without the sample.

Standard curve and $E^{1\%}_{1cm}$ *for Pure Capsaicin*

A 2 gms/litre solution of pure capsaicin in ethyl acetate (AR/GR) is prepared. 50, 40, 30, 20 and 10 ug of capsaicin corresponding to 25, 20, 15, 10 and 5 ul of this solution is spotted on strips of Whatman No. 3 paper. These strips are developed, the capsaicin spot visualized and eluted and the standard curve/graph is prepared.

The % of capsaicin from this graph is calculated or by $E^{1\%}_{1cm} = 640$ at 615 nm.

In the case of chilli fruit, whole or powdered, the capsaicin estimation is done by extraction of a known mass of the powdered chilli powder (fineness not more than 300 micron) with ethyl acetate in a Soxhlet apparatus for not less than 2.5 hours. The extract is desolventised and weighed and then proceeded as before.

XXIV. Thin-Layer Chromatographic method of detection of true cinnamon (*C. zeylanicum*) from *China Cassia* (*C. cassia*) & Indian cassia (*C. tamala*)

a) Theory

Advantage is taken of the presence of eugenol in true cinnamon and its absence in the other cinnamons. Eugenol is separated and identified through TLC and spraying it with solution of vanillin in ethanolic H_2SO_4.

b) Apparatus

TLC set of plates measuring (20 cm)², applicator, TLC glass

chamber and hot air oven thermostatically controlled.

Reagents

i) Silica gel-G (BDH grade) ii) Conc. H_2SO_4 iii) Ethanol 95% iv) Eugenol AR) v) Vanillin Reagent : 5 gms of vanillin is dissolved in 90 ml of ethanol + 5 ml conc H_2SO_4 and the volume made upto 100 ml with ethanol. vi) Cinnamic aldehyde (pure) vii) True barks of *C. zeylanicum, C. cassia* and *C. tamla* viii) Benzene (AR) ix) Methanol (AR)

Procedure

The glass plates are coated with paste of gel : H_2O::1:2, air dried and activated at 100°C for 1 hour. Samples of the petroleum ether extract of different cinnamon spieces are spotted on one end of the TLC plate, 2 cms above the bottom along with pure standards of eugenol and cinnamic aldehyde.

The plate is developed in benzene: methanol:: 80:1 upto 10 cm height. The removed plate is sprayed with vanillin reagent (v) and kept at 110°C for 2 minutes.

The true cinnamon (*C. zeylanicum*) gives 6 spots including cinnamic aldehyde and eugenol spot. The eugenol spot is just below the cinnamic aldehyde spot at the solvant front. The Chinese and Indian cassia gives 4 spots, the dominant being cinnamic aldehyde with the eugenol spot..

Ref. I.S.I. Bulletin, 1977, 29, 307-312

XXV. Detection by mucilage content determination

Procedure

4 gms of powder (passing through 140 sieve, retained on 230 sieve) is mixed well with 5 ml of isopropanol and 70 ml of H_2O in a 100 ml, stoppered, graduated cylinder. The contents are set aside for 2 hours and volume made upto 100 ml with H_2O. Sediment column height is max 98.0, minimum 81.0, average 93.6, True Cinnamom sediment columes is 36.0.

Ref: J. Inst. Chemists (India), 1980, 52, 125–126.

XXVI

III. Detection of Papaya Seed in Pepper

a) Theory

Paper chromatography of the alcoholic extract of papaya seeds gives a characteristic yellow coloured band at the solvent front when sprayed with diazotised sulphanilic acid. In contrast pepper extract gives a pink coloured band at lower Rf.

b) Apparatus

Whatman No. 1 chromatographic paper (10x25 cm) strips and descending chromatographic glass chamber.

c) Reagents

i) Sulphanilic acid reagent:

4.5 gms sulphanilic acid is dissolved in 45 ml of 12 N HCl and diluted to 500 ml with H_2O. To 10 ml of this ice cooled acid is added 10 ml of cold 4.5% $NaNO_2$. The resulting reagent is kept at 0°C for 15 minutes. An equal volume of 10% aqueous Na_2CO_3 solution is added just before spray.

ii) Butanol iii) Acetic acid iv) Hyflosupercel

d) Procedure

25 gms each of black pepper, papaya and sample mixture containing 5 to 25% or more of papaya seeds are pulverised. 10 gms of powdered sample is mixed with 150 ml of 75% ethanol in a 250 ml beaker and kept aside overnight. The contents are filtered through a Büchner funnel containing a layer of hyflosupercel. The solid residue is washed twice or thrice with aqueous ethanol (50-70%). The combined filterate is concentrated on a water bath. The residue is redissolved in 1 ml of isopropanol. Each Whatman filter paper strip is marked a horizontal line 4 cms from one end of the paper. Extract of each sample is streaked on a separate strip and then air dried. The chromatogram is developed using solvent system of butanol: acetic acid: H_2O:: 12:3:5 in a descending method allowing the solvent to reach upto 20 cms. Individual strips are removed, air dried and sprayed with diazotised sulphanilic acid reagent and are again air dried. In case of papaya seeds a yellow band appears on the chromatogram at the solvent front (Rf. 0.93) while with pepper a pink band is observed 2 cm below the solvent front (Rf-0.87). The mixture containing 10% papaya seeds in pepper could be detected by this method. The yellow colour formed is stable for more than 15 days.

Source: Society of Public Analysts and Analytical Chemists (India), CFTRI, Mysore, New letter 1989, 8, 142.

XXVII. Determination of Gingerol in Ginger Oleoresin

Gingerols and other pungent principles of ginger are separated on TLC silica plates and estimated colorimetrically by reaction with *Folin-Denis reagent*. This reagent is prepared by refluxing 750 ml of H_2O + 100 gms of sodium tungstate + 20 gms of phosphomolbydic acid + 5 ml of phosphoric acid for 2 hours. The cooled reactants are diluted with H_2O to 1000 ml.

Procedure

i) Preparation of TLC Plates

30 gms of silica gel having $CaSO_4$ as binder + 60 ml H_2O are mixed thoroughly and spread over 6 plates each 20 cm², thickness of the spread gel being 150 mu. effected through a TLC spreader. The plates are air dried for 4.5±0.5 hours and are subsequently activated by oven drying at 100 to 105°C for 1/2 hour and stored in a desiccator.

ii) Preparation of Standard Graph

A vanillin standard solution is prepared by dissolving 100 mgm of vanillin (AR/GR) in 100 ml of H_2O. 0.1 ml = 10 ug of vanillin. 0.1 to 0.6 ml of this vanillin solution is accurately pipetted and mixed with 1 ml of Folin's reagent prepared as above and 1 ml of saturated solution of Na_2CO_3 and the volume made upto 5 ml. Its optical density is measured and a standard graph is drawn for gingerol after multiplying the optical densities obtained at various concentrations with factor 322/152, plotting the quantity of vanillin against optical density.

5.00 gms of the alcohol dissolved material is diluted to 100 ml in a measuring flask. 3 to 5 ul of this solution is spotted on a TLC plate and developed with the solvent in an all glass chamber already thoroughly saturated with solvent vapours. The plate is kept in the chamber for about 8±2 minutes after the solvent has reached the maximum height. The plate is exposed for 10 to 15 minutes to remove solvent and sprayed lightly with Folin-Denis reagent. 2 major blue spots get developed. High Rf spot (0.54 to 0.71) is of waxes and colouring matter. Lower Rf spot (0.36 to 0.49) is of gingerols.

The gingerol area is scooped into a 10 ml. centrifuge tube using a small stainless steel scooper/spatula encircling the spot + 2 mm more on all sides. 3 ml H_2O is added and contents shaken well before and after addition of 1 ml of Folin-Denis reagent. After 4 minutes 1 ml of Na_2CO_3 solution is also added, reactants shaken well again and kept for one hour.

A blank is prepared by using nearly same area from the silica gel plate plus reagent mixing. The tubes are centrifuged after one hour till the solids are separated. The optical density is read in a spectrophotometer at 725 mu or in colourimeter using 660 to 690 mu. The gingerols quantum is determined in the spots from the standard graph (ii) above derived by using vanillin at different concentrations.

Calculation

Gingerol content % by mass = 100 A/B. where
A = graph reading for gingerol in 5 ml solution in ug.
B = quantity of oleoresin in spot.

XXVIII. Determination of Residual Solvents

I. Apparatus

i) Clevenger's apparatus with a trap meant for water heavy volatile oils.

ii) A gas chromatographic unit with the following essentials:

a) Differential type detection device and recorder.

b) Separate thermostats for the cell and columns. The columns to be maintained between 70 to 80°C and all temperature shall be constant at 150°C.

c) One column shall have impregnated packing consisting of 20% by weight of a liquid phase like Ucon LB - 135 on 35 to 80 mesh fire brick.

d) Another column should have impregnated packing consisting of 17% by weight of a liquid phase like Ucon-75-H 90000 lubricant on 35 to 80 mesh fire brick.

e) Each column should be 2 to 2.5 metres in length and contain between 50 to 80 ml of the liquid phase.

f) Hydrogen carrier gas at the flow rate of 50 to 70 ml/minute.

II. Reagents

i) Na_2SO_4, anhydrous ii) K_2CO_3, anhydrous iii) Benzene AR (iv) Detergent and Antifoam bath free of volatile compounds. v) Toluene - pure by chromatographic analytical standards, otherwise interfering impurities will appear as peaks prior to toluene hence are removed by fractional distillation.

Reference Solutions

a) Acetone solution, 0.63% (v/v) in H_2O.

b) Benzene solution — Prepare 2.85 ml benzene/litre of toluene. If only benzene is already present as an impurity, quantify the same and adjust its level as above (i.e. 2.85 ml).

Benzene in toluene is determined by determining the benzene area in a suitable sample size of toluene at constant carrier gas flow rate, column temperature as well as other conditions. Known quantities of benzene are added to this toluene and the corresponding areas determined under aforesaid identical conditions. The results are plotted on linear graph paper, area v/s concentration of benzene. The plot should be linear and the negative intercept on concentration of benzene will give the concentration of benzene in the original toluene.

III Instrument Calibration

Known mixtures of solvents and benzene in toluene are injected. The resulting response of the detector in the instrument for the above known quantities of solvents is determined. However, the levels of benzene and the solvents must be of equal magnitude as present in the analysis. The solvents areas are calculated corresponding to benzene. The calibration factor A of the detector for a particular solvent is

$$A = \frac{\text{wt. of solvent}}{\text{wt. \% of benzene}} \times \frac{\text{benzene area}}{\text{solvent area}}$$

The recovery of various solvents from the oleoresin corresponding to benzene recovery, by the distillation procedure is:

Name of solvent	*Recovery % (w/w)*
Acetone	85
Ethylene dichloride	102
Hexane	52
Isopropanol	100
Methanol	87
Methylene chloride	87.5
Trichloro ethylene	113

IV Procedure

Sample Solution

In a 250 ml flask is placed a small amount of detergent and antifoam,

10 gms of anhydrous Na_2SO_4, 50 ml H_2O, 1.00 ml of benzene solution and finally 50.0 gms of the oleoresin. The distilling assembly is completed and nearly 15 ml of the distillate is collected to which is added 15 gms of K_2CO_3, contents cooled while shaking and then set aside to permit separation of the two phases. The toluene layer has all the solvents but no methanol.

The drawn aqueous layer in a 50 ml flask with boiling chips + 1.00 ml of acetone solution is distilled to collect nearly 1.0 ml of distillate which shall contain methanol, if present in the oleoresin and acetone as the internal standard.

Through column (iid) acetone and methanol are separated from the aqueous solution. Also are separated and analysed, hexane, acetone and trichloroethylene in the toluene layer from the distillate. The observed elution order on this column is as under:

i) Aqueous layer	acetone, methanol, water
ii) Toluene layer	Hexane, acetone, isopropanol plus methylene chloride, benzene, trichlor oethylene, ethylene dichloride plus toluene.

Through column (iic) methylene chloride + isopropanol and ethylene dichloride are separated. The elution order on this column is:

Hexane+acetone, methylene chloride, isopropanol, benzene, ethylene dichloride, trichloroethylene, toluene.

Sufficient sample solution in size is injected to peroxide, an accurately measureable deflection of the internal standards of benzene in the toluene phase or of acetone in the aqueous phase. When the detector is a katharometer then nearly 40 ul will give an adequate deflection. In the event of argon ionization detector nearly 0.4 ul or less shall suffice. The peak areas of solvents and internal standards are measured.

V. Calculation

The level of the internal standards related back to the 50 gms of the oleoresin used is:

benzene	43.4	ppm
acetone	100	ppm

The level of residual solvents other than methanol using benzene as an internal standard is computed as below:

$$\text{Residual solvent (ppm)} = \frac{\text{Ax}43.4 \times 100}{\%\ \text{solvent recovery}} \times \frac{\text{solvent area}}{\text{benzene area}}$$

where A is calibration factor of the detector for the particular solvent (see III above).

The level of the residual methanol using acetone as an internal standard is computed as below:

$$\text{Residual methanol ppm} = \frac{100 \text{ A methanol}}{0.87} \times \frac{\text{methanol area}}{\text{acetone area}}$$

where A methanol is calibration of the detector for methanol.

XXIX. Detection of Ethylene Dibromide in Black Pepper Berries

1. Though many countries have banned the use of ethylene dibromide (EDB) as a fumigant for foods and food products, yet it is still in use in Indian warehouses. Foods kept in cold storages have less desorbtion of EDB and the fumigant remains unchanged. *Hussain et. al.*, have evolved the ensuing simple, fairly accurate and rapid method for the fumigant's detection even at ug levels.

2. Reagents

i) Chloramine - T:- 1% aqueous solution

ii) KOH 10% aqueous solution

iii) 1,2 EDB 99% purity

iv) 2-4 dichloro fluorescein 0.01%; 10 mgm dissolved in 25 ml of 0.1N NaOH and the volume made upto 100 ml with H_2O.

v) Acetate buffer (pH 5.3 to 5.4):- 6.6 gms of anhydrous sod. acetate is dissolved in H_2O and 1.2 ml of glacial acetic acid added - the volume made upto 100 ml with H_2O.

3. Procedure

a) 10 gms of black pepper sample (whole) is extracted repeatedly using 2x15 ml and 1x10 ml of absolute alcohol through soaking for 30 minutes everytime. Each extract is filtered through Whatman No. 1 filter paper into the same porcelain dish. 0.1 ml of KOH solution (ii) above is added to the filterate and the contents are evaporated on a water bath to about 2 ml. This concentrate is carefully neutralized with glacial acetic acid to pH 7 and transferred to a 20 ml graduated cylinder and diluted to 20 ml with H_2O.

b) 1 ml of this solution is transferred to a clean 25 ml porcelain dish. 5 ml of (v) buffer is added followed by a drop of fluorescein reagent (iv) and 1 drop of chloramine-T (i). On stirring with a glass rod a yellowish-pink colour indicates the presence of EDB. Untainted berries give a greenish yellow colour fading withing 10 minutes, while the former persists for more than 20 minutes.

(c) A standard solution of EDB 1000 ug/ml is prepared in absolute alcohol. 0.1 ml to 0.5 ml of this solution equivalent to 100 ug to 500 ug of EDB is added to a series of beakers containing 10 gms of whole pepper sample. The contents are well shaken and the alcohol is evaporated at room temperature allowing the EDB to be absorbed on the-sample.

(d) Colour is developed as in (b) and compared with the test sample. The small amount of oleoresin extracted along with alcohol interferes neither with the sensitivity of the method nor with the colour development. Sensitivity upto 5 ug. The method can be adopted for cumin, coriander, fenugreek, celery and other similar seeds etc.

(Source: N.I. Hussain; M.D. John and C.L. Adinaryanaiah, *Spice India*, 1990, S(III), 8-9.)

XXX. Detection of mineral oil in Black Pepper (Whole)

I. Apparatus

1. TLC set including glass plates, applicator, developing tank etc.
2. Hot air oven with thermostat to main temperature at 105±2°C.

II. Reagents

a) Silica gel G,TLC quality (preferably Stahl grade)
b) Ethanol 95%
c) Chloroform A.R.
d) Benzene A.R.
e) Ethyl ether (anaesthesia grade)
f) Fluoroscein A.R.

III. Procedure

10 gms of the sample is mixed by stirring with 3x25 ml of ether (e) and filtered immediately in 100 ml beaker. Solvent is evaporated cautiously on a water bath. The solute (mineral oil) is dissolved in 1 ml of benzene (d).

The plates having gel thickness of 250 um are activated for 1 hour in oven (2) and preserved in desiccator, 5 ul of the benzene solution is spotted at a distance of 2 cms from the bottom. The TLC plates are positioned in chromotographic tank containing chloroform (c): benzene (d)::7:3 as the developing solvent mixture. The plates are developed upto 10 cms from the application point, then taken out, air dried and finally sprayed with 0.10% ethanolic solution of fluoroscein.

A yellowish green fluoroscence at Rf 0.7 indicates the presence of mineral oil upto 0.1%.

9

Analysis of Insecticide and Pesticide Residues in Spices

In Western countries it was the preservative action of spices that was of primary importance. Meat could be preserved for even a year without refrigeration by pickling it with cloves. Cured Pork was well spiced and so was sausage. Mustard seed and ground mustard were, likewise, used to prolong the life of perishable foods.

In India, spices are even more widely employed in foods cooked every day where it is the flavour, taste and colour of these materials that are of primary concern.

Rule 65 of the PFA Rules, 1955, under the P.F.A. Act, 1954; notification No. GSR 790 (E) dt. 10.10.83 mentions the following insecticides commonly used on spices along with their maximum tolerance limits.

	Name of insecticide	*Spices on which used*	*Tolerance max. limit ppm.*
1.	Formothion determined as dimethoate and its oxygenated analogues expressed as dimethoate	Pepper	1.00
2.	Inorganic bromide determined and expressed as total bromide from all sources	Spices	100.00
3.	Monocrotophos	Onion	0.10
4.	Carbendazim	Mango	2.00
5.	Benomyl	Mango	2.00
6.	Fenthion	Onion	0.10

(Source: Prevention of Food Adulteration Act, 1954. And P.F.A. Rules, 1955, 2nd Edn. amended upto 15.12.92. pub. by Associated Chambers of Commerce and Industry of India. New Delhi

However, this list is quite small as seen from the following list arranged alphabetically of the names of insecticides used as mentioned in various monographas issued by National Research Centre for Spices, Calicut, India.

Aldrin (0.1%); Bavistan (2 gm/litre), BHC (0.05%), Bordeaux mixture (1%); Carbary (0.1%), Carbofuran Captofolcarb, Chlor pyrifos; Copper Oxychloride; Dimethoate, Diofal, Dithane, Durofume; Endosulfan, Ethylene dibromide; Fenthion, Formalin, Formothion, Inorganic bromides; malathion, Mancozeb, Methyl bromide, Methyl demeton, Methyl parathion, Monocrotophos; Phorate, Phasalone, Phasphomidon; Quinalphos; Ridomil-ziran and Zineb.

Frequently a residue of these pesticides remains in the spices for consumption which needs to be determined accurately and for which sampling and preparation of sample is equally important.

Sampling

Scientifically based sound sampling techniques are a must to determine true data on residues. The FAO project "Food Contamination Monitoring — India and Nepal" has suggested that for spices a minimum sampling weight of 500 gms is a must. Further, the sample should not be in a container having rubber sealing rings. For ground spices, the best container is wide mouth glass bottle. However, whole spices can be kept in polythene (300 gauge) bags also. The sample should be subjected to analysis as early as possible after collecting, otherwise the sample should be stored preferably in a deep freezer (-15°C), alternatively in a refrigerator (4°C) taking the precaution that the sample does not absorb any moisture as a result of storage. Since deep freezing delays, not prevents deterioration, storage should be an interim measure only.

Extraction and Clean up Methods

Spices samples are ground and blended to 300 micron size for extraction. The pesticides' residues in substrates are of micro quantity, therefore, a relatively large portion of sample in/on which it is present, is necessary for extraction to obtain the pesticide. But, simultaneously a large quantity of other extractions also accompany which may interfere in the final analysis hence need to be removed by clean up procedures fulfilling the following criteria:-

(i) Enabling estimation of the particular pesticide at the desired limit of detection.

(ii) Recovery of pesticide should be assured at 80% and above level.

(iii) Reduction of background interferences should be reasonable.

(iv) The method/procedure should be simple and the results reproduce able.

For these clean up procedures the following special precautions are essential.

Scrupulously clean glass ware is mandatory for pesticide residue analysis work. Suggested basic cleaning steps are:

a) Surface residues are removed immediately after use. The glass apparatus are flushed with acetone before putting them in the hot detergent soak to check any cross contamination.

b) Selected detergent must be free from contamination likely to interfere in pesticide residue analysis. The detergent base should not be a fatty acid base. The test material is soaked in hot bath containing the above type detergent.

c) Thorough rinsing with water is a must followed by soaking in an oxidising agent like chromic acid and rinsing with tap water fol lowed by rinsing with distilled water, then with acetone and n-hexane immediately before use. There is always a possibility that between the time of washing and the next use, the glass apparatus may pick up some contaminate hence is to be rinsed again with some of the above mentioned solvents.

Detection and Determination of Pesticide Residues in Spices

Reagents

i) Petroleum Ether (60°C-80°C)
ii) Acetonitrile
iii) Anhydrous sodium sulphate
iv) 1% Otolidine in acetone
v) Florisil diethyl ether

Apparatus

a) Vaccum evaporator
b) Glass column (30x2 cms)

Purification of Solvents and Reagents

(a) Acetonitrile

Reagent grade acetonitrile is distilled over reagent grade silver nitrate (3 g/litre) with all glass fractionating column equipped with water cooled condenser. The first 10% of distillate and the last 20% of solvent in the flask is discarded. The flask is rinsed and fresh silver nitrate and boiling chips are used for each distillation.

Alternatively, to 4 litres of acetonitrile, 1 ml of 85% phosphoric acid, 30 gms phosphorous pentoxide and boiling chips are added and distilled in all glass apparatus at 81-82°C. The distillate is tested for suitability. Similarly all other solvents are distilled and checked for suitability.

(b) Sodium Sulphate

Sodium chloride/and glasswool may cause interfering peaks. Consequently as a routine and good practice, these are extracted in a Soxhlet apparatus with solvents to be used later during analysis and dried at 130°C before use. 50 extraction cycles are usually sufficient to remove impurities.

Procedure for Ascertaining the Solvent Purity

30 ml of solvent under test is evaporated to dryness at 35°C under a gentle stream of nitrogen. Alternatively, 30 ml of solvent is evaporated in a rotary vacuum evaporator at 35°C. When the volume becomes less then micro synder concentrator is used for effecting complete dryness. The dried residue is dissolved in 5 ml of n-hexane of ensured purity.

A 5 microlitre aliquot is injected into a chromatograph previously set at the desired operating parameters and detector response is recorded for 20 to 30 minutes. The resulting chromatograph is examined for any extraneous peaks.

If no interferring peaks elute at or near the retention sites of the compounds of interest on the chromatogram, the solvent is deemed acceptable. If the solvent gives more than 2% full scale deflection at the retention sites of any test pesticide, the solvent may be discarded. Some batches of solvents resist purification. In such instances, if after re-distillation the distilled solvent does not qualify purity test, it is more expedient to try another lot or solvent from another source.

Procedure for Testing Substances Causing Degradation of Pesticides

Solvent impurities not detected above may cause degradation and loss of pesticides during analysis. Consequently, solvent(s) is (are) also detected by spiking it(them) with carrying known quantums of pesticides under test in the absence of any commodity procedures detailed later on.

Procedure for detection and determination of pesticides residues in spices as practised in standardisation and quality control laboratories has been prominently adopted from AOAC.

50 gms of the sample is extracted with 3x100 ml (65:35 :: acetronitile : H_2O). The acetronitrile extract is washed thrice successively with 50 ml of petroleum ether (60-80°C). The ethereal layers are discarded. The acetonitrile layer is diluted nearly three times of its volume. This layer is also extracted as before with the 3x100 ml of pet. ether (60-80°C) and this extract is dehydrated with the help of purified anhydrous sodium sulphate (b) above. The dehydrated extract is concentrated to 1 ml at 40°C in a vacuum evaporator.

The aforesaid glass column (30x2 cms) should have a stop cock at the bottom end containing glass wool to plug the column base. Florisil is activated at 100°C for one hour and then filled in the column. Alternatively BDH silicagel of 80 to 120 mesh is filled upto 12 ±3 cms column height followed by 1 cm thick layer of anhydrous purified sodium sulphate. Now the concentrated 1 ml extract is poured on the top of the column diluting it with 200 ml of 6% solvent ether in petroleum ether containing organochloro insecticide residues like BHC, DDT, heptachlor and epoxide etc. The column is eluted with another 200 ml of 15% solvent ether in pet. ether containing Endrin and Parathion. The column is eluted for the third time with 200 ml of 50% solvent ether in pet. ether containing only melathion. The three eluates are mixed to make a single elute which is further concentrated like before to 1 ml in the vacuum evaporator. This concentrate is subjected to Thin Layer Chromatography (TLC) to detect, organochlorine, Organophosphorous and carbamate insecticides.

Thin Layer Chromatographic Analysis

The glass plate is coated with silica gel G (gel: H_2O::1:2) maintaining the gel thickness to 0.25 mm. The plate is activated for 60 minutes at 100 ± 2°C. The sample is spotted on the plate employing a glass capillary tube thoroughly cleaned and dried just before use. Along side are spotted organochlorine standards of DDT, BHC, aldrin and dieldrin. The plate is developed upto a height of 15 cms in petroleum ether. The developed plate is taken out of the solvent, air dried followed by spraying with 10% O-tolidine in acetone. The plate is exposed for five minutes to sunlight and then observed under ultraviolet light. DDT gives greenish-blue spot, BHC gives 3 to 4 blue spots while aldrin and dieldrin give light yellowish-blue spots. However, the final identification is confirmed by comparing the Rf values of the sample with the standards.

The suspected organophosphorous insecticides are to be spotted (parathion, malathion, fenitrothion, etc) along with the sample and the plate is developed in 5% acetone in pet. ether. Plates are then sprayed with 1% brilliant green in acetone, and are exposed immediately to bromine vapours. If any sample spot comes in view, its Rf is compared with the Rf of the standards.

Insecticide Residue' Quantification by Gas Liquid Chromatography (GLC)

Apparatus

Basic gas-liquid chromatography (GLC) equipment for pesticide analysis is supplied with electron-capture having H^3 (tritium) or N^{63} as radiation source and alkali modified flame ionization (AFID) detectors. Flame photometric detector provided with 526 nm and 394 nm emission filters may also be used in phosphorous or sulphur mode, respectively for the quantitative estimation of organo-phosphorous and organo-sulphur insecticides.

Flow System

The flow system comprises an entire system through which inert carrier gas like nitrogen flows from the point of entry to the flow controller, to the column and thence through the detector. Leakage even of a minute nature has no place in the system. It has to be detected scrupulously with the help of soap water called "snoop" at the joints and couplings. Besides, regular air and hydrogen supplies are provided additionally with the basic equipment for AFID detector.

Hamilton micro syringes 701; 10 microlitre or equivalent are also a part of the flow system. High purity nitrogen (TOLAR-1) from M/s Indian Oxygen Ltd) is quite suitable as a carrier because the purity of nitrogen materially affects the sensitivity of electron capture detector. Compressed air and hydrogen in cylinders is quite usable for AFID detector.

GLC Columns

Pyrex glass columns

Commercially available silanized glass columns and silanized glass wool are preferred. In the event of non-availability, glass wool and glass column can be silanized by treating them with 10% dimethyl dichlorosilane in toluene for 10 minutes. The column as well as the glass wool heated above is to be rinsed with toluene, then treated with methanol for 10 minutes, finally rinsed with menthol and allowed to dry in air.

Column packing materials

The undernoted have been found quite satisfactory for pesticide analysis.

(a) 1.5% SP 2250/1.95% SP-2401 (liquid phase) on 80-120 supelco port (solid support), from M/s SUPELCO, USA.

(b) 5% (OV-17) coated on 80-100 mesh chromosorb W

(c) 5% DC-200 on 100-120 mesh Gaschrom

(d) 3% DEGS (diethylene glycol succinate) on 100-200 mesh Gaschrom Q from M/s Applied Science USA

(e) 5% OV-210 on 100-120 mesh Gaschrom Q.

Principle

Gas-Liquid chromatography is a sophisticated tool or system for quantitative estimation of trace quantities of pesticide residues introduced into a column maintained at high temperature where the constituents are resolved and eluted into an appropriate detector for quantitative response. Routinely, electron-capture detector is used for organochloride compounds but modified thermionic or flame-photometriç detector is used for organo-phosphates. Individual pesticide in each class may respond to more than one type of detector. The response depends on the compound, its concentration and conditioned state of the column. Despite the capability of this technique to identify and measure picogram quantities, the several practical problems are attendant in the state of its art. These are surmounted through laboratory experience. The analyst is expected to know the operating specificity of GLC equipment in his laboratory to ensure its working.

Preparation of column packing materials

i) 5% DC-200 on Gaschrom Q

2.0 gms of DC-200 are dissolved in 250 ml of ethyl acetate in a 400 ml beaker. 38.0 gms of 100-120 mesh Gaschrom Q is added and allowed to remain for 10 minutes with occasional gentle stirring. This material is transferred to a clean stainless steel flat pan or to a glass petri dish. Pan or the petridish, as the case may be, is placed in a hood and the solvent is allowed to evaporate spontaneously, mixing the material by shaking the pan/dish forward and backward gently. A slurry shall be formed. More material is added till the material flow stops. The contents are airdried and then heated for one hour at 50° + 1° C in an oven. This material is now ready for packing in the column.

ii) 3% DEGS on Gaschrom Q

The above procedure is followed with the variation that the liquid phase DEGS (1.2 gm) be dissolved in chloroform.

iii) 5% OV-17 on Chromosorb W

Proceed as above dissolving the liquid phase OV-17 (2gms) in acetone, 80-100 mesh Chromosorb W being the support.

iv) 5% OV-210 on Gaschrom Q

Here the liquid phase OV-210 (2gms) is dissolved in chloroform.

Column Packing

The free flowing coated material is poured gently in the column. Broken particles are not conducive, hence the emphasis on gentleness. The column is tapped with a rubberised pencil followed by tapping mildly on a wooden table. This settles the coated material.

Packing material is settled in coiled column by applying a low vaccum at the exit plugged with glass wool and operating an electric vibrator. This shall help in having the packing material devoid of cracks and pores at the same time the packing is neither too tight nor too loose. Gaps are filled up by adding more material. Silanised glass wool is packed at either end of the column, compact enough to prevent dislodging of the packing material at the time of flow of the carrier.

Column Conditioning

Column conditioning eliminates bleeding and improves the resolution process of GLC for several compounds by conditioning it slightly above operating temperatures for nearly 3 days. Columns need conditioning keeping the carrier gas flow on. The suggested temperatures for conditioning of columns with the following materials are tabulated as under:

Liquid Phase	*Conditioning Temperature (oC)*	*Conditioning Time (hrs)*
1	*2*	*3*
a) 1.5% SP-2250 + 1.95% SP 2401 on Supelcoport	245	48
b) OV-17 on Chromosorb W	245	48
c) 5% DC-10 on Gaschrom Q	220	48
d) 3% DEGS on Gaschrom Q	200	20
e) OV-210 on Gaschrom Q	245	48

Initial injection of large quantities of compounds that are difficult to chromatograph may improve their efficiency.

Nevertheless, contamination or deterioration of column results in significant decrease in peak height, loss of resolution, loss or re-arrangement of peaks, and appearance of non-symmetric peaks. Column deterioration is frequently caused by injection of poorly cleaned up samples. On a contaminated column p.p. – DDT peak is decreased and a peak with the same retention time as TDE may be formed. Further, losses by degradation on the column and unclean samples cause changes in detector response.

The oven, detector temperature and carrier gas flow rates are set at the optimum operating levels for column in use. The instrument is left to equilibrate under these conditions.

Procedure

i) The entire system must be leak proof. In case leakage persists the septum is changed if found not in good condition.

ii) The range is set. The attenuator is also set to the pre-select positions. Recorder is switched on. The parameters of the instruments are so set that at least 0.5 ng of p,p. – DDE and 2 ng of methyl-parathion give half scale deflection with electron capture and AFID detector, respectively.

iii) The cleaned syringe is rinsed meticulously with n-hexane. Rinse the syringe thoroughly and afresh before proceeding to a new sample.

iv) A 5 microlitre aliquot of n-hexane is injected and the response is recorded for 10 minutes.

v) The chromatogram response on examination should have a minimum time response of hexane. It should return to the baseline within 30 seconds.

vi) It is imperative to "prime" the idle column before attempting quantification. The idleness is there if the chromatograpbic system has remained idle for several hours like overnight or over the weekend. This priming is affected by successive injections of working standard mixture.

vii) Atleast 30 minutes suffice for chromatogram response. Steps (vi) & (vii) above are repeated and their chromatograms are studied for reproduceability. If reproduceability is missing it is imperative to resolve the difficulty before proceeding further. Injections of the standards should be injected frequently but in no case the same standard injection be used for comparison after the 5th sample has been injected.

viii)The sample extract likely to contain pesticidal residue is injected only after the same has been cleared up through florisil and concentrated. The injection volume is also chosen to obtain approximately the same peak height as that of the standards. In no case the variation between the heights of peaks of sample and standards exceeds 25%.

ix) Finally the chromatograms of these samples are compared with those of the standard compounds retention time to know the suspected pesticides. The concentrations are calculated on peak height and on peak area basis.

Operating parameters for GLC (electron-capture detector)

Below are tabulated operating parameters for GLC (electron capture detector). These are, however, for guidance, therefore each analytical unit is expected to establish its own optimum conditions for their respective instruments:-

Liquid phase	1.5% SP-2250+ 1.95% SP-2401	5% OV-17	5% DE 200	20% DEGS
Solid Support	Supelcoport 100-120 mesh	Chromosorb W HP-80-100	Caschrom Q 100-200	Gaschrom Q 80-100
Column size	1.84 m long 3 mm i.d.	1 m long 3 mm i.d.	1 m long 3 mm i.d.	1 m long 3 mm i.d.
Temperatures °C				
Detector	205	185	200	200
Column	200	180	190	190
Injection port	210	190	210	210
Carrier Gas flow nitrogen, ml/min	70	70	70	100

The pattern of resolution of organo-chlorine pesticides obtained on several columns employing the above reported operating systems usually are as tabulated here:-

Retention time (minutes) of Organo Chlorine/Pesticides on different GC columns

Pesticide	*Liquid Phase*	
	5% D-200 on Gaschrom Q	*2% DEGS on Gaschrom Q*
1	*2*	*3*
α–HCH	0.34	1.5

(Continued)

1		*2*	*3*
β-HCH		0.37	5.5
γ-HCH		0.42	2.0
Δ-HCH		0.42	-
Aldrin		-	2.2
Endosulfan	A	2.30	-(better resolution can be obtained
-do-	B	3.30	-by using longer (2m) columns.
-do-	Sulphate	4.30	-However this will give longer retention times.
p,p' - DDE		3.0	3.5
o,p' - DDT		3.55	5.0
Dieldrin		3.0	4.5
o-p'- TDE		3.0	6.5
p-p' - TDE		3.55	10.0
p-p' - DDT		5.15	8.0

Operating Parameters of AFID Used for Organophosphorous Insecticides

Ceaesium bromide, sodium sulphate, rubidium sulphate or potassium chloride are alkali salts. Presence of any of these salts modifies AFID and increases selectivity for organophosphorous pesticides. Operating parameters are generally specified but for optimum performance viz. sensitivity and selectivity as well as operational stability the analysts are, as before, deemed to work out optimum conditions for their equipment.

For guidance sake the operating parameters are:-

Liquid Phase	1.5% SP 2250+ 1.95% SP -2401	5% DC-200
Column size	1.9 m long x 3mm i.d.	1.9 m long x 3 mm i.d.
Solid Suport	Supelcoport 100-120 mesh	Gaschrom Q 100-120 mesh
Gas Flow (ml/min)		
Nitrogen (carrier)	60	60
Air	400	400
Hydrogen	40	40
Temperatures (°C)		
Column	200	200
Detector	210	210
Injection port	210	210

Colorimetric Determination of Insecticide Residues

DDT (dichlorodiphenyl trichloroethane)

Schechter - Haller - nitration and colorimetric method.

Theory

DDT is nitrated to the tetranitro derivative which produces a coloured solution in benzene with a max. absorption at 596 mu when reacted with methanolic sodium methylate.

Reagents:

i) Nitrating mixture is prepared by mixing 30% fuming HNO_3: conc. H_2SO_4::2:1.

ii) Sod. methylate is prepared by refluxing absolute alcohol over calcium hydride for 4 hours. The dried alcohol is distilled into a dry flask containing metallic sodium, previously weighed and washed with methanol. Since the reaction is exothermic, it is necessary to have cooling arrangements.

Procedure

An aliquot of the stripping solvent containing the DDT sample is evaporated to near dryness on a steam bath followed by complete evaporation with airstream. In the wake of an aromatic solvent having been used, 5 ml of ethanol is added and evaporated as before. The residue is treated with nitrating mixture; excercising caution when excessive quantities of organic material has resulted from the stripping solution. If deemed essential, the nitrating mixture and the residue be cooled and slowly raised to hot condition on a steam bath. Nitration on the steam bath is carried out with occassional shaking for one hour followed by addition of ice water to the nitration mixture. This prevents the reaction completely.

The solution is quantitatively transferred to a 250 ml separating funnel with the help of cold ethyl ether having its final volume nearly 50 ml. The mixture is shaken vigorously for 1 minute. Completely separated lower aqueous layer is discarded. The clear ether layer is rinsed with 2x10 ml portions of saturated NaCl and dried by passing over anhydrous Na_2SO_4. The separating funnel is rinsed with 3x10 ml portions of ethyl ether passing each rinse through Na_2SO_4 as before and collecting ether in a flask. The ethyl ether is evaporated completely in an air stream. The resulting residue is dissolved in a known volume of benzene and is followed by the addition of 2 vols. of sod. methylate. The solutions are mixed by swirling and filtered into the spectrophotometric tubes. A reading is made within 15 minutes at 596 mu. 2.5 ml benzene suffices for the analysis of most of the residues, for micro work only 0.5 ml shall be enough.

Interferences

Any aromatic compound that may be nitrated is a potential source of interference. Fats and oils present in the extraction solvent interfere despite the oxidising conditions during the nitration step eliminate some of these. Besides the above, DDT, DDE, methoxy chlor, pertheme, tedion, etc. also interfere. Simultaneous determination of both DDT and DDE have been carried out by using separate readings at 596 and 540 mu absorbances.

Benzene Hexachloride (BHC) residue

Principles

Benzene hexachloride (BHC) is extracted from the sample with CCl_4. The solvent is removed. The residue solute BHC is dechlorinated to benzene by Zn + glacial acetic acid (HOAC) in presence of malonic acid which slowly liberates CO_2, sweeping formed benzene into nitrating mixture. Benzene is converted to m-dinitro benzene (nearly 85%) which is extracted and treated with buta-none-2+alkali and absorbance of magenta coloured compound formed is measured at 565 nm.

Reagents

a) Malonic acid — Reagent grade

b) Glacial acetic acid

c) Ether — redistill before use

d) Nitrating acid — Mix fuming HNO_3 with equal volumes of H_2SO_4.

e) KOH, 40% w/v, dissolve 470 gms KOH (85%) and dilute to 1 litre.

f) Mineral oil — refined and free from aromatic compounds.

g) CH_3-C_2H_5 Ketone — fractionated and portion distilled at 79 to 81°C.

h) Absorbant cotton: to be purified by immersing in ether and stirring for five minutes and sequeezing out the solvent. This treatment is to be repeated twice. The entire cotton is either air dried or heated in an air oven maintained at 110°C ±2°C. The dried cotton is stored in a closed container.

(i) Trichloroethylene

(j) BHC standard solution: 40 mg/ml. 100 mg of BHC is disolved in 100 ml of HOAC. 4 ml aliquot is diluted to 100 ml with HOAC.

Preparation of Standard Curve.

0, 1, 2, 3, 4 and 5 ml of the standard BHC solutions are poured in separate reaction flasks. Each solution is diluted to 15 ml with HOAC 1.5 gm powdered zinc and 2 gm malonic acid is transferred to each flask with funnel help to ensure that no particle sticks to the flask necks. Stop cocks and the corresponding ground joints are moistened with H_3PO_4 avoiding its mixing with the reaction mixture: 5 ml nitrating acid (d) is transferred to nitrating tube. The outer jacket is filled 1/4 with trichloro ethylene and for smooth boiling little granular zinc is also added. The reaction flask is connected to the apparatus and gentle heat is applied initially and then full heat is turned on for 2 to 5 hours to enable trichloroethylene vapours to just reach cold finger condenser. Heat is turned off, reaction flask withdrawn quickly to prevent liquid from nitrating tube being drawn too far into inner tube.

100 ml ice cold water is added to 250 ml separator and nitrating liquid is drained into this water. The inner and nitrating tube is rinsed with portions of cold water but the total rinsing cold water volume remains 50 ml followed by rinsing with 3 portions (50 ml like water) of ether culminating in rinsing with 50 ml of cold water.

The separator is shaken vigorously for one minute and the lower acid layer is drained into another separator of 250 ml capacity. This acid is extracted with 30 ml ether, discarding the aqueous layer. The etheral layers in both the separators are mixed with single 30 ml portion of 2% NaOH solution by shaking. The ethereal extract is packed in glass holder and fitted through a plug of purified cotton. The separators along with respective cotton plugs are washed with ether (3x15 ml), ether evaporated and colour developed. The two ethereal extracts are mixed. 1 drop of mineral oil along with glass beads is added to the extract and evaporated on a steam bath till the volume is just 3 ml. The steam bath should remain covered while swirling flask till the volume is further evaporated to 1 ml. The flask is transferred to warm section of hood to remove ether. The residue is dissolved with 1.0 ml of methyl ethyl ketone swirling the reactants followed by the addition of 1.0 ml of 40% KOH solution and reshaking vigorously for not less than 60 seconds.

In the event of determination of absorbances in column or Beckmann Model instruments, the contents are transferred to stoppered matched tubes and left in darkness for 20 minutes to permit colour development. The absorbance is read at 565 nm against blank of 10 ml of the ketone shaken vigorously with 1 ml of 40% KOH solution. If Beckmann Model DV sepectrophotometer is used then colour is developed in original flask for 20 minutes in dark, the upper ketone layer is carefully decanted into absorption cell. The absorbance is determined immediately since colour stays only in the presence of alkali solution.

Aldrin

Phenylazide Photometric Method

Principle

The method is useful for aldrin estimation in plant materials and animal tissues etc. Chromatographically cleaned up extract of aldrin in purified hydrocarbon solution is essential to preclude interferring substances. This aldrin solution is mixed with phenyl dihydrotrizole. Excess phenylazide is removed under vaccum. Thiazole is dissolved in ethyl alcohol reacted with HCl. The resulting secretory amine is coupled with diazotised dinitroamine. H_2SO_4 is added. Blank is taken. The corrected absorbancy is taken as a measure of HADN content.

Reagents

(i) Diazotised 2, 4 — dinitroaniline :- 1.5 ± 0.05 gm of 2, 4 — dinitroaniline and 30 ± 0.01 ml of Conc. H_2SO_4 (sp.gr. 1.84) are agitated to effect solution in a 250 ml conical flask. The reaction being exothermic, hence this solution is cooled in an ice bath below 5°C. 0.7 ± 0.01 gm of finely powdered $NaNO_3$ is added continuoulsy in a span of atleast 45 minutes. For stabilisation and completion of reaction the flask is kept in the ice bath (less than 5°C) for a further period of 2 hours. It is pertinent that this cooling step commences only after the entire nitrate has dissolved. 40 ± 0.01 ml. of 85% H_3PO_4 is gently and slowly added, keeping the reactants stirred and maintained below 40°C. This solution is kept at room temperature for a further period of 2 hours before putting it to use. Finally this solution must be stored in brown coloured bottles having glass stoppers.

(ii) Phenylazide reagent

The reaction flask required is of 2 litre capacity having 24/40 standard tapered joint. To 600 ml of H_2O is poured slowly and gently 110 ml of Conc. HCl. To negate the exothermicity of the reactants, the flask is immersed, as usual, in an ice bath. 67.5 ± 0.1 gm of phenyl hydrazine is added dropwise, stirring the contents non-stop with a stirrer driven by air. 200 ml of ether is added to the slurry followed by addition of a solution of 50 gms of $NaNO_2$ in 60 ml of H_2O. The nitrite solution addition is so regulated that the temperature of reactants does not rise above 5°C. The reaction flask is brought to room temperature away from the bath. 400 ml H_2O is further added, ether and 600 ml H_2O distilled into a chilled receiver, using an electric heating mantle. The ether and water distillate is transferred to a 1 litre separating funnel, mixture shaken, phases allowed to separate, aqueous phase drained into portions of ether and finally ethereal extracts combined. The aqueous phase is discarded, ethereal solution dried with anhydrous Na_2SO_4 and filtered in a 500 ml wide mouthed conical flask immersed in a 40°C bath to evaporate the ether by employing nitrogen stream.

Phenylazide is dissolved in the extraction solvent and diluted to obtain a 30% solution. This solution is washed with 2x50 ml portions of 4% NaOH solution in H_2O, alternatively till the washings are colourless. The washed azide solution is further washed with H_2O till alkali free, ascertained by phenolapthalein remaining colourless when added to washings. The azide solution is dried over anhydrous Na_2SO_4, filtered and stored in an amber coloured bottle kept in a cool place.

Prior to use, 25 ml portions of phenylazide are daily withdrawn, purified by percolating through an 8 gm column of 4:1 MgO — Celite adsorbant mixture. The loss of volume due to adsorbancy is made up with skellysolve B before use.

(iii) HHDN recrystalized: A HHDN known standard sample is used.

(iv) Chromatographic adsorbant: Celite 545: Attagel-3::2:3 by weight are mixed and heated for 16 hours between 180-200°C

Apparatus

a) Spectrophotometer
b) Air evaporator
c) Vacuum evaporator
d) Chromatographic column
e) Oil bath assembly
f) Distillation assembly
g) Reaction tube

Procedure

Sample Preparation

Advantage is taken of the fact that a mixture of skellysolve B and isopropyl alcohol assures quantitative extraction of aldrin from macerated crops. Materials containing saponifiable oils and fats are defatted by saponifying the oil/fat present with alcohlic KOH for 2-4 hours and aldrin extracted from the aqueous phase into skellysolve B.

Either an extract portion equivalent to 100 gm sample is used or if a residue level more than 0.4 ppm is expected then a portion likely to contain 20-40% HHDN is used.

The extract is desolventised of polar solvent with the help of H_2O where isopropyl alcohol — skellysolve B has been used, drying the skellysolve B with Na_2SO_4. Where ether, chloroform etc. are present it is diluted with skellysolve B and evaporated. The process is repeated untill skellysolve B alone remains as solvent. Evaporation to dryness is not done lest a loss of aldrin may occur.

Skellysolve B solution of the sample extract is adjusted to 100 ml volume prior to chromatography. For extent in excess of 100 ml a 3 ball synder column is attached to the flask, two boiling chips added and evaported on the steam bath to 100 $\pm$ 5 ml. For extracts measuring less than 100 ml the same is diluted to the desired volume in a graduated cylinder with skellysolve B.

Chromatographic Separation

The bottom of the chromatograph column is attached to a 250 ml flask and a vacuum is applied to the side arm. A 3 cm layer of anhydrous Na_2SO_4 is added, simultaneously keeping the column tapped followed by 24 gms of the chromatographic adsorbant mixture. The surface is levelled and pressed with the flat end of a wooden rod. A top layer of 3 cm of anhydrous Na_2SO_4 is added. 100 ml of hydrocarbon solvent to the reservoir is added and allowed to pass through the column until the liquid falls within 10 mm of the top of the upper Na_2SO_4 layer. Vacuum is released, flask removed from the column and replaced with a clean and dry flask.

The concentrated extract is transferred to the reservoir of the column with the help of several small portions of the hydrocarbon solvent to complete the transfer. The solution is made to pass through the column at a flow rate of approximately 200 ml/hr by applying vacuum untill the liquid level just drops below the top of the upper Na_2SO_4 layer. The sides of the reservoir are washed down with 10 ml portions of the hydrocarban solvent, drawing the liquid level each time just below the top of Na_2SO_4. 400 ml of hydrocarbon solvent is added and drawn 200 ml/hr through the column untill the liquid level just drops below the top of the Na_2SO_4 layer.

Concentration of Effluent

Vacuum is released, flask is detached from the column, 2 to 4 boiling chips are added and the 3 ball synder is attached to the column. The hydrocarbon solvent is evaporated on the steam bath until about 5 ml of solution remained. In no case concentration should result in less than 5 ml level.

Colour Development

The prepared skellysolve B extract containing not more than 40 ug of the essentially pure HHDN is transferred to a reaction tube. A gentle stream of air is directed on the surface of the solution using an air evaporator until 0.20 to 0.60 ml of the extraction solvent remains. 0.40 ml of freshly cleaned (through MgO) phenylazide reagent, reaction tube is transferred to the oil bath and heated at 85 $\pm$ 1°C for 30 minutes. The cuvette is attached to the vacuum evaporator manifold. The entire assembley is sunk in hot water previously brought to a temperature between 60-70 °C so that the lower 3/5 of the cuvette is under the water and system is evaporated below 0.1 mm of mercury for 5 minutes. The assembly is taken out of the bath, vacuum is gradually released and reaction tube removed.

5 $\pm$ 0.1 ml of 95% ethanol is added into the tube, the lower end is warmed in a 40°C bath to dissolve any residue present. It is essential that the entire triazole is completely dissolved. To this solution is added 1 $\pm$ 0.01 ml of Conc. HCl, the mixture allowed to stand for 20 minutes.

5 ml of skellysolve B solvent is added to the solution and stirred vigorously for 60 $\pm$ 5 seconds. The layers are allowed to separate and the upper layer is sucked out with a hypodermic syringe. 0.3 ml of diazotised 2,4-dinitroamine reagent is added, mixed well and the solution allowed to stand for 30 minutes to assist full colour development; 4 ml of 75% H_2SO_4 is added from a burette, mixed well and transferred for centrifuging at 1500 $\pm$ 500 rpm for 5 minutes to clarify the solution.

The coloured solution is transferred to a cuvette and then inserted in the spectrophotometer, absorbancy measured with H_2O as reference at 515 mu.

Note: The intensity of the pink coloured solution increases

significantly upon prolonged standing at room temperature. It is essential that readings of the final coloured solution are made not later than one hour of colour formation.

Blanks

(a) Hydrocarbon solvent blank

100 ml of hydrocarbon solvent treated as detailed above.

(b) Sample blank

Though not obligatory yet desirable for the highest accuracy. An equivalent quantum of an aldrin free spice sample is analysed and its apparent aldrin content is applied as a correction to the aldrin content of the spice sample under test.

Calibration Curve

400 mgm of the crystalline standard is accurately weighed separately twice and each is transferred quantitatively into separate 1 litre volumetric flasks. It is dissolved in skellysolve B (hexane), diluted to volume and mixed. Working standards of 5, 10, 20, 30 and 40 ug/ml are prepared by pipetting 5, 5 and 10 ml aliquots into 200, 100 and 100 ml volumetric flasks respectively and diluting the volume to give concentrations of 10, 20 and 40 ug/ml. The 5 ug/ml standard is obtained by diluting the 10 ug/ml standard with an equal volume of skellysolve B, the 30 ug/ml standard is obtained by mixing equal volumes of 20 ug/ml and 40 ug/ml standards. 1 ml aliquot is pipetted from each set into separate 16 mm reaction tubes. 2 blank tubes are also prepared by pipetting 1 ml of skellysolve B.

The material is reacted in the tubes as above for colour development and absorbancy of each is measured with reference to H_2O at 515 mu. The average absorbance of the zero standards is lessened from the absorbance of each of the HHDN standards, net absorbancy is plotted against ug of HHDN and the most suitable curve touching all points is drawn.

Calculation

Aldrin (ppm) = W/S x 1.053

Where

W = weight of HHDN found in the aliquot taken for analysis in micrograms.

S = weight of the sample represented by the aliquot taken for analysis in grams.

1.053 is the factor to convert the HHDN content to aldrin content since aldrin is defined as containing 95% HHDN (100 + 95 = 1.0526 rounded off to 1.053).

DIELDRIN: Phenylazide Photometric Method

Principle

The dieldrin contained by the sample is extracted in solution form in a non-polor solvent. This solution is chromatographed to separate the HHDN from interfering sample extractives. The fraction containing the HEOD is reacted with HBr to open the epoxide group of the HEOD, the resulting bromohydrin or bromoacetoxy derivative is heated with zinc dust to form an olefinic double bond. This ensuing olefin is reacted with phenylazide to form a phenyldihydroazole derivative. The triazole is reacted with HCl to open the ring and form a secondary amine. The amine is coupled with diazotised dinitroaniline to form a dye which has an intense characteristic colour in acid solution. The intensity of this colour is taken as a measure of the HEOD content.

Reagents

a) HEOD - 1,2,3,4,10,10 - hexachloro, 6-7 - epoxy - 1,4,4a,5,6,7, 8,8a - Octohydro - 1,4, - endo, Oxo - 5,8 - dimethanonapthalene is recrystallized. HEOD content known sample is used as standard.

b) Extraction solvents: Conc. HCl (Sp.gr. 1.19) and ethanol 95%

c) Diazotised 2,4 - dinitroamine

d) Phenylazide reagent

e) NaOH 4% in H_2O

f) H_2SO_4 (75%W). It is prepared by cooling H_2O in an ice bath and Conc. H_2SO_4 is crept slowly down the walls of the vessel containing chilled H_2O. Acid volume poured is twice of the H_2O.

g) Zinc dust

h) Na_2SO_4 anhydrous granular

i) NaCl 20% solution

j) Reduction acid Mixture: 10 ml of 48% HBr is taken in a glass stoppered 50 ml conical flask kept in an ice bath. 20 ml of acetic anhydride is gradually transferred into this flask. The flask is removed from the bath and stoppered. 15 minutes is the minimum induction period required before using it, but never after six hours. Daily fresh solution is advised.

k) *Chromatographic adsorbant mixture*

Magnesium: Celite 545::4:1. Only fresh magnesium kept in tightly closed containers, protected from moisture and CO_2 or other acid gases is suitable for this work.

Procedure

i) Sample preparation:

Mixture of isopropyl alcohol and skellysolve B extract quantitatively dieldrin from macerated samples. Saponifiable oils and fats are refluxed in alcoholic KOH for 2 to 4 hours, H_2O added and dieldrin extracted in skellysolve B.

100 gm sample equivalent extract portion is used. In case a residue more than 0.4 ppm is anticipated, then a portion likely to contain between 20 to 40 ug of HEOD is used.

The extract is desolventised if solvent is polar. In the case of isopropyl-alcohol-skellysolve B mixture, alcohol is washed off with H_2O and solve B is dried over Na_2SO_4. Ether and or chloroform etc, solvents are driven off by diluting the extract with solve B, evaporated to small volume, rediluted and evaporated to small volume till only solve B remains as solvent. *Only evaporation and no drying to check loss of dieldrin.*

The above solution is adjusted to 100 ml before subjecting it to chromatography. For extracts in excess of 100 ml a 3 ball synder is attached to the flask, 2 boiling chips added, contents evaporated on the steam bath till the volume becomes 100 $\pm$ 5 ml. For extracts below 100 ml the volume is brought up again to the desired level in a graduated cylinder with solve B.

Calibration of the chromatographic adsorbant Mixture

The bottom of the chromatographic column is connected to a 500 ml conical flask having a 24/40 standard taper joint. Vacuum is applied through the side arm, 3 gms of anhydrous Na_2SO_4 is added to the column succeeded by 24 $\pm$ 1.0 gm of the adsorbent mixture while tapping the column to obtain definite uniform packing. The adsorbant surface is lightly pressed with a wooden rod having a flat end, followed by a top layer of 3 cm of anhydrous Na_2SO_4. 100 ml of the purified extraction solvent is added and drawn through the column untill the liquid falls to the top of the Na_2SO_4 layer. These washings are discarded and the bottom flask replaced afresh.

100 ml of skellysolve B solution containing 200 ug. of dieldrin is quantitatively transferred to the reservoir of the chromatographic column. To wash down the sides of the reservoir and effect complete transfer a small quantity of the purified hydrocrabon solvent is used as a stream from a wash bottle. A slight vacuum helps the solution to pass through the column @ 200 ml/hr culminating in the dropping of the liquid level just below the top of the Na_2SO_4. The first 100 ml of the effluent are discarded.

A 100 ml cylinder with a 24/40 standard taper outer joint replaces the flask. The reservoir is again washed down in the column and filled with purified hydrocarbon solvent which is drawn through the column @ 200 ml/hr until 100 ml has been collected. After withdrawing the vacuum the cylinder is removed from the column. This entire operation is repeated eight (8) times. Each effluent fraction is analysed as detailed here.

Fractions having absorbances less than 0.100 are to be deemed essentially free of dieldrin. Fractions having dieldrin in the sample are spotted. The volume of effluent to be collected when analysing sample ought to be equivalent to this second group of fractions plus 50 ml immediately preceeding and suceeding.

The weight of the adsorbant mixture is so adjusted for subsequent determination made with the same batch of adsorbant mixture that dieldrin begins to be eluted from the column at about the 250-300 ml point including the 100 ml volume of hexane derived by virtue of the addition of the sample to the column. This enables a 200 ml dieldrin free fraction to be discarded.

Chromatographic Separation

A chromatograph column is prepared like before. The concentrated extract is transferred to the reservoir of the column without entailing even a minute loss. This is accomplished by using several small portions of the purified extraction solvent. By a slight vacuum the solution passes through the column @ 200 ml/hr till the liquid level has come below the Na_2SO_4 top layer.

The necessary solvent volume is added to remove all the dieldrin and drawing under vacuum @ 200 ml/hr is continued till 200 ml has been collected. As a forecut it is discarded. A clean flask is placed on the column and elution continued at the same rate of 200 ml/hr until the volume essential to elute the dieldrin has been collected.

Concentration

The skellysolve B solution is evaporated on a steam bath till 100 ml is left by attatching a 3 ball synder column to the conical flask. The concentrated solution is completely transferred to a reaction tube. This is further concentrated to nearly 0.5 ml but never less than 0.3 ml by impinging a gentle stream of air on the solution surface using an air evaporator.

Conversion of HEOD (Hexachloroepoxy Octahydro-demethonapthalene).

2 ml of the reduction acid mixture is pippetted into each reaction tube. The acid-mixture is percolated, simultaneously rinsing the tube sides. A taper 24/40 joint with nearly 12 cms extension is attached. Tubes are now placed in oil bath maintained at 120 ± 1°C for 1/2 hour. The tubes removed from the oil bath are kept to cool to room temperature. 400 mgm zinc dust is added, away from the ground joint, through a funnel and distributed by shaking. The tube is replaced in the bath and heated for 15 minutes. The tube is again removed from the bath, cooled to room temperature, the sticking bath oil washed away with the hydrocarbon solvent. The mouth and inside of the tube is rinsed with the hydrocarbon solvent until the tube contains 5 ml of the solvent. Zinc dust agglomerates, if any, are broken with a glass rod which is removed, washed with hexane into the tube; 5 ml of NaCl added, tube stoppered and vigorously shaken for 10 seconds. Zinc agglomerates, if again formed, are again broken up with the glass rod. The entire trapped organic solvent is carefully pressed out from the zinc.

The reaction tubes are inserted 8 cms deep into a pan of crushed dry ice to freeze and solidfy within 15 minutes the bottom aqueous layer, decanting the top hydrocarbon extract into a cuvette. Without wetting the bottom layer the sides of the tubes are rinsed with 2-3 ml of skellysolve B delivered from a wash bottle; the washing added to the cuvette. The contents are allowed to thaw, aqueous phase extracted a second time with 5 ml of skellysolve B like before. Similarly, the entire extraction solvent is evaporated with the help of an air evaporator.

Colour Development

Less than 40 ugm of the essentially pure and reduced HEOD contained in the prepared skellysolve B is transferred into a reaction tube. The volume of extraction solvent is reduced to 0.60 ml or less by passing a gentle air stream. 0.40 ml of the freshly cleaned (through MgO) phenylazide is added, the reaction tube transferred immediately to the oil bath and heated at 85 ± 1°C for 1 hour. Cuvette is attatched to the vacuum evaporator many fold, the assembly immersed in hot water maintained at 65 ± 5°C, 3/5 of the cuvette being under hot water. The system is evacuated for 5 minutes at less than 0.1 mm of Hg. The assembly is carefully taken out of the bath, vacuum released and reaction tube removed. 15 ml of 95% ethanol is added into the tube, the lower end is warmed in a bath maintained at 40°C to dissolve any residue. Dissolution of entire triazole is imperative. 1 ml of Conc. HCl is added and the mixture allowed to stand for 20 minutes.

5 ml of the skellysolve B solvent is added to the solution and stirred vigorously for 1 minute. The layers are separated, the upper layer is syringed out and discarded. 0.3 ml of the diazotised 2,4-dinitroaniline reagent is added, the reactants mixed well and kept aside for 1/2 hour to permit complete colour formation. 4.0 ml of 75% H_2SO_4 is gently delivered from a burette, the reactants again mixed well and centrifuged for 5 minutes, for clarity at 1800±200 rpm.

The coloured solution is transferred to a cuvette for measuring absorbancy in a sepectrophotometer at 515 mu against H_2O standard.

It is obligatory that the final colour reading is taken within one hour because the intensity of the pink colour of the solution increases significantly upon prolonged standing at room temperature. 2 blanks with skellysolve B are essential using 100 ml of the solvent. More than 0.13 absorbancy means the solvent is not pure enough hence needs redistillation.

Calibration Curve

2x400 mgm of the crystallised HEOD is weighed and quantitatively transferred into 2x1 litre flask separately. Each is dissolved in skellysolve B, diluted to 1 litre and mixed. Portions of both the stock solutions are diluted (400 ug/ml) to give working standard of 5,10,20,30 and 40 ug/ml. This is accomplished by pipetting 5,5 and 10 ml aliquots into 200,100 and 100 ml volumetric flasks respectively and diluting to volume to give concentrations of 10,20 and 40 ug/ml. 5 ug/ml standard is obtained by diluting the 10 ug/ml standard with an equal volume of skellysolve B. The 30 ug/ml standard is prepared by mixing equal volumes of 20 and 40 ug/ml standards. 1 ml aliquot is pipetted from each set into separate 16 mm reaction tubes. Two blanks 1 ml each of skellysolve B are a must.

Procedure as described above, the absorbancy of each is determined at 515 mu. Net absorbancy is plotted against ug content of HEOD of each standard, the best fitting curve is drawn. Difference upto 1% is ignored for concordance considerations.

Calculation

From the calibration curve the weight of HEOD is determined.

Dieldrin content ppm (sample) $= \frac{W \times 1.18}{S}$ where W = wt(ug) of HEOD found in the aliquot taken for analysis. S=wt(gm) of sample represented by aliquot of the extract taken (gms). 1.18 is the factor to convert the estimated HEOD to dieldrin containing 85% HEOD (100/85 = 1.176, rounded to 1.18). Personal variation upto 15.0% (maximum) tolerated.

Endosulfan

Colourimetric Method

Principle

The evolved SO_2 is absorbed and by addition of p-rosaniline dye the developed colour is read spectrophotometrically.

Reagents

i) *Stock Solution:* Conc H_2SO_4: H_2O :: 4:456 ml is cooled to room temperature. 16 ml of 3% p-rosaniline solution in ethanol is added and the reactants shaken vigorously for a few minutes, 249 ml of H_2O +4 gms of NORITE activated carbon are thoroughly mixed, refrigerated overnight and filtered through 2 whatman No 42 filter papers.

ii) *Stock Solution* 2: 5 ml of 40% HCHO in an 100 ml volumetric flask is diluted with H_2O upto the mark.

iii) *Standard* SO_2 *Solutions*:

a) *Sod. bisulphite solution* $Na_2S_2O_5$ (150 mgm)/litre of

H_2O is standardised against 0.01 N iodine immediately before use.

b) SO_2 solution is prepared by diluting solution (a) to obtain 10 ug/ml of SO_2 in 2% glycerol and 0.5N NaOH. From this and the absorbing solution are prepared solutions containing 1.0, 2.0 and 4.0 ug SO_2/2ml.

iv) *Absorbing Solution*: 2% glycerol in 0.5 N NaOH diluted to volume with H_2O.

v) *Acid Reagent*: 304 gms of p-toluene sulphonic acid (CP) is dissolved in 1 litre of isopropanol + 200 ml H_2O. This solution is gently refluxed with 50 gm of activated chacoal for 20 minutes. After cooling it is filtered through a fluted filter paper prior to use.

vi) *Skellysolve B* Pet. ether 35-60°C + isopropylalcohol

vii) *Colour Reagent*:: Stock solution (i) :Stock solution (ii) ::20:1 by volume.

viii)Iodine solution 0.01 N

ix) Nitrogen of high purity

x) *Phenolpthalein* Standard solution 0.5%

xi) *Alcoholic KOH 2% Solution*: It is freshly prepared by dissolving 20 gms USP grade KOH pellets in 1 litre of anhydrous alcohol. It is kept over night to facilitate complete precipitation of solid K_2CO_3.

xii) *Acetone-KCN Solution*: 500 mgm of KCN is dissolved in 25 ml H_2O and 475 ml of acetone added. Turbidity may be there but fades away upon keeping the solution standing for a few hours.

Sample preparation: Surface residues likely to contain insecticides/ pesticides are extracted with skellysolve B in a tumble or roll type extraction apparatus. In case of hard fruits 2 kgs of the sample is extracted with 500 ml of skellysolve B for 10 minutes in tumble type extractor. Insoluble solids are separated by filteration through a fluted quick filter. Leafy crops have greater surface area therefore more solvent is used for periods upto one hour.

Leafy whole spices like curry leaves, coriander leaves, tejpat, celery leaves etc.:- 500 gms sample is chopped with a Hobert food cutter and placed in a 5 litre capacity food blender with 500 ml of isopropanol. After maceration for 5 minutes 1 litre of hexane is added and macerated for 5 minutes. 1 litre of hexane is added and maceration is repeated for another 5 minutes. The sample and solvent are washed into 5 litre capacity tumbling jar with 1 litre of H_2O and tubmbled for 10 minutes. The mixture is filtered through a Whatman filter paper. The filterate is washed twice with equal volumes of H_2O, the water layer is discarded. Hexane solution is dried over Na_2SO_4.

Determination of Thiodan From Crop Extract

25 ml aliquot from the skellysolve B standard solution is taken in a 250 ml separating funnel, 50 ml of acetone - KCN solution added, contents shaken, 100 ml of 2% NaCl in H_2O added and contents thoroughly shaken and allowed to separate in different layers. The turbid aqueous layer is drained off. To the remaining loosely emulsified skellysolve B layer, 25 ml H_2O is added, contents swirled and the lower separated H_2O layer is drained off. To obtain a clear skellysolve B layer, 2-3x25 ml H_2O washings are carried out.

Colorimetric Determination

In an 40 ml evolution tube, aliquot from the above clear skellysolve B layer containing 5 to 50 ug thiodan is added along with about 9 ml of isopropanol + 1 ml of the 2% ethanolic KOH solution. Hexane is distilled off through thc Vixgreux column. The tube with the cooled isopropanol residue is placed on the evolution apparatus with nitrogen passing through the system @ 100±10 ml/minute. 2 ml of the absorbing solution is added to the absorption tube then connected to the gas delivery tube. A hot water bath 89 ± 1°C is placed around the evolution tube, 5 ml of the acid reagent is added through the adopter, sweeping the apparatus for 10 minutes. To the removed absorbing tube 1 ml of colour reagent is added, contents shaken, colour allowed to develop during the next 5 minutes and transmittance is read at 570 mu with a spectrophotometer.

Preparation of Standard Extinction Curve

In separate 15 ml test tubes are pipetted 2.0 ml in duplicate of the standard SO_2 solution containing 0,1,2,3,4 and 8 ug of SO_2/2.0 ml. To each tube is further added 1 ml of colour reagent, each tube contents well mixed. Full colour develops within 5 minutes. In a 3 ml spectrophotometric tube transmittance at 570 mu of each tube is read using no SO_2 tube as blank for 100% light transmittance.

The standard curve is obtained by (i) ug SO_2 x 6.35 = Thiodan content (ii) Thiodan content is plotted against the net proper transmittance value.

Parathion Estimation

Averell — Norris Colorimetric Method

The reduction of parathion nitro group is achieved with HCl and zinc dust. The resulting amine is diazotised and coupled with N-1-napthyl-ethylene diamine to produce a colour with a maximum absorbance at 560 mu.

Reagents

(i) Ethanol 95% (ii) $NaNO_2$ Solution 0.25% w/v prepared fresh (iii) Ammonium Sulphamate 2.5% solution (only week old solution to be used) (iv) Benzene (v) N-1 napthalene diamine dihydrochloride 1% w/v solution prepared afresh daily (vi) HCl 5 N (vii) Zn dust.

Apparatus

Spectrophotometer capable of measurements at 545 to 575 mu.

Procedure

Benzene stripping solutions are evaporated to dryness in a 250 ml standard taper, ground glass conical flask or a 300 ml beaker. The last 10 ml of benezene is removed with an air stream at room temperature. The dried residue is taken in 10 ml of 95% ethanol +10 ml H_2O, 2 ml of 5 N HCl and 200 mgm of zinc dust. The resulting solution is boiled gently on a steam bath or hot plate without much volume loss. The container (flask/beaker above) is rinsed down with H_2O cooled and contents are quantitatively transferred through Whatman No. 42 filter paper into a 50 ml flask. The volume is adjusted approximately to 40 ml with H_2O, 1 ml of 2.5% $NaNO_2$ solution is added, the resulting solution mixed well and allowed to stand for 10 minutes. 1 ml of 2.5% of ammonium sulphamate is added, the solution mixed well and again allowed to stand for 10 minutes. 2 ml of 1% N-1 napthylethylene diamine dihydrochloride is added, volume of flask adjusted to 50 ml. The solution is mixed well and allowed to stand for 10 minutes again. The absorbance of the resulting solution is determined at 560 mu using a simultaneously prepared blank to adjust the instrument to zero absorbance.

Interference comes from plant pigments unless removed prior to the colorimetric determination as well as from plant extractives that produce a colour during analysis. Heavy concentrations of oils, fats and waxes interfere by way of turbidity produced.

Sensitivity

The above described analytical procedure detects 20-200 ug of parathion in a final volume of 50 ml. Modifications of this procedure increase sensitivity of detection to less than 5 ug even by using smaller final volumes.

Recovery

The recovery of parathion from plant residues depends upon the magnitude of interferring substances present, however, in most crops, recoveries are quite adequate for residue estimation (0.1 ppm).

Standard Curve

A standard curve is prepared using pure parathion (20-200 ug) by adopting the aforesaid procedures. The curve has its basis on colour development in a 10 ml volume instead of the described 50 ml volume.

Calculation

Parathion (ppm)=ug parathion in sample/gms tissues.

The developed colour is converted to ug of parathion by extrapolation of the standard curve.

Malathion

Principle

Malathion is extracted from the spice plant(s) with CCl_4 and decomposed by alkali in a CCl_4 - ethanol solution fumarate. The $Na(CH_3)_2$-phosphorodithionate is extracted with H_2O and converted to a copper complex and extracted in CCl_4 wherein it forms an intense yellow colour measured at 418 mu. The corresponding quantity of insecticide is obtained from a standard curve prepared by carrying weighed quantities of the pure insecticide through the same procedure.

Reagents

i) Copper sulphate reagent: 1 gm of $CuSO_4 5H_2O$ (CP) dissolved in 100 ml H_2O

ii) NaCl: 20 gms of NaCl (C.P.)/litre of H_2O.

iii) CCl_4

iv) Alcohol absolute

v) NaOH aqueous 7N

vi) Malathion (AR)

Special Apparatus

(i) Glass extraction jars of about + 5 litre cap. with plastic screw caps lined with tin or Al foil.

(ii) Spectrophotometer

(iii) Tumbling machine, motor driven rollers geared to produce agitation at about 40 rpm for end-over-end tumbling, glass extraction jars placed sideways in a large cylinderical container which can then be placed on rollers.

Procedure

Total Residue

Nearly 750±250 gms representative sample is chopped into small pieces. These are macerated in a Waring blender with enough H_2O to develop into a thick slurry, finally transferred to the aforesaid 5 litre jar. Measured CCl_4 added, jar mouth tightened with tin foil lined cap and extracted for 4 hours by end-over-end agitation @ nearly 40 rpm. Jar removed, mixture allowed to separate CCl_4 layer and then siphoned off. Stable, unbreakable emulsions even after an overnight standing are centrifuged. However, the following alternate procedure has also been employed especially found very effective in potatoes.

The sample is macerated and extracted as above, but limiting to an absolute minimum the H_2O used for slurrying. Anhydrous Na_2SO_4, thrice the weight of the sample is added to the extraction to form a paste or a crumbly mass. The solution is slowly stirred lest the localised exothermic heat may volatilise the solvent and or crack the jar. With the lid on, the sample is again tumbled for 10 minutes to obtain a broken emulsion and an aliquot of CCl_4 enough for analysis. This extract is dry filtered to remove water or suspended solids and an aliquot immediately analysed to avoid possible decomposition of malathion during prolonged storage.

Surface Residue

0.5 to 1.0 kg of accurately weighed representative sample is extracted with measured CCl_4 taken @ 1-3 ml/gm of the sample in the 5 litre glass jar as above by mechanical shaking. Materials having relatively small surface areas need to be treated for short periods. Short periods are also employed to distinguish strictly surface residue. Longer periods extract residues found in waxy surface layers.

Malathion in CCl_4 Extract

Appropriate CCl_4 extract aliquot containing malathion (0.25 to 2.5 mg) is transferred to a dry 250 ml separating funnel, diluting to 100 ml with CCl_4. If more than 100 ml of the extract is required for analysis, the extract solution is concentrated in a beaker to about 90 ml by evaporation on the steam bath with the help of an air jet blowing across the surface. The concentrate is quantitatively transferred to the separating funnel and the volume made up to 100 ml with CCl_4. 25 ml of ethanol is added, the contents mixed well by swirling. 1 ml of 6 N NaOH added and separating funnel shaken vigorously for about 60 seconds. NaCl solution, 75 ml (cooled to about 15°C) is added and funnel reshaken vigorously for 60 seconds. The completely separated CCl_4 layer is drained off. 25 ml of CCl_4 added, contents shaken, layers separated and CCl_4 layer rediscarded along with small emulsion layer and trapped suspended solids.

25 ml of CCl_4 + 1 ml of 7N HCl is added to the separating funnel, contents shaken again vigorously for 30 seconds discarding the CCl_4 layer as before. CCl_4 extractions are continued till the CCl_4 phase is colourless. The absence of yellow colour is confirmed by measuring

absorbance of CCl_4 at 418 mu. The entire CCl_4 is drained off using pipette even. A fresh 25 ml of CCl_4 + 2 ml of $CuSO_4$ reagent is added, contents vigorously shaken for 1 minute and phases allowed to separate but retaining the CCl_4 extract this time.

The absorbance of thc yellow colour in CCl_4 layer is immediately measured at approximately 418 mu using a 1-1.5 cm cell and distilled CCl_4 as the reference solution. From the standard curve, the quantity of malathion corresponding to the absorbance observed is read and the ppm of malathion in the sample is calculated.

Interferences

Compounds like O, O-O, O - $(CH_3)_4$, 2,3-dithio-tetraphosphane, 1, 1-4, 4-dithiotetroate which are converted to O, O-dimethyl dithiophosphoric acid by the alkali treatment interfere with the described method. Either one or both of the half esters of malathion namely S-(carboxyl 1-3, carbethoxy ethyl) O,O-dimethyl dithio phosphate and S-(2-carboxy-1-carbethoxy ethyl), O-O dimethyl dithio phosphoric acid also interfere. However, the compound S-(2-dicarboxy ethyl) O, O-dimethyl dithiophosphate is not converted to O-O-dimethyl dithio phosphoric acid by the alkali treatment, hence does not interfere.

$(Cu)^+$ interferes by forming a colourless complex with the dithiophosphate which is more stable than the $(Cu)^{++}$ complex. Readily oxidisable materials e.g. mercaptans (thiols) if not removed prior to addition of the copper reagent, will reduce $(Cu)^{++}$ hence give low results. Consequently in the adopted method mercaptans and other acidic impurities are removed by CCl_4 extraction made on acidified aqueous solution just before addition of the copper reagent.

Small amounts of $(Fe)^{++}$, $(Fe)^{+++}$, $Zn/(Ni)^{++}$, Cd, Al,

$(Sn)^{++}$, $(Pb)^{++}$, $(Pb)^+$, wettable sulphur, ferbam, zineb, Cu_2O, toxaphene, parathion, ovex, DDT and methoxy chlor do not interfere.

Sensitivity

Control values on most untreated plant materials have usually indicated less than 0.1% of apparent malathion.

Recoveries are generally about 80% on a variety of crops, ranging between 70-90%.

Preparation of Standard Curve

Nearly 250 mgm of pure malathion is dissolved in ethanol and the volume made up and contents mixed.well. 25 ml aliquot is further diluted to 250 ml with ethanol so that 1 ml contains 0.1 mgm of malathion. This is the standard solution for use. 0,2.5,5,10,15,20 and 25 ml aliquots are transferred in separate 250 ml separating funnels individually. Each separating funnel already containing 100 ml of distilled CCl_4, 25 ml ethanol added to each and all swirled for thorough mixing. 1 ml of 6N NaOH is added to each, and each shaken vigorously for 60 seconds exactly. The ensuing procedure is to be carried out UNINTERRUPTED.

Aqueous alkali and acid solution of dimethyl dithiophophoric acid are stable for short periods only. Requirements to produce maximum decomposition of the insecticide by alkali to dimethyl dithiophosphoric acid are critical. Reaction periods beyond 30 to 120 seconds produce low results. Water addition limitation to 6N NaOH quantum shall avoid low results. 95% ethanol also gives results low by about 10-20%.

75 ml NaCl solution (cooled to 15°C) is added immediately and contents shaken vigorously for 60 seconds, phases separated, the CCl_4 layer drained and discarded. 25 ml of CCl_4 is poured in the separating funnel, reshaken for 30 seconds and CCl_4 separated layer again discarded. 25 ml of CCl_4 ± 1 ml of 7N HCl are added to the separating funnel, shaken vigorously for 30 seconds, phases separated, CCl_4 layer discarded like before. 25 ml of distilled CCl_4 is pipetted along with 2.0 ml of $CuSO_4$ reagent, contents shaken vigorously for 60 seconds and the phases are left to separate. A small quantity of CCl_4 is used in a more sensitive procedure however decreasing the accuracy.

The absorbance of the yellow colour in CCl_4 is measured immediately at 418 mu using like before, 1 to 1.5 cm cell and distilled CCl_4 as the reference solution. A standard curve is plotted from aliquots absorbance against mgm of malathion present.

Fenitrothion

Principle

Fenitrothion in formulations and on plant materials like spices is determined colorimetrically as 4-nitro-3-methyl phenoxide and its absorbance measured at 398 nm. The time involved in alkaline hydrolysis under reflux is an inconvenience. Peroxide ion is a nucleophile by + 1000 factor, than OH^-, it was deemed reasonable to investigate the use of alkali peroxide for determination of fenitrothion in formulations as well as at residual level.

Extraction

Powdered spices (300 micron size) are kept immersed for 16 hours in

90 ml of 75% ethanol: H_2O::95:5 or acetone with occasional shaking or 60 gms of the sample is pulverised with 180 ml of 95% aqueous ethanol in a kitchen blender. The superanatant from these powdered spices is filtered through Celite. 40 ml of this filtrate is poured down a tube (dia 2.5 cms) containing 3 cms of anhydrous Na_2SO_4 above 5 cm basic alumina grade.

Hydrolysis of Fenitrothion

20 ml of filterate from the alumina columns is mixed with 5 ml of 1N Na_2O in a 25 ml volumetric flask and shaken. Two boiling chips are added, contents are left like that for 15 minutes (min) before 100 mgm of $BaCl_2.2H_2O$ is added, and shaken well. Filterate (Whatman No. 4) absorbance is measured without additional work up.

Standard Preparation

Primary standard is resublimed 4-nitro methyl phenyl phenol. Cresol standard dilution is similar to those used for formulations or commodities. Optical blank is .02 M NaOH in 99% aqueous ethanol for formulations and 0.2 M Na_2O in 75% aqueous ethanol for commodity extracts. Beer's law plots are prepared from data obtained in 10 mm cells for the concentrated range of 0.2×10^{-5} M (0.3×10^{-3} gms/litre). Each 0.53 gm cresol corresponds to 1 gm of fenitrothion.

10

Gamma Irradiation of Spices and Condiments in India

Introduction

THE declaration by the "Joint WHO/IAEA/FAO Expert Committee" on "whole-someness of Irradiated Foods" in 1980 that all foods irradiated at 10 KGy are safe for human consumption and that they present no toxicological, nutritional or microbiological problems, has really set the ball in motion regarding food irradiation. Consequent to the above interesting development, the Codex Alimentarius Commission adopted the "General Standard for Irradiated Foods" and "Recommended International Code of Practice" for operation of Irradiation Facilities for the Treatment of Foods in 1983. Since then legislation and clearance have increased. Presently, many countries have given clearances of one or more food products for public consumption.

Present Scenario:

Considering the potential of food irradiation processing, 36 irradiation facilities in 23 countries are being used for treating foods for commercial use. The total quantity of foods treated annually in these countries is around 500,000 tonnes out of which 400,000 tonnes of grains are being treated annually at the Odessa Port of the USSR. Other countries which treat reasonable quantities of foods are Belgium, China, France, Japan, Netherlands and South Africa. India is to follow soon on onions, seafoods and spices for export.

So far as Indian scenario is concerned regarding spices and condiments sterilization, it is imperative because overall ground spices may well be unhygienic because of contamination with a heavy load of saprophytic and thermophilic bacterial spores, moulds and yeasts, ranging from 10^2 to 10^7 per gram, as tabulated below:-

Table

Microbial Count in Ground Spice*

Ground Spice	*Total Count/gram (Suspension plated & incubated at 37°C)*
Pepper	2,190,000
Celery seed	1,150,000
Cinnamon	8,000
Clove	190
Coriander	410,000
Ginger	60,000
Nutmeg	1,200
Black Pepper	10,400,000
White Pepper	42,000

* Health, H.B., Source Book of Flavors, AVT Pub. Co. Inc., Westport, Conn., 1981.

Further contamination by microbes in dockside warehouses and godowns due to humid condition as well as access to rodents and insects when stored prior to shipment needs to be taken note of. Obviously, the use of even a small quantity of such spice leads to the spoilage of the preparation. It is, therefore, imperative to decontaminate these spices for purposes of safety as well as economy. For better marketing also the marketed whole spices should have reduced bacterial count to acceptable limits in the ground form. The three methods employed for sterilisation are:-

1. Sterispice Process
2. Sterilant Gases
3. Gamma Irradiation

1. Sterispice Process:

Sorenson and Scanflavor of Denmark developed this process on request from the Danish Food Industry. The process is based on coating the spice with a specific fraction of extract from food grade beef bones, to prevent loss of flavours. The level of coating material is less than one micron on dry weight of the material to be treated. Then the batch is sterilized by injecting steam at more than 100°C. The temperature depends upon the type of spices and heat stability of their flavor components. For example, for pepper, temperature is kept low enough to avoid decomposition of piperine and the treatment is given for longer duration to reduce the bacterial count. By this process, bacterial count in different spices and herbs is reduced considerably according to treatment carried out by Danish Food Industries as shown in this table:-

Table

Bacterial Count Before and After Sterispice Process*

Spice	*Viable count per gram*	
	Before	*After*
Black Pepper	10,000,000	50
White Pepper	1,000,000	50
Coriander	1,000,000	20
Allspice	100,000	20
Nutmeg	100,000	10
Ginger	1,000,000	10
Cloves	1,000,000	10
White mustard	1,000,000	40
Fennel	100,000	20
Poppy seeds	100,000	100

Spores after treatment observed were 3/g in all spices.

* Sorenson, S. and Scanflavor, A.S., 1987, 9(1), 41.

The major advantages of this process are:-

(a) Viable bacterial count is reduced to acceptable level.

(b) Enzyme activity is eliminated by the high temperature.

(c) Gives same flavor strength as that of spices treated with ethylene oxide or irradiated.

(d) Releases flavor much more quickly than untreated or ethylene oxide-treated spices when used in the dry form and the level of spices can be reduced quite substantially.

(e) Due to steam treatment, spice is moistened by condensation during processing and obviously some pigment is dissolved, which on drying, distributes more evenly near the surface which gives bright color to the spice. Some of the disadvantages are:-

(i) Loss of volatiles to the extent of 3 to 11%.

(ii) Darkening of some spices like paprika, due to the high temperature.

(iii) Loss of 'green' flavor in some herbs like dill.

(iv) Development of cooked or roasted taste in the case of onion or garlic.

2. Sterilization by sterliant gases:

This has been well described by Raghavan et. al., 1992 "Guide on Food Products," Volume II, page 66. The same is being reported adverbitim.

"Fumigant gases like formaldehyde, carbon disulphide, carbon tetrachloride, chloropicrin etc. have limited value bacause they impart undesirable odors to the resultant spice. Also they have less penetration in the whole spice. Whole or ground spice can be treated with ethylene oxide or a mixture of ethylene oxide and carbon disulphide (1:9). It is in commercial use since 1972. In this process, the spice is spread inside a chamber, evacuated and the temperature raised to 60°C. A pre-determined dose of the above gas (es) is introduced. Time of contact and processing condition may vary with the individual spice and its physical character. According to 'Food Additives Amendment'; contact time for propylene oxide is limited to 4 hour at a temperature of less than 50°C, but for ethylene oxide, it is not precisely prescribed. After effective sterilization the gas is withdrawn and the chambar space is sprinkled with sterilized air to remove all residual gases. There should not be any residual gas which can be detected.In the U.S., the limit of ethylene oxide is 50 ppm and for propylene oxide, 300 ppm. The method is effective in reducing the bacterial load to acceptable levels. However, there are some drawbacks like (i) it does not get rid of any extraneous filth or rodent hairs, which, however, sterile, are still objectionable in the finished food products, (ii) there is some loss of volatile oil (nearly 1%), since sterilants are to some extent solvents, (iii) in presence of moisture, the gases ethylene oxide and propylene oxide react with chlorine present as organic chlorides in the ground spices and form the corresponding chlorohydrin which is toxic. Ethylene oxide as a fumigant is banned in some countries. It is mutagenic and causes chronic toxic effect.

3. Gamma Irradiation:

Certain radioactive isotopes emit electromagnetic radiation called gamma-rays which are extremely effective in killing micro organisms and they can be used for preserving food. At present, however, the preservation of food by irradiation is not permitted in Britain.

Cobalt-60 and caesium-137 are two radioactive isotopes available as byproducts of the nuclear power industry. Both of them emit gamma-gays with sufficient energy to kill all the micro-organisms found in food but not of such high energy that the irradiated food is itself made radioactive.

The unit of radiation dose is the gray (Gy). One gray is the dose of radiation received by one kilogram of matter when it absorbs one joule of radiation energy.

Gamma-rays are able to penetrate food (or any other substance, for that matter) to a considerable depth. Consequently, food can be processed in bulk or in packages made of any material and of any size without fear that the innermost parts will not be properly processed. The food is carried past the radio-isotope on a conveyor and after a very brief exposure the process is complete. Three levels of radiation treatment, known in order of severity as radurization, radicidation and radappertization are used for extending the storage life of food.

Radurization (low doses - below 1 kGy)

Inhibits sprouting of vagetables such as onions and potatoes.

Retards ripening of fruit.

Kills insects in grain, rice and spices.

Radicidation (moderate doses - 1 - 10 kGy).

Kills most micro-organisms and so extends storage life and reduces risk of food poisoning.

Kills parasites in meat (e.g. larvae of *Trichina spiralis* which cause Trichinosis).

Radappertization (high doses - above 10 kGy).

Completely sterilizes food by killing all micro-organisms.

Irradiation equivalent of canning; for a 12D process a dose of about 50 kGy is required.

As well as inhibiting sprouting and ripening, and killing pests and micro-organisms, irradiation causes minor chemical changes. Some large molecules, such as those of carbohydrates or proteins, may be split and some destruction of vitamins may also occur. New compounds - called *radiolytic products* - may be formed, but they will be present to only a very minor extent - perhaps one or two parts per million. Nevertheless, it is possible that they might be carcinogenic or be harmful in other ways. Even such minor changes in the composition of a food can affect its flavour and texture. Irradiated meats, for example, have been said by some to have a 'goaty' flavour or, more vividly, a 'wet dog' taste. Vegetables may become soft and spongy after drastic irradiation owing to partial breakdown of their cellulose cell walls. An official committee - The Advisory Committee on Irradiated and Noval Foods (ACINF) - has exhaustively examined all the information currently available about the safety of irradiated food. It came to the conclusion that there are no health hazards associated with eating food which has been irradiated upon an average overall dose of 10 kilograys by gamma-rays of energy below 5 million electronvolts.

Nevertheless, there is still a great deal of suspicion about irradiated food. Because of fears that it may be harmful its sale is not at present permitted in Britain. Irradiated food, however, is sold in several other countries and no harmful effects have been reported.

Nevertheless, after 30 years of research and development, gamma irradiation is now proving to be most effective for the commercial decontamination of spices.

As reported earlier, although an irradiation does of 20 kilogray may be required to achieve commercial 'sterility' (= viable cell count of 10 per gram), treatment of spices with 3 - 10 kGy can reduce the viable cell count to an acceptable level of 10^4 per gram without affecting the sensory properties of almost all the spices tested. The storage life of properly packaged spices is improved by irradiation decontamination; this treatment also prevents the growth of moulds and insects, since these are more sensitive to this treatment. An average does of 10 kGy is recommended by the Joint FAO/IAEA/WHO Expert Committee for treatment of spices. The acceptable limit of microbes in spices is 10^4 per gram. Now FDA has recommended dose upto 30 kGy only for disinfestation of spices, seasoning and blends.

Insects are highly susceptible to gamma irradiation. Bhabha Atomic Research Centre, Trombay found that a minimum dose of 1 kGy prevents insect emergence in prepacked spice and spice products. The safety of irradiated spices upto a dose of 1 kGy for consumers has been assured by International Joint Committee on Food Irradiation of spices as tabulated here:-

Irradiated Spices Cleared for Human Consumption in Different Countries*

Country	*Nature of clearance*	*Dose (kGy)*	*Date of Clearance*
Australia	Unconditional	10	-
Bangladesh	Unconditional	10	28 Dec., 1983
Belgium	Provisional	10	29 Sep. 1983
Brazil	Unconditional	10	07 Mar. 1985
Canada	Unconditional	10	Sep. 1984
Chile	Unconditional	10	29 Dec. 1982
Denmark	Provisional	10	01 Jun. 1986
France	Unconditional	11	10 Feb. 1983
Germany	Provisional	10	29 Dec. 1982
Hungary	Test Marketing	5	1983
India	Export only	10	Jun. 1986
Israel	Unconditional	10	06 Mar. 1985
Netherlands	Provisional	10	15 Feb. 1980
New Zealand	Provisional	8	Mar. 1985
Norway	Unconditional	10	1982
South Africa	Unconditional	10	22 Jul. 1983
U.S.A.	Unconditional	30	10 Apr. 1986

*Rigney, C.J., Indian Spices 1987, 24(1), 12.

Spice irradiation is quite simple and can be made a continuous operation unlike fumigation. It can be applied to prepacked spices. Although the technique is characterised by relatively high capital costs, the operational costs are low since the dosage requirement is very moderate. Further, it can be conducted in centralized or service irradiator, due to the compactness in relation to value, stability and transportability.

11

Specifications of Spices and Condiments

as Amended upto 15.12.1992 Under the P.F.A. Act 1954 & P.F.A. Rules 1955. (Appendix B)

A.04 --- ASAFOETIDA (Hing or Hingra) means the oleogum — resin obtained from the rhizome and roots of *Ferula alliaces, Ferula rubricaulis* and other species of Ferula. It shall not contain any colophony resin, galbanum resin, anmmoniaccum resin or any other foreign resin. Hing shall conform to the following standards, namely:-

(1) Total ash content shall not exceed 15 percent by weight.

(2) Ash insoluble in dilute hydrochloric acid shall not exceed 2.5 per cent by weight.

(3) The alcoholic extract (with 90 per cent alcohol) shall not be less than 12 per cent as estimated by the U.S.P. 1936 method.

(4) Starch shall not exceed 1 per cent by weight.

Hingra shall conform to the following standards, namely:-

(1) The total ash content shall not exceed 20 per cent by weight.

(2) Ash insoluble in dilute hydrochloric acid shall not exceed 8 percent by weight.

(3) The alcoholic extract (with 90 per cent alcohol) shall not be less than 50 per cent as estimated by U.S.P. 1936 method.

(4) Starch shall not exceed 1 per cent by weight.

Compounded asafoetida or *Bandhani Hing* is composed of one or more varieties of asafoetida (*Irani* or *Pathani Hing* or both) and gum arabic, edible starches or edible cereal flour.

It shall not contain:-

(a) colophony resin,

(b) galbanum resin,

(c) ammoniaccum resin,

(d) any other foreign resin,

(e) coal tar dyes,

(f) mineral pigment,

(g) more than 10 per cent total ash content,

(h) more than 1.5 per cent ash insoluble in dilute hydrochloric acid,

(i) less than 5 per cent alcoholic extract (with 90 per cent of alcohol) as estimated by the U.S.P. 1936 method

A.05.01 --- CARAWAY (*Siahjira*) Whole means the dried seed of the plant *Carum carvi (L)*. Extraneous matter including foreign edible seeds, chaff, stem, straw, dust, dirt, stones, and lumps of earth shall not exceed 5 per cent by weight.

A.05.02 --- CARAWAY BLACK (*Siahjira*) means the dried seeds of *Carum bulbocastanum*. It shall conform to the following standards:-

Foreign edible seeds	Not more than 5.0% by weight.
Total ash	Not more than 9.0% by weight.
Ash insoluble in dilute HCl	Not more than 1.5% by weight.

A.05.03 --- CARDAMOM (*Chhoti elachi*) Whole means the dried and nearly ripe fruits of *Elettaria cardamom (L)*. The percentage of extraneous matter shall not exceed 5.0 per cent by weight. The cardamom seeds obtained from the capsules shall contain not less than 3.0 per cent (v/w) of volatile oil.

A.05.03.01 --- CARDAMOM (*Chhoti elachi*) Seeds means the seeds obtained by separating the seeds from the capsules of *Elettaria cardamomum (L)*. The percentage of extraneous matter in the seeds shall not exceed 2.0 per cent by weight. The seeds shall contain not less than 3.0 per cent (v/w) of volatile oil.

A.05.04 --- CARDAMOM AMOMUM (*Badi elachi*) Whole means the dried and nearly ripe fruit of *Amomum subulatum (Roxb)* in the form of capsules. The proportion of calyx pieces, stalk bits and other extraneous matter shall not exceed 5.0 per cent by weight. The cardamom amomum seeds obtained from the capsules shall contain not less than 1.0 per cent (v/w) of the volatile oil.

A.05.04.01 --- CARDAMOM AMOMUM (*Badi elachi*) Seeds means the seeds obtained by separating the seeds from the capsules of *Amomum subulatum (Roxb)*. The percentage of extraneous matter in the seeds shall not exceed 2.0 per cent by weight. The seeds shall contain not less than 1.0 per cent (v/w) of the volatile oil.

A.05.05 --- CHILLIES (*Lal Mirchi*) Whole means the dried ripe fruits or pods of *Capsicum annum/Capsicum frutescens (L)*. The proportion of extraneous matter including calyx pieces, loose tops, dirt, lumps of earth, stones shall not exceed 5.0 per cent by weight. The pods shall be free from extraneous colouring matter, coating of mineral oil and other harmful substances.

A.05.06 --- CINNAMON (*Dalchini*) Whole means the dried pieces of the inner bark of *Cinnamomum zeylanicum (Blume)*. It shall not contain any other foreign vegetable matter or colouring matter. It shall contain not less than 0.5 per cent (v/w) of the volatile oil.

A.05.06.02 --- CASSIA (*Chinese Cinnamon) (Taj)* Whole means dried pieces of bark of *Cinnamomum cassia (Blume). Syn. Cinnamomum aromaticum (Nees) or (Cassia lignea)*. It shall not contain any other foreign vegetable matter or colouring matter.

A.05.07 --- Cloves (*Laung*) Whole means the dried, unopened flower buds of *Eugenia caryophyllus (C. Sprengel) Bullock and Harrison*. The inorganic extraneous matter shall not exceed 0.5 per cent by weight and the organic extraneous matter, which includes vegetable matter of plants other than cloves, tendril cloves (peduncle), mother cloves or other matters of plants of cloves, shall not exceed two per cent by weight. (Headless cloves shall not be considered as extraneous matter). The amount of insect damaged clove shall not exceed 1.0 per cent by weight.

The cloves (on dry basis) shall contain not less than 15.0 per cent (v/w) of the volatile oil.

A.05.08 --- CORIANDER (*Dhania*) Whole means the dried mature fruits (seeds) of *Coriandrum sativum (L)*. The proportion of extraneous matter including dust, dirt, stones, lumps of earth, chaff, stalk, stem or straw, edible seeds of fruits other than coriander and insect damaged seeds shall not exceed 8.0 per cent by weight.

A.05.09 — CUMIN (*Safed jeera*) Whole means the dried seeds of *Cuminum cyminum (L)*. The proportion of extraneous matter including dust, stones, lumps of earth, chaff, stem or straw shall not exceed 7.0% by weight. The proportion of edible seeds other than cumin seeds shall not exceed 5.0% by weight.

A.05.10 — CUMIN BLACK (*Kalonji*) Whole means the dried seeds of *Nigella sativa (L)*. The proportion of extraneous matter including dust, dirt, stones, lumps of earth, chaff, stem or straw shall not exceed 7.0 per cent by weight. The proportion of edible seeds other than cumin black shall not exceed 5.0 per cent by weight.

A.05.11. FENNEL (*Saunf*) Whole means the dried ripe fruits of *Foeniculum vulgare (Mill)*. The proportion of extraneous matter including dust, dirt, stones, lumps of earth, chaff stem or straw shall not exceed 5.0 per cent by weight. The proportion of edible seeds other than fennel shall not exceed 5.0 per cent by weight.

A.05.12 — FENUGREEK (*Methi*) Whole means the dried ripe seeds of *Trigonella foenum-graecum (L)*. The proportion of extraneous matter including dust, dirt, stones, lumps of earth, chaff, stem or straw shall not exceed 5.0 per cent by weight. The proportion or edible seeds other than fenugreek shall not exceed 5.0 per cent by weight.

A.05.13 — GINGER (*Sonth, Adrak*) Whole means the rhizomes of *Zingiber officinale (Rose)* in pieces, irregular in shape and size with peel not entirely removed, washed and dried in the sun. The proportion of extraneous matter shall not exceed 2.0 per cent by weight. It shall contain, on dry basis, not less than 1.0 per cent (v/w) of its volatile oil. If the ginger is limed, the lime (Calcium Oxide) content shall not exceed 4.0 per cent by weight (on dry basis).

A.05.14 — MACE (*Jaepatri*) Whole means the dried coat or arilus of the seed of *Myristica fragrans (Houtt)*. It shall not contain the arilus of any other variety of *Myristica malabarica* or *Fatua* (Bombay mace) and *Myristica argentea* (wild mace). The proportion of extraneous matter shall not exceed 3.0 per cent by weight.

A.05.15 — MUSTARD (*Rai, Sarson*) Whole means the dried seeds of *Brassica alba (L), Boiss (Safed rai), Brassica compestris (L) var. dichotoma (Kali Sarson), Brassica Compestris (L), var.*

yellow Sarson, syn. Brassica compestris (L), var. glauca (Pili Sarson), Brassica compestris (L), var. toria (Toria), Brassica juncea (L) Coss-et. Czern (Rai, Lotni) and *Brassica nigra (L) Koch (Benarasi rai).* The proportion of extraneous matter which includes dust, dirt, stones, lumps of earth, chaff, stem, straw, edible foodgrains, edible oilseeds of any other variety or any other impurity shall not exceed 7.0 per cent by weight. It shall be free from seeds of *Argemone maxicana (Linn).*

A.05.16 --- NUTMEG (*Jaiphal)* Whole means the dried seeds of *Myristica fragrans (Houtt).* The proportion of extraneous matter and infestation shall not exceed 3.0 per cent by weight.

A.05.17.01 --- PEPPER BLACK (*Kalimirch*) Whole means the dried berries of *Piper nigrum (L)*, brown to black in colour with wrinkled surface. The proportion of extraneous matter including dust, stalks, leafy matter and other foreign matter shall not exceed 3.0 per cent by weight. The proportion by weight of light berries and pinheads shall not exceed 10.0 per cent and 4.0 per cent respectively.

A.05.17.02 --- *LIGHT BLACK PEPPER* --- Light black pepper means the dried berries of *Piper nigrum (L)* dark brown to dark black in colour. It shall be well dried and free from mould or insects and shall not contain more than 6 per cent extraneous matters including dust, stone, lumps of earth, stalks, leafy matter and other foreign edible seeds and 10 per cent pinheads.

A.05.17.03 --- PINHEADS --- Pinheads shall be wholly derived from the spikes of *Piper nigrum (L).* They shall be reasonably dry and free from insects. The colour shall be from dark brown to black. The extraneous matter shall not exceed 6 per cent.

A.05.18 --- (*KHAS-KHAS*) Whole means the dried seeds of the ripe fruit of *Papaver Somniferum (L).* The seed may be white or greyish in colour. The proportion of extraneous matter shall not exceed (5.0) per cent by weight. It shall contain not less than 40.0 per cent by weight of non-volatile ether extract.

A.05.19 --- *SAFFRON (Kesar)* means the dried stigmata or tops of styles of *Crocus sativus (L).* It shall not contain any foreign colouring matter or any other extraneous matter. It shall conform to the following standards:-

Total ash	Not more than 8 per cent by weight.
Ash insoluble in dilute HCl	Not more than 1.5 per cent by weight.

Volatile matter at 103° ± 1°C	Not more than 14 per cent by weight.
Aqueous extract	Not less than 55 per cent by weight.
Total Nitrogen	Not Less then 2 per cent by weight. (on dry weight basis)
Foreign matter such as sand, earth, dust, leaf, stem, chaff and vegetable matter.	Not more than 1 per cent
Floral waste defined as yellow filaments, pollen, stamens parts or ovary and other parts of flowers of Crocus sativus Linn.	Not more than 15 per cent

Saffron shall be free from living insects, moulds and shall be practically free from dead insects, insect fragments and rodent contamination visible to the naked eye.

A.05.20 --- TURMERIC *(Haldi)* Whole means the dried rhizome or bulbous roots of the plant of *Curcuma longa (L)*. It shall be free from lead chromate and other artificial colouring matter. The proportion of extra-neous matter shall not exceed 2.0 per cent by weight.

A.05-21.01 --- MIXED MASALA (Whole) means a mixture of clean, dried and sound aromatic herbs and spices. It may also contain dried vegetables and/or fruits, oilseeds, garlic, ginger, poppy seeds and curry leaves. It shall be free from added colouring matter. It shall be free from mould growth and insect infestation. The proportion of extraneous matter shall not exceed five per cent by weight, out of which the proportion of organic matter including foreign edible seeds, and inorganic matter shall not exceed three per cent and two per cent respectively.

A.05.22 --- ANISEED or *SAUNF* imported means the dried ripe fruit of *Pimpinella anisum*. Foreign edible seeds or matter shall not exceed 5.0 per cent by weight. It shall conform to the following standards:-

Total Ash	Not more than 9 per cent by weight.
Ash insoluble in dilute HCl	Not more than 1.5 per cent by weight.
Volatile Oil	Not less than 1.0 per cent (v/w).

A.05.23 --- (Bishops' weed) or *AJOWAN* means the dried ripe seeds of *Trachyspermum ammi (Linn) Sprague*. The proportion of organic and inorganic extraneous matter shall not exceed 3 per cent and 2 per cent respectively. The seeds shall be free from living insects, insect fragments and rodent contamination visible to the eyes.

A.05.24 — Dried Mango Slices — Means the dried wholesome, edible part of raw mango fruit with or without the outer skin. It shall be free from fungus, moulds and insect infestation, rodent contamination, added colouring, flavouring matter. It shall also be free from deleterious substances injurious to health. It shall not contain any preservative except edible common salt which may be added to the extent of 5 per cent by weight on dry basis. It shall have characteristic taste and flavour. The proportion of extraneous substance shall not exceed 4 per cent by weight out of which inorganic matter shall not exceed 2 per cent by weight.

It shall also conform to the following standards, namely :-

Moisture — Not more than 12 per cent by weight.

Damaged Slices — Not more than 5 per cent by weight.

Seed Coatings — Not more than 6 per cent by weight.

Explanation:

(i) Seed coatings shall be exterior covering of the seed.

(ii) Damaged slices mean the slices that are eaten by weevils or other insects and includes slices internally damaged by fungus, moisture or heating.

Notes:

All these whole spices shall also conform to the following also.

(i) The amount of insect damaged matter shall not exceed 5 percent by weight except cassia (*taj*) whole (A.05.06.02), Nutmeg (A.05.16), light black pepper (A.05.17.02), pin heads (A.05.17.03), saffron (A.05.19), mixed masala (Whole) (A.05.21.01) and Bishop's weed (*ajwain*) (A.05.23). For these spices this limit has been specified under their respective heads.

Explanation

The term "insect damaged matter" means spices that are

(i) partially or wholly bored by insects.

(ii) Shall be free of added colouring matter.

P.F.A. Act 1954 and Rules 1955

Specifications for powdered spices and condiments as amended up 15.12.1992

Name of Spice/ Condiment	*Moisture (max)%*	*T.Ash (max) %*	*A.I.Ash (max) %*	*Volatile Oil (mini) %*	*NVEE (mini) %*	*Crude Fibre (max) %*	*Cold Water sol. extract, (mini)%*
1	2	3	4	5	6	7	8
Caraway (Siahjira)	13.0	8.0	1.5	-	-	-	
Cardamom (Choti Elaichi)	14.0	8.0	3.0	3.0	-	-	
Cardamom Ammomum (Badi Elaichi)	14.0	8.0	3.0	1.0	-	-	
Chillies (Lal Mirch)	12.0	8.0	1.3	-	12.0	30.0	
Cinnamon (Dalchini)	12.0	8.0	2.0	0.5	-	-	
Cloves (Laung)	12.0	7.0	1.5	15.0	-	-	
Coriander (Dhania)	12.0	7.0	1.5	-		-	
Cumin (Safed Jeera)	12.0	9.5	1.5				
Cumin Black (Kalonji)	12.0	7.0	1.5	0.5			
Fennel (Saunf)	12.0	9.0	2.0	1.0			
Fenugreek (Methi)	10.0	7.0	2.0	-	-	-	30.0
Ginger (Sonth, Adrak)	13.0	8.0	1.0	1.0	-	-	10.0
Mace (Jaepatri)	10.0	3.0	1.0	-	20.0 to 30.0	10.0	
Mango (dried Amchur)	12.0	*6.0		1.5		6.0	
Mustard (Rai, Sarson)	7.0	8.0	2.0	0.25	22.0	8.0	
Nutmeg (Jaiphal)	8.0	5.0	0.5	-	25.0	10.0	
Pepper Black (Kali Mirch)	12.5	8.0	1.2		5.5	18.0	
Turmeric (Haldi)	13.0	9.0	1.5				
Curry Powder	14.0	-	2.0	0.25	7.5	15.0	

* (Salt free basis)

(Continued)

Name of Spice/ Condiment	*Water sol. Ash (mini)%*	*Calcium as CaO (max)%*	*Alcohol, 90% V/W sol. ext. (mini)%*	*Starch (max)%*	*Lead Chromate test*	*Edible common salt (max)%*	*Lead (max) ppm.*	*Rem-arks*
9	*10*	*11*	*12*	*13*	*14*	*15*	*16*	*17*
Caraway (Siahjira)								
Cardamom (Choti Elaichi)								
Cardamom Ammomum (Badi Elaichi)								
Chillies (Lal Mirch)								
Cinnamon (Dalchini)								
Cloves (Laung)								
Coriander (Dhania)								
Cumin (Safed Jeera)								
Cumin Black (Kalonji)								
Fennel (Saunf)								
Fenugreek (Methi)								
Ginger (Sonth, Adrak)	1.7	4.0	4.5					
Mace (Jaepatri)								
Mango (dried Amchur)								Acidity as anhydrous tartaric acid (12.0-26.0% by weight)
Mustard (Rai, Sarson)								
Nutmeg (Jaiphal)								
Pepper Black (Kali Mirch)								
Turmeric (Haldi)				60.0	Neg			
Curry Powder						5.0	10.0	all on dry wt. basis

N.B. Moisture % is on wt. basis.

All spices and condiments whole as well as powdered, shall be free from added colouring matter.

12

Agmark Specification for Export

I. Grade designation and definitions of quality of Chillies

(Heading)

1. Variety

Special Characteristics

2. Length in cms
3. Colour

Maximum Limits of tolerance (percent)

4. Damaged or Discoloured Pods
5. Stalkless Pods
6. Moisture
7. Loose Seeds
8. Foreign Matter
9. Broken chillies
10. Grade Name
11. Pods with Stalks
12. Pods with Calyx
13. General characteristics

1	2	3	4	5	6	7	8	9	10	11	12	13
1. Sanam (Jan.- August)	5+	Light red shining	2.00	2.00	11.50	1.00	1.00	5.00	Special			@@
	3 to 5	-do-	4.00	3.00	11.50	2.00	2.00	7.00	General			
	-do-	Dull Red	6.00	4.00	11.50	2.00	2.00	7.00	Fair			

(Continued)

1	2	3	4	5	6	7	8	9	10	11	12	13
2. Sanam (Sep.-Dec.)	5+	Light red shining or	5	10.00	-do-	3.00	1.00	0.50	Special			
	3 to 5	dull red	5	20.00	-do-	-do-	-do-	2.00	General			
3. Mundu	2.5 –	Deep red Shining	2.0	5.0	-do-	1.00	1.00	1.00	Special			
	-do-		4.0	10.0	-do-	1.00	1.00	1.00	General			
4. Rari (Patarki or Patli)	8+	Bright red	1.0	2.0	-do-	-do-	-do-	5.0	Special			
	6 to 8		2.0	2.0	-do-	-do-	-do-	5.0	General			
5. Gaspurea	5+	Bright Red	-do-	-do-	-do-	-do-	-do-	-do-	Special			
	3 to 5	-do-	3.0	-do-	-do-	-do-	-do-	-do-	General			
6. Non-specific	Typical of Variety	Typical of Variety	2.0	2.0	-do-	2	-do-	4.0	Special			
			4.0	3.0	-do-	3	2.0	6.0	General			
			6.0	4.0	-do-	3	2.0	8.0	Fair			
7. Stalkless*	-	-	-	-	11.00	5.0	0.5	-	General	1.0 by count	5.0 by count	
8. Clipped++	-	-	-	-	-do-	3.0	0.5	-	-do-		-do-	

@@ Chillies shall-

(a) be the dried ripe fruits belonging to the species ***Capsicum annum (L)***

(b) have shape, pungency and seed contents normal to the variety

(c) be free from mould or insect damage and be in sound condition and fit for human consumption

(d) be current year's crop and should be free from extraneous colouring matter, oil and other harmful substances.

Basis of quantitative determinations

All determinations and percentages shall be reckoned on the basis of total weight representative samples.

Length

Tolerance specified in col. 2 shall be based upon the average length of 20 fruits selected at random. The measurement will be taken from the tip of the fruits to the pedicel point (where the stalk is attached).

Discoloured pods

Pods having brown, black, white and other coloured patches will be considered as discoloured pods.

Foreign matter

All extraneous matter including calyx pieces and loose stalk will be treated as foreign matter. In accidental errors, a tolerance of 0.5 per cent under col. 4 and 1 per cent under col. 7 is permissible for both the grades.

Moisture

For accidental errors, a tolerance of 0.5 per cent for moisture content will be allowed over the above 11.5 per cent only.

Foreign matter

* All extraneous matter including calyx pieces and loose stalk will be treated as foreign matter. A tolerance is permissible upto 0.25% in excess of the tolerance specified under columns 4 and 8 and 0.5% in column 5.

++ Foreign matter

All extraneous matter including calyx pieces and loose stalk will be treated as foreign matter. A tolerance is permissible upto 0.25% in excess of tolerance specified under columns 4 and 7.

++ Moisture

A tolerance of 0.5% for moisture content will be allowed over and above the stipulated limit. Clipped chillies means chillies having the stalks clipped from the very base but having the calyx.

II. Grade designation and definitions of quality of Ginger

Variety	*Grade Designation*	*SpecialCharacteristics*				*General Characteristics*
		Size of rhizomes (minimum) (mm) in length	*Ex. Matter % by maximum*	*Very Light wt. pieces % by maximum*	*Lime as CaO % by maximum*	
1	2	3	4	5	6	7
1. Ungarbled Bleached Calicut Ginger	Special	15	3.0	4.0	4.0	The ginger, whole 1. shall be the dried rhizomes of *Zingiber officinale Rose*, in pieces, irregular in shape and size, pale brown in colour, with fibre content charac teristic of the variety, with the peel not entirely re moved.
	Good	-do-	4.0	6.0	6.0	
	Non-specified	-do-	As specified in contract			

(Continued)

1	2	3	4	5	6	7
2 Ungarbled Bleached Cochin Ginger	Special	-do-	3.0	4.0	4.0	2. shall have characteristic taste and flavour, be wholesome, and shall not have rancid or bitter taste or musty odour
	Good	-do-	4.0	6.0	6.0	
	Non-specified	-do-	-As specified in contract			
3. Garbled Bleached Calicut Ginger	GBKG	-do-	2.0	-	3.5	3. shall be reasonably dry and reasonably free from moulds and insect infestation.
4. Ungarbled Non-bleached Cochin Ginger	Special	-do-	3.0	4.0	-	
	Good	-do-	4.0	6.0	-	
	Unspecified	-do-	As specified in contract			
5. Garbled Bleached Cochin Ginger	BGC	-do-	2.0	-	3.0	
6. Ungarbled Non-Bleached Calicut Ginger	Special	-do-	3.0	4.0	-	
	Good	-do-	4.0	6.0	-	
	Unspecified	-do-	As specified in contract			
7. Garbled Non-Bleached Cochin Ginger	NGC	-do-	2.0	-	-	
8. Garbled Non-Bleached Calicut Ginger	NGK	-do-	2.0	-	-	

Notes: For varieties at S.No. 1, 2, 4, 6 (ungarbled).

1. Extraneous matter means all foreign matter including the exhausted or spent ginger.

2. A tolerance for size due to accidental errors may be allowed up to 7 per cent in the case of grade 'Special' and 15 per cent in the case of grade 'Good'. In the case of 'Non-specified' grade, no tolerances is prescribed; however, it may depend upon the terms of the contract with the buyer.

3. Non-specified grade is not a grade in its strict sense, but has been provided for the produce not covered by the other two grades. Ginger under this grade shall be exported only against a *firm order*.

4. *Firm order* means that the entire value of the goods contracted for shall have been obtained in advance by opening a cent per cent

irrevocable letter of credit in India, which is encashable on the production of a shipping bill supported by receipt of shipment or is guaranteed in any other way.

Note: Tolerance for size

For varieties at S.No. 3, 5, 7, 8 (Garbled)

Maximum tolerance of 3 per cent shall be allowed.

III. Grade designation and definition of quality of Garlic

	Variety	*Grade designation*	*Diameter mm (Minimum)*	*General characteristics*
1.	Madurai Hill (Smoked or unsmoked)	Big Medium Small Mixed	35 25 10 Assorted but not less than 10 mm.	The bulbs shall: 1. have resonably uniform shape,colour and pungency characteristics of variety/ type,
2.	Madurai Plain	Big Medium Small Mixed	20 15 10 Assorted but not less than 10 mm.	2. be mature, thoroughly cured and dried, 3. be compact with cloves well filled and fairly plump, 4. be free from damage caused by moulds, decay, shattered cloves,
3.	Jamnagar	Big Medium Small Mixed	35 25 12 Assorted but not less than 12 mm	dirt or stain, sunburn, sunscald, cuts, sprouts, tops, roots, diseases, insects, mechanical or other injuries & 5. each bulb shall be fairly well enclosed in its outer sheath.
4.	Poona/Nasik	Big Medium Small Mixed	30 25 10 Assorted but not less than 10 mm.	

Notes:

1. *Tolerance for size* — For accidental errors in sizing not more than 5 per cent by weight may be of the next lower grade.
2. *Tolerance for requirements in respect of General characteristics:* To allow for variations other than size, incidental to proper grading and handling not

more than 10% by weight of garlic in any container may be below the requirements specified under General characteristics but not more than a total of 1/5th of this tolerance or 2% shall be allowed for garlic which is affected by decay.

3. Mixed - This Grade may be packed against a *"Firm Order"* only.
4. Smoked/Unsmoked - The fact whether the bulbs are smoked or unsmoked would be indicated on the labels.

IV. Grade designations and definitions of quality of Pin-heads+

Grade Designation	*++Extraneous matter not exceeding (per cent)*	*General characteristics*
1	*2*	*3*
pH Grade Special	3	Shall be wholly derived from the spikes of *Piper nigrum* grown in South India.They shall be reasonably dry and free from insects. The colour shall be from dark brown to black.
pH Grade 1 +++	6	

\+ Pin-heads are under-developed and/or broken berries of black pepper.

++ These comprise dust, chaff, pickings and other foreign matter.

+++ This grade is for export only.

V. Grade designations and definitions of quality of Black Pepper (Non-specified)

Grade designation	**Extraneous matter not exceeding (per cent)*	*General characteristics*
1	*2*	*3*
NS Grade X	4**	Shall be wholly derived from the spikes of *Piper nigrum*, grown in South India. Different qualities of pepper can be mixed in different proportions in accordance with the orders from buyers.

*These comprise dust, chaff, pickings and other foreign matter. Pin-heads will be regarded as extraneous matter.

**Extraneous matter determined on analysis of any sample shall be specified in the Certificate of Grading, if so desired. *This grade is for export only.*

VI. Grade designations and definitions of quality of Tellicherry Garbled Black Pepper

Grade designation	*Size* (diameter of holes in m.m. of the sieve on which retained*	***Extraneous matter not exceeding (per cent) by weight*	****Light berries not exceeding (per cent) by weight*	*Moisture content not exceeding (per cent) by weight*	*General characteristics*
1	*2*	*3*	*4*	*5*	*6*
TGSEB (Tellicherry Garbled Special Extra bold)	4.75	0.5	3.0	11.0	Shall be the dried mature berries of *Piper nigrum* grown in South India. Garbled dark brown to dark black in colour, nearly globular, with a wrinkled surface, the deepest wrinkles forming a network on the dried berry. It shall be free from mould or insect or any other adulterant.
TGEB '(Tellicherry Garbled Extra Bold)	4.25	0.5	3.0	11.0	
TG (Tellicherry Garbled)	4.25 (50% min) and 4.00 (50% max)	0.5	3.0	11.0	

* Tolerance allowed for the next lower size 5 per cent in T.G. (Tellicherry Garbled); the tolerance for both the sizes taken together will not exceed 5 per cent.

** These comprise dust, chaff, pickings, and other foreign matter.

*** Light berry content to be tested by floatation method in alcohol or methylated spirit of 0.80 to 0.82 specific gravity at room temperature (around 25°C).

During monsoon months, i.e., from the 1st of May to 30th of September, a tolerance of 0.5 per cent is allowed in respect of moisture.

VII. Grade designations and definitions of quality of Malabar Black Pepper

Variety	*Grade designation*	**Extraneous mater not exceeding (percent)*	***Light berries not exceeding (percent)*	****Moisture content not exceeding (percent)*	*General characteristics*
1	*2*	*3*	*4*	*5*	*6*
Garbled	M.G. Grade 1	0.5	2.0	11.0	shall be the dried mature berries of *Piper nigrum* grown in South India, dark brown to dark black in colour, nearly globular with a wrinkled surface, the deepest wrinkles forming a network on the dried berry. It shall be free from mould or insects or any other adulterants.
	M.G. Grade 2	0.5	5.0	11.0	
Ungarbled	MUG Grade 1	2	7.0	12.0	
	MUG Grade 2	2	10.0	12.0	

* These comprise dust, chaff, pickings and other foreign matter. Pinheads will be regarded as an extraneous matter.

** Light berry content to be tested by floatation method in alcohol or methylated spirit of specific gravity 0.80 to 0.82 at room temperature (around 25°C).

*** During the monsoon months, i.e., from the 15th of May to 30th of September, a tolerance of 0.5 per cent is allowed in respect of moisture.

VIII. Grade designations and definitions of quality of Light Black Pepper*

Grade designation	***Extraneous matter not exceeding (percent)*	*Pinhead not exceeding (percent)*	*General characteristics*
1	*2*	*3*	*4*
UGL Special	3	-	Shall be the dried berries of *Piper nigrum* grown in South India, dark brown to black in colour and ungarbled. They shall be well dried and free from insects.
UGL 1	4	5	
UGL 2""	7	10	
GL Special	2	-	
GL 1	3	5	
GL 2	6	10	

* Pepper in which 50 percent or more float when stirred in alcohol or

methylated spirit of 0.80 to 0.82 specific gravity at room temperature (around 25°C).

** These comprise dust, chaff, pickings and other foreign matter.

"" This grade is for export only.

UGL Connotes- Ungarbled whereas GL Connotes - Garbled

IX. Grade designations and definitions of quality of Turmeric Bulbs (Round, *Gathas* or *Golas*) produced in India

Grade designation	*Special Characterisics*		*General characteristics*
	Foreign matter percentage by weight maximum	*Chura and defective bulbs, percentage by weight maximum*	
1	*2*	*3*	*4*
Special	1.0	1.0	1. The turmeric bulbs shall be primary rhi zomes of the plant *Curcuma longa L. (Syn. C. domestica (Val)*
Good	1.5	3.0	2. They shall:
Fair	2.0	5.0	a) be well developed, smooth, sound, soft and free from rootlets;
Non-specified	–	–	b) have the shape, length (not below 15 mm) and colour characteristic of the variety;
			c) be perfectly dry
			d) be free from damage caused by weevils, moisture, over boiling or fungus attack except that 0.1 per cent and 0.2 per cent by weight of rhizomos damaged by moisture and overboiling shall be allowed in grades Good and Fair respectively,
			e) have not been artificially coloured with chemicals and dyes.

Notes - Foreign matter includes chaff, dried leaves, powder, clay particles, dust, dirt and any other extraneous matter.

Chura and defective bulbs include immature small fingers and/or bulbs internally damaged, hollow bulbs except weevilled bulbs.

The length shall be reckoned at the points of greatest thickness of the bulbs.

The colour of core shall be reckoned in bulbs freshly broken with hands.

Non-specified: This is not a grade in its strict sense, but has been provided for the products not covered by the other two grades. Turmeric bulbs under this grade shall be exported only against a **'firm order'**.

X. Grade designations and definitions of quality of the varieties of turmeric commercially known as Finger Turmeric produced in India

Variety	Grade designation	Flexibility	Special Characteristics				General characteristics
			Pieces* percentage by weight maximum	Foreign matter percentage by weight maximum	Chura and defective bulbs percentage by weight maximum	Percentage of bulbs and cut bulbs by weight maximum	
1	2	3	4	5	6	7	8
Alleppey	Good	Should be hard to touch	5	1.0	3.0	4.0	1. The turmeric 'fingers' shall be secondary rhizomes of the plant *Curcuma longa (L)*.
	Fair	-do-	7	1.5	5.0	5.0	2. They shall
Non-Alleppey	Special	Should be hard to touch and break with metallic twang	2	1.0	0.5	2.0	a) be well set and closely grained and free from bulbs (primary rhizomes) and ill developed porous fingers;
	Good	-do-	3	1.5	1.0	3.0	
	Fair	Should be hard	5	2.0	1.5	5.0	b) have the shape, length, wrinkles, colour and other characteristics of the variety;
	Non-specified						c) be perfectly dry and free from damage caused by weevils, moisture, over-boiling or fungus attack except that 1.0 per cent and 2.0 per cent by weight of rhizomes damaged by moisture and over boiling shall be allowed in grades Good and Fair respectively. d) not have been artificially coloured with chemicals or dyes.

* Pieces are fingers, broken or whole, of 15 mm or less in length.

Note - Foreign matter includes chaff, dried leaves, clay particles, dust, dirt and any other extraneous matter. The length shall be reckoned from one tip of the finger to the other tip longitudinally.

The colour of core and flexibility shall be reckoned from fingers freshly broken with hands. Chura and defective bulbs include immature small fingers and or bulbs internally damaged, hollow and porous bulbs, cut bulbs and other types of damaged bulbs, except weevilled bulbs.

Non-specified:- This is not a grade in its strict sense but has been provided for the produce not covered by the other grades. Turmeric fingers under this grade shall be exported only against a **'firm order'**.

XI. Grade designation and definition of Indian Onions for Export

Variety	*Grade Designation*	*Special characteristics*		*General characteristics*
		Size (dia) in mm (min)	*Colour*	
1. Red Motluru for seed purposes from Tamil Nadu and Andhra Pradesh	Special	15	Light purple to Pink	The bulbs occur in bunches or clusters of two or more, joined together at the base.
	Good	20	-do-	They shall :
2. Dindigul/Kar/ Podisu Red.	Special	15	-do-	1. be reasonably uniform in shape, colour and pungency characteristics of the variety type;
	Good	10	-do-	
3. Bangalore	Big	30	Light purple to purple	2. be mature, solid in feel, reasonably firm with tough clinging skin free from bottle-necks.
	Medium	20	-do-	
	Small	15	-do-	
	Mixed	Assorted but not below 15 mm	-do-	
4. Krishanapuram (Chitty bellary)	Big	35	Light rosy to dark rosy	3. be thoroughly cured and dried.
	Medium	25	-do-	4. be free from damage caused by seed-stems, moisture, mechanical or other injuries and staining dirt or other foreign material; and
	Small	15	-do-	
	Mixed	Assorted but not below 15 mm	-do-	

(Continued)

Variety	Grade Designation	Special characteristics: Size (dia) in mm (min)	Special characteristics: Colour	General characteristics
5. White from Maharashtra and Karnataka	Big	40	White to silvery white	5. be free from moulds, diseases, soft, rots, decay and insect attack.
	Medium	25	-do-	
	Mixed	Assorted but not below 20 mm	-do-	
6. Nasik/Saurashtra/Bellary	Extra Big	55	Light to rosy	
	Big A	45	-do-	
	Big B	45	-do-	
	Medium A	35	-do-	
	Medium B	35	-do-	
	Small A	20	-do-	
	Small B	20	-do-	
	Mixed A	Assorted but not below 20 mm	-do-	
	Mixed B	-do-	-do-	
7. Poona	Extra Big	60	Light to deep red	
	Big	45	-do-	
	Medium	35	-do-	
	Small	20	-do-	
	Mixed	Assorted but not below 20 mm	-do-	

Note:- for 1 and 2 only

1. Tolerance for size:- For accidental errors in sizing not more than 10% by weight of the bulbs may be smaller than the minimum diameter prescribed. In this case it is the smallest onion in the bunch that would be taken for measuring the diameter for the purpose of grading.

2. Tolerance for requirements in respect of General characteristics - To allow for variations other than size, incident to proper grading and handling not more than 10% by weight of onions may fail to meet the requirements of the grade.

NOTE: (For Rest Grades)

1. Tolerance for size - For accidental errors in sizing, not more than 5%

by weight of the bulbs in any lot may be of next lower grade than the minimum diameter prescribed.

2. Tolerance for requirements in respect of General characteristics - To allow for variations other than size incident to proper grading and handling, not more than 10 per cent by weight of the onions in any lot may fail to meet the requirements of the grade.

3. Mixed - This grade may be packed against a Firm Order only.

XII. Grade designation and quality of seed spices

(Heading)

1. Name of seed spice
   Grade Designation

Special characteristics (percentage by weight)

2. Extraneous matter Maximum
3. Spilt Seeds Maximum
4. Damaged, Blackened, Insect Bored seeds Maximum
5. Shrivelled and Immature seeds Maximum
6. Moisture Maximum
7. Other seeds maximum
8. Jeeralu content Maximum
9. Inorganic Extraneous Matter Maximum
10. Organic Extraneous Matter Maximum
11. Light seeds Maximum
12. Weight G/L Minimum

1	*Grade Designation*	*2*	*3*	*4*	*5*	*6*	*7*	*8*	*9*	*10*	*11*	*12*
1. Coriander	Special	1.5	10.0	1.0	1.0	10.0	-	-	-	-	-	-
	Good	3.0	15.0	2.0	2.0	10.0	-	-	-	-	-	-
	Fair	7.0	30.0	4.0	3.0	10.0	-	-	-	-	-	-
	X	7.0	-	4.0	3.0	10.0	-	-	-	-	-	-
2. Cumin	Special	1.5	-	1.5	1.5	10.0	0.5	1.0	-	-	-	-
	Good	2.5	-	2.5	3.0	-do-	1.0	3.0	-	-	-	-
	Fair	3.5	-	3.5	4.0	-do-	1.5	3.5	-	-	-	-
	Average	5.0	-	5.0	5.0	-do-	-	5.0	-	-	-	-

(Continued)

1	Grade Designation	2	3	4	5	6	7	8	9	10	11	12
3. Fenugreek	Special	1.00	-	0.5	1.5	-do-	-	-	-	-	-	-
	Good	2.00	-	1.00	3.0	-do-	-	-	-	-	-	-
	Fair	4.00		2.5	5.0	-do-	-	-	-	-	-	
4. Fennel (saunf)	Special	-	-	1.5	2.0	-do-	-	-	0.25	1.5	-	-
	Good	-	-	4.0	4.0	-do-	-	-	0.5	2.5	-	-
	Fair	-	-	6.0	6.0	-do-	-	-	1.5	3.5	-	-
5. Poppy	I	1.5	-	-	-	11.0	0.5	-	-	-	-	-
	II	3.0	-	-	-	-do-	1.0	-	-	-	-	-
6. Ajowan	Special	-	-	-	1.0	-do-	-	-	0.25	0.5	-	-
	Good	-	-	-	2.0	-do-	-	-	0.5	0.75	-	-
	Fair	-	-	-	3.0	-do-	-	-	1.0	1.0	-	-
7. Cardamom	CS1	1.0	-	-	-	-	-	-	-	-	3.0	675
	CS2	2.0	-	-	-	-	-	-	-	-	5.0	650
	CS3	10.0	-	-	-	-	-	-	-	-	-	-
8. Celery	Special	1.0	-	-	-	10.0	-	-	-	-	-	-
	Good	3.0	-	-	-	-do-	-	-	-	-	-	-
	Fair	5.0	-	-	-	-do-	-	-	-	-	-	-

Definitions:

1. Extraneous matter comprises dust, dirt, stones, earth, chaff, stalks, stems, straw or any other foreign matter.

2. Split seeds are those fruits which have split longitudinally.

3. Damaged and blackened seeds are those fruits or split fruits which are damaged or blackened materially affecting the quality.

4. Insect bored seeds are those fruits or split fruits which are partially or wholly bored or eaten by weevils or other insects.

5. Shrivelled and immature seeds are those fruits which are not properly developed.

6. Inorganic extraneous matter means dust, dirt, stones, earth or any other inorganic foreign matter.

7. Organic extraneous matter means chaff, stalks, stems, straw, other seeds or any other organic foreign matter.

8. Weevilled seeds are those seeds that are partially or wholly bored or eaten by weevil or other insects.

XIII. Grade designation and definitions of quality of small cardamoms

(Heading)

1. Variety
2. Trade Name
3. Colour
4. Empty and malformed capsules - % by wt. Maximum
5. Immature and shrivelled capsules - % by wt. Maximum
6. Blacks and splits - % by count Maximum
7. Sieve size for retention of capsules (mm)
8. Weight in gm/litre
9. Unclipped capsules % by count Maximum
10. General characteristics

1	*2*	*3*	*4*	*5*	*6*	*7*	*8*	*9*	*10*
1. Alleppy Green Cardamom	Extra Bold	Deep Green or	2.0	2.0	0.0	7.0	435	-	1. The cardamoms shall be the dried capsules of *Elettaria* cardamom grown in South India, capsules being three cornered and having a ribbed appearance.
	Bold	light green	2.0	2.0	0.0	6.0	415	-	
	Superior	-do-	3.0	5.0	0.0	5.0	385	-	
Shipment	Green 1	-do-	5.0	7.0	10.0	4.0	350		
	Green 2	-do-	7.0	9.0	12.0	4.0	320		
	Light	-	-	-	15.0	3.5	260	-	
	AGN	-	-	-	-	-	-	-	
2. Coorg Green	Extra Bold	-	0.0	0.0	0.0	8.0A	450	0.0	
	Bold	-	2.0	3.0	0.0	7.5	435	0.0	2. The capsules shall be free from insect infestation and visible mould.
	Superior	-	3.0	5.0	0.0	6.5	415	0.0	
	Mota	Green	5.0	10.0	0.0	6.0	385	3.0	
	Shipment	-	10.0	15.0	10.0	5.0	350	5.0	
	Light	-	-	-	15.0	3.5	280	-	
	CGN	-	-	-	-	-	-	-	3. Thrip marks alone on the cap sules shall not lead to the conclusion that the capsules have been infested by insect

(Continued)

1	2	3	4	5	6	7	8	9	10
3. Bleached or Half Bleached	BL1*	-	0.0	0.0	-	8.50	340	-	
	BL2*	-	0.0	0.0	-	7.00	340	-	
	BL3	-	0.0	0.0	-	5.0	300	-	
	BLN	-	-	-	-	-	-	-	
4. Bleachable Mysore/Mangalore Cardamom	Clipped A	-	1.0	0.0	-	7.0	460	-	
	Unclipped A	-	1.0	0.0	-	7.0	460	-	
	Bulk Clipped	-	2.0	0.0	-	4.3	435	-	
	Bulk Unclipped	-	2.0	0.0	-	4.3	435	-	
	BWN	-	-	-	-	-	-	-	
5. Mixed Cardamom	Mixed Extra Bold	-	2.0	2.0	0.0	7.0	435	-	
	Mixed Bold	-	2.0	2.0	0.0	6.0	415	-	
	Mixed Superior	-	3.0	5.0	0.0	5.0	385	-	
	Mixed Shipment I	-	5.0	7.0	10.0	4.0	350	-	
	Mixed Shipment II	-	7.0	9.0	12.0	4.0	320	-	
	Mixed Light	-	-	-	15.0	3.5	260	-	
	MN(a)	-	-	-	-	-	-	-	

Definition of Terms

1. *Empty and malformed capsules:-* Capsules which have no seeds or are scantily filled with seeds. For this purpose 100 capsules selected at random from the sample shall be opened out and the number of empty and malformed capsules counted.

2. *Immature and shrivelled capsules*:- Capsules which are not fully developed.

3. *Blacks and Splits*:- The former will include capsules having visibly blackish to black colour and the latter will include those which are open at corners for more than half the length.

4. *Colour*:- Cardamoms shall be packed separately according to the colour as (a) Deep green, (b) Green, (c) Light Green and also Pale Brownish. The relevant colour of the cardamoms shall be indicated on the Agmark Lables provided at least 95% of the capsules correspond to any of the colour groups. Where the cardamoms are not of any one uniform colour mentioned above, there will be no indication of the colour on the labels.

5. *AGN* :- The cardamom which does not conform to any of the grades AGEB to AGL shall be packed under the grade AGN against a "Firm Order". "Firm Order" means that the entire value of the goods contracted for, should have been obtained in advance by opening a cent per cent irrevocable letter of credit in India which is encashable on the production of shipping bill supported by receipt of shipment or guaranteed in any other way.

6. *Unclipped capsules*:- Capsules in which the tips have not been trimmed.

7. *CGN* :- The cardamom which does not conform to any of the grades CGEB to CG4 shall be packed under the grade CGN against a "Firm Order.

* Coorg cardamoms shall be packed separately according to colour e.g. (1) Golden to light Creamy, (2) Creamy, (3) Light Greenish to Greenish and (4) Brownish to Brown in respect of grade designations CGEB to CG3 provided at least 95% of the capsules correspond to any of the colour groups. Where the cardamoms are not of any uniform colour there will be no indication of colour on the Agmark label.

(A) A tolerance upto 5% of the next lower size is permissible.

8. *BLN*:- The cardamom which does not conform to any of the grades BL1 to BL3 should be packed under the grade BLN against a "Firm Order".

9. Cardamoms shall be packed separately according to whether they are fully bleached or half-bleached. In the later case the colour of the capsules may be indicated at the request of the packer on Agmark label as (1) Pale Creamy or Dull white.

10. The word "Special" would be affixed to grades BL1 and BL2, if atleast 95% of the capsules do not have thrip marks over 50% of their body surface.

11. *"BW Non-specified*"- The cardamom, which does not conform to any of the Grades BW1 to BW4 may be placed under the grade "BW Non-Specified" against a "Firm Order".

12. MN(a) - The cardamom which does not conform to any of the grades from MEB to ML shall be packed under this grade against a "Firm Order."

Chemical Specifications for Powdered Spices and Condiments for Export Under Agmark

Headings

1. Name of the Spice/Condiment
2. Moisture % Maximum
3. T.Ash % Maximum
4. Acid Insoluble Ash % Maximum
5. Volatile oil % Minimum
6. NVEE % Minimum
7. Crude Fibre % Maximum
8. Coldwater sol. extract % Minimum
9. Water soluble Ash % Minimum
10. Calcium (CaO) % Maximum
11. Alcohol (90%) sol. extract v/w % Minimum
12. Starch % Maximum
13. Chromate test
14. Edible salt as NaCl % Maximum
15. Lead ppm Maximum
16. Added colouring Matters
17. REMARKS

1	2	3	4	5	6	7	8	9	10	11	12	13	14	15	16	17
1. Cardamom (small)	14.0	8.0	3.0													Passes through 500 microne sieve
2. Chilly	10.0	8.0	1.25		12.0	30.0									absent	Free from oils, flavouring matters, preservatives, foreign substances or substitute
3. Coriander	10.0	7.0	1.5												absent	Adopted from ISI–2444-1963
4. Cumin (white)	12.0	8.0	1.5													Standard grade
5. Cumin (black)	12.0	9.5	1.5													General grade
6. Fennel	12.0	9.0	2.0													Passes 500 micron sieve
7. Fenugreek	10.0	7.0	2.0													Passes 500 micron sieve
8. Ginger	13.0	8.0	1.0				10.0	1.7	2.0	4.5						
9. Pepper Black	12.0	7.0	1.2			18.0										Standard grade Passes
	12.5	8.0	1.2			18.0										General grade passed through 500 micron sieve
10. Turmeric	10.0	7.0	1.5								60.0	neg		2.5	absent	Passes 300 micron sieve. Standard grade (Adopted from IS:2446-1963)
	10.0	9.0	1.5								60.0	neg		2.5	absent	Coarse grade passes 500 microns sieve
11. Curry Powder	10.0	-	1.0	0.25	7.5	15.00							5.0	10	absent	Standard
	10.0	-	-	-	-	-							10.0	10	absent	No preservative allowed General

ANNEXURE 12.1

American Spice Trade Association (ASTA) Cleanliness Specifications (Effective from August 1, 1992)

For purposes of these Specifications, extraneous matter is defined as everything foreign to the product itself and includes, but is not restricted to: stones, dirt, wire string, stems, sticks, nontoxic foreign seeds, excreta, manure and animal contamination.

The limits of the various contaminants permitted under these Specifications are shown on the following table:

Cleanliness Specifications	*Whole Insects, Dead*	*Excreta, Mammalian*	*Excreta, Other*	*Mold*	*Insect Defiled/Infested*	*Extraneous/ Foreign Matter*
Name of Spice, Seed or Herb	*By Count*	*By Mg/Lb*	*By Mg/Lb*	*% By Wgt.*	*% By Wgt.*	*% By Wgt.*
All spice	2	5	5.0	2.00	1.00	0.50
Anise	4	3	5.0	1.00	1.00	1.00
Sweet Basil	2	1	2.0	1.00	1.00	0.50
Caraway	4	3	10.0	1.00	1.00	0.50
Cardamom	4	3	1.0	1.00	1.00	0.50
Cassia	2	1	1.0	5.00	2.50	0.50
Cinnamon	2	1	2.0	1.00	1.00	0.50
Celery Seed	4	3	3.0	1.00	1.00	0.50
Chillies	4	1	8.0	3.00	2.50	0.50
Cloves	4.	5	8.0	1.00	1.00	1.00
Coriander	4	3	10.0	1.00	1.00	0.50
Cumin Seed**	4	3	5.0	1.00	1.00	0.50
Dill Seed	4	3	2.0	1.00	1.00	0.50
Fennel Seed	SF(2)	SF(2)	SF(2)	1.00	1.00	0.50
Ginger	4	3	3.0	SF(3)	SF(3)	1.00
Laurel Leaves	2	1	10.0	2.00	2.50	0.50
Mace	4	3	1.0	2.00	1.00	0.50
Marjoram	3	1	10.0	1.00	1.00	1.00
Nutmeg (Broken)	4	5	1.0	SF(4)	SF(4)	0.50
Nutmeg (Whole)	4	0	0.0	SF(5)	SF(5)	0.00
Oregano***	3	1	10.0	1.00	1.00	1.00
Black Pepper	2	1	5.0	SF(6)	SF(6)	1.00
White Pepper	2	1	1.0	SF(7)	SF(7)	0.50
Poppy Seed	2	3	3.0	1.00	1.00	0.50
Rosemary Leaves	2	1	4.0	1.00	1.00	0.50
Sage	2	1	4.0	1.00	1.00	0.50
Savory	2	1	10.0	1.00	1.00	0.50
Sesame Seed	4	5	10.0	1.00	1.00	0.50
Sesame Seed, Hulled	4	5	1.0	1.0	1.00	0.50
Tarragon	2	1	1.0	1.00	1.00	0.50
Thyme	4	1	5.0	1.00	1.00	0.50
Turmeric	3	5	5.0	3.00	2.50	0.50

* Clove Stems A 5% allowance by weight for unattached cloves stems over and above the tolerance for other Extraneous Matter is permitted.

** Cumin Seed - 9.5% total Ash, 1.5% acid insoluble ash.

*** Oregano - sumac negative.

(2) Fennel Seed: In the case of fennel seed, if more than 20% of the subsamples contains any rodent, other excreta or whole Insects, or an average of 3 mg/lb of mammalian excreta, the lot must be reconditioned.

13

Judiciary and Spices

under P.F.A. Act 1954 and P.F.A. Rules 1955

(Amended upto 15.12.1992)

Prevention of Food Adulteration Act, 1954

THE Act No. 37 dated 29th September, 1954, was passed by the Indian Parliament (Lok Sabha) with the noble purpose of curbing and remedying the widespread evil of food adulteration and also to ensure the availability of wholesome food to the people.

It is well settled that the language of such a statute should be construed in a manner which would suppress the mischief, advance the remedy, promote the objects of the statute, prevent its suitable evasion and foil its artful circumvention.

1987 (II) FAC, 297

Section 2(m)

The basic aspect emphasized is that the additive is an adulterant if it effects injuriously the nature, substance or quality of the food. However, there is an exception to the rule which states in para (m) of Section 2 as:-

"Provided that where the quality or purity of the article, being *primary* food, has fallen below the prescribed standards or its constituents are present in the quantities not within the prescribed limits of variability in either case, solely due to natural causes and beyond the control of human agency, then such article shall not be deemed to be adulterated, but the burden shifts to the accused to establish that the adulteration was solely due to natural causes and beyond the control of human agency."

1981(1) FAC, 49; 1981(2) FAC, 100

Primary Food, Section 2(xii)(a)

Primary food as defined in Sec 2(xii) (a) of the Act means any article of food being produce of agriculture or horticulture in its *natural form. Natural* means normal, existing in nature; not artificial or made, manufactured or obtained by artificial process. *Form* means the shape in which it manifests itself.

Thus (coriander) powder is not a primary food. *1981(1) FAC, 312.*

Similarly turmeric powder is not a primary food. *1980, FAJ, 437 and 1981(1) FAC, 16.*

Khas-khas is a primary food (Public prosecutor vs. P. Ponniah) Madras High Court FAC 1986 (I) 399.

Dhania whole is a primary food and hence extraneous matter present due to natural causes and beyond control of human agency (Krishan Kumar vs. State of Haryana), FAC 1987 (II) 255.

Primary Food:— Whether the sample is a "primary food" or not and whether the sample contained pin heads more than the maximum quantity prescribed under the PFA Act which is not injurious to health and would constitute offencc under the provisions of PFA Act; Held Black Pepper (Kali Mirch) is "primary food" and as opined by the Public Analyst, mixture of pin heads in Kali Mirch is not injurious to the health. (Kishore Kumar Venilal Patel Vs. Dayaswarup Bhailabhai Rao and another) GUJARAT HIGH COURT—FAC, 1991(1), 234.

Sonth Ginger — a primary food not for sale. (Shiv Charan Rai vs State of Haryana) FAC, 1983 (II), 309.

Explanation

When two or more articles of primary food are mixed together and the resultant article of food:-

a) is stored, sold or distributed under a name which denotes the ingredients thereof; and

b) is not injurious to health, then such resultant article shall not be deemed to be adulterated within the meaning of clause (m).

Notwithstanding the above explanation, the standard fixed under the rules, made under the Act, *are certain and not variable,* to avoid the vagaries of fluctuation.

Section 2(ia)(f), Insect Infestation

1. Under the above clause are prescribed various substances the presence of which shall make an article of food adulterated. All these grounds are to be read disjunctively and the mere proof that the article of

food being filthy, putrid, rotten, decomposed or insect-infested would be *per se* sufficient to bring the case within the above meaning of adulteration. (The word 'disgusting omitted from Section 2 w.e.f. 1st April, 1976). It would not be necessary in such cases to prove further that the article of food was unfit for human consumption.

1980, FAJ, 257 (Kerala)

2. For the purpose of determining whether an article of food is insect-infested and therefore adulterated within the meaning of above clause, or whether the sample contains insect damaged matter in excess of the prescribed limit, the time lag between the date on which the sample is taken and date of analysis by itself would be of no consequence. There should be sufficient materials in evidence from which it can be reasonably inferred that the sample at the time of sale would not have been insect-infested on could not have contained insect-damaged matter in excess of the permitted limit. In the absence of such materials the report of the Public Analyst (where Section 13(2) has not been involved) or the Certificate of the Director, Central Food Laboratory (CFL), as the case may be, shall be taken as indicative of the quality and standard of the article of food at the time of sampling.

1987 (II), FAC, 297

This overruled the earlier ruling that it would be the duty of prosecution to show that insects were present at the time of sampling in some form. 1979, FAJ (Bomb), 445-556.

3. Public Analyst reported presence of living meal worms but neither reported specifically that it was insect-infested nor that it was unfit for human consumption. The court held that the prosecution had not established that *mirch* (Chilly) powder was adulterated. *1985(2) SCC 589; 1985, SCC cri 289; 1985 Cr.LJ, 921; 1985 (I),FAC, 161*. Later on, *FAC, 1988 (II), 43*.it was again decided that it is not necessary for the prosecution to prove in the case of insect-infested food that the same was unfit for human consumption. This is just a bald submission of the learned counsel and it has not been supported by any principle or precedent. It is the duty of the prosecution to show that the article is adulterated as defined in Section 2(1) (f) of the Act.

4. Mere presence of eggs in an article of food and with no living insect visible to the naked eye cannot be held that the article of food is insect-infested (Municipal Corporation Delhi vs. Badrinath) Delhi High Court, FAC 1982 (I) 211. The term insects-infested means a swarm of insects or at least a large number of insects. (Municipal Corpn. Delhi vs. Shri Ramji Das) Delhi High Court, FAC 1988 (II) 20.

5. An egg normally takes 1-14 days to develop into insect. *Susris* and *Sundis* are fully developed insects hence cannot enter in the sample earlier than this period.

1989 (II), FAC, 331

6. There is no justification for the view that insect-infestation could continue so long as the insect continues to be active. In the insect-infested food article, if for same reason those insects die, the mere fact that the article of food has no longer living insects would not change its character of being insect-infested.

1975, FAJ, 388; 1976 AIR SC 394

7. Though the opinion of the Public Analyst would be a legal evidence, yet it is not conclusive and binding on the court. The *final judge is the Court.* There was no evidence that the sample was insect damaged and unfit for human consumption. It was held that mere presence of insects (dead or alive) in the sample would not render the same adulterated unless there is *unassailable* evidence that it is unfit for human consumption.

1983, FAJ, 185 (Pb)

It is for the *Court to decide* whether the insect found was of such a nature to make the article unfit for human consumption. 1981(1), FAC, 41; 1981, FAJ, 285. (Pb. and Haryana).

But the correctness of the above decision was doubted by the Supreme Court in her decision *1980, AIR, SC. 360.* The court observed that the mere proof of the fact that the article of food being filthy, putrid, rotten, decomposed, or insect-infested would be *per se* be sufficient to bring the case within the meaning of the word adulterated as defined in sub-clause (f) and it would not be necessary in such a case to prove futher that the article of food was unfit for human consumption.

However, in case of insect infestation that prosecution should invariably strengthen its case by adducing evidence to show that the sample in question has been rendered unfit for human consumption due to the presence of insects in number, as found. *Failure to adduce* such evidence *perse* cannot, however, be fatal to the prosecution case if the Court can justifiably conclude from the mere extent and degree of infestation that the article of food has become unfit for human consumption.

Conclusion

8. The law is now settled that the various clauses under sub-clause(f)

should be read disjunctively and the mere proof of the article being insect-infested would be *per se* sufficient to attract this definition. It would not be necessary in such cases to prove further that the article of food was unfit for human consumption 1979(2), FAC, 143, 218, 1980(1) FAC, 219; 1982(2), FAC, 60, 376; 1985(1) FAC, 161 and 1987 (II), FAC, 297.

Application of Sub-clauses (f) and (m)

"Even if there is no notification showing standard of any food thereby clause(m) not attracted but if the food, even primary food, is found unfit for human consumption, by virtue of clause (f) and despite the charge sheet not specifying the charge under the above two sub-clauses (f) and (m), the accused is guilty of offence under the PFA Act and Court must punish the accused".

1988 (II), FAC, 13 (Supreme Court of India)

Nevertheless, "Interest of justice demands that an opportunity *must* be given to the respondent to discharge the burden to prove that quality/ purity of the food in question has fallen OR is below the prescribed standard due to natural causes and beyond the control of human agency".

1988 (II), FAC, 203 (Kerala High Court)

Section 2(ia) (l)

When no standard has been prescribed under the Rules then the provisions under sub-clause (l) will not apply. *Further, the Courts are not competent* to alter the standard of quality prescribed by the government.

1972(1), Cr.L.J., 326. (Supreme Court of India)

1980, FAJ, 123. (Rajasthan High Court)

In other words, the standard of food must be specifically prescribed and scope for any presumption from the prescribed standard of food for any other food article is strictly discouraged.

1966, Cr. L.J. 1347

1982, FAJ, 75 (Allahabad High Court)

1982(1), FAC, 93.

Garam Masala — not a variety of curry powder — Two entirely different articles used for entirely different purposes, their constituents are also different. No standards fixed for garam masala.

(Sardari Lal & Co. vs. State of Punjab and Haryana High Court, FAC 1983 (1) 207.

No standard for garam Masala — standards for curry powder can not be applied.

(Banwari Lal vs. State of Haryana) Punjab and Haryana High Court, FAC, 1984 (I), 249.

Kala Masala is not curry powder and hence standard of curry powder cannot be applied to it.

(State of Maharashtra vs. G.S. Murry) Bombay High Court, FAC, 1982 (I), 37.

Ajwain khurasani — no standards laid down and does not appear to be for human consumption — accused rightly aquitted.

(Medical Officer of Health vs. Satish Chander) Allahabad High Court, FAC, 1982 (I), 93.

Amchur powder — no standard or quality or purity prescribed, hence prosecution uncalled for (M/s Garg Masala Co. vs. State of Punjab) & Haryana High Court; FAC, 1983 (1), 47.

However, if a standard is fixed subsequent to collection of sample and prosecution initiated, it was held that the prosecution is liable to be quashed.

1985, FAJ, 152 (H.P. High Court)

Section 2(v)

Definition of Food: Under section 2(v), food is defined any article used as food or drink for human consumption other than drugs and water — *it is immaterial* whether the accused has sold it for human consumption or not.

1988 (II), FAC, 27 (Orissa High Court)

1988 (II), FAC, 102 (M.P. High Court)

Contextually the Supreme Court of India had made detailed observations as under:-

"In order to be *food* for the purpose of PFA Act, an article need not be fit for human consumption, it need not be described or exhibited as intended for human consumption, it may even be otherwise described or exhibited, it need not even be necessarily intended for human consumption, *it is enough* if it is generally or commonly used for human consumption or in the preparation of human food. Where an article is generally or commonly not used for human consumption or in the preparation of human food but for some other purpose, notwithstanding that it may be capable of being used on rare occassions for human consumption or in the preparation of human food, it may be said, depending upon the facts and circumstances of the case, that it is not food. In such a case the question whether it is intended for human consumption or in the preparation of human food may become material. But where the article is one which is generally or commonly used for human consumption or in the preparation of human food there can be no question but that the article is food 1980(1), FAC, 7

Section 2(ix)(a)

It is well settled that what constitutes breach of Section 2(ix) (a) of the P.F.A. Act is a food article which is found to be immitation or substitute of another article of food.

Mere close resemblance of the package used by the accused to that of some other manufacturer cannot, by itself, constitute breach of this provision of law and, consequently, the *misbranding referred to in the above sub-clause is with relation to the contents of the package and not to the container.*

1984(2) PFA cases 99 (Bombay High Court)

1987(II), FAC, 105 (Pb & Haryana High Court)

Section 2(xi)(e) - Marginal Deviation Effect

Under this section an article of food shall be deemed to be misbranded if false claims are made for it upon the label or otherwise.

In a food article the edible salt % declared under Rule 42(1) was 4% while actually it was found to contain 5% edible salt. The Court decided that *marginal deviation* of 1.0% does not make the article of food adulterated. *1986, FAJ, 353.*

Section 2(xiii)

The definition of 'sale' under this section and sub-clause of the P.F.A. Act covers not merely a sale for human consumption but also the sale for analysis.

1987(I), FAC, 226

Business not yet commenced-furniture making was in progress-Food Inspector asked the accused to sign certain papers and he obliged-the licence to do business issued just one-day before-it cannot be said that the appellant had commenced business in the shop and was selling adulterated oil. (Ahmed Dadabhai Advani vs. State of Maharashtra) Supreme Court of India-FAC 1991(I) 222.

Section 7

Analysis report clearly points out that it is not cinnamon but some foreign bark and is adulterated under section 2(i) (c) of the P.F.A. Act. This was not the case of the prosecution that it was a case of misbranding and as held by the learned magistrate that the defence of the accused is supported by the prosecution evidence itself that the said article was used for the purpose of medicinal preparation. Rs.1.80 for 450 gms is enough to indicate that it was cinnamon but of an inferior quality which the food Inspector had asked for.

1987(II), FAC, 29

PFA Act not applicable to foods for export — tea kept in the godown for blending and thereafter for export is not covered under the PFA Act. It is now well settled that storage simplicitor or storage otherwise than for sale is not an offence (Food Inspector vs. Suwert Dholakia (P) Ltd. Kerala High Court, FAC 1982 (II) 159.

Applicability of-There is neither a whisper nor a shred of evidence even to remotely indicate that the first petitioner was in charge of and responsible for the day-to-day affairs of M/s Parry and Company Limited. It is settled law that unless allegations were found in the complaint to attract the provisions of section 17 of Act, the prosecution against the first petitioner, cannot be allowed to survive. (Chief Executive, Parry's Confectionery Limited, Madras, vs. The Food Inspector of Udhagamandalam Municipality) — Madras High Court-FAC 1991 (1) 295.

Sections 7 and 16

1. Certificate of the Central Food Laboratory supersedes the report of a Public Analyst, a charge will have to be framed in terms of the Central Food Laboratory certificate and the Court cannot do so unless there is sanction for the offence disclosed by the Certificate of the Central Food Laboratory.

1978(2), FAC, 136 (Bombay High Court)

2. Conviction on the basis of the report of the Public Analyst is bad after the certificate of the Director of Central Food Laboratory for the reason that the ground for prosecution in the complaint based on the report of the Public Analyst was negated by the Certificate of the Director; therefore, the bottom was knocked out of the prosecution case as stated by the complaint and the liability eventually was sought to be fastened on the accused is on an entirely different ground not mentioned in the complaint.

1979 (1), FAC, 256 (Allahabad High Court)

3. Only on the basis of paper chromatography the Public Analyst opined that non-permitted Yellow basic coal-tar dye was present in the sample and that no other data has been given about that opinion and therefore on the basis of that report the petitioner could not have been convicted — conviction set aside.

1987(I), FAC 161

4. Sample of curry powder was found to contain 3.3% common salt whereas 3.00% was printed on the label-5% allowed as per rules (Rule A.05.21, Appenxix B). An article of food can be declared to be misbranded only if its label is false or misleading in any material particular. This can by no means be said to be the case here, with the deviation in the sample from the declaration on the label being of such an insignificant nature, that is, of only 0.3% and that too of merely edible common salt. The prosecution of the petitioners in such circumstances is clearly uncalled for and consequently the charge framed against them under Section 16(1)(a)(i) of the Act cannot be sustained.

1987(I), FAC, 317

5. A very look at Section 16(1) of the Act will show the offence being one under section 7/16(1) of the Act is to be tried in a summary way by a judicial Magistrate of First Class, *specially empowered in this behalf by the* State Govt. Section 16A starts with the wording "Notwithstanding anything contained in the code of Criminal Procedure". Therefore an offence under Section 16(1) of the PFA Act cannot be tried in a summary way by the Judicial Magistrate (Railways). The Judicial Magistrate (Railways) had no jurisdiction to try.

1987(II), FAC, 13 (Rajasthan High Court)

6. Complaint cannot be withdrawn for refiling - there is no such provision in law that any complaint can be withdrawn for refiling with the permission of the Court. When once a person has been acquitted, any prosecution sought after removing the lacuna cannot be said to be in the universal rule of fair trial... After acquittal all the consequences and advantages of a person acquitted of the charge have to be with that person and those cannot be snatched away in the above manner.

1987(II), FAC, 26 (Patna High Court)

7. Second and third sample sent to the Director, Central Food Laboratory, who reported each sample decomposed, hence unfit for analysis — effect — the continuation of the proceedings against the accused is nothing *but an abuse* of the process of the Court — in the face of the

latter two reports by the Director, Central Food Laboratory, the earlier report of the Public Analyst was of no consequence and could not be treated even *prima facie* as evidence of adulteration in question. In the absence of any such adulteration, the petitioner could obviously not be chargesheeted.

1985(1), FAC, 120; Punjab & Haryana High Court

1987(II), FAC, 226 -do-

8. Sample of turmeric found adulterated. Accused respondent pleaded that it is meant for pooja and rangoli. This plea is of no avail since any article of food mentioned in the Appendex 'B' shall be deemed as edible stuff fit for human consumption otherwise adulteration of any food stuff would become permissible by merely stating that the same was meant for a different use other than human consumption. There is no evidence, however, on record to show that the turmeric sample for rangoli and or pooja is a different kind of article which is other than food stuff turmeric (haldi). In the circumstances, if food stuff under reference has been sold under the brand of turmeric powder, it must conform to prescribed standards.

1987(II), FAC, 40. (Patna High Court)

Mens rea

9. The question of *Mens rea* arises when the legislature has omitted to prescribe mental conditions as an ingredient of the offence. Knowledge is not the necessary ingredient of the offence. Under Section 7 of the Act the liability of the person contravening any provision is an absolute liability and is not dependent upon any particular intention or knowledge. The distributor of an adulterated food is *per se* liable whether he knows the same to be adulterated or not.

1960, AIR (Mysore), 80) Mysore High Court

1961, Cr.LJ, 499

10. A delegatee cannot legally delegate his authority to another person.

1986(3), FAC, 66 Punjab & Haryana High Court

1987(II), FAC, 254-255

Valid sanction for Prosecution

11. The sanctioning authority must apply its mind to the record placed before it and before according sanction, to find out the nature of offence committed by the accused. The omnibus sanction granted for breach of Section 7, therefore, shows non-application of mind on the part

of the sanctioning authority. Besides, it is expected of the sanctioning authority to mention *one or two* of the various types of adulterations as are described in section 2(ia) (a to m). Consequently, it is deemed that non-application of mind on the part of sanctioning authority *VITIATES trial.*

1986, FAJ, 275

Section (10b) Sample Despatch

"The sample and the specimen impression of the seal had not been sent separately to the Public Analyst. The contravention of this rule equally entitles the respondent accused acquittal."

1988(I), FAC, 110-111

"If the rule lays down that the sample should be sent to the Public Analyst in a dry and clean container, it is not open to the Food Inspector to send the sample in the form of a packet, which is likely to be tampered with".

1988(II), FAC, 224 State of Haryana V/s Gordhandas

1988(II), FAC, 225 Maharaja Exports, Amritsar V/s U.T. Chandigarh.

Section 11

This section deals with the procedure to be followed by Food Inspector.

1. Accused ought to have made the sample representative before selling it to the Food Inspector. He cannot blame anybody and raise it as a technical defence to escape liability.

1989(I), FAC, 371

2. **Section 11(b)(1)** connotes that what is required is to divide the sample *then and there* into three parts. It is not mandatory and or obligatory that the three parts must be equal in weight also. This equality of weight even is not contemplated by the law.

1989(II), FAC, 49 (M.P. High Court)

Sample of meat masala was wrapped in a strong thick paper and not in a sealed container as required under Rules (Nasib Chand vs. State of Punjab) Punjab & Haryana High Court FAC, 1986 (I) 88, 310 (Also Pritam Singh vs. U.T. Chandigrah) FAC, 1986 (I), 313, (Chand Ram vs. State of Punjab) FAC, 1986 (II), 1 Punjab and Haryana High Court.

Sample — not representative — the Food Inspector did not follow the method of quartering as described in authoritative book Chemical Analysis of Food and Food Products (Second Edition) by Morris B Jacobs, importance of which has been very pertinently emphasized in the Division Bench Judgement of this court reported in Bhagat Ram etc. vs. State of H.P. It can, therefore, be said that the sample taken by the Food Inspector in this case is not a representative sample. (State of Himachal Pradesh vs. Sandeepan Kumar) Himachal Pradesh High Court — FAC, 1991 (1), 182.

Section 13

Report of Public Analyst

1. It is mandatory that Public Analyst must perform all the specified tests *at least*. It is his imperative duty. Public Analyst is required to give opinion in respect of all the standards laid down and the Public Analyst cannot leave out any of the tests at his discretion.

2. "The fact that the foreign material was not found in the process of adulteration is of no consequence. If the prescribed standards of food stuff and its purity are not found then once the chemical analysis of adulteration is done, it is not the duty of the judiciary to probe into the chemical contents of adulteration to find out as to what type of adulteration is there".

1988(I), FAC, 65

3. Chemical constants of any spice sample viz. moisture%, volatile oil%, Acid insoluble ash %, etc. cannot be ascertained with any degree of accuracy by mere occular examination under a microscope. Chemical analysis would be a must. Since in the instant case the sample was not subjected to any chemical test or analytical process, the opinion of the Public Analyst was not entitled to any weight whatsoever.

1981(1), FAC, 33, 1981 AIR (SC) 123

1982(1), SCC, 350; 1982 SCC Cri, 221

4. To declare a sample of coriander powder sub-standard merely on the basis of microscopic examination is not adequate and the report of the Public Analyst is fit for rejection.

1987(I), FAC, 120

5. Microscopic examination by itself is insufficient.

1989(I), FAC, 371

6. The well settled view of this court is that the report of the Public Analyst under Section 13 of the PFA Act need not contain the mode or particulars of analysis nor the test applied but should contain the test of analysis namely, data from which it can be inferred whether the article of food was or was not adulterated as defined under Section 2(1) of the Act.

1985, FAJ, 321 (Supreme Court of India)

Section 13(2)

1. "Period provided in Section 13(2) is not an inflexible one and it is further laid down that there is no bar under Section 13 for the Court to allow the application, if submitted, beyond ten days for getting the alleged adulterated sample re-analysed by the Central Food Laboratory".

1985(2), FAC, 184

1986(1), FAC, 238

1988(I), FAC, 195

2. A hypothetical argument does not command acceptance because petitioner did not, as a matter of fact, move any court to send a sample for analysis. Prejudice is a question of fact. There must be basis to think that prejudice was caused. One who never made attempt to get the sample analysed cannot complain of prejudice.

1988(I), FAC, 365 (Kerala High Court)

3. Sanction granted by Dy. CMO merely written "seen" held — this was no sanction. Conviction set aside.

(Ramji vs. State of U.P.) Allahabad High Court, FAC 1981 (I) 182.

4. Sanction accorded by CMO without persuing the relevant documents on record hence without applying his mind. Such sanction is no sanction.

(Roshan Lal vs. State) Allahabad High Court. FAC 1980 (II) 193.

5. The Chief Medical Officer signed the cyclostyled form, gaps were filled by a clerk, the CMO did not even put the date underneath his signature. The sanctioning authority therefore did not apply his mind for signing document.

Habib vs. State of U.P.) Allahabad High Court, FAC, 1985 (I), 104.

6. The Joint Commissioner, Foods and Drugs Administration, Nagpur Division, has not perused the relevant papers i.e. Chemical Analyser's report which should have been mentioned in particular and there is non application of mind in sanctioning (Administrator of City of

Nagpur vs. Hari)

Bombay High Court, FAC 1986 (I) 100.

7. Effect of delay in instituting prosecution, if the delay is inordinate or unreasonable leading to the decomposition of sample and rendering it unfit for analysis by the Central Food Laboratory, the conviction of the accused cannot be sustained. However, delay *per se* is no ground to vitiate a trial. To prove the delay leading to illegal conviction it must be shown that prejudice was caused to the defence resulting in deterioration of the sample by the time summons were received by the accused thereby depriving him of his right under Section 13(2) of the Act to get it analysed by Central Food Laboratory.

1983 (I), FAC, 142. (M.P. High Court); 1982 (I), FAC, 285, Allahabad High Court.

8. Delay in sending the report of the Public Analyst-effect-the conviction of the accused cannot be sustained-the right granted to the accused under Section 13(2) of the Act is very valuable. The local health authority is bound to send a copy of the report of the result of the analysis to the accused informing him that he, if so desired, could make an application to the court within a week to send the second sample for fresh examination by the experts. In case the accused is deprived of this right due to the lapses or shortcomings on the part of the authorities concerned including local authority, no conviction of an accused can be sustained. (Jagdish vs. State of U.P.) Allahabad High Court — FAC, 1991 (1), 96.

9. Fee for Analysis at CFL — accused not under obligation to pay.

Has the accused any legal obligation to remit the free for sending part of the sample to the Director of Central Food Laboratory for a certificate under Section 13(2) of the Prevention of Food Adulteration Act? Held in the absence of any clear statutory insistence an accused cannot be asked to bear the expenses to bring in a document having greater probative value and a substitution for the earlier documents of the prosecution. Hence, the deletion of the words "*on payment of the prescribed fee*" from Section. 13(2) coupled with the other charges, conveys the message that it is no longer obligatory for the accused to bear the expenses for such analysis. (George Kutty vs. State of Kerala) — Kerala High Court-FAC, 1991(1), 133.

10. Accused cannot be asked to bear the expenses for sending the sample for analysis by the Central Food Laboratory. It is the duty of the Court to send the sample to the Central Food Laboratory when a valid

application is made to the effect. The court was not justified in directing the party to produce packing materials to enable the court to send the sample to the Central Food Laboratory — the mistake committed by the trial court cannot be rectified at this stage. So the only possible way is to acquit the accused. (Remann vs. Food Inspector) Kerala High Court-FAC, 1991 (1), 266.

Section 13 (3)

It specifically provides that the certificate issued by the Director, CFL shall supersede the report given by the Public Analyst provided that:

a) the certificate is a complete report, and

b) the certificate is original and duly signed by the Director.

To be specific, only the original signed certificate is admissible as evidence and not its copy. This is in pursuance of rule about the admissibility of the documents as provided under Section 13(5) of the Act. Though it is at variance from the normal rule about adducing evidence in criminal trials because the evidence furnished by the certificate is not given by the person issuing the certificate in the presence of the accused where the opportunity to examine him is not there, so the certificate itself becomes the evidence of the analysis conducted in the laboratory.

Section 13(5)

This Section provides that the certificate of the Director shall be final and conclusive evidence of the facts stated therein. However, this does not prevent the Court of Law record a finding of its own after taking into consideration the facts stated in the certificate as well as other evidence on record. Simultaneously, the courts of law are not to make a comparative study of the certificate of the Director, Central Food Laboratory with that of the report of the Public Analyst.

Thus convictions have been set aside where the courts have on record that the Director's certificate based on the analysis of sample whose specimen impression of seal sent to him did not tally with the seal on the container in which the sample under dispute was sent to him.

1. Where the reports of Central Food Laboratory and Public Analysts appear to be absolutely divergent and different from each other, then the report of public analysts can be looked into (MCD vs. Lala Ram) Delhi High Court, FAC, 1980 (II), 147.

2. Divergence in the analysis of sample by Public Analyst and Director, Central Food Laboratory—Acquittal justified (Uma Shankar Sharma Food Inspector vs. Raman Chona) Delhi High Court, FAC, 1981

(II), 206.

3. Difference in the reports of Public Analysts and Central Food Laboratory—sampling defective, Acquittal upheld (Municipal Corporation of Delhi vs. Bhishan Sarup) Delhi High Court, FAC, 1984 (I), 169.

4. It is true that the report of Director, CFL is conclusive and supersedes Public Analyst report but the pre-requisite is that he has examined a representative sample. The evidence does not indicate that the sample could have been representative as shown by the conflicting report of the Public Analyst and Central Food Laboratory (Mahadev vs. Food Inspector) M.P. High Court, FAC, 1985 (II), 294.

5. Vast defference between the report of Public Analyst and of Central Food Laboratory—defence must succeed (State of Maharashtra vs. Padam Shee WALEJI Chheda), FAC 1987 (II) 45.

6. The report of the Central Food Laboratory has totally shaken the prosecution case which was based on the report of the Public Analyst. In such circumstances the complaint can no longer proceed. The initial grounds having failed the complaint has become infructuous. If the food inspector wanted to file a complaint on the basis of report of Central Food Laboratory, then he was competent to do so by filing a fresh complaint (N.S. Jain vs. State of Punjab) Punjab and Haryana High Court, FAC, 1987 (I), 127.

7. The report of Public Analyst on the basis of only the Paper Chromatographic Test that non-permitted yellow basic coaltar dye was present and no other data given and hence on the basis of that report the petitioner could not have been convicted (Rajender Kumar vs. State of Haryana) Punjab and Haryana High Court, FAC, 1987 (I), 160.

8. Public Analyst found a sample of Dhania containing approximately 30% of foreign pulse and millet starch, the respondant was called upon by the magistrate to meet those allegations based on the report of Public Analyst. In the certificate of Central Food Laboratory sample contravened SECTION 2 (Ia) (m) as it is not within the prescribed limits and as this certificate supersedes the report of Public Analyst hence the report of Public Analyst non-set. The accused cannot be charged on the non-existing facts hence prosecution fails (State of Assam vs. Subkaran Aggarwala) Gauhati High Court, FAC, 1987 (I), 99.

Section 16A

1. Not in accordance with law-the Trial Magistrate neither applied his mind that greater sentence was to be awarded to the offender, than could be awarded as a result of the summary procedure, nor, any such order was passed

in writing. It was, thus, obligatory on the part of the Trial Magistrate to try the accused summarily, and, follow appropriate procedure in that regard. Thus, in the instant case, the trial, which was held as a warrant case, was not in accordance with law-the trial, which is held in violation of the procedure would be illegal, and, not merely irregular. (Giridhar Lal vs. The Govt. Food Inspector) Punjab and Haryana High Court — FAC, 1991 (1), 26.

2. Failure on the part of the Trial Magistrate to follow procedure meant for summary trial goes to the root of the case-trial which is held in violation of the procedure, would be illegal, and, not merely irregular-in the present case the Trial Magistrate neither applied his mind that greater sentence was to be awarded to the offender than could be awarded as a result of the summary procedure, nor any such order was passed in writing-obligatory on the part of the Trial Magistrate to try the accused summarily, and follow appropriate procedure in that regard-the trial which was held as a warrant case was not in accordance with law. (Jaipal vs. State of Haryana) Punjab and Haryana High Court-FAC, 1991 (1), 33.

3. The legislature intended that all offences under Section 16(1) of the Act be tried summarily by specially-authorised Magistrate, unless such a Magistrate in writing opines that the accused deserved greater dose of sentence and so he be tried in accordance with the procedure prescribed by Criminal Procedure code. But the Judicial Magistrates can hold summary trial only if they are specially so empowered. (Naresh Kumar vs. State of Haryana and another) — Punjab and Haryana High Court — FAC, 1991 (1), 82.

4. Trial-held as a warrant case-not in accordance with law-failure on the part of the trial court to follow procedure meant for summary trial goes to the root of the case. (Jaswant Singh vs. U.T. Chandigarh) Punjab and Haryana High Court-FAC 1991 (1) 98.

5. Retrial ordered on 16th Feb. 1990 — Sample of milk taken on 26th February, 1986 — procedure of warrant case adopted ...held retrial abuse of the process of court. (Krishan Lal vs. State of Haryana) Punjab and Haryana High Court — FAC 1991 (1) 101.

6. Remand Order-whether could be passed after 13 years of the taking of sample-in a case of present nature when the accused petitioner is a petty milk-vendor and the sample of milk was taken from his possession on 12th May, 1976 almost more than 13 years ago, the learned Sessions Judge should not have remanded the case back to fresh trial to the learned Trial Court. In this case, the criminal trial had remained pending for six years. The accused had to appear in the Court on all dates on which the case is fixed and has to incur expenses as the trial did not conclude within the reasonable time. Therefore,, in a case of present nature, if 13 years have elapsed and if by the

time the learned Appellate Court decides the case, 12 years elapsed, it is not a case for exercise of discretion of the learned Session's Judge when he ordered for remand of the case. (Man Singh vs. State of Rajasthan) Rajasthan High Court— FAC, 1991 (1), 102.

7a. The Trial Magistrate neither applied his mind that greater sentence was to be awarded to the offender, than could be awarded as a result of summary procedure, nor, any such order was passed in writing. It was, thus, obligatory on the part of the Trial Magistrate to try the accused summarily, and follow appropriate procedure in that regard. Thus, in the instant case, the trial, which was held as a warrant case, was not in accordance with law. (Mohan Lal vs. State of Haryana) —

Summary. Procedure-failure to follow-trial in violation of the procedure would be illegal and not merely irregular. (Mohan Lal vs. State of Haryana) Punjab and Haryana High Court FAC, 1991 (1), 110.

8. Every offence under Section. 16 in the first instance to be tried in a summary way. (Piare Lal vs. State of Haryana) — Punjab and Haryana High Court — FAC, 1991 (1), 162.

9. Trial-as a warrant case-illegal-the case under Section 16(1) of this Act shall be tried in a summary manner by the Judicial Magistrate unless during the pendency of the case he feels that under the circumstances of the case a sentence of more than one year is warranted the Trial Court has not recorded any such order of trying this case as a warrant case-the trial stands vitiated on this score alone.

Petitioner suffered agony and pangs of the pendency of the trial for more than 6 years....court should not have remanded case. (Mahinder Singh vs. State of Haryana) Punjab and Haryana High Court — FAC 1991 (1) 164.

10. Magistrate started the case as a warrant trial and framed charges — magistrate at a later stage found that he had adopted a wrong procedure and started a fresh trial as a summary case — Held that once the Magistrate had adopted the procedure of a warrant trial, he had no power under the Code of Criminal Procedure to recall that order, to wash off the charge-sheet and start retrial.

Protracted trial — Petitioners have a right to a speedy trial and the case should not linger on for years and the petitioner should not be made to suffer the agony of a protracted trial. (Ramesh Prasad and another vs. State of Haryana) Punjab and Haryana High Court — FAC, 1991 (1), 168.

11. Validity of-case remanded to the trial for retrial in conformity with summary procedure after six years-Held not fair to order retrial after remand and appropriate orders in such cases would be to record acquittal of the accused (Ramesh Kumar vs. State of Haryana) Punjab and Haryana High Court — FAC, 1991 (1), 209.

12. The occurrence took place about more than 8 years back. Records show that the appellant has already suffered a part of the imprisonment — no useful purpose would be served in sending the appellant to jail at this point of time for undergoing the remaining period of the sentence though ordinarily in an anti-social offence punishable under the Prevention of Food Adulteration Act the court should take strict view of such matter. (Ram Lal vs. State of Haryana) Punjab and Haryana High Court-FAC, 1991 (1), 316.

13. Summary trial-procedure violated-in the present case the Trial Magistrate neither applied his mind that greater sentence was to be awarded to the offender, than could be awarded as a result of summary procedure nor any such order was passed in writing. It was, thus, obligatory on the part of the trial magistrate to try the accused summarily, and follow appropriate procedure in that regard. Thus in the instant case, the trial was not in accordance with law. (Ashok Kumar vs. State of Haryana) Punjab and Haryana High Court-FAC, 1991 (1), 319.

14. Procedure not followed. After several years at the stage of final arguments the sub-divisional Judicial Magistrate passed the impugned order and wanted that procedure for summary trial may be adopted-the petitioner should not be required to undergo the agony of the trial afresh-prosecution quashed. (Babu Ram vs. State of Haryana) Punjab and Haryana High Court-FAC, 1991 (1), 334.

Sections 22 A & 23

An administrative instruction issued under Sec 22A of the PFA Act cannot have any statutory force and, consequently, a prosecution based on such an instruction is not sustainable.

Instruction under Section 22A could be only with regard to carry into execution, all or any, of the provision of the Act; Central Government has no power to modity or amend the rules by administrative instructions (State vs. Charanjit Singh) Delhi High Court, FAC, 1982 (II), 174.

Administrative instructions issued under Section 22(A) of the Act not binding (R.N. Gujaral vs. M/s Mahabir Trading and others) Delhi High Court, FAC, 1982 (II), 10.

FAC, 1987(II), 141 — S.H. Patra V/s State of Orissa

Iron filing found in a sample of tea were within the tolerance limits of size and quality of letter issued by Ministry of Health. Complaint as well as process issued quashed. (Claude Victor Lawrence Godwin vs. State) Punjab and Haryana High Court, FAC, 1982 (II), 257.

Instructions issued regarding size and quantity of iron filing in tea could be issued by the Central Government under Section 22A of the Act and being statutory in nature are binding on the Government (Brooke Bond India Ltd. vs. State of Himachal Pradesh) Himachal Pradesh High Court, FAC, 1984 (I), 289.

Section 23

Section 23 confers upon the Central Govt. the power to make rules in consultation with the "Committee" to carry out the provisions of the Act after observing the formality laid down therein. The power to make rules carries with it also the power to amend the rules. If in the opinion of the Central Govt. some additional standards with regard to quality or purity are required to be prescribed the same may be done by suitable amendment.... of Appendix B by virtue of the legislative power conferred upon it by Sec 23 of the Act. It is, however, not open to Central Govt. to circumvent the provisions of Sec 23 of the Act and to achieve the above object by issuing administrative instruction because such instruction can neither amend nor supersede the statutory rules.

In this connection, an important aspect must also be borne in mind. A person concerned in any way with the manufacture, sale or storage of an article of food to which the Act applies has the right to know the standards prescribed by the Central Govt. in regard to such food article because non-conformity with the prescribed standards will expose him to the risk of prosecution. Unless, therefore, the standards are laid down in the rules which are required to be notified in the official gazette under Sec 23 of the Act, it may not be possible for him to know the prescribed standard of such article of food and his prosecution for non-conformity of the article of food with the standards laid down in administrative instructions to which he cannot possibly have any access will be unfair, unjust and opposed to the principle of natural justice.

Court in determining whether an article of food is adulterated or not, can not take into account the standards of quality or purity laid down in any administrative instruction in this behalf.

FAC, 1987(II), 77-80 — Annapurna Stores and another v/s Corporation of Calcutta and another Calcutta High Court.

Prevention of Food Adulteration Rules, 1955

Rule 7(3)

Duties of the Public Analyst

1. "It is all the more necessary that the Public Analyst must express his opinion in the report which he submits on Form III of Rule 7(3) of the

aforesaid rules, as to whether the foreign impermissible ingredients present in the sample of analysis is deleterious to health or unfit for human consumption.

1975, FAJ (Allahabad), U.P. State V/s Radhey Shayam

2. Held that public analyst must find out whether the adulterated sample renders it injurious to human health or not, when a sample falls below the prescribed standard or its constituents are not present within prescribed limits of variabilities (Nizamuddin Sddikbhai Tiqala vs. State of Maharashtra) Bombay High Court, FAC, 1985 (II), 88.

Report to be sent to vendor-compliance mandatory.

3. Non-compliance would vitiate the report of the Public Analyst and benefit would go to the accused. (State of Assam vs. Shiew Kumar Jain and another) — Gauhati High Court — FAC, 1991 (1), 21.

Rule 9A

If the Local Health Authority fails to send the report of Public Analyst to the accused i.e. the petitioner is not informed of his right to apply to the Court to have the sample analysed by the Central Food Laboratory then it means that the entire proceedings are vitiated. This provision of Section 13(2) is mandatory and to report again, non-compliance of this provision would vitiate the entire proceedings.

The State of Assam V/s Anukul Chand Dey & others FAJ, 1986, 419

Rule (9f)

Sale & Storage

1. Definition of Food (Section 2) (v)—Sample of khari haldi meant for puja purposes and not for sale-respondant rightly acquitted (Nagar Mahapalika. Varanasi, vs. Hira Lal) Allahabad High Court, FAC, 1982 (I), 121.

2. Dhania stored for seed, not for human consumption — no offence (State of Orissa vs. Chiranji Lal Sharma) Orissa High Court, FAC, 1983 (II), 116.

3. Chilli powder kept in a tin box in a kitchen meant for preparation of food articles stored for sale (State of Maharashtra vs. Jaman Das Vansimal Pariyan) Bombay High Court, FAC, 1981 (II), 92.

4. Storage simplicitor — the food inspector cannot take sample of primary food stored for sale or stored for manufacture of any other article of food for sale or exhibited for sale, unless such article was intended for sale as such food (State of Haryana vs. Ramanand) Punjab and Haryana High Court, FAC, 1982 (II), 167.

5. Sonth ginger — a primary food not for sale had become unfit for human consumption and had not been intended for sale, the food inspector having been aware of the curb put on his powers in spite of protests by the petitioner-Acquitted, FAC, 1983 (II), 67 (Shivcharan Rai vs. State of Haryana) Punjab and Haryana High Court FAC, 1983 (II), 309.

6. Chilli powder not stored for sale but kept for preparing *samosas*. The word 'store' in Section 7 means storing for sale and storing of adulterated article of food for purposes other than sale is no offence. (Joginder Singh vs. State of Haryana) Punjab and Haryana High Court, FAC, 1985 (I), 261.

7. Chilli powder kept in restaurant for use as an ingredient in other products is not stored for sale. (State of Maharashtra vs. P.M. Mohuddin) Bombay High Court, FAC, 1987 (II), 23.

8. Keeping of an adulterated food a little away from the shop front 3 to 4 cubits (cubit 18"-22" approx. (author) is itself no proof for the defence contention that the accused had already rejected that stock and so it was set apart at the corner — the *haldi* (turmeric) powder was stored inside the grocery shop hence shall be deemed for sale"

FAC, 1989(II), 339.

9. The sale of adulterated food, actually or purported, ought to be within the country. If the stored food is not meant for local sale than the storage of adulterated food or article of food is not *per se* an offence.

Food Inspector V/s Sunwet & Dholakia (P) Ltd.

Cr.LJ 1982, 1707; FAC, 1982(2), 159; FAJ, 1982, 646.

Rule 12 A Warranty

"The Warranty would come to his rescue only if the article of food, while in his possession, was properly stored and when he sold it in the same state as he purchased it. The mere production of a bill or invoice or warranty is of no help to the vendor.

FAC, 1975(I), 41 — The Commissioner of Police V/s Goverdhanlal

FAC, 1987(I), 41 — Food Inspector Changancherry V/s Augusty

Rule 16. Manner of packing and sealing the samples:-

A sample of ajwain not made homogeneous and hence not a representative sample. This duty is cast on the food inspector and not on the vendor (Sham Sunder vs. State of Haryana) Punjab and Haryana High Court, FAC, 1986 (I), 160.

Sample of meat masala was wrapped in a strong thick paper and not in a sealed container as required under Rules (Nasib Chand vs. State of Punjab) Punjab & Haryana High Court FAC, 1986 (I), 88., 310, (Also Pritam Singh vs. U.T. Chandigarh) FAC, 1986 (I) 313 (Chand Ram vs. State of Punjab) FAC, 1986 (II), 1 Punjab and Haryana High Court.

Rule 22

The provisions of Rule 22 are not mandatory.

Rule 22A

This rule provides that when the article is sold in sealed container, the sealed container bearing the same label should be treated as sample and the article be sent in the same condition to the Public Analyst. But the Supreme Court of India has observed that when the sealed container contains quantity larger than that required under the Rule, the sample may be collected by opening the container and as such there is no irregularity. It was observed that Rule 22A is corollary to Rule 22 and is directory in nature.

1983 AIR (SC), 545; 1983, Cr.LJ 980 -- State of Punjab v/s Devinder Kumar

Rule 23

1. Rule 23 prohibits the use of colouring matter in any article of food excepting those which are specially permitted under the rules.

2. It is not necessary for the Public Analyst to investigate and to report the identity of the substance that has actually been used for colouring. Suffice for the Public Analyst to report that the colouring matter(s) used is/are other than the permitted ones.

1970, Cr.LJ, 221.

Later on the Rajasthan High Court decided that it is incumbent upon the Public Analyst to state the type of coal tar dye he actually found in the sample which the Public Analyst had reported unaccountable. Such a report of the Public Analyst was held vague and the accused acquitted.

1977, FAJ (Raj), 213 — State of Raj. v/s Tulsa Ram

It is sufficient to sustain conviction that colouring matter used is not one of those which had specifically been permitted by the Rules. It is irrelevant to find as to what actually was the substance (Municipal Corporation of Delhi vs, Ram Dayal) Delhi High Court, FAC, 1983 (II), 255.

Rule 27 v/s Rule 62

Rule 27 states that the inorganic colouring matters and pigments shall not be added to any article of food and black gram *dhall* with husk contained inorganic pigment $MgSiO_3$ which is a forbidden inorganic pigment. Rule 62, Notification No. GSR 764(E) dated 15-11-84 permits the addition of following anticaking agents not more than 2.0% either singly or in combination namely, $CaCO_3$, $MgCo_3$, $Ca_3(PO_4)_2$, $Mg_3(PO_4)_2$, $CaSiO_3$, $MgSiO_3$, Al_2SiO_3 or SiO_2, myristates, palmitates, or stearates of aluminium, calcium, potassium or sodium. Nevertheless, it was held that the aforesaid *dhall* is adulterated.

FAC, 1986(2), 198.

Rule 28

Permissible Coal Tar Food Colours

1. Public Analyst has opined that there was a red, non-permitted, coal-tar dye, but he has not specified on the basis of the chromatogram the name of the dye present nor he has made any effort to exclude the possibility of all the under detailed five permitted coal-tar dyes pertaining to the red colour.

S.No.	*Colour*	*Common Name*	*Colour Index 1956*	*Chemical class*
1.	Red	Ponceau 4R	16255	AZO
2.	"	Carmoisine	14720	"
3.	"	Fast Red E	16045	"
4.	"	Amaranth	16185	"
5.	"	Erythrosine	45430	"

Notification No. GSR 133 dt. 23.1.1973.

Consequently, the report of the Public Analyst cannot be taken as the gospel truth, thereby, outweighing normal judicial balancing. If the courts were to blindly follow the report of the Public Analyst then it would be in the nature of abdication of judicial functions. *It is to be borne in mind that the Public Analyst is just an expert* and his opinion evidence should normally be clear and unambiguous so that it is understandable, if not to all, atleast to a sizeable section of the people who are non-experts.

1987(II), FAC, 320. Maya Ram v/s The State of Punjab

2. "Mere stating basic coal tar dye is not enough for the Public Analyst. He ought to give the nature of dye which the Public Analyst has failed to give. Under the circumstances, a doubt still remains and which could have been cleared had the Public Analyst given the report with more precision. Despite the fact that the Public Analyst did mention that

the use of Basic Coal tar `dye' is prohibited *in all articles of food.* But Rule 28 mentions certain exemptions regarding the specific coal tar dyes which can be used".

1989(1), FAC, 249.

(N.B.) All spices and condiments must not contain added colouring matter irrespective of these being in whole form, seed form or powder form.

Rule 29

Rule 29 is subordinate to the Rule 5 of Appendix B relating to definition of standard quality. However, if any article of food lies beyond the name under common parlance viz. *dhania dal*, which is specifically not mentioned in Rule 29. then under Section 105 of the Evidencve Act, the burden of proving existence of circumstances for bringing the case within an exception in any law defined in the Act is upon the PFA Act authorities. The Court shall presume the absence of an article like any of the article specifically mentioned in clauses (a) to (o) or a product similar to them, it will have to be presumed that *dhania dal* does not fall under Rule 29 test.

1979(1), FAC, 325 (Bombay) — State of Maharashtra V/s Vilas Dashrath Sethe

Rule 30

Maximum limit of any permitted coal tar food colour or mixtures of coal tar food colours which may be added to any food enumerated in Rule 29 shall not exceed 200 mgm/kg i.e. 200 ppm of the final food or beverage for consumption.

"Public Analyst does not state in his report as to the percentage of tartrazine Sunset Yellow FCF found in the sample. In the absence of proof that the permitted colour is in excess of the quantity mentioned in Rule 30 has been used by the respondent, the respondent cannot be held guilty for selling the adulterated food article in question".

1989(1), FAC, 22-23 — State of Maharashtra V/s A.B. Varejile

Rule 28, 29 & 30

"The report of the Public Analyst discloses neither the colour, nor does it specify the extent of colouring material used therein. It merely reads that the article has impermissible coal tar dye. According to Rajasthan High Court decision in State V/s Tula Ram (Supra), it was

necessary for the Public Analyst to disclose in his report the type of coal tar dye used and that in the absence of this report was vague and could not be used to characterise the food article adulterated".

1977(2), FAC, 82 — State of Rajasthan V/s Tula Ram

1987(1), FAC, 29 — Karam Chand V/s State of M.P.

1988(II), FAC, 67 — State of MP V/s Prem Chand

A recent Gazette Notification has been published in the Gazette of India. Extraordinary Part II Section 3(i) under SSR 267(E) dated 11.3.93 regarding Rules 28 to 30. The text is:—

In Rule 28 of the Prevention of Food Adulteration Rules, 1955 (hereinafter referred to as the Principal Rules) for the words "Coaltar food colour", wherever they occur, the words "Synthetic colour" shall be substituted.

For Rule 29 of the Principal Rules, the following shall be substituted, namely:-

"29. Use of permitted synthetic colour prohibited:-

Use of permitted synthetic colour in or upon any food other than these enumerated below is prohibited:-

a) Ice-cream, milk lollies;
b) Biscuits, pastries, cakes, sugar boiled confectionary, lozenges and thread candies;
c) Bottled or canned peas, fruit syrup, fruit squash, fruit cordial and jellies, fruit bar, fruit beverages and fruit drink, jam, marmalade, candied crystallised or glazed fruit and synthetic soft drink concentrates;
d) Non-alcoholic carbonated and non-carbonated ready-to-serve synthetic beverages including synthetic syrups, sherbets;
e) Custard powder; and
f) Jelly crystal and ice candy,"

For Rule 30 of the Principal Rule, the following shall be substituted, namely:-

Rule 30, Maximum limit of permitted synthetic colours

The maximum limit of permitted synthetic colours or mixture of permitted synthetic colours which may be added to food articles enumerated in Rule 29 shall not exceed 100 parts per million of final food beverages for consumption, except in case of articles listed in sub-clause (c) where the maximum limit of synthetic colours shall not exceed 200 ppm.

Miscellanious Decisions

1. PFA Act v/s FPO, APGM Act and Essential Commodities Act.

Supreme Court in criminal Appeal No. 151 of 1966 in the case of MCD v/s Shiv Shanker had decided that FPO, APGM Act and Essential Commodities Act, singly or jointly, do not by implication repeal the PFA Act.

2. Cr.P.C. Section 313

Extent of adulteration not put to the accused hence the above section is violated leading to the acquittal.

1986(2), FAC, 6 — Mangaldas v/s The State of Haryana

1987(I), FAC, 150 — Amarnath v/s The State of Haryana

1987(I), FAC 321 — Sarup Chand v/s The State of Haryana

3. Latest decision Binding

When an earlier judgement of the Supreme Court is analysed and considered by a later Bench of the Court, then the view taken by the later as to the true ratio of earlier case is authoritative and binding on High Courts.

FAC, 1987(I), 53 — State v/s Bahadurchand

Borderline Exemption not allowed

4. "The Act does not provide for exemption of marginal or borderline variation of the standard from operation of the Act (loc. cit).

5. *Dhania* powder is distinct and different from *dhania* whole, both in common parlance and in commercial circles.

Chilli powder is distinct and different from chilli whole.

FAJ, 1987(2), 99 — Ambica Provision Stores v/s State of Kerala

6.(a) "Chilli seeds are an article of food by virtue of their use in one form or other in the preparation of food. Because chilli seeds are not sold alone does not preclude them as an article of food provided seeds were stored as such for sale".

FAJ (Bombay), 1979, 445-446 *State of Maharashtra v/s Jetha Lal Devshi.*

6.(b) "But chilli seeds taken as sample from the whole chillies stored in bags does not amount to sale under Section 2(1)(6), 7 and 16. Chilli powder is a condiment and not a spice

FAJ (Raj), 1979, 202, State of Rajasthan v/s Tejmal

6.(c) "Chilli pods, if it continues in its `natural form' then it is primary food. The processing of original commodity brings into existence a commercially distinct form. Chilli powder can thus never be considered a product of agriculture in its natural form"

FAC, 1988(II), 89 -- Rajan v/s Food Inspector, Kerala High Court.

Select Bibliography

Achaya, K.T., *Everyday Indian Processed Foods* (1986), Second Edn., National Book Trust, India, New Delhi.

Anita, F.P., *Clinical Dietetics and Nutrition* (1986), 2nd Edn., 5th impression, Oxford University Press, New Delhi.

D.S. Chaddha, *Prevention of Food Adulteration Act 1954* (1993), Assocham, New Delhi.

De, D.J., *Notes on the P.F.A. Act 1954* (1988), S.C. Sarkar and Sons, Calcutta.

Harold Egan, Ronald S. Kirk, Ronald Sawyer, *Pearsons' Chemical Analysis of Foods,* (1981), 8th Edn, Churchill Livingstone, London.

Homoeopathic Pharmacoepia of India, Vol. I to V, Ministry of Health and Family Welfare, Govt. of India, New Delhi.

Mahindru, S.N., *Spices in Indian Life, 6500 BC-1950 AD,* (1982), Sultan Chand and Sons, New Delhi.

Mahindru, S.N., *Hand Book of Food Analysis,* (1987), Swan Publishers, New Delhi.

Nadkarni, K.M., *Indian Materia Medica,* Vol. I, (1989), Popular Prakashan, Bombay.

Natarajan, C.P., *Processing of Pepper and Pepper Products - A Workshop,* (May 1981), Central Food Technological Research Institute, Mysore.

Pearson, D., *Laboratory Techniques in Food Analysis*, Butterworth, London.

Prevention of Food Adulteration Act, 1954, (1990), 4th Edn., International Law Book Co., Delhi.

P.F.A. Act (1986), Gazette of India, Part II, Section I, dated 26.12.86.

Potty, V.H. and Balakrishnana, P.S., *Indian Spices,* 1989, 26 (4), 14-21.

Pruthi, J.S., *Spices and Condiments*, (1987), 3rd Edn., National Book Trust, India, New Delhi.

Pruthi, J.S., *Bibliography on Spices and Condiments (1974-86)* Association of Food Scientists and Technologists, (India), Delhi Chapter, Delhi.

Richard, J. Lewis, Food Additives Hand Book (1989), Van Nostrand Reihold, New York.

The Consumer Protection Act, 1986, Gazette of India Extraordinary, Part II, Section I, dated 26.12.86.

S.O. 390(E), Gazette of India, Extraordinary, Part II, Section 3(ii) dated 15.4.1987.

Wealth of India (Raw Materials), Vol. I to X, Council of Scientific and Industrial Research, New Delhi.

Index